THE ORKNEY BOOK

Books Edited/Written by Donald Omand

The Caithness Book	Inverness	1972
The Moray Book	Edinburgh	1976
Red Deer Management	Edinburgh	1981
The Sutherland Book	Golspie	1982
The Ross & Cromarty Book	Golspie	1984
A Kaitness Kist (with J. P. Campbell)	Thurso	1984
The Grampian Book	Golspie	1987
The New Caithness Book	Wick	1989
A Northern Outlook:		
100 Essays on Northern Scotland	Wick	1991
Caithness Crack	Wick	1991
Caithness: Lore and Legend	Wick	1995
The Borders Book	Edinburgh	1995
The Perthshire Book	Edinburgh	1995
Caithness: Historic Tales	Wick	2001
The Fife Book	Edinburgh	2001
The Argyll Book	Edinburgh	forthcoming

Monograph
The Caithness Flagstone Industry
(with J. D. Porter)   University of Aberdeen 1981

With kindest Regards
Donald Omand

THE ORKNEY BOOK

edited by

DONALD OMAND

Birlinn

First published in 2003 by
Birlinn Limited
West Newington House
10 Newington Road
Edinburgh
EH9 1QS

www.birlinn.co.uk

ISBN 1 84158 254 9

British Library Cataloguing-in-Publication Data
A catalogue record for this book is available from the British Library

Designed and typeset by Carnegie Publishing Ltd, Lancaster
Printed and bound by MPG Books, Bodmin

Contents

Lists of Plates, Figures, Tables and Maps

Plates

Knap of Howar, Papa Westray

Skara Brae, Sandwick

The Stones of Stenness

The Ring of Brodgar, Stenness

One of the standing stones at the Ring of Brodgar

The Broch of Gurness, Evie

The Broch of Gurness, aerial view

Midhowe Broch, Rousay

Maes Howe runes

Knowe of Burrian, Pictish symbol stone

Beachview, Birsay

Pictish symbol stone, St Peter's Church, South Ronaldsay

Marwick Head with Kitchener's memorial and the Brough of Birsay

Cubbie Roo's Castle, Wyre

Norse Mill, The Bu, Orphir

St Boniface Church, Papa Westray

St Magnus Cathedral, Kirkwall, from the air

St Magnus Cathedral, Kirkwall, side door

St Magnus Cathedral, Kirkwall, east end

St Magnus Cathedral, Kirkwall, tower and transept

Figures

Tables

Maps

Conversion: Metric/Non-metric

1 metre = 3.28 feet   1 foot = 0.30 metres

1 kilometre = 0.62 miles   1 mile = 1.61 kilometres

1 hectare = 2.47 acres   1 acre = 0.40 hectares

Acknowledgements

THE PUBLISHER AND EDITOR would like to express thanks to the following, who assisted in the production of this book.

Mr David Abenheimer and Mrs Ethel Ross for permission to reproduce excerpts from the works of Edwin Muir; John Murray (Publishers) Ltd for permission to reproduce excerpts from the works of George Mackay Brown; Alistair Cormack for his assistance in compiling Chapter 19; Dr R. P. Fereday for guidance towards some materials; Ms A. Fraser, Orkney County Archivist, for her help with a number of chapters in this book; Ms J. H. Beattie, Keeper of Hudson's Bay Archives, Winnipeg; Mr P. Leith and Mr M. Payne for texts which would not otherwise have been consulted; Mr J. P. Robertson for access to Mrs Christian Robertson's business records; Mr S. MacCubbin and Mr J. Bruce, fishery officers, Kirkwall, for information on modern developments in the Orkney fishing industry; Mr T. Muir, for his considerable help with picture research.

It was decided not to include a chapter on well-known Orcadians as Bill Hewison had written an excellent publication, *Who Was Who In Orkney*, Bellavista Publications, 1998.

Foreword

ORCADIANS ARE FASCINATED by the world about them. A walk along the shore opens up so many questions. Why has the sand shifted along the beach from last year? What makes the line of the waves bend round the distant headland? Where do the little polished pieces of flint come from?

Or you could be coming out of a hall after an evening out, and suddenly you are hit by the sheer expanse of open frosty sky, with the full power of the stars, and the Northern Lights rippling above. How, you wonder, do such phenomena come about? And your neighbour tells you, explaining how all his life he has tried to find out more, and has been doing so from books, or going to talks by visiting speakers.

So it is not surprising that Orcadians have a deep love of books, and it is not surprising that lectures on just about every subject you can think of get a keen response from an Orkney audience.

Aberdeen University's Continuing Education Department has contributed greatly to Orkney, and particularly through Donald Omand. From his base in Halkirk, Caithness, he developed an annual programme through the whole Northern area which brought in speakers and also gave the initial encouragement to many local people who have gone on to become experts in their own right.

Donald has the skill of bringing out the best in people – of seeing their potential, encouraging them, giving them confidence – and for many years he was doing this for a vast area of scattered communities across the Highlands and Islands. Every year there were not only lectures but also summer schools, conferences, seminars, and a range of new courses that for many people was the opportunity of a lifetime to take up university study.

It was a model of how a university can serve a rural community.

Amidst it all, he brought out a series of books on the counties of the north – *The Caithness Book, The Sutherland Book, The Ross-shire book, The Grampian Book, The Moray Book* – and more besides. In each case, he brought together a team of the people whom in his work he had identified as true experts and able communicators to provide a treasure chest of knowledge and insight on each chosen county.

When he reached the stage of well-earned retirement, we wondered what would happen about the gap in the series – an *Orkney Book*. But Donald has been quietly working away, and now it is a delight to view the fruits of one more set of labours. This book will enrich the study of Orkney and inspire a new generation of Orcadians and Orkney-lovers.

Howie Firth

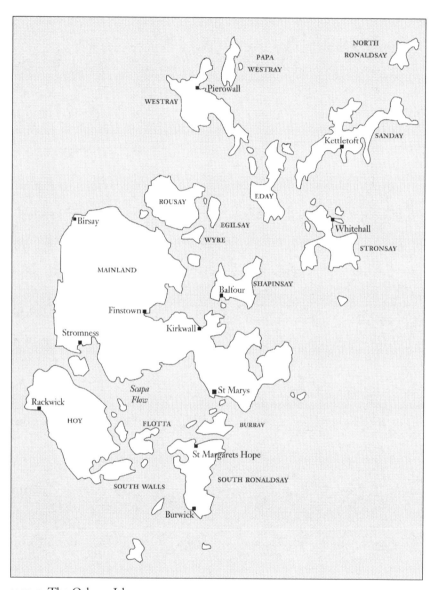

MAP 1 The Orkney Isles

CHAPTER ONE

Geology and Landscape

Introduction

This chapter will endeavour to present an overview of the processes forming the low rolling landscape of Orkney. Previous articles by this author concentrated on geology (*Orkney Nature*, 2000) and the human history aspects of climate and Ice Ages (*The Faces of Orkney, Stones, Skalds and Saints*, 2003).

The landscape is a function of the underlying geology and the processes that have acted upon it over many millennia, including erosion, which is removal of rock and soil material by natural processes, principally running water, glaciers, waves and wind. Erosion carves the surface of the earth into new landscapes.

In Orkney, several major factors controlling landscape development are present. The last glacial episode (the Devensian 115,000 to 11,500 years ago) dominated the overall form of the islands. In the Holocene (the last 11,500 years) climate change, vegetation and human interaction modified this form inland, while coastal erosion by wind and waves coupled with relative movements in sea level created the dramatic seascapes of the islands.

Geoindicators of environmental change

Landforms generally develop over longer timescales than a human lifetime. Measurement of processes therefore requires the use of geoindicators that can quantify environmental change. Humans are without doubt an integral part of the environment, but it is essential to recognise that nature and the environment are ever changing, regardless of the presence of people. Environmental sustainability must therefore be assessed against a moving background.

Particular indicators such as shoreline position and the aerial extent of lakes can be used to reflect climate change, tectonic movement and human interference, or some combination of each. Some geoindicators have the capacity to record and store evidence of environmental changes. Such natural recording systems are useful in determining how the local environment has changed. Ice sheets such as Greenland provide an invaluable

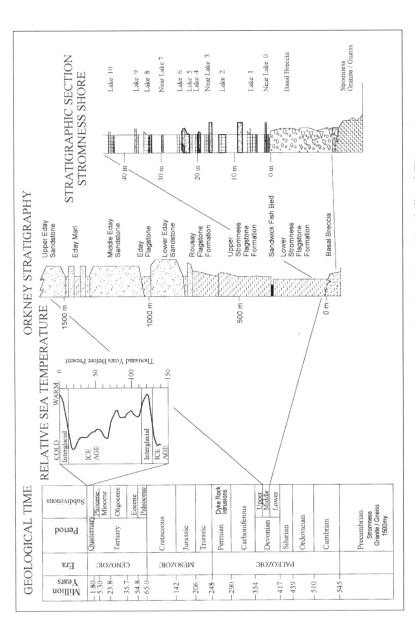

FIGURE 1 Geological time scale and Orkney stratigraphy (after J. E. A. Marshall and T. Aston)

archive of past climates (this record extends back into the Pleistocene), where the ice and air bubbles between ice crystals provide a record of past changes in atmospheric composition.

Continental ice sheets and glaciers, with their capacity to store water for extended periods, exert a significant control on the surface water cycle. The ice volume has generally decreased worldwide over the past 11,500 years. It is well understood that ice volume changes directly affect global sea level so that warmer climate gives less continental ice and therefore higher global sea level.

In attempting to understand the effects of environmental change over the history of an area like Orkney, it is important to remember that natural processes work at global and local levels as well as interacting with human activity. Many of the indicators developed for present-day environments are equally important in the reconstruction of more ancient environments as recorded in the sediments of Orkney. Prevailing themes throughout this chapter will be related to cyclical processes in the paleoenvironment and climatic changes interpreted from their observed effect in the geological record.

Climatic cycles controlled the depositional environment in the Devonian, 380 million years ago. The eccentricity of the Earth's orbit about the Sun controlled the sedimentary rhythmic repetition of 'wet period' deep-lake deposition approximately every 100,000 years. The effects of this same 100,000-year orbital eccentricity cycle combined with the shorter obliquity and precession of the equinox cycles can explain the waxing and waning of glaciation and stadial ice sheets over the past 2 million years (Figure 1). Much finer-scaled insolation parameters give the 2 to 3 degree temperature changes observed during the latest Holocene interglacial period.

Underlying geology

The rocks of the Orkney archipelago (Figure 2) are poorly representative of the immense stretch of geological time from 4.5 billion years ago to the present. Mineral resources such as copper, iron, coal and flint are not native except in trace amounts. Sulphides of lead, zinc and silver (galena) in veins are widely distributed but difficult to extract from the ore.

Stratigraphy

1 *Precambrian Basement Complex*
The basement rock exposed at Graemsay, Stromness and South Yesnaby consists of a pinkish-grey *granite-gneiss complex*.

FIGURE 2 Geological sketch map of Orkney (after Geological Survey of Britain and T. Aston)

2 *Lower Devonian Sediments*

The *Harra Ebb* formation Yesnaby, attributed to the early Devonian, consists of breccia, conglomerates, sands and mud deposited on an uneven surface of eroded basement gneiss.

3 *Lower Middle Devonian Sediments*

The Orkney flagstone group is 752 m thick and consists of grey and black thinly bedded flagstones laid down in an extensive lake of variable salinity. This group is subdivided into three parts:

Lower Stromness flagstone formation: 277 m (43 cycles) of flagstones, sands and silt. The distinctive Sandwick fish bed 10 m to 30 m thick marks the top of the formation.

Upper Stromness flagstone formation: 285 m (25 cycles) of lake cycle deposits as above with higher content river sand and sheet flood deposits.

Rousay flagstone formation: 170–190 m (18 cycles) of lake cycle deposits similar to the underlying Upper Stromness flagstone formation.

4 Upper Middle to Upper Devonian Sediments

The Eday group including the Hoy sandstones (up to 800 m thick) is composed largely of yellow and red sandstones with intervening grey flagstones and red/green marls. Contemporary tectonic movements in the region released alkaline volcanic deposits of ash and lava flows near the base of the Lower Eday and Hoy sandstone.

There are five separate units in the Eday group above the basal volcanic sequence.

Lower Eday sandstone, formed during an arid period when there was local faulting and folding. It varies from 35 m at the margin to nearly 180 m in the core of the Eday syncline basin.

Eday flagstones mark a return to wetter conditions with the establishment of up to 12 lake cycles. Westwards from South Ronaldsay the lake cycles pass laterally into aeolian (desert) deposits.

Middle Eday sandstone in Eday alluvial sands returned after only four lake cycles. The Middle Eday sand is confined to the northern part of Orkney.

Eday marl is a distinctive unit of red and green silt and mud. Recent discovery of halite pseudomorphs, marine microfossils, dolomite, gypsum, anhydrite altered to limestone and beds with worm burrows indicate a marginal-marine floodplain.

Upper Eday sandstone represents a return to sandy river deposits. The uppermost fluvial sands of the Eday Group in Hoy and Dunnet Head (Caithness) could be as young as Lower Carboniferous.

5 Post Devonian Rocks

No sedimentary rocks younger than Devonian have been identified definitely on land in Orkney.

Geological History

Basement

The oldest rocks found in Orkney are 'basement' granitic-gneiss and schist exposed in the West Mainland (Figures 3 and 4) at Yesnaby, Stromness and Graemsay. Although these rocks have never been directly dated, their similarity to metamorphic rocks in Sutherland led to their being assigned a Moinian Age.[1]

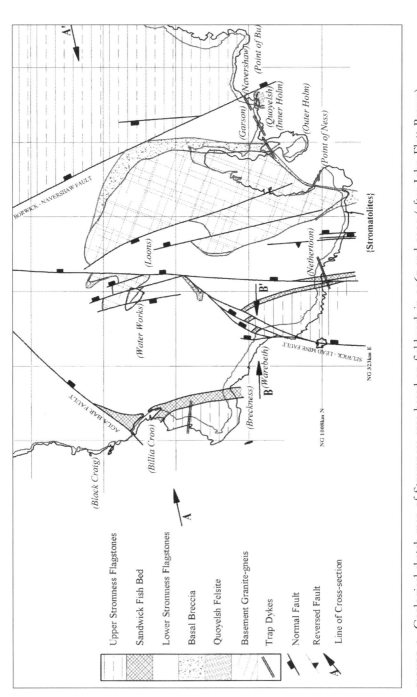

Upper Stromness Flagstones

Sandwick Fish Bed

Lower Stromness Flagstones

Basal Breccia

Quoyelsh Felsite

Basement Granite-gneiss

Trap Dykes

Normal Fault

Reversed Fault

Line of Cross-section

FIGURE 3   Geological sketch map of Stromness area based on fieldwork in 1967 and 1999 (after John Flett Brown)

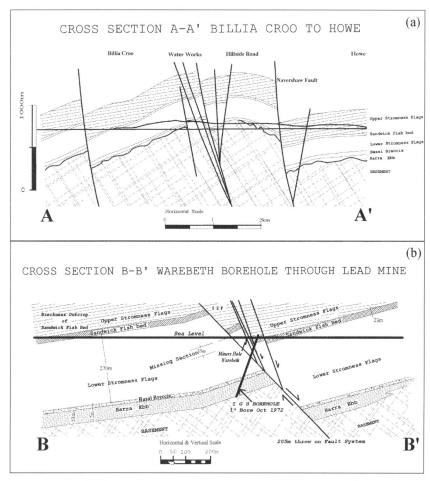

FIGURE 4 (a) Regional west to east cross section, times two vertical exaggeration (b) Cross section through I. G. S. Warebeth borehole 1972 used to reconstruct the lower Stromness flagstone stratigraphy identifying a 35-m missing section cut by a reversed fault on the west shore (after John Flett Brown)

After a long period of burial in the crust of the Earth, these rocks were thrust to the surface during the Caledonian mountain building episode (500 to 400 million years ago).

Middle Devonian Flagstones

Paleomagnetic studies of rocks show that Orkney was located approximately 16 degrees south of the equator during the middle Devonian in the centre of a large continental mass called 'Euramerica'. At this latitude, the Orcadian basin would have been climatically located within the southern hemisphere continental desert belt.

The locally observed Devonian sand dune bedding, salt crusts and gypsum crystal pseudomorphs (often in the form of desert rose) are typical of deserts. Rain pits, mud cracks and wind ripple marks are indicative of marginal lake mud flat conditions in a wetter environment while finely laminated dark-coloured rocks containing fossil fish and plants are formed in a 'permanent lake' environment. Current rippled sandstones, trough cross-bedding and sand sheet-floods demonstrating the presence of river systems are also common.

By middle Devonian times an extensive relatively flat area stretching from the Moray Firth to the east coast of Greenland and across to Norway was established. At times of maximum flood, this basin filled with a fresh water lake. At other times, the basin almost totally dried out and small saline lakes formed at the lowest topographic levels. The basin also contained internal ranges of hills, consisting of metamorphic basement rocks, extending along the upthrown sides of major normal faults.

This area, known as the 'Orcadian basin' when dry or 'Lake Orcadie' when substantially covered by shallow waters, was fed by large rivers originating in the surrounding high mountains and continental plateaux. These rivers cut gorges through the elevated margins of the Orcadian basin, filling the lake depression with mud, silt and sand. The primitive freshwater fish that were swimming around in the lake would die and settle to the anoxic bottom where they were covered by mud and preserved as fossil fish in the dark coloured laminate rock.

All the flagstones were formed in a lake environment. The stratigraphy of Orkney's sedimentary rocks show a regular repetition from the freshwater permanent lake conditions of Lake Orcadie to a mud/sand flat or desert environment every 10 to 15 m of vertical section. The evidence strongly indicates oscillations (108 cycles) between climatically wet and dry conditions in the 10.5 million years of Lake Orcadie's existence, to give an average of about 97,000 years for each Milankovitch cycle.

Permian Dyke Rocks

More than 200 igneous 'trap dykes' crosscut the Devonian sediments in Orkney. These dyke intrusions vary in width from 1 to 2 m and can be traced over lengths of 2 to 3 km. The Orkney dyke rocks are 252 +/- 10 million years old, making them late Permian in age. Some of these dykes contain an exotic collection of lower crust and mantle-derived xenolithic inclusions.

The Ice Age

The smooth rolling landscape of Orkney was sculpted by the scraping transit of vast ice sheets passing over the islands at various times during the Quaternary Glaciation (Ice Age). Over the last 2.4 million years, in excess of 20 glaciations worldwide have been detected, each lasting about

100,000 years and interspersed with interglacials lasting approximately 15,000 years. Each glaciation consists of several Stadials (shorter cold episodes) and Interstadials (short warm periods). We are presently approaching the end of the current Interglacial warm period (Figure 1).

Glacial to interglacial oscillation involves a potential exchange of up to 50 million cubic kilometres of water between the oceans and the ice caps. This exchange is calculated to have produced a global change in mean sea level of about 150 m, with stadial–interstadial cycles producing smaller changes. Concomitant changes in seawater salinity, oxygen isotope composition and ocean surface temperature also occur.

Several major 'ice age periods' appear in the geological record. Reconstruction of the Earth's past climate indicates that global temperatures were probably 8 to 15 °C warmer than today. During the last billion years of Earth history these warmer conditions were interrupted by relatively short glacial periods at 925 my, 800 my, 680 my, 450 my, 330 my, and 2 million years BP (Before Present). The causes of such ice ages are complex and a combination of factors such as continental distribution, volcanic activity, jet stream directions in the upper atmosphere and astronomical orientation of the Earth all contribute. During the coldest periods of the Ice Age average global temperatures were probably 4–5 °C colder than they are today.

On a world scale the timing and extent of ice coverage during the Ice Age varies with respect to geographic position and the local climatic environment at that time. The driving mechanism for these variations is the amount of solar radiation (insolation) reaching the surface of the Earth in a particular area. Insolation changes with the cosmic positioning of the Earth with respect to the Sun and alterations in the orbital parameters of the Earth.

This solar variable, Milankovitch cycles, relates to the three major components of the Earth's orbit about the Sun:

1. The orbital eccentricity of the Earth around the Sun, varying from a circular orbit to an elliptical orbit with a change in seasonal incoming solar radiation of about 30 per cent, takes 95,800 years.

2. Changes in the inclination (obliquity) of the Earth's axis alternate between extreme values of 21.39 degrees and 24.36 degrees with a periodicity of 41,000 years. An increase in axial tilt results in lengthening the period of winter darkness in polar regions.

3. The precession of the equinoxes over a period of 21,700 years requires the northern hemisphere to be tilted towards the Sun at successively different points on the Earth's annual orbit, affecting in the northern hemisphere the lengths of summer and winter.

The Ice Age in Orkney

Although the Ice Age started about 2.4 million years ago, there is no evidence of glaciation in Scotland until about 850,000 years ago. The first presence of small glaciers on Hoy may actually date from this period. About 750,000 years ago, the Cromerian Glaciation was probably the first time that the Scottish ice sheet reached Orkney. During the Anglian Glaciation 440,000 years ago, when the Scottish and Scandinavian ice sheets were confluent, they almost certainly covered Orkney. Approximately 300,000 years ago, the Saalian ice sheet was present in the northern North Sea and Orkney was again probably covered by ice.

The Devensian Ice Age, which started approximately 115,000 years ago, is characterised by at least four ice advances (stadials) interspersed by shorter intervals of ice retreat with consequent changes in global sea level of between 20 and 40 m. The late Devensian Glaciation removed most of the evidence of earlier events from Orkney as it passed across the islands. This ice sheet, which built up and advanced from about 30,000 radiocarbon years ago, reached its maximum about 24,000 radiocarbon years ago. The ice retreated and thinned around 15,000 radiocarbon years ago, with its final retreat from Orkney about 13,000 radiocarbon years ago.

This ice sheet carried rock materials, sand and mud derived mainly from local sources. Erratics are also present and include chalk, flints and shells from the bed of the North Sea and granites and metamorphic rocks from as far away as Norway. The rocks ingrained in the ice left scratch marks, known as striations, on the bedrock, giving the movement direction of the ice sheet (Figure 5).

The rocks, sand and mud frozen in the ice sheet were deposited as the ice melted, forming a layer of boulder clay (or till) in most of the low-lying areas of Orkney. This boulder clay varies from a few centimetres thick up to 20 m. Small rounded hills or 'morainic mounds' of boulder clay cover substantial regions of Orkney.

The north-west end of the island of Hoy exhibits most of the classical valley-glacier mountain landforms. Towards the end of the Devensian, the short cooling period of the Loch Lomond stadial, 13,000 to 11,500 years ago (about 11,500 to 10,000 radiocarbon years ago), marked the end of the last Ice Age.

Following this there appears to have been a long period of very cold climatic conditions when the ground was still without vegetation. This is demonstrated by frost shattering, churning and solifluction on the top of the boulder clay deposits and barren rock surfaces. Arctic tundra conditions continued to between 11,500 years and 10,500 years ago, when the climate changed to warmer conditions than the present time and sea water levels rose rapidly.

Environment and landscape of the Holocene

The Holocene Interglacial, in which we are now living, started 11,500 years ago with the final retreat of the polar ice caps and rapid global warming.

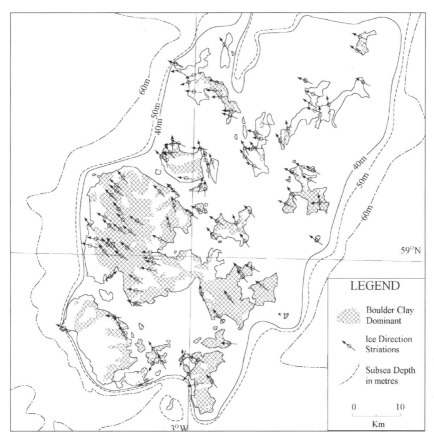

FIGURE 5 Distribution of boulder clay in Orkney with direction vectors from striation marks

Evidence from southern Greenland ice cores suggests that a 7°C warming may have taken less than 50 years. The recession of the ice sheet uncovered vast areas of new land in higher latitudes, which then became available for human occupation. Rapid flooding of the low-lying coastal plains due to rising sea levels put further pressure on the human population to move.

The major change to the landscape of Scotland at the beginning of the Holocene was the establishment of a forest cover. Once established, extensive open forest woodland consisting of hazel, birch and willow with a more restricted distribution of alder in the West Mainland continued until 5600 BP. During the Mesolithic, the Orcadian landscape may have been a mixture of thick forest in the lower regions with open woodland, grassland and heath on the hillsides (Figure 6). The scarcity of Mesolithic archaeological sites may relate to this distribution of tree cover with communities established in clearings at the edge of the forest, along the seashore and on the hillsides.

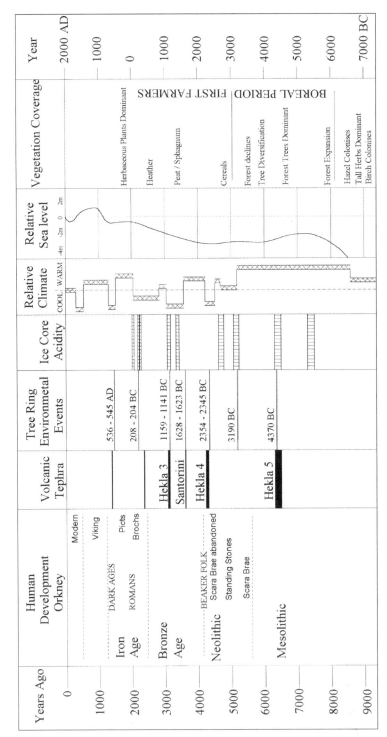

FIGURE 6 Correlation diagram to show related features during the Holocene Orkney. Relative climate and related sea-level columns are indicative (after John Flett Brown)

Post Mesolithic sea level rising would have inundated many of the coastline settlements, leaving only the hillside sites for modern archaeology to discover beneath the blanket peat now covering these areas. The abundance of wood at this time means that they would have made all their tools and buildings from this perishable material. Fossil wood of this period is observed at low spring tides in sheltered bays within Scapa Flow as the 'submerged forest' peat deposits.

Peat bogs persisted in Orkney from the early Holocene. Nevertheless, by the middle of the Bronze Age (1500 BC), the pollen record shows a dominance of heather species indicative of a landscape of heath and blanket peat bog although there was still double the present tree cover.

The environment and climate of the late Holocene contained warm periods such as the 'Roman period' from 300 BC to AD 400, the medieval 'Little Optimum' (AD 750 to AD 1300) and the current warm period that started in AD 1850; temperatures were one to two degrees more than today. In the Orkney context, the 'Little Optimum' contained the Viking period and likewise the Picts flourished in Orkney during the earlier warm period. The last cold period (AD 1300 to AD 1850) known as the 'Little Ice Age', reached its peak between AD 1650 and AD 1750.

During the Holocene vegetative cover, human occupation and climate appear to be interrelated. Historians and archaeologists have perhaps underestimated the effect of climate change on population dynamics in the Northern Isles.

Climate controls the range and extent of colonisation by human farming groups. The viability of such settlement requires a stable or improving climate. Deterioration in climate may lower crop yields in southern communities, while at the same time marginal areas may suffer famine, disease and population migration. Where the marginal area is an island such as Orkney, worsening climate could lead to decimation of the indigenous people and leave behind an impoverished culture. This has happened several times in Orcadian prehistory.

Climatic History

Climatologists believe that only a limited number of factors are primarily responsible for most of the past episodes of climate change on the Earth. These factors include:

- Variations in the Earth's orbital characteristics.
- Variations in the solar output.
- Volcanic eruptions.
- Collision and near collision by interstellar bodies.
- Atmospheric carbon dioxide variations.

Computer models and historical evidence suggest that the Milankovitch cycles exert their greatest cooling and warming influence when the troughs and peaks of all three cycles coincide with each other. These cycles control the incoming solar radiation (insolation) and the broad climatic configuration. Cycles at 95,800 years, 41,000 years and 21,700 years are associated with temperature changes in the tens of degrees and mark the onset of glacial and interglacial climatic conditions.

Shorter cycles dominate the Holocene climate pattern and tend to cause variations of 1 to 3°C (Figure 6). Sunspot abundance and solar flaring is one such 22-year cycle. Cycles of 70 to 90 years are also evident. Longer-term climate oscillations are noted in ice cores at 78, 181, 400 and 2400 years. These may relate to zones of fine interstellar matter, through which the Earth passes, combined with the sunspot activity. Although most of these changes are gradual, there is increasing evidence from ice core data that some major climatic shifts involve rates of one to two degrees per year. This could be potentially catastrophic for farming populations in marginal areas.

Superimposed on the cyclical changes in local and global climatic regimes is the effect of natural geological processes. Volcanic eruptions can adversely affect the local climate for one or two seasons. Orkney has had an increased potential for major shocks to the local climate throughout history, as it is 900 km down wind from the active Icelandic volcanic regions. Mount Hekla intermittently put vast amounts of volcanic ash into the upper atmosphere (Figure 6). Some of these ash fragments (tephra) are distinguished in the peat deposits of Orkney (Hekla 5 about 4400 BC, Hekla 4 in 2340 BC and Hekla 3 in 1140 BC).

Major catastrophic explosive eruptions such as Santorini (1628 BC) and Krakatoa (AD 1823) affect not only local climate, but can have major consequences for the global climate over a period of decades.

The Earth has been in contact with various interplanetary objects such as comets, asteroids and meteorites in the past. There are many historical records of comets affecting the climate regionally and globally, followed by disease and famine. Evidence from the tree ring record of Irish bog pine and German oak shows climatic crises (narrow growth rings) lasting several years. Seven such events (4370 BC, 3190 BC, 2354–2345 BC, 1628–1623 BC, 1159–1141 BC, 208–204 BC and AD 536–541) may be due to near misses by comets. Where these tree ring events show coincidence with tephra and ice core acidity, from volcanism, there has to be an element of doubt about the causal agent (Figure 6).

The tree rings show a global environmental downturn lasting several years that peaked in AD 540, the beginning of the Dark Ages. Could this climate change have led to the end of the Pictish Broch culture and virtual abandonment of the Northern Isles? Slow recovery of the economy and population could explain why the subsequent Viking occupation during the next warming was relatively peaceful.

Erosion and coastal processes in modern landscape development

The global climate depends largely on the carbon cycle and carbon dioxide in the atmosphere. The more erosion happening on land, the faster carbon is buried and removed from the cycle. This consequently lowers the level of atmospheric carbon dioxide. The relatively cool climate of the late Cenozoic (Ice Ages) was thus reinforced by erosion and the most effective type of erosion was by glacier action.

Erosion is the process that turns rock into sediment and carries it from high to lower elevations. Erosion is responsible for the shape of the land around us. Erosion fills rivers with silt and mud and piles the beaches with sand, developing our modern landscape.

Cliffs exceeding 15 m in height make up nearly a fifth of Orkney's extensive 800 km-long shoreline, whilst sand or shingle beaches make up another 10 per cent. The remaining 70 per cent consist of low rock and boulder clay cliffs and rocky shores. The interior coasts consist of low-energy marine environments, while the outer fringes are exposed to high-energy wind and waves. This section will show how the complicated coastline of cliffs, beaches, bays and sand dune systems superimposed on a submerged glacial landscape gives us the ever-changing coastal beauty of these Orkney Islands.

The westward-facing coasts are fully exposed to the destructive forces of the open Atlantic, with deep water extending close inshore and waves breaking directly on the cliffs, a solid rock wave-cut platform, with many rock pools formed on these exposed shores with boulder beaches being created in the bays. In places wind-blown sand has collected behind the beaches to form extensive dune and machair areas.

Within historical times, the sea has encroached on some shores such as the Bay of Skaill, exploring weaknesses of rock structure and exploiting valleys formed by the moving ice sheet. Within living memory at Birsay, Skaill and Warebeth, 5–10 m of sand and boulder clay shore have been lost. An average rate of 10 m per century is estimated for erosion on the exposed coastlines.

Not all the actions of the sea, wind and waves are destructive. The fourth Churchill Barrier, linking South Ronaldsay to Burray, has an expanding beach formed by creating an offshore sand bar and filling in the lagoon behind it with beach and blown sand. Such bay-mouth bars (ayres) are formed by a combination of factors including sea-level change, wave refraction and storm beaches. Major storms over hundreds or thousands of years have lifted rocks to form boulder beaches on cliff tops at Sacquoy Head, Rousay and at the Nev in Westray.

The major dynamic agent for changing coastal landscape is waves. As wind-generated waves approach the coastline, the wave may change shape and break while at the same time picking up rock and sand materials which increase their abrasive action on the coast. When waves arrive at the coast at an angle they set up currents that can move sand and rock materials laterally (long-shore currents). Wave-driven currents are the driving force of much coastal landscape development, yet it is not the only force capable of moving coastal sediments and altering the landform's shape.

Tidal currents are the second major energy input into the coastal zone, moving vast volumes of water in and out twice a day. Tide waves respond to the same physical laws as the smaller wind-generated waves. Orkney has about a 3 m tidal range. Generally, if the tidal range is less than 2 m it may be assumed that wind waves provide the dominant coastal process forming beaches, spits and barrier islands as the predominant features of the coast. Where the tide range is greater than 4 m funnel-shaped estuaries, mudflats and salt marshes are predominant. As Orkney exhibits tidal ranges between those two limiting ranges a mixed coastal process regime is expected, which may oscillate between tidal wave-dominated features and wind wave-dominated features.

Cliffs and Shore Platforms

The existence of a cliff face in a slope profile is probably very short-lived. Marine action plays a dual role in the cliff process. The obvious role is in cliff erosion, undercutting the slope base and thus forming debris both directly and indirectly due to mass failure of the over-lying rock. The debris produced is removed by a variety of marine processes including long shore drift.

Cliff formation and erosion relate directly to the formation of a notch at the base of the cliff. The development of the cliff notch through time is important as it controls both the rate of cliff recession and the form of the shore platform left behind. Experiments have shown that breaking waves are much more effective than broken waves at notch cutting. When cliffs plunge into deep water, waves are reflected and very little other erosion takes place. When waves break some distance offshore, owing to a low beach or shore platform angle, erosion occurs slowly. Cliffs whose base have a relatively narrow steep beach are more likely to experience the maximum erosive forces of breaking waves.

When the shore platform is relatively mature, only very short steep waves are capable of progressing to the cliff face without breaking. When such abnormal waves do occur, they will cause accelerated cliff erosion. Cliff erosion is therefore dependent on a critical height of wave such that waves lower than this critical height merely remove the loose debris. Waves larger than the critical height occur more and more infrequently until the effect on cliff erosion becomes so rare as to be negligible.

This continued erosion of the coastal slope and the subsequent removal of the debris by near-shore currents causes the shoreline to retreat to form a sub-horizontal wave cut or shore platform. In Orkney, the coastal wave cut shore platforms show a relatively steep aspect ending in relatively deep water. This is related to the general rising sea level over the past six millennia.

Superimposed on this process of cliff erosion is the subsidiary process creating cliff morphologies. Along the exposed coasts of Orkney, this gives an endless succession of headlands, bays and geos, with caves, gloups or blowholes, arches and sea stacks in every stage of development and destruction. The process starts with wave-induced erosion of the rocks along fracture lines at the base of the cliff and initiates a small opening following the weakness. Cave enlargement proceeds by hydraulic action of the waves enhanced by the pneumatic action of entrapped air and the abrasive action of sand and pebbles. When long caves are formed, collapse of the roof at the inward end forms a gloup, while total collapse of the roof forms a geo. Intersection of geos can leave isolated sea stacks and arches. The Old Man of Hoy is only one of many sea stacks and castles along the Orkney shoreline and may be the result of relatively recent erosion no more than 250 years old.

Sea level change during the Quaternary has meant that cliff development in many areas has had a stop–start history such that it is difficult to decide whether a given cliff is a product of present-day processes or whether it is a fossil feature relating to previous sea levels.

Beaches

Stable beaches of sand and boulders would appear to be the most unlikely landform to be found facing the high-energy environment of the open ocean. Because it can adjust shape rapidly in response to changing wave energy, the beach maintains a dynamic equilibrium with its environment. Beaches are thus essentially energy sinks and act as a buffer between waves and the coast. High energy is best dissipated by wide flat beach profiles that spread the oncoming wave energy. On the other hand, low-energy flat waves are easily dissipated by a narrow steep beach. Shingle or rocky beaches can dissipate wave energy in interparticle friction so that the beach particle size will modify the slope requirement.

A feature of Orkney beaches is that low flat swell waves, typical of summer, bring in 1–2 m of offshore sand to fill the beach area, forming a steep profile. During winters, the high steep storm waves erode this beach face and transport the sand seaward where it forms as a long-shore bar near the base of the beach profile, reducing the gradient. In Orkney, with about 3 m tidal range, beach gradients can vary from 0.5 degree to 11.0 degrees, giving beach widths of 300 m in the winter and 15 m in summer.

Shoreline beaches generally follow the coast but the beach does not reflect any irregularities of cliff or coastal slope as it adopts a smooth curved seaward limit. The alignment of such beaches is parallel to the wave crest curvature of the dominant wave approach direction maintaining a dynamic equilibrium with input and output of sediment.

Detached Beaches

When a coastline turns abruptly landwards, as at the entrance of a bay, and the long shore current does not turn with the coastline, sand and gravel accumulate in the direction of the current as a spit. In Orkney, this is called an ayre (aire) which is defined as a gravelly point or shingle spit often found in a tidal estuary (Figure 8). An ayre also commonly encloses a small salt-water lagoon or oyce (uiss).

The ayre and oyce feature is very common around Orkney, it is often backed by a grass-covered cliff and raised beach about 1–2 m above mean high water. It is considered to have been formed during a recent sea-level high.

Barrier islands are formed by the long shore extension of spits that are subsequently broken through by storm waves forming a series of discon-nected islands such as Mirkady and Scarf Points in Deer Sound.

Tombolos usually reflect conditions where waves are reflected around an obstruction such as an offshore island joining them with a shingle beach. Copinsay and Corn Holm are examples.

Coastal Sand Dunes

Coastal sand dunes differ markedly from desert dune systems although both are formed by aeolian (wind) transport of sand. Coastal dunes normally exist in a wide zone bordering the high tide mark on a beach and may extend up to 10 km onshore. The conditions necessary for dune growth are strong on-shore winds, abundant sand supply, vegetation cover and sand grains (less than 1 mm) that can be displaced by winds combined with a tidal range that permits sand to dry out.

Sand moves by several processes in coastal dune systems. The first is saltation, in which sand grains are picked up by the wind after being dislodged by the impact of another sand grain. Surface creep takes place when larger sand grains are impacted by smaller grains. Finally, sand grains smaller than about 0.2 mm are suspended by the wind and blown clear of the beach and dune system. The other side of the equation allowing deposition of this moving sand is the presence of vegetation, commonly marram grass, which provides shelter between the leaves, lowering wind velocities while grains hit the leaves and fall to the ground.

Growing landward of the active fore-dunes is the first dune ridge. Older ridges become lower and lose the straight parallel to shore characteristic of the first ridge. This lowering and flattening of the older ridge systems is because fresh sand supplies are usually trapped in the younger dunes and sand is generally removed from the older dunes to fill the valleys between dune ridges.

In Orkney, fresh dune systems are present at Dingieshowe, Aikerness, Scapa, Stronsay and Sanday among others. Along the western seaboard, the Birsay Links, Skaill Bay and Warebeth Beach (Figure 7), the dune ridge systems are less obvious. Given the time scales of approximately 100 years between each ridge, they probably relate to sand movement and dune formation from a much earlier time and a beachfront much farther west than today. The links at Skaill and Warebeth in particular show dune sands that overlie fresh water loch peat deposits dated at 6,580 +/– 80 years at Skaill and directly overlie the boulder clay at Warebeth.

Mudflats and Salt Marshes

Tidal sediments are composed mostly of silt and clay. These sediments form mudflats and marshes, in areas with medium to large tidal ranges (greater than 3 m) and usually in areas sheltered from the effects of wind-driven waves.

Mudflats are not necessarily flat, but the inner parts are usually held at about the high tide level. Salt marshes are vegetated mudflats. Marsh surfaces are much higher, relative to mean tide level, than mud flats and are consequently flooded less frequently. The exact height at which mud flat surfaces become vegetated is dependent on suitable plant species and the salinity levels of the tidal water. After plant colonisation, the rate of deposition will increase on the marsh surface. As the marsh surface rises a succession of plants can occur – *Halimione portulacoides* (sea purslane), *Aster maritima* (sea aster), *Puccenelia maritima* (salt marsh grass) and *Limonium vulgare* (sea lavender), ending with *America maritima* (sea pink) on the highest levels.

The marsh height will increase by the addition of organic matter from the dying plants forming a silty peat and eventually just peat on the surface. Over time, the accretion rates on salt marsh surfaces show a gradual decrease as the surface height rises. In young marshes (0–100 years), the accretion rate may be as high as 10 cm per year But on older marshes (200–1,000 years) this may drop to less than 0.001 cm per year. Salt marshes are often enclosed by spits and bays, which provide sheltered conditions for deposition.

During the development of salt marshes, a small cliff may be formed at the marsh edge, sometimes as much as one metre in height. Sea-level drop may cause accretion to resume seaward of this cliff so that several terrace-like features are to be seen in some marshes. This explains the two peaty salt marsh terraces we observe in the Hamnavoe area of Stromness harbour, Brig o' Waith and many other locations (Figure 7).

Estuaries

The absence of great rivers in Orkney means that these landforms are not present but the Stenness Loch–Bay of Ireland system probably most closely represents a true estuary. Small local burn mouth estuaries do exist and provide habitats for many species of birds.

Sea-level change and coastal geomorphology

World coasts have seen sea-level variation of approximately 100 m within the past 11,500 years through melting of the ice caps. When the ice caps melt the sea level rises globally (eustatically). The relative sea level at any location is measured proportionate to the nearby land, which is itself subject to tectonic movement both up and down.

During the Ice Age, there was approximately 2 km of ice over central Scotland. On melting, the downward pressure was released and the land surface moved up (isostatic rebound) quicker than the eustatic sea level rose. This gives the appearance of a relative sea-level drop over much of Scotland during the Holocene.

In Orkney, where the ice thickness may have been considerably less, eustatic sea-level rise was greater than isostatic rebound, giving a local appearance of sea levels rising. This is responsible for the archipelago's present drowned topography.

Where the relative sea level is dropping, evidence of emerged shorelines consists of platforms backed by steep cliff slopes (raised beaches), marine shell beds and stranded beach deposits. Where the relative sea level is rising, evidence of submerged coastal features consists of drowned river valleys, submerged dunes, remnants of forests and peat layers below sea level (noted in Scapa Flow) and notches with benches in the submarine topography. In Orkney waters, a well defined notch is seen between 40 m and 50 m (Figure 5) with a less well-defined notch at about 10 m. Both of these features may relate to pauses during the early Holocene sea-level rise but equally may have formed at any time during the last Ice Age.

Coastal landforms develop towards equilibrium with their environment. When a major change in sea level occurs, old coastal landforms are completely abandoned and a new set initiated. After about 6,000–7,000 years ago, when sea-level rise slowed down (Figure 6), coastal deposition probably managed to keep pace with sea-level rise so that migration of coastal features could take place, producing local transgressions and re-gressions of the shoreline intimately associated with the vertical changes of relative sea level.

Climatic change affects the amount of snow melting, snow precipitation and ice accumulating on the polar ice caps and mountain glaciers. This in turn affects the volume of water in the sea and thus accordingly the global rise or fall in sea level. Therefore, local relative sea-level change should reflect the global climate at that time.

Significant fluctuations in sea level have occurred around Orkney in the recent past. This is inferred from features observed near Stromness (Figure 7) and many other parts of Orkney. There is compelling evidence from widespread raised beach features for an approximately 1–2 m higher relative sea level in the past, while the large number of Oyces backed by grass-covered cliffs, and raised beaches around Orkney's coastline confirm

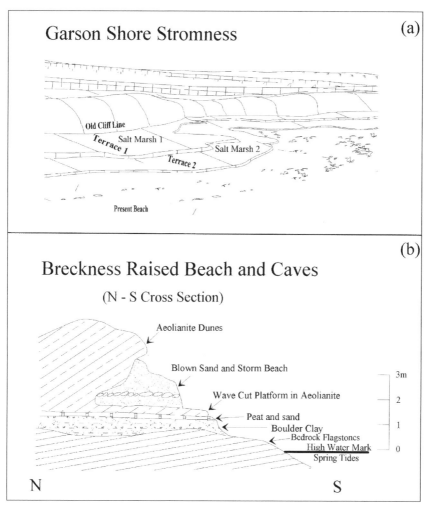

Garson Shore Stromness (a)

Old Cliff Line
Terrace 1   Salt Marsh 1
            Salt Marsh 2
        Terrace 2

Present Beach

Breckness Raised Beach and Caves (b)

(N - S Cross Section)

Aeolianite Dunes

Blown Sand and Storm Beach   3m

Wave Cut Platform in Aeolianite   2

Peat and sand   1
Boulder Clay
Bedrock Flagstones
High Water Mark   0
Spring Tides

N   S

FIGURE 7 (a) Garson Shore Stromness showing grass-covered cliff line possibly relating to 1-m higher sea-level around the Viking period in Orkney. Also shown are two terraces separated by only a 25-cm peat cliff indicating falling relative sea level and salt marsh development between AD 1000 and the present (b) Cross section through the Aeolianite dunes at Breckness indicating the relationship between the raised beaches, with caves approximately 1 m above present sea-level (after John Flett Brown)

a similar story. Although not dated, it is inferred that this particular high stand occurred about 1,000 years ago in the Viking Period. It is postulated that as sea level dropped ayres grew across the mouths of small bays enclosing the oyce and developing the new equilibrium coast line. This relationship between raised beach, ayre and oyce is well demonstrated at Rothiesholm Head on Stronsay (Figure 8).

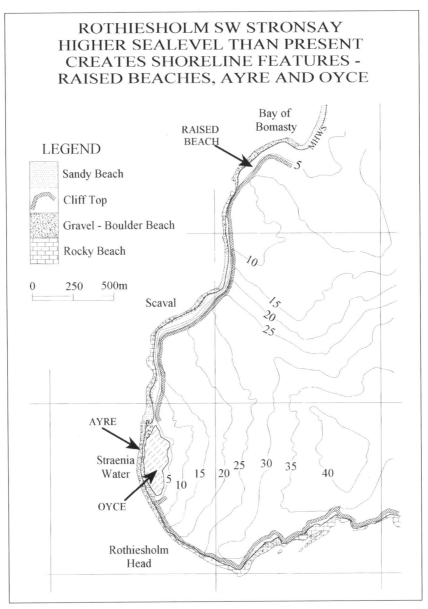

ROTHIESHOLM SW STRONSAY
HIGHER SEALEVEL THAN PRESENT
CREATES SHORELINE FEATURES -
RAISED BEACHES, AYRE AND OYCE

FIGURE 8   Sketch topographic map showing the relationship between an ayre, oyce and raised beach system SW Stronsay (after John Flett Brown)

The 'fossil forest' and submerged peat reported below the sand to the east of the Inner Holm, Stromness and from the Sands of Wright, South Ronaldsay, probably date from the Mesolithic. Approximately 4 m in altitude separate this feature from the raised beaches indicating an average rate of rise in relative sea level of at least 10 cm/100 years between 3000 BC and AD 1000. A subsequent drop of about 2 m with a return to the present level followed.

A raised beach deposit at about 7 m in the cliff face near Braebuster, North Hoy, is covered by glacial till. This is considered evidence of higher relative sea level during one of the interstadial episodes of the last Ice Age and not part of the current phase. Since approximately equal volumes of ice forms and subsequent depression of sea level occurs during glaciations over many hundreds of millennia it will not be an unusual coincidence to have ancient sea-level features (raised beaches etc.) that are at about the same level as observed today.

Notes

1 The Age of the Orkney Basement Rocks: The basement metamorphic rocks in Orkney bear a strong likeness to migmatised Moine rocks found within the Kirtomy Nappe above the Swordly Thrust in eastern Sutherland. These rocks, and by inference the Orkney inliers, with mica schists, psammites and subordinate semipelites belong to the Loch Eil Group of Moine sediments with a sedimentary age of about 950 million years. Rims of Zircon crystals, which grew during migmatisation, have given ages of 461 +/- 13 million years for the Kirtomy assemblage and 467 +/- 10 million years for the Naver assemblage. This shows the presence of a middle Ordovician (Taconic) tectonothermal event. This is in contrast to the age of migmatisation found in Moine rocks of the central Highlands where the main tectonothermal event is 840 +/- 11 million years. Detrital Zircons within the sedimentary forerunners of these migmatites fall in the age range of 1,850 to 1,000 million years showing that depostition of the Moinian sediments in Sutherland probably occurred later than 1,000 million years ago.

Legend:
▲ Maes Howe-Type Tombs
● Stalled and Related Tombs

N. Ronaldsay

Papa Westray

Westray

Eday

Sanday

Rousay

Stronsay

Mainland

Shapinsay

Flotta

Burray

Hoy

S. Ronaldsay

Pentland Firth

Caithness

0   20Km

MAP 2 Distribution map of the chambered cairns in Orkney (after Ritchie 1995, 46)

CHAPTER TWO

The Early Peoples

T HE EARLY PEOPLES of Orkney have left us traces of the tools they used and the monuments that they built, but we know nothing of their languages and little of the intricacies of their evolving society. Frustratingly, we have no information about the sorts of boats that the earliest folk used, although they must have been skin boats or log boats. Seafaring must have played an important part in the settlement of Orkney from the first moment that the islands were spied from the north coast of Scotland and the decision made to see what the land held. Just when this happened is, however, uncertain. It is likely that these first people had a way of life that depended on the seasonally available natural resources by hunting, fishing and harvesting from the land; archaeologists describe this as a Mesolithic economy. Among the earliest radiocarbon dates for their settlements in Scotland are those from excavations on Rum in the Inner Hebrides and they indicate that occupation there was under way by the eighth millennium BC. As with the settlement of islands off the west coast we must assume that boating technology in the north was sufficiently advanced to allow the journey from Caithness to Orkney to have been made in Mesolithic times, though we do not know exactly when. The majority of the surviving artefacts are characteristic flint implements known as microliths (small carefully-fashioned tools), many collected a long time ago, but only recently studied in detail (Saville 1996; 2000). Saville's conclusion was that the artefacts were sufficiently distinctive to confirm that Orkney had indeed been inhabited well before the arrival of the earliest agricultural communities some time around 4000 BC. The resources at their disposal might in faunal terms have been more restricted than on the mainland, but both in fishing and in the adventitious beaching of whales there would surely have been compensations. There is evidence to suggest the presence of oak, alder and pine as well as birch and hazel woodland. It is quite likely that this period saw an ever-increasing awareness of the seasonal potential of the land and a respect for the moods of the sea, wind and weather, which can only have assisted new people who arrived centuries later with their livestock, seeds and notions of farming.

Our impression of the way of life of the earliest agricultural communities in Orkney is dominated by the settlement of Skara Brae, an icon of the Scottish Neolithic period, 'the new stone age' so-called because of a

distinctive tool-kit, including ground stone axe-heads. Skara Brae is not
the earliest Neolithic settlement, however, for radiocarbon determinations
have placed that at Knap of Howar, on the island of Papa Westray, at
about 3600 BC to 3100 BC, and the initial settlement of the islands by
agricultural colonists is likely to have been some centuries earlier. At Knap
of Howar two stone-built houses are broadly rectangular on plan with
rounded corners and are set side by side with their main doorways to the
seaward ends (Ritchie, A. 1983). The outer doorways were carefully designed with upright jamb-stones, against which a portable door of wood
and skin would be placed; the doorway of the larger house was additionally
provided with a sill-stone to reduce draughts further. Upright slabs were
used to divide the larger house into two areas and in the outer there were
traces of a low slab-built bench or platform. Upright slabs create three
areas in the second house with a hearth in the central one; the inner
compartment is interpreted as a storage area with cupboards and three
aumbry-like recesses in the thickness of the wall. The site is not only of
structural interest, for the associated middens provide information about
the environment, the economy, stone and bone tools and round-based
pottery in a style known as 'Unstan ware'. They grew barley and wheat,
and reared cattle and sheep as well as a few pigs.

The animal bone at Knap of Howar was well-preserved. Cattle and
sheep were found in about equal proportions. The cattle were large beasts;
Noddle compared them in scale to recently domesticated aurochs (in
Ritchie, A. 1983, 97). The use of adult bone for tool-making, the possibility
that primitive cows might not breed annually, and the scarcity of winter
feed are several of the possible reasons for the large number of young
animals represented. The majority of the sheep were also killed young as
a source of food and skin; primitive sheep are not considered to have been
usefully wool-bearing.

Fishing and exploitation of seabirds would have played important roles
in the economy. The range of species represented is wide, suggesting the
exploitation of both freshwater lochs and streams (conger eel and flounder)
and offshore in deeper waters to obtain some of the larger species. The
presence of turbot, a fish now found only farther south, may indicate
warmer sea conditions in Neolithic times than at present. The numbers
of birds identified is unusually wide (40 species were noted), including
divers, gulls, guillemots, puffins and great auks. The seabird oil would
doubtless have been useful for lighting. Deer were also hunted. The
preservation of deer, fish, and bird bone in the Knap of Howar middens
provides some impression of the importance within this farming economy
of the contribution of what is essentially a hunting and foraging way of
life.

The findings from Knap of Howar have been described in detail, as they
offer a fairly full picture of daily life and get us close to the people themselves in practical terms. Skara Brae is better known and the chronology

and development of the settlement has been clarified by the excavations of 1972–73. The span of the settlement is between 3100 BC to 2500 BC (Clarke and Maguire 2000). The settlement is more complex, with super-imposed phases of building. One of the unusual aspects of the site is that it appears to have been constructed within deliberately collected midden material, possibly to ensure that the houses were wind-tight. The internal features of the houses, hearths, beds and the like, are in stone; the major difference between the earlier and the later phases of building is that in the former the beds are set into the thickness of the walls, whereas in the latter they project into the living space. The dresser of House 7 is a built-in piece of furniture in stone. All the houses have central hearths. Several have stone boxes set into the floor, the joints of which were smeared with clay, apparently in an attempt to make them water-tight; it is usually suggested that these held limpets that were being prepared as fish bait. Saithe and cod bones have been recovered. Farming activities included the keeping of cattle, pigs and sheep/goats, and the growing of barley and wheat. At a comparable settlement at Rinyo, Rousay, the base of a clay oven was recovered, and it is likely that this was used for baking bread (Childe and Grant 1939, 14–15). The pottery from both sites belongs to the grooved ware tradition with flat bases and a range of incised decorative motifs and impressed cordons. Some of the most tantalising objects from Skara Brae are in carved stone, both intricately decorated balls and spiked objects. An unusual aspect of the Skara Brae settlement is the large number of structural stones that have decorative motifs, particularly lozenges and criss-crosses (Shepherd 2000).

Neolithic settlement studies in Orkney have benefited from recent excavations not yet fully published and a greater range of house types and environmental adaptations seems likely to be demonstrated. More irregular plans were found in excavations at the Links of Noltland, Westray (Clarke and Sharples 1985). At Barnhouse, the lowest courses of small houses with central hearths and bed-recesses have been identified, but there is also a larger and more sophisticated house with six recesses and very straight wall lines. A larger building, Structure 8, had a complex entrance arrange-ment (Richards 1990). Pool, Sanday, is important as it offers an archaeological sequence with artefactual material and thermoluminescence dates (Hunter 2000). Crossicrown was discovered by examining ploughed fields to gather artefacts; Stonehall was reported as a result of increasing local awareness of the importance of reporting material (Downes and Richards 2000).

The burial places of the agricultural communities in Orkney are among their most lasting testimony to their skills in the use of stone (Davidson and Henshall 1989). In all cases the tombs are set within mounds of stone and earth and appear to have been designed for use over a long period of time with a covered passage from the edge of the mound leading to a chamber within it. Two broad categories of tomb are known as the

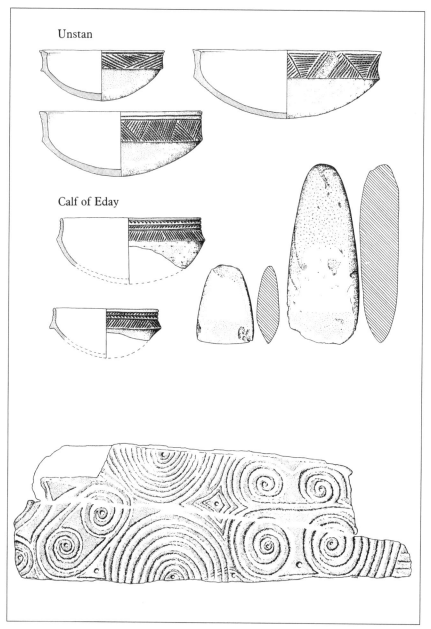

FIGURE 9 Pottery and stone artefacts from the chambered cairns of Unstan and Calf of Eday (after Davidson and Henshall 1989, 68 and 72); the decorated slab from the chambered cairn at Pierowall, Westray (drawn by Marion O'Neill)

Orkney–Cromarty and Maes Howe groups; in the former the chamber is rectilinear and is divided by upright slabs set into the side walls into a series of compartments, or stalls, whereas in the latter a series of individual cells are entered from the central chamber. Stalled cairns of Orkney–Cromarty type have a widespread distribution across north and west Scotland, but tombs of Maes Howe type are found only in Orkney. Two examples of the former class, Unstan and Midhowe, may be taken as representative. Unstan on the south shore of the Loch of Stenness is an oval mound with a central drystone chamber with five divisions, as well as a little cell; excavation in 1884 produced at least 30 pottery vessels of Unstan ware. Human bones were found in each of the stalls and in the side cell there were two crouched skeletons. It is likely that such tombs were in use over a period of time and that what the archaeologist recovers is merely evidence of the last period of use. Midhowe is a much larger chamber situated on the island of Rousay. Here there are 12 compartments within a long central chamber fully 23 m long. Several of the compartments had low stone settings or benches and skeletons were found on these, in some cases in a crouched position. There are variations in cairn shape and chamber length, but there is no doubt that there are many structural similarities with monuments in Caithness. Until recently excavators concentrated on the chambers, often with unsatisfactory results because they had been plundered long ago. In Orkney, work on cairn formation was pioneered at Point of Cott, Westray, where a cairn at risk from coastal erosion was carefully excavated and recorded in 1984–85, before the sea took it away little by little (Barber 1997). The core cairn around the chamber, a series of box-like structures to lengthen the monument, and finally a number of stepped encasing walls and forecourt combine to make it all the more an impressive monument in the landscape. The excavation and publication in both popular and academic formats of work at Isbister raised public awareness of interpretations of such sites in terms of a Neolithic society's approaches to burial rites, totemism and ritual (Hedges, J. W. 1893; 1983).

The second major category of tomb is named after the most famous example, Maes Howe. A long low passage leads from the outside of the cairn to a central chamber and entrances in the chamber walls give access to cells. Maes Howe was cleared out long before it was excavated in 1861; indeed Norsemen had entered the tomb in the twelfth century and left many runic inscriptions on the walls of the chamber (Farrer 1862; Davidson and Henshall 1989, 142–6). Quanterness was excavated in 1972 and on the floor of the chamber and in the cells there was a thick layer of soil with human bones, along with those of animals, fish and birds. The number of people represented in the excavated area was estimated as 157. Artefacts recovered included sherds of grooved ware vessels, an antler hammer and bone points (Renfrew 1979). Vinquoy Hill on Eday is a less well-known example, but it illustrates the disposition of passage, central chamber and cells and the building technique known as corbelling, where stones are set slightly oversailing inwards to create a vaulted structure. At Pierowall, Westray, a chambered cairn probably of Maes Howe type had been largely destroyed by later building and by quarrying, but a finely decorated slab bearing spirals and concentric rings was discovered, motifs that may be paralleled in the art of passage-graves in Ireland (Davidson and Henshall 1989, 83).

Recent excavations show that the classification of cairns should not be seen as too rigid. A very small burial chamber was found within a little cairn at Setter on Eday, and at Crantit a small chamber had been inserted into a natural mound. The greater variety of the Orkney burial monuments and houses is becoming apparent, and as more excavation is undertaken with sophisticated recording and scientific back up, this variation is likely to increase.

That Neolithic people had an interest in the movement of celestial bodies has long been recognised. One of the most dramatic pieces of evidence for this is the fact that around the time of the midwinter solstice the sun's rays travel along the passage of Maes Howe and strike the back wall of the chamber, although this is not such a precise calendrical event as has sometimes been suggested and occurs for some weeks on either side of the actual solstice (Ruggles and Barclay 2000, 67–8). Nevertheless, that this happens at all is a remarkable piece of observation, ground layout and construction, even if absolute precision was not the aim.

In the later Neolithic period a major centre of ceremonial in Orkney was certainly the twin peninsulas between the Lochs of Stenness and Brodgar, where the stone circles of the Stones of Stenness and the Ring of Brodgar have long attracted archaeological visitors. We know about the lay-out of the Stones of Stenness as a result of excavations in 1973–74 (Ritchie, J. N. G. 1988) and of the Ring of Brodgar at the same time (Renfrew 1979). Both stone circles are surrounded by deep rock-cut ditches. Stenness has an external bank, now very low (and in part reconstructed by Historic Scotland), and Renfrew felt that on balance the slight traces recorded at Brodgar did indeed show that there had been a bank here also, perhaps originally as much as 3 m in height. Both circles are thus parts of 'henge monuments', the archaeological term for ditched enclosures with outer banks with one or more entrance causeways across the encircling works; Stenness probably has one causeway and Brodgar certainly has two opposing causeways. Dating to around 3000 BC, Stenness is also much smaller than its north-west counterpart with a circle of 12 stones having a diameter of 30 m whereas Brodgar has had some 60 stones with a diameter of about 104 m (Ritchie, J. N. G. 1988; Renfrew 1979). The Brodgar circle has been most carefully laid out. But perhaps the most impressive con-structional feat was the digging out of the ditch, as it is cut into the bedrock and measures some 9 m across the top and over 3 m in depth. Altogether 4,700 cubic metres of rock were dug away. Estimates of how long

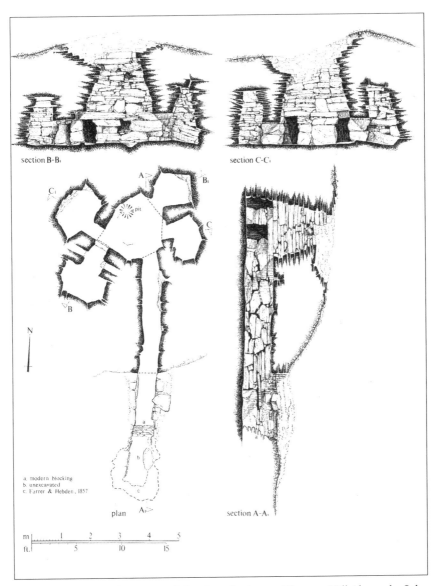

section B-B₁

section C-C₁

a. modern blocking
b. unexcavated
c. Farrer & Hebden, 1857

plan

section A-A₁

FIGURE 10 Plan and sections of chambered cairn on Vinquoy Hill (drawn by John Borland. Crown Copyright RCAHMS)

construction of any monument took in prehistoric times are clearly difficult, for it is likely that such work was seasonal, but Ralston suggested a figure of some 50,000 man-hours for Stenness, and Renfrew put forward the figure of some 80,000 man hours for Brodgar, admittedly taking rather different approaches to construction (Ralston in Ritchie, J. N. G. 1976, 51;

Renfrew 1973, 231). What is not in doubt is the huge scale of such operations for societies without the knowledge of metals.

The large number of excavated sites of the Neolithic period in Orkney has made it possible for the relationships of the monuments to be drawn together in a number of theoretical approaches, linking landscape and cosmology, monumentality and situation. This is no place for a critique of individual theories. But there is no doubt that study of archaeology must go beyond mere description and these approaches allow us to think of the possible ways in which prehistoric peoples thought about their surroundings and the immensely time-consuming monuments that they were creating. The prehistory of Orkney, as in any part of Scotland, was undoubtedly very much more complex than any broad-brush account can offer, and creating over-rigid compartments for monument- or artefact-types underestimates the many possibilities of approach (Ritchie, A. 2000). Indeed, uniquely, Orkney has a broadly representative chronological span of monuments in state guardianship, and there are several guidebooks designed to encourage general interest in them. The intricacies of different approaches may be inappropriate in this sort of consideration, but the level of detail that is possible in the careful excavation of monuments such as Point of Cott chambered cairn or the Howe mound show that the islands still remain a challenging archaeological laboratory, particularly with regard to those sites that have been discovered as a result of field-walking and artefact scatters.

The second millennium BC in Orkney is seen as something of a disappointment after the splendid monuments of the third millennium and as a contrast to the many hoards of bronzes and the array of artefacts that are associated with burial deposits in other parts of Britain (although this is the state of affairs in northern Scotland generally). There are certainly very few examples of objects made of the newly available metal, bronze. Two knives of Early Bronze Age date are known, one of which from Wasbister, Rousay, still retains a horn hilt, but the place where the other was found is known only to be somewhere in the parishes of St Andrews and Holm. The Wasbister implement is described as a working tool with hammered surfaces and much whetted edges (Henshall 1968, 177), and thus is perhaps unlikely to be an isolated example in Orkney. The rich finds that are associated with the Early Bronze Age in other parts of Britain are missing from Orkney, with one important exception. In 1857 at the Knowes of Trotty, a group of mounds in Harray parish, a cist was uncovered; it contained burnt bones, four gold discs and a number of pieces of amber, which may originally have been part of a spacer-plate necklace (Clarke *et al.* 1985, 282). The gold discs, possibly covers for buttons, are elaborately decorated with concentric bands of ornamentation. Such rich grave-goods of Early Bronze Age date indicate long-distance contact, for which there is very little other evidence at this time. Another import is the jet button with a distinctive V-perforation found with a little cache of stone tools beside the revetment wall of the chambered cairn at Isbister (Hedges, J. W. 1983, 45–6). Examples of Middle and Late Bronze Age metal-work are equally few in number, but there are finds that show that well-made bronze objects of recognisable type were making their way into Orkney, for example the socketed bronze knife and 'razor' found while casting peats on Quoykea Moss, St Andrews parish. A sword made from yew wood replicates recognisable Late Bronze Age types of around the 9th century BC and is presumably an import. In many other parts of Scotland the tradition of depositing pottery vessels with burials continued, although chambered cairns went out of use and individual burial, either by cremation or inhumation, became the norm. This was not so in Orkney, and there are thus few examples of those readily identifiable forms such as beakers and food vessels, although fragmentary examples from deposits in chambered cairns and a beaker from Rinyo demonstrate that some knowledge of the southern ceramic traditions did exist (Davidson and Henshall 1989, 79). There are a few beaker sherds at Howe. The discovery of steatite (or soapstone) vessels indicates trade contact with Shetland.

Until recently very little was known about the burial sites of the second to first millennia BC, for few had been excavated to modern standards, and the associated finds had been few and unremarkable. There are, however, several large mounds in the vicinity of the Ring of Brodgar, and this suggests that the old ceremonial complex remained important in the Bronze Age. Not one of the larger mounds in Orkney has been excavated under modern conditions. But the completion of Plumcake Mound for example, to the north-east of the Ring of Brodgar, which measures about 19 m in diameter and was recorded as being 3 m in height, implies a social order in which manpower could still be galvanised to build impressive monuments. The fact that the two cists that were found in the rudimentary excavations in 1854 were well above the original ground surface implies that there is still a great deal to learn. Both cists contained cremation burials, one within a pottery vessel and the other in a steatite urn.

The Orkney flagstone allows a range of cist-construction that is of considerable variety. This is well illustrated at Quandale on Rousay, where Grant excavated a number of mounds and carefully planned the cists, one containing a steatite vessel with a cremation as well as three objects of shaped steatite described as bag-stoppers (Grant 1937). The most extraordinary cist was discovered at Sand Fiold, in west Mainland. Here, a rock-cut chamber held a large free-standing slab-built cist, which had been cleverly designed so that one of the side-slabs could be folded back to allow later burials to be inserted, then replaced and held in position by a small wedge. Good conditions of preservation meant that it was possible to record aspects of the burial rites that do not normally survive. The earliest deposit was material from a cremation pyre which had been placed outside the cist itself, and this dated to the first half of the third millennium

BC. A cremation urn dated to between 2200 and 1900 BC and further cremated bones were added some 900 years later. This was covered by the remains of a mat made of the fibres of grass and sedge. Thus the radio-carbon dates show that the cist was in use over some two millennia (Dalland 1999).

Careful excavation of the Knowes of Quoyscottie revealed the complex nature of such mounds and here a date in the early first millennium was proposed (Hedges, M. E. 1977). This set the scene for the Orkneys Barrows Project that began to examine the less distinguished mounds of Orkney, many at risk from ploughing and cattle damage (Downes 1999). The project identified some 700 mounds, but 150 of these had been destroyed in recent years and more than half had been damaged in some way. Excavation of one of the mounds at Linga Fold, beside the Loch of Stenness, extended over a much larger area than the mound itself and revealed a cremation pyre and a number of secondary burials in cists and pits (Downes 1995). One of the pyre sites still had the remains of the body at its centre (McKinley 1997). Gathering enough material for the funeral pyres cannot have been easy, but birch and hazel and peat were used. Associated finds are few: a pot-lid or a steatite vessel. The sort of detailed research that is now being undertaken on the burial deposits and the rituals surrounding them will greatly enhance our understanding of society in the second and early first millennia BC.

There is no doubt, however, that at this time, for a variety of reasons, including deteriorating weather conditions, there was an increase in the growth of peat. The evidence for settlement is represented by mounds of burnt stones that result from a particular cooking method. The mounds, which are between 5 m and 15 m across and up to 3 m in height, vary from shapeless masses of stone to distinctly crescentic forms, and often have evidence of a large trough or water container. This may lie within the opening of the crescent. Mounds are invariably sited close to a source of water. The mounds are of burnt stone mixed with peat ash and soil. Experiments have shown that a troughful of water can be heated by dropping hot stones into the water, but that these stones will crack, and it is the clearing out of the fractured stones and casting them onto the adjacent pile of debris that creates the mound. Our understanding of burnt mounds was revolutionised by the excavations of Liddle and Beaquoy, where for the first time detailed analysis of the structures was undertaken (Hedges, J. W. 1975). At Liddle, for example, the trough was within a compartmented structure. Other items of the contemporary tool-kit include plough points, indicating agriculture, hammer-stones, pot-lids and undecorated pottery, perhaps suggesting nearby settlement. Other mounds may have been more in the way of field-kitchens and in use only occasionally; the range of possibilities of interpretation, including that of saunas, is intriguing (Barber 1990). With the latter interpretation the inhabitants of Orkney in the later Bronze Age were poor, but clean.

Domestic structures of the later Bronze Age are known at Quanterness, Bu and Pierowall, Westray. At Quanterness a substantial house was built against one side of an earlier chambered cairn around 700 BC. At Pierowall a circular structure of about 600 BC was excavated in advance of quarrying. But it is the Bu building, near Stromness, that most completely illustrates this type. It was originally some 16.3 m in diameter overall, with a wall 3.6 m thick enclosing a central area 9.1 m in diameter. The walls were solid and there was a single entrance passage to the interior. The interior had used flagstone to advantage with a series of compartments round the walls. There was a large central hearth. The artefacts include stone tools such as plough points, grinders and pounders; the radiocarbon dates indicate an occupation around 600 BC.

The brochs of the Northern Isles are among the most impressive prehistoric monuments of Scotland. In using the term 'broch' we run counter to some modern nomenclature that links many of the round houses and forts of the north and west of Scotland as 'Atlantic round-houses'; while it makes good sense to draw attention to the broad connections, many brochs are sufficiently distinct to retain the term, which has a good archaeological ancestry. These circular towers enclose an area between 9 m and 12 m in diameter within a wall up to 4.5 m in thickness. The height of the best preserved, Mousa on Shetland, is 13.3 m, but it is unlikely that all were originally as tall as this. The walls use an ingenious constructional technique to help to achieve height, in that there is both an inner and an outer thickness of walling bonded with cross slabs at intervals. The entrance passage is the only opening in the outer wall, and it is usually checked for a stout door. Inside there may have been openings to cells and to take light into the wall galleries. Excavation has indicated the former existence of a ring of posts that had probably supported internal timber ranges that rested on a ledge or on a series of jutting out stones some distance above the broch floor. Often there are traces of a central hearth. But many features are uncertain or contentious. Broch roofing is a subject for which there may never be a satisfactory solution; there may indeed have been many different ways of roofing in use at the time. The currently fashionable idea of an all-over conical cap seems to the present writer to be unlikely from both structural and storm-effective points of view, while a snugged down inner roof protected by the height of the broch wall from the gales seems more practical, either overall or as an internal range.

Brochs are such a distinctive form of architecture that their origin too is a matter of debate. One school favours the invention of the type following experimentation with forms of drystone walled fortifications, perhaps in Skye. The other school suggests that brochs evolved from the drystone round-houses of the later first millennium BC such as Bu. The date of broch construction and use is also a matter of discussion, but a consensus might see their origin in the last centuries BC and a change in building and social conditions by the 2nd century AD. The social imperative for building such substantial structures is equally uncertain. There was perhaps a perceived external threat, and for those brochs near the coast the risks of skirmishes involved with pirates seeking slaves is plausible, but for inland defences the rationale of prestige, of keeping up with the neighbours, is surely more likely. But, whatever the imperative for broch construction, it evaporated around the 2nd century AD and in many cases the stonework was used to build houses round about the once proud structure.

Excavation of a large mound at Howe has revealed a sequence of structures with three major periods of occupation in the Iron Age. The earliest was a thick walled round-house which was occupied in the 4th to 3rd century BC; this was overlain by a broch, which was itself replaced by a more massive broch with outlying settlement on one side. In the final phase a complex series of structures dating from the 4th to around the 8th centuries AD take us into the realms of the following chapter (Ballin Smith 1994). The importance of Howe is that it demonstrates a degree of structural experimentation on one site. Together with the evidence from Pierowall, Quanterness and Bu, Howe shows the existence of a structural tradition from which the features of distinctive broch architecture might emerge (summarised in Ritchie, A. 1995, 96–7).

More domestic structures are assumed to be associated with underground store-houses, known as souterrains or earth-houses. Such structures generally involve a passage leading to a chamber covered by stone slabs or lintels. Often discovered in the course of agricultural or building operations, they were initially thought to be houses, but it is now clear that they are the cellars of houses of timber and stone that have long since disappeared. One of the best preserved, at Rennibister, was later used as a burial place.

The archaeology of Orkney never ceases to surprise with new discoveries, and never more so than the excavation of Mine Howe. Here a shaft dug into a natural mound had been stone-lined in order to create a precipitous stair leading to a chamber some 7 m below the top of the mound. Further work has shown that the mound is surrounded by a ditch. Metal working of great sophistication took place in the vicinity and there is evidence of slag, furnace-linings and finished brooches. The purpose of the shaft remains a mystery, although a ritual function is probable.

Orkney enters history at the time of Roman invasion of Britain (Maxwell 1975; Fitzpatrick 1989). The name of the islands, Orcades Insulae, is related to Latin 'pig' or 'boar', but cognate words suggest that 'sea monster' may also be related. Tacitus in describing the final stages of Agricola's campaigning after Mons Graupius in AD 83 says that the fleet was sent north to circumnavigate Britain and that they 'found and conquered islands, hitherto unknown, which are called the Orcades'. The 'conquering' is a political puff, for there is no evidence of Roman military presence. But we can envisage the consternation that the sight of the Roman fleet sailing round the islands must have caused. Trading vessels with access to

Roman markets may have produced the Roman amphora of 1st century date from the broch of Gurness and the glass vessel of 4th century date found in a cist on Westray. Little by little Orkney entered the historical world of the Picts.

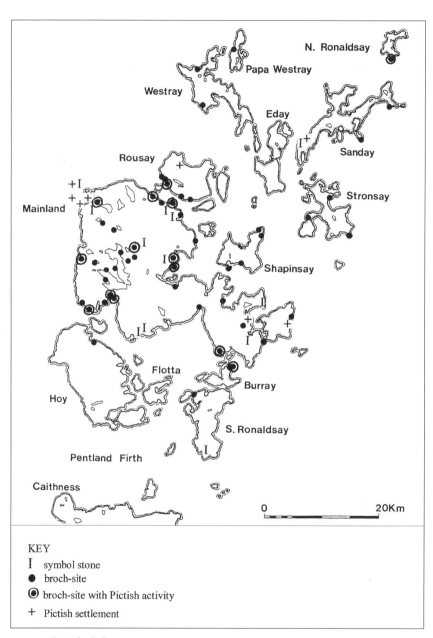

KEY

I   symbol stone

●   broch-site

◉   broch-site with Pictish activity

+   Pictish settlement

MAP 3   Pictish Orkney

CHAPTER THREE

The Picts

Perhaps the single most tantalising aspect of Pictish Orkney is that we know that there was an Orcadian ruler in attendance at the royal court of the Pictish high king near Inverness in AD 565, but we know neither his name nor where he lived in Orkney. A best guess is that he was based at Birsay, because this appears to have been a power-centre in both Pictish and Viking times, and one of his successors in the 7th or 8th century may be portrayed on the symbol stone from the Brough of Birsay. But the importance of this historical reference, in Adomnan's *Life of St Columba* (Sharpe 1995, Book II, chapter 42), is that it backs up the archaeological evidence for the status of Orkney as part of Pictland.

The Picts were the descendants of the Celtic tribes who in lowland Scotland encountered the Roman army and who in the far north built the brochs. Opposition to the might of Rome seems to have encouraged these Celtic-speaking tribes to co-operate with one another and to form political federations with the strength to prevent the Roman army from adding the far north of Britain to the Empire. By the end of the 3rd century AD, the name Picti was in use among classical authors, and soon afterwards the name became a blanket term for all the tribes north of the Firths of Forth and Clyde. By the 6th century the Picts had developed kingship, with a high king and regional kings and chieftains. The fact that Adomnan used the term *regulus* for the Orcadian king suggests that his royal lineage was one of those from which the high king might be chosen (Ritchie, A. 1985, 185) and that Orkney should not be regarded as a peripheral area in which Pictish cultural traditions were in some way diluted. Raymond Lamb has argued on ecclesiastical grounds that Orkney was not absorbed into the Pictish kingdom early in the 8th century (Lamb 1995, 18), but this approach seeks to separate the archaeological evidence in Orkney for Pictish cultural identity from the mid 6th century onwards from a notional political Pictish identity. Nationalism is a relatively recent concept, and it may be doubted whether material culture and political identity can be separated for communities living some thirteen or fourteen hundred years ago.

Overall, the history and archaeology of the Pictish kingdom cover three centuries, from the mid 6th to the mid 9th, when much of mainland Pictland was taken over by the Gaelic-speaking warlords of Dalriada in Argyll under Kenneth mac Alpin. At the same time the Northern Isles fell under the domination of the Norsemen, and Pictish traditions and language were largely replaced by those of the new overlords.

In material terms, the Picts are distinguished from contemporary peoples principally by their use of a unique system of symbols carved on stone slabs (and probably wood, but that does not survive). Symbol stones effectively delineate the geographical extent of Pictland, for they have been found from the Firth of Forth north to Shetland and west to the Outer Hebrides. The symbols themselves are uniform over this wide area, and they testify to the unity of the Pictish kingdom. They range from the abstract to the realistic, from the baffling 'crescent and V-rod' (one of the terms for these symbols that were invented by scholars early last century) to the recognisable goose or bull. The symbols were clearly a means of communication in a society that was largely illiterate, and much has been written in modern times about their purpose and identity (well summarised in Foster 1996, 71–9 and Carver 1999, 18–21). It is a sad but nonetheless true fact that we cannot, and probably will never, be certain of what each symbol represented for the Picts. The meaning of the symbols was certainly flexible, in that they could be used on standing stones, silver jewellery, bone artefacts and in caves (as well as on non-durable materials about which we can only guess, such as leather shields or wooden house-posts). and there is no need to assume that standing stones, the most prolific surviving use for the symbols, all served one function. Some were grave-stones, others were boundary markers and at least one seems to have commemorated a battle.

Compared with mainland Pictland, Orkney has yielded relatively few symbol stones (12), despite the abundance of stone suitable for carving (Mack 1997) (Map 3). On the other hand, none of the surviving stones had remained upright in the landscape, and only four were found in potentially their original location (Brough of Birsay, Greens, Gurness and Pool). Of the rest, three had been re-located in antiquity (Knowe of Burrian, Orphir and Oxtro) and two in recent times (Firth and St Peter's, South Ronaldsay). These circumstances suggest that there may be any number of symbol stones still to be discovered. On the other hand, even fewer symbol stones are known in Shetland (three; Ritchie 1997), and it may be that the nature of society in these northern islands had less need of this particular form of communication. More surprising is the lack of symbol-bearing cross-slabs in Orkney, given the strong links with the Roman Church of south-east Pictland in the 8th century (Lamb 1998).

Among the known stones from Orkney, the crescent and V-rod is the most commonly used symbol (it occurs eight times) as it is for Pictland as a whole (Figure 11). The rectangle occurs five times, the mirror case four times, the mirror and eagle each three times, and the double disc, Pictish beast and divided rectangle are each used once. Symbols were also used on small artefacts, such as a bone pin from Pool carved with a double disc and Z-rod, and knuckle bones that were probably playing pieces from Pool

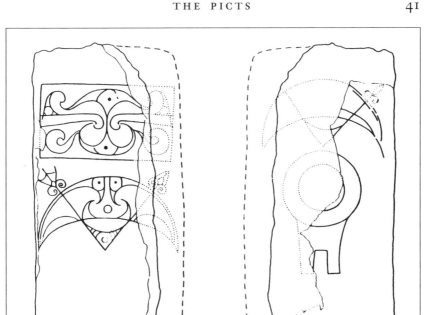

FIGURE 11 Symbol stone from St Peter's Church, South Ronaldsay, with a crescent and V-rod and rectangle on one side, and a crescent and V-rod and mirror case on the other

(crescent and V-rod and rectangle) and Burrian in North Ronaldsay (crescent and V-rod, mirror case). Again the emphasis is upon the crescent and V-rod, rectangle and mirror case. Overall, Orcadian Picts are known to have used just 10 of the 44 designs that were available.

The earliest scientific date that we have for Pictish symbols is the mid 6th century radiocarbon date associated with a crude and possibly unfinished stone from the settlement at Pool in Sanday (Hunter 1997, 32). Otherwise, dating depends upon art-historical analysis of the designs, and here the finely executed eagle on the Knowe of Burrian stone is critical. The style of the eagle is so close to that used as the symbol of St John in an illustrated gospel-book of the early 7th century (known as the Corpus MS 197B) that the Burrian stone-carver and the monk who painted the manuscript must have been copying the same prototype, thought to have been a Pictish gospel-book that has not survived (Henderson 1987, 95–6). The Burrian eagle is thus likely to date from around the same date as the Corpus manuscript and to have been created within a Christian community. It has also been suggested that the 'prototype' was an item of Pictish silverwork that found its way south as a diplomatic gift (Lamb 1998, 44).

The fact that, in mainland Pictland, symbols occur alone on undressed slabs (known as Class I) and on dressed cross-slabs alongside the Christian cross (Class II) has often led to the assumption that the former are earlier and pagan, while the cross-slabs are later and obviously Christian. Only the Christian nature of cross-slabs is certain, and the rest is truly assumption. The Knowe of Burrian stone proves that symbol stones can have Christian associations (and the rectangle is thought to represent a monk's book satchel), but equally other symbol stones may be pagan. And some symbol stones may be contemporary with symbol-bearing cross-slabs, the earliest of which belong to the early 8th century. Christianity had certainly reached Orkney by the 6th/7th century through the influence of Irish monks, who also brought the ogham alphabet, which proved quite popular in the Northern Isles for brief inscriptions. Ogham was invented in Ireland by the 4th century AD as an easy alphabet for carving in wood or stone, for the letters are formed by groups of strokes arranged on either side of a medial line. It was used on memorial stones (Broch of Burrian, North Ronaldsay), on the walls of buildings (Brough of Birsay), and on artefacts. The inscription on a stone spindle-whorl (the weight for a wooden spindle used to spin thread) from the settlement at Buckquoy (Figure 12.1) has been recognised as Irish and reads 'A blessing on the soul of L' (Forsyth 1995). The owner's name presumably began with L, and one can only wish that the whole name had been included. But the importance of this inscription is that it is Irish and Christian.

The precise design of the latest of the Pictish houses at Buckquoy in Birsay also has an Irish/Western Isles link. In essence, it consisted of two main elements: a living hall with low platforms flanking a central hearth and a storage chamber opening off one end. The same type of house was built, for example, in the Western Isles at the Udal in North Uist and in Ireland at Deer Park Farms in Co. Antrim. Together with items of personal adornment such as bronze dress-pins which are also found over the same area, these contacts along the western seaways indicate a cultural climate of which monks following in the footsteps of Cormac were part. Merchants as well as monks may have spoken Irish in Orkney, but most people spoke a form of Celtic as did the Picts in mainland Scotland (Forsyth 1997).

Painted pebbles were not, however, decorated with symbols. These are small white pebbles of quartzite, which were painted with dots, circles and squiggles, but nothing remotely like a symbol (Figure 12.2), and the implication must be that symbols were not considered appropriate for use on pebbles. The tradition of painting pebbles went back into the pre-Pictish, pre-symbol, Middle Iron Age, and the purpose may thus have had its own parameters, which did not include symbols. Painted pebbles are thought to have been charmstones (Ritchie 1972; the current total of painted pebbles found in Orkney, Shetland, Caithness and North Uist is 31) or, less likely, playing pieces (Sharples 1998, 172). As yet, scientific attempts to identify the nature of the paint have failed, but haematite has

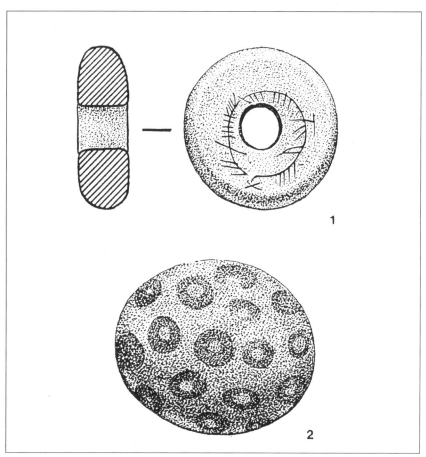

FIGURE 12 Ogham-inscribed spindle whorl (1) and painted pebble (2) from Buckquoy, Birsay

been suggested as a likely element (Isbister 2000, 194). If the symbol-bearing bones from Pool and Burrian were indeed playing pieces rather than ritual objects, a magic use for painted pebbles might be strengthened by their very lack of symbols.

Two outstanding artefacts have survived from this period in Orkney, both made of organic materials that help to illustrate the richness of what we have lost through natural decay. In both cases, the objects were preserved by being buried in peat, whether by accident or design. One is a beautifully carved wooden box that was found near the farm of Howe in Evie in 1885. It was carved from a block of alder, with a sliding lid, and it held leather-worker's tools. The other is an extraordinary high-fashion garment that was found in the very deep peat of St Andrews parish south-east of Kirkwall in 1867: a woollen shoulder cape with a hood, which is edged with a deep fringe about 300 mm long (Figure 13). This well-worn and oft-repaired garment has been dated by radiocarbon analysis to the years between AD 250 and 615 and thus belonged to someone who lived in earliest Pictish times. St Andrews has proved to be a very interesting area of Iron-Age Orkney, not least because of the remarkable underground stair in Mine Howe near Toab and the Pictish settlement excavated on the lower flanks of the mound in 2000. Like the complex of subterranean chambers beneath the floor of the broch at Gurness (Hedges 1987, 35–6; Ritchie 1995, 113–14), the Mine Howe stair with its low side-cells is best seen as a ritual site associated with pagan religious beliefs. The Knowe of Burrian stone was found re-used at the entrance into a well inside a broch (Ritchie 1997, 38, 44) and thus reinforces an enduring interest in wells and shafts.

Little is known about Pictish paganism, but it is likely to have shared many of the aspects of Celtic beliefs and practices recorded by Roman authors and Irish legends and saints' Lives. Natural cult foci included springs, bogs and lochs, while artificial foci included shrines, wells and shafts. Pictish *magi* or wizards figure in Adomnan's acount of Columba's visit to the court of King Bridei in AD 565, and the wolf-headed human carved on the stone from Mail in Shetland may represent a masked wizard or shaman of the early 7th century (Turner 1994). Although Christian ideas were known in Orkney by the end of the 6th century, the conversion process was undoubtedly slow and paganism is likely to have persisted into the 7th century and probably longer. Unfortunately for the archaeologist, pagan burial rites among the Picts did not involve gravegoods, thereby depriving us of artefacts, such as weapons, that might otherwise have survived. Unfortunate, too, because it is difficult to distinguish between pagan and Christian burials, unless the latter are associated with a chapel. At Westness in Rousay, for example, the 9th-century pagan Norse graves are preceded by Pictish graves of the 7th and 8th centuries (Sellevold 1999), but were the latter Christian or pagan? The only clue is their east/west orientation, which might suggest that they were Christian if it were not for the fact that, for all we know, pagan ritual may also have called for that orientation.

The Westness Pictish burials were inhumations in slab-lined long cists, which was the common grave-form for this period. The number of graves that have been discovered throughout Pictland suggests, however, that the bulk of the population was not given formal burial in durable structures. In some cases elsewhere the cist was marked at ground-level by a low stone cairn, round or square in shape and edged by low upright slabs, and this seems to have been a Pictish speciality. Two such cairns as well as long cists without cairns were found on the Point of Buckquoy in Birsay (Morris 1989, 287–92).

Marking the grave with a cross or an inscribed gravestone seems not to have been as important in early Christian times as in more recent centuries,

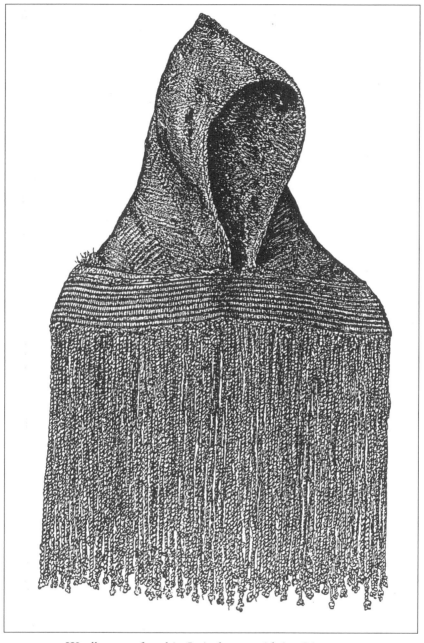

FIGURE 13 Woollen cape found in St Andrews parish in 1867

although of course many simple gravemarkers of wood or stone may have vanished. One very unusual gravestone has survived from Papa Stronsay, in the form of an incised cross with spiral terminals and a Latin inscription, DNE DI for *Domine Dei* (Lord God), and excavations have uncovered traces of a monastic site of Pictish origin, which continued in use into Norse times (Buteux et al. 1999). The excavations in Papa Stronsay have also yielded a fragment of green porphyry to add to those known from the Brough of Birsay, Hunday and Westness in Rousay. Green porphyry was imported into Britain from the Mediterranean in early Christian times, perhaps in the luggage of pilgrims.

Other early cross-slabs indicate pre-Norse chapels at St Boniface in Papa Westray, St Colm's Chapel in Walls, Skaill in Deerness, Burrian in North Ronaldsay and Brough of Birsay, while an impressive slab carved with an interlace-decorated cross from the tiny island of Flotta is part of an altar or a shrine within a church of the 8th century. Excavations at the broch of Burrian in North Ronaldsay yielded evidence of post-broch Pictish activity, along with the cross-slab and a small iron hand-bell of Irish type (MacGregor 1974). The cross-slab also bears an ogham inscription, and it was found in the late levels towards the south side of the broch, in the vicinity of a rectangular slab-lined feature that may have been a large long cist, which was apparently empty at the time of the excavation (ibid. 69). There is thus the intriguing possibility that the ogham-inscribed cross-slab marked a Christian burial in a long cist. Isolated long cists are known from elsewhere in Orkney, for instance at Buckquoy in Birsay (Ritchie 1977, 183–4) and Sandside, Graemsay (Hedges 1978), and it is clear that burials could be made outside formal graveyards.

Lovers of place-name studies will already have picked up the connection between early Christian sites and islands with the prefix *papa*, such as Papa Stronsay and Papa Westray. Originally the Latin name for 'father', *papa* was adopted by the incoming Norsemen to describe monks of the early Church. Palsson sees the *papi* as Irish priests whose presence led to *papar*-place-names in the Isle of Man, the Hebrides, Caithness, Orkney, Shetland, Faroes and Iceland, and even one name in western Norway (Palsson 1996, 18). On the other hand, Lamb has argued from the location of these place-names in Orkney and Shetland that they were clerics of the Roman Church, who had high social status and rich estates attached to their churches (Lamb 1995, 21).

Contacts across the North Sea in pre-Viking times have proved elusive, and even the one *papar*-name in Norway cannot be taken to indicate pre-Viking missionary activity. Reindeer antler has been identified as the material from which several Pictish combs were made, but this identification is not universally accepted (Weber 1992; Ballin Smith 1994), and the dating of the combs is imprecise. The same problems of date and ultimate origin beset artefacts made of steatite, which could have been imported either from Shetland or from Norway. Fine metalwork of Pictish and Irish manufacture has been found in early Viking graves in Norway and could have reached Norway from the mid 8th century onwards (Myhre 1998). Only a limited amount of fine metalworking seems to have been carried out within Orkney (Brough of Birsay, Skaill, Gurness), despite the wealth indicated by the lost hoard of silver vessels, pins, brooches and combs, as well as amber beads, from Burgar (Graham-Campbell 1985). The trickle of imported items of jewellery into Pictish Orkney was no greater than that of Roman times, but it is difficult to judge whether this was the effect of indifference or general impoverishment.

Orkney leads the field in excavated Pictish settlements, and the pattern is clear: the nucleated villages of broch-times gave way to dispersed individual family farms (Hunter 1997, 5). Some of these farms were new establishments of the 5th and 6th centuries (Skaill, Pool) or of the 7th and 8th centuries (Buckquoy, Red Craig, Saevar Howe), and others represent the final phases of occupation on old broch-sites (Howe, Gurness). All belonged to an essentially self-sufficient farming economy, growing barley and oats and breeding cattle, sheep and pigs (but surprisingly few horses), as well as exploiting on a limited scale marine resources such as fish, shellfish and sea-birds (Hunter 1997, 16–22). Deer were hunted and the occasional stranded whale was a welcome source of food, oil and bone. Quite a variety of building forms can be seen among these sites, and large areas of good-quality paving are a feature at Pool and Skaill, where they appear to mark a deliberate and tangible break with the past. At both these sites in the 5th century AD there was a stone-built roundhouse, but, whereas at Skaill this was levelled and covered by paving, at Pool the roundhouse continued in use into the early Viking period (unique evidence of structural overlap between Pictish and Viking times). Otherwise, all the known Pictish houses were built as multi-cellular structures, apart from the figure-of-eight house already mentioned in connection with Irish influence at Buckquoy. Open yards are part of the settlements at Pool and Howe, and these are reminiscent of the earlier yards in the broch-period village at Gurness.

In mainland Pictland, forts were a strong element of the landscape, especially fortified promontories such as Burghead and Portknockie on the Moray coast. Domestic settlement around abandoned brochs in Orkney continued into Pictish times, but it is difficult to judge how functional were the encircling defences at this period. The overall impression is that normal domestic farms were unenclosed. But most Orcadian promontory forts have not been excavated or dated, and it is possible that some were high-status residences in Pictish times. The Brough of Deerness was almost certainly a promontory rather than a detached stack when its rampart and oblong houses were built, and the tidal Brough of Birsay may also have been a promontory 1,300 years ago, when its inhabitants were wealthy enough to commission fine brooches and a Pictish symbol stone. The Castle of Burwick in South Ronaldsay remains a promontory (just – the next hundred years may see it become detached), with four lines of rampart and ditch guarding its landward approach. It may not be a coincidence that a foot-marked stone was found in the vicinity. This is the Ladykirk stone, now to be seen in St Mary's Church at Burwick. A flat rounded boulder is carved with a pair of shod footprints, similar to the stone at Clickhimin in Shetland, and both are part of a tradition that is likely originally to have been of Irish origin and which was involved with the inauguration of kings (the new king stepping literally into the footprints of his predecessor). Its presence in the Burwick area suggests that a prestigious power-centre may have existed here in Pictish times.

Orkney is essential to our understanding of the Picts and in particular of everyday Pictish life. It is also in Orkney that the clearest picture has emerged of the social transition from Pictish province to Norse earldom in the 9th century, in which Viking colonists usurped political control without displacing the indigenous population.

CHAPTER FOUR

Viking and Late Norse Orkney

Introduction

Towards the end of the 8th century, Western Europe witnessed seasonal attacks from Scandinavia. This was the beginning of the Viking Age, recorded vividly by the clerics whose monasteries were prime sources of wealth and portable loot.

Alcuin wrote of the attack on Lindisfarne in AD 793: 'never before has such terror appeared in Britain as we have now suffered from a pagan race'. This sentiment could well have been repeated at several more northerly centres.

The earliest reference to attacks on a Scottish monastery, recorded in the Annals of Ulster in AD 617, refer to 'the burning of Donnan of Eigg with 150 martyrs'. Whether this was Viking activity, or more likely sea-borne Pictish raiders, we cannot really confirm. In 795 Skye was attacked by Vikings *en route* for Ireland, and Iona was repeatedly attacked in AD 795, 802 and 806. Plundering in the Hebrides is noted in 798 and the period which followed, into the 830s, saw a series of seasonal raids in the west.

It is clear, however, that the activity was not all in one direction! *Orkneyinga Saga*, the saga of the Orkney earls, written in the late 12th century tells that: 'One summer Harald Finehair sailed west to punish the Vikings, as he had grown tired of their depredations, for they harried in Norway during the summer, but spent the winter in Shetland or the Orkneys.'

However, the period of raiding was a preliminary to more lasting contacts commencing with over-wintering and then more permanent settlement. With no surviving contemporary Viking sources, the role of archaeology is thrown sharply to the fore; layers of destruction, breaks in artefact or building sequences could represent the advent of the Vikings.

Orkney was inhabited by the Picts on the eve of the arrival of the Vikings, and archaeology in the islands has demonstrated that these indigenous people had a distinctive material culture. The most cited excavations of Pictish buildings are those at Buckquoy, Birsay in the north-west Mainland (Ritchie 1977), but more recent work for example, at Pool on Sanday (Hunter 2000; 1997) and Skaill, Deerness (Gelling 1984; Buteux

1997) has demonstrated that this evidence is more widespread. Burial evidence in the form of kerbed cairns, overlying a sealed long cist and extended inhumation have been noted at Birsay (Morris 1989). The artefactual elements of the culture are also well-represented in Orkney, with painted pebbles, symbol stones and short composite antler combs. However, penannular brooches of a smaller, but similar form to those found in the St Ninian's Isle treasure in Shetland, a massive Pictish hoard deposited in the late Pictish period, were being manufactured in Orkney.

The Arrival of the Vikings

The low-lying fertile lands of Orkney, with good land in the right coastal location, commanding sea routes, marine resources and farming potential, would have been a welcome sight to the Scandinavian incomers; the only drawback may have been the sitting tenants! With milder winters than in Norway, cattle could be overwintered outside, reducing the hay requirement and autumn slaughter.

The overwhelming density of Norse placenames in Orkney – demonstrated on each road sign you pass (Skaill, Kirbister, Quoyloo for example) – provides an indication of the extent to which the incoming Norse population overpowered the pre-existing native population. It is important to remember, however, that a dialect of Norwegian, Norn, was spoken in the islands into the 18th century, ensuring the currency of Scandinavian naming traditions. The Norse earldom (centred in Orkney, but encompassing also Caithness and Shetland), saw Thorfinn establish his base at Birsay in the 11th century and ensured close political ties with Norway throughout the Late Norse period.

Although the majority of the recent excavations in Orkney have focused on the settlement traces, there have been some discoveries of outstanding pagan graves. At Westness on Rousay, for example, Dr Sigrid Kaland excavated a major pagan cemetery which included two boat burials with male warriors, as well as rich female graves, one of which included the famous Westness brooch (Kaland 1993). More recently, the amazing discovery of the Scar boat burial on Sanday has provided an insight into the wealth and cultural variety brought to Orkney in the Viking period (Owen and Dalland 1999). Prior to these discoveries, isolated examples such as a male pagan burial at Buckquoy or the earlier, and somewhat muddled accounts of several graves from Pierowall in Westray, serve to broaden the field of study.

Within the last 25 years the general picture of Viking and Late Norse settlement and economy in Scotland has altered radically and a number of the most significant excavations have taken place in the Orkney Islands. Excavations around Birsay Bay in Western Mainland, Skaill and Deerness in the eastern Mainland, Orphir in south Mainland as well as on the islands such as Westness on Rousay, Pool on Sanday and Tuquoy on Westray have combined to revolutionise our understanding of the Viking (c. 800–1050) and Late Norse (c. 1050–1350 and beyond) periods in Orkney.

There is an imbalance in the amount of information available for the Viking period, in terms of settlement evidence, although this is in part compensated for by the rich pagan burials in the islands, as well as massive silver hoards such as Skaill in the West Mainland. This may have been the property of a wealthy landowner and was deposited c. 950–970, comprising silver ingots and hack silver as well as ornaments (Graham-Campbell 1993).

Western Mainland

Buckquoy

At this site, three distinct phases of Norse settlement were distinguished by the excavator, Dr Anna Ritchie. Built on top of, and adjacent to, an important complex of Pictish cellular dwellings, three fragmentary 9th-century Norse buildings were identified as being of succeeding phases. Ritchie points out that 'Each of the three buildings represents a stratigraphically and chronologically separate phase of the farmstead, and each must originally have been accompanied by at least one other building which has vanished into the sea' (Ritchie, A. 1977).

The primary Viking-age farmstead is represented by the remains of a sub-rectangular structure (House 3), with traces of an eroded byre at the seaward end. Its plan may indicate a small dwelling with integral byre – a true long house. The two interior zones of the building were divided by a stone partition, and high phosphate readings from the drain-fill at its seaward edge support the presence of animals in the structure. When the building fell out of use it was used as a midden dump.

The artefactual material from this phase, as also the succeeding phases of activity at Buckquoy has assumed considerable significance with the benefit of hindsight. Was it Pictish or Norse? The cellular nature of the Pictish buildings was distinctive, but rectangular structures may also have been built before the Norse arrived (cf Skaill, Deerness discussed below or Wag of Forse in Caithness. Curle 1941). Unfortunately, the building had no clearly-defined floor deposit and 'it was impossible to attribute finds from its interior to the period of its occupation'.

The next Norse phase (House 2) comprised a small rectangular building to the north which was very fragmentary; its walls had straight wall-faces and angular internal corners. This building has been interpreted as a threshing barn on the basis of the carefully paved floor and its orientation at right angles to the prevailing wind. This is the only evidence at the site for arable activity. Following the deliberate dismantling of this

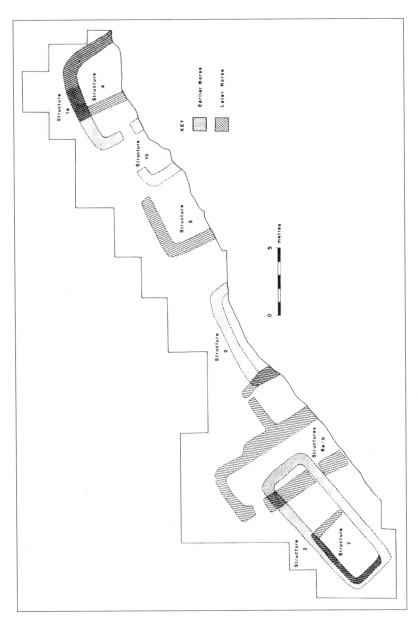

FIGURE 14 Birsay, after Hunter 1986, ill. 60

intermediate structure, the later Norse farmstead and its paving were built on the site.

The few artefacts from this second phase of Norse activity came predominantly from the midden infilling the earlier structure, an assemblage dominated by a range of well-crafted bone pins, several of which appear to be of native rather than specifically Norse manufacture. The suggested cross-over nature of this assemblage – an admixture of Pictish and Norse – has provided a central element in the discussion about the nature of the takeover of Pictish settlement by the Norse.

The final Norse phase (House 1) was identified as a dwelling-house, which had been partially removed by the sea. Only the inner stone faces of the walls survived with sufficient 'turf backing', or wall-core, to show that they had been c. 1 m wide; the north-east corner was squared and the gable-end was constructed of more substantial stone blocks; there had been some remodelling of the structure. The house probably had a central hearth. A potential foundation deposit, in the form of an infant burial under a slab, was also recorded in this building.

The artefactual assemblage from this phase had been widely scattered by ploughing activity. However, the admixture of Pictish material continues into this phase. A single male pagan Norse burial had been inserted into the mound created at the site by infilling middens.

It seems safest to suggest that the Norse phases are all developments of a single farmstead, occupied by one family group, and modified to suit its changing requirements. However, the occupants were not without neighbours, as excavations on the Brough Road, the Brough of Birsay and Saevar Howe to the south have all shown.

The Brough of Birsay

Excavations on this tidal island off the north-west coast of Mainland Orkney have been undertaken since the 1930s (e.g. Orkney Heritage 1983). With the exception of the detailed study of Pictish and Viking artefacts recovered from the work prior to 1974 by Mrs Cecil Curle (Curle 1982), very little is available in published form for this earlier work. The excavations undertaken after 1974 by Professor John Hunter and Professor Christopher Morris concentrated on apparently previously undisturbed areas of the Brough, and revealed considerable structural complexity, spanning the Pictish and Viking periods.

To the west of this complex are the turf-covered remains of sub-rectangular buildings, and in the eastern part there are Viking buildings overlying Pictish ones. It is from this area of the site that much of the important Pictish metalworking evidence has been recovered. However, up the slope to the west the sub-rectangular buildings appear to be more readily intelligible as single phase Viking long houses or hall buildings. Recent re-examination of parts of this area proves that this view is too simplistic – here too there are structural modifications. Work undertaken between 1956 and 1961 concentrated on the Viking buildings to the west of the church and the first phase of these was dated to the 9th century by the excavator Dr Stewart Cruden, with modifications taking place in the 10th–11th centuries. The two earlier structures were about 15 m long by 5 m wide and the long walls appeared to be bowed. Internal divisions were marked by upright flagstones and Cruden suggested an aisled roofing construction on the basis of the internal postholes. Nearby were three structures of the same period range; each structure in this part of the site replacing another, and the earliest of which lay along the contour (the only one identified in this part of the site). The natural slope of the island and the naturally high level of precipitation would have necessitated a swift modification of this building to reduce flooding of the interior. Many of the other structures in the western part of the site were equipped with an efficient external drainage system which reduced this problem.

Other buildings to the west of the churchyard have been examined by Morris in the renewed work at the site since 1974 (Morris 1996). It is clear that this whole area had been examined in the 1930s, but the interiors of the buildings had been of greatest interest and the walls examined only with a view to enable coherent presentation to the public. The renewed activity concentrated on the areas between the obvious structures, as well as a detailed examination of remaining internal features. Considerable structural complexity in these areas was superimposed in places on top of massive post holes and timber remains of the pre-Viking period.

To the north of the church, a relatively undisturbed part of the site, suffering from severe coastal erosion, was examined by Hunter and revealed a number of structures. Several stone and timber pre-Viking buildings were superseded by stone, double-walled buildings of Viking age date (Hunter 1986). Amongst the buildings examined were three structures which could be dated to the earliest Viking activity on the Brough (Figure 14). The next phase of Viking buildings on this part of the site was characterised by buildings which were aligned at right angles to the earlier ones – they were gable-end on to the sea and had consequently suffered badly from erosion. One of these buildings may have been a smithy – with iron slag, fragments of burnt clay and a series of open hearths dominating the area.

Away from this part of the complex on the Brough, several hundred metres to the south, Morris has distinguished a number of additional structures aligned along the cliff-edge, each having suffered through erosion. The most thoroughly examined and complete lies on the Peedie Brough, a narrow neck of land today surrounded by sea on both sides.

Brough Road, Birsay

In the course of excavations undertaken by Morris on the Brough Road sites, Birsay, significant Pictish remains were found to overlie Viking building fragments, middens and a Viking burial (Morris 1989). These are likely to be peripheral to settlement to the north. Severe coastal erosion and the actions of Hurricane Flossie in 1978 wrought havoc on the remaining evidence.

Saevar Howe, Birsay

Excavations undertaken in 1977 by Dr John Hedges demonstrated the importance of the eroding settlement mound of Saevar Howe which is located only a few hundred metres to the south of Birsay Village. Excavations by James Farrer in 1862 and 1867 identified a long cist cemetery, and some fragmentary structures. The 1977 work demonstrated that a Viking settlement had indeed overlain a Pictish one and that the cemetery was most likely of the Christian Norse period (Hedges 1983a).

Farrer's excavations had revealed both fragments of buildings and middens; Hedges identified three superimposed Viking sites above either destroyed or abandoned buildings. The earliest structure was apparently aligned almost east–west and on its uneven floor lay a series of 13 unbaked clay loom-weights. This building fell into disrepair and was covered by blown sand, prior to the construction of a new Viking building above it. Within the succeeding building was central paving of large flags, a burnt area representing the position of the hearth and suggestions of an internal partition. Twenty-eight loom-weights were recovered from the floor level. Following sand blow onto the abandoned building, reoccupation of its upstanding fragments took place and the north wall was completely rebuilt. After the abandonment of this structure, the area became a dumping ground for midden waste.

East Mainland

Skaill, Deerness

Excavations at Skaill, Deerness, were undertaken by Dr Peter Gelling over several seasons during the 1960s and '70s (Gelling 1984). During this period, a large complex of buildings was excavated which indicated occupation in the area of Sandside Bay from the Early Iron Age to the present day (Buteux 1997). On Gelling's Site 2, the earliest Norse building to be identified (House 2) was built from the fragmentary remains of an underlying, roughly rectangular, structure which was identified as Pictish (House 1) (Figure 15). Rebuilding on this site provided a temporary structure which was replaced, after its dereliction, by another which he described as being 'more like a conventional long house' (House 3). There were several structural modifications, indicating that this building was used over an extended period, which Gelling suggested as AD 850–1000.

The main structure, House 3, with its possible adjacent room and enigmatic squared structure incorporating upright stone slabs, was dominated by a long hearth. House 4 – a short rectangular building – replaced House 3, lying partially over one end of the earlier structure. Fitted out

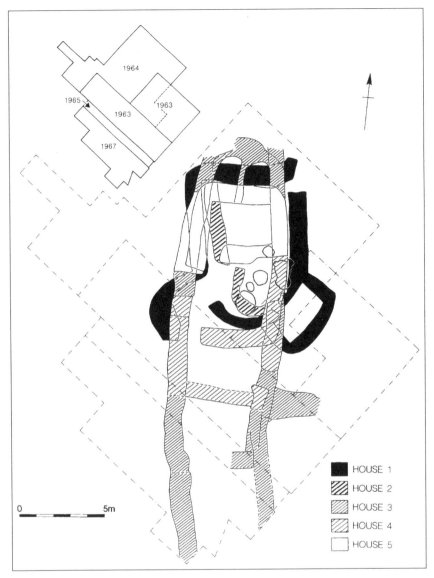

FIGURE 15   Skaill, Deerness, after Buteux 1997, fig. 7.1

with opposing benches and drain, this short rectangular structure was identified provisionally as a kitchen building and was itself subsequently remodelled into a smaller structure (House 5), tentatively suggested as being for livestock. The excavated middens were rich and included antler combs of Norse types as well as bone and antler pins.

Site 4 lay to the south of Site 2 and included substantial remains of

Norse origin, with a building which Gelling suggested was 'erected rather late in the Viking Age'. A further building was examined on Site 1, immediately south of Site 4, '. . . in all probability ... dated not later than the 11th century' (Gelling 1984).

The relationship suggested between the Picts and the incoming Vikings is interesting – Gelling proposed that the Norse settlement brought about a regression in material culture rather than an enhancement. This is likely to be a simplification as there were few finds from the 9th century recovered during this work, possibly due to coastal erosion having removed the earlier deposits. Gelling himself noted 'that there was considerable integration between the two peoples can hardly be doubted, but the sense of a clean break, and of a change for the worse in many material respects, is very strong at Skaill' (Gelling 1984).

Isle of Sanday

Pool

Excavations undertaken in the late 1980s by Professor John Hunter centred on the large man-made mound which had been sectioned by the sea at Pool on Sanday (Asmit 1990; 1997). The mound itself was made up of burnt peat, or turf-like material, and included massive structural activity from the Neolithic into the Iron Age. Immediately, pre-Viking settlement at Pool focused on a sub-circular building, with an internal diameter of c. 6 m, which had been formed out of a remodelling of an earlier building. Many of the features of this structure survived the subsequent Viking activity on the site. Further pre-Viking features included an extensive area of paving which allowed access to a series of cellular units. Large parts of the area which had been occupied in the Neolithic period were than paved over in the 6th century. As an integral part of this phase, Hunter notes 'a courtyard-type component of rectangular form more in keeping with Norse architectural styles than with expected native traditions'. This represented the maximum extent of the Pictish settlement, for there followed a slight contraction.

On the arrival of the Vikings at the site, which radiocarbon dating has indicated may possibly have been as early as the period of the late 8th to early 9th century, the site was partially levelled and a sub-rectangular building (of stone and turf) was created out of fragments of existing structures. The artefacts were not in general culturally specific, showing an admixture of both native and Norse types and Hunter notes this 'serves additionally to cast at least some shadow of doubt over the cultural pedigree of the building itself'. However, some changes in material culture (such as the introduction of steatite vessels), and also changes in the economy, such as the introduction of flax, suggest a cultural change.

Hunter distinguished an interface period at the site when other

Viking-period structures were built to the north-east; one building, although badly damaged by ploughing, was not fully excavated but is likely to have been of c. 14.5 m internal length, and approximately 5 m wide (Structure 25). This building was of timber construction, and survived only in the plan of the post-holes and slots. Of particular interest in this structure are the remains of an inner timber framework, comprising traces of sockets and slots. The floor level comprised burnt deposits, but lacked paving or hearth; Hunter suggests an industrial purpose for this structure, as was also the case for a structure 10 m to the south.

Structure 27 falls within the later part of the interface period distinguished by Hunter. Internally measuring only 9.5 m by 3.5 m, it is about half the size of Structure 25. Hunter suggests that this must have had a turf superstructure, probably of very limited height. The interior was dominated by a rectangular stone-sided hearth, and the artefact assemblage dominated by iron items, mostly rivets. Other finds include hipped pins of pre-Norse types alongside Viking items. Grass-tempered pottery is found throughout all phases – pre-Viking to Late Norse – and certainly underlines that care is needed in ascribing this type of pottery to the arrival of the Norse. Ecofactually, the material is dominated by animal and fish bone, leading to the suggestion that this may have been an area for the processing of meat.

Late Norse Settlement

In recent decades many new settlement sites have been excavated from the Late Norse period (c. 1050–1350) and it is now the case that considerably more Late Norse sites are known than those from the Viking period. The explosion of information concerning the Late Norse activity is, however, yet to be fully realised as many of the sites are still in the process of reaching full publication – the corollary of working in large multidisciplinary teams on large, rich assemblages with extensive environmental sampling programmes.

In the Late Norse period, buildings appear to have been more substantial than before, often made with coursed stonework and with squared corners which may indicate a different roofing construction. The use of flagstone in the north in place of the previous predominance of beach pebbles has enabled a better survival of building plans.

A change in settlement layout, with the use of byres and separate annexes, has been shown at sites such as Jarlshof in Shetland. More recently, Bigelow has argued that the inclusion of an internal byre – to create a true 'long house' – may also be a feature of the Late Norse period. Individual settlements in the Late Norse period distinguished by their associated rich midden dumps, have resulted in an explosion of information, particularly in the north of Scotland. Before the 1970s, later Viking-age settlement had been published from Jarlshof and Underhoull in Shetland, Birsay in Orkney and Freswick in Caithness. However, since then, Sandwick and Da Biggings (in Shetland), Birsay, Beachview, Orphir, Pool, Tuquoy, Westness and Skaill, Deerness (in Orkney); Robert's Haven and Freswick (in Caithness), as well as Whithorn (in the south-west of Scotland), have all been the subject of detailed work. The picture has changed beyond recognition, and in all cases this new evidence has been not only structural or artefactual, but also ecofactual.

Although there must have been close cultural links among Orkney, Shetland and Caithness, which were all parts of the same Northern earldom for several hundreds of years, there is considerably more evidence available from Orkney. Could this simply be a function of the concentration of archaeological work in those islands? Or does it result from the better agricultural prospects there? Orkney was the heart of the Northern earldom, and it has provided the bulk of the new evidence.

Brough of Birsay

Amongst the most obvious group of buildings visible on the Brough of Birsay today, the small 12th-century church, dedicated to St Peter, and its associated buildings, are perhaps the most evocative. This became a major focus of the earls of Orkney in the mid 11th century following periods of both Pictish and Viking activity on the island.

Late Norse secular activity on the Brough of Birsay has been distinguished by Mrs Curle (1982) as the Upper Norse horizon and by John Hunter (the Later Norse phases of Sites VII and VIII at the northern cliff-edge, see Figure 14).

In the area located to the east of the ecclesiastical buildings, Curle reported limited occupation in the Upper Norse horizon, lying to the side of the earlier Viking buildings. Of perhaps greater interest in the light of Hunter's subsequent work are two buildings which are isolated to the north, one of which is virtually square while the other may have been either square or more likely rectangular, similar in form to Hunter's Structure 2 nearby.

Hunter recorded seven structures of the Later Norse period in the area of the cliff top north of the visible complex, including a deliberate reorientation of the buildings, potentially as one simultaneous building programme. In each case, it appears that there had been a deliberate pairing of a major building with an outhouse. One of the buildings produced extensive quantities of metal-working debris, but others may have served as store houses.

Beachview, Birsay

Excavations in the village of Birsay revealed the remains of a substantial stone structure infilled with midden (Morris 1996). This formed the final phase of activity on a totally man-made mound, some 10 m high. The highly fragmented nature of the artefacts – steatite sherds, whalebone, industrial material and distinctive types of antler comb – suggests dumping activity from a building in the immediate vicinity in the Late Norse period. However, the form of the structure, which was ruinous by the time this material was deposited within its walls, is of some considerable interest. The main structure had five major building phases, resulting from the need to extend and then shorten the length of the building and also the need to incorporate a corn-drying kiln at one corner (the earliest so far recorded of this type).

Earl's Bu, Orphir

The site of the Earl's Bu at Orphir lies on the north side of Scapa Flow, and encompasses the remains of the Round Church and the adjacent Norse 'Hall', so often equated with references in the *Orkneyinga Saga* for the year 1135 to the drinking hall of earls Paul and Harald (Taylor 1938, chapter LXVI). The *bu* element in the site's name has a great significance: it indicates that this was *bordland* i.e. earldom property. There are 30 such sites mentioned in *Orkneyinga Saga*, of which 20 are on Orkney, such as Sweyn's *bu* on Gairsay, the *bu* at Paplay, *bu* of Cairston and, probably the best known, the Bu of Orphir.

Today, the visible structural remains, which were largely uncovered in the 1930s, are difficult to interpret. They are an amalgam of different structural phases, probably all or mostly dating from within the Late Norse period. It is, however, clear that these fragmentary buildings are not specifically *the* drinking hall of the saga, but parts of several other structures, only some of which are partially exposed. Geophysical survey has clearly shown that several other buildings lie in this area.

The first recorded investigation at the site took place as early as 1758, and other archaeological activities are recorded in 1899–1901; excavations were undertaken in the 1930s, when the site was taken into guardianship. Nothing further happened until 1978, when excavation began on a dry-stone linear construction which had slab lintels. This feature was identified in 1988 as the remains of a horizontal water-mill – chamber, leat (tail race) and lade – infilled with Late Norse midden debris from the adjacent Earl's Bu to the south (Batey 1993). These excavated deposits are the first to have been recovered from stratified contexts at the Earl's Bu site, comprising the debris thrown away from the 'Earl's Hall' and its associated buildings, which was noted only in a cursory manner in the earlier excavations.

The mill's underhouse survived to over 1 m in height but there were few traces of the upper house above it. This upper room would have contained the workings of the mill – the millstones and working floor. The lade or head race was distinguished as a narrow chute-like feature with substantial slabs standing on end, which gradually sloped eastwards towards the underhouse, where later examples of this mill-type often have a wooden chute. The existence of a small pond to allow a build-up of water pressure was indicated at the west end. The lintel-covered leat or tail race – the original feature to be found in 1978 – allowed water to flow away to the east towards the burn.

The underlying deposits suggest that the feature may have been built in the late Viking period and it had certainly fallen out of use within the Late Norse period. A rather later example of the type can be seen at the Click Mill near Dounby.

This is the first horizontal water-mill in the north to have been dated to the period of Norse presence, although the technology certainly existed in the preceding centuries in Ireland, where several timber mills have been examined.

Skaill, Deerness

The structural remains identified by Peter Gelling at the site of Skaill, Deerness, span a long period. There are several structural elements which may belong to the Late Norse period, including the substantial remains of a rectangular building, 11.6 m × 4 m, with walls of turf core and 'relatively well-built facing on the inside' (Gelling 1984). The structure could have been a large bath-house, or more likely a heated building for grain storage.

Westness, Rousay

Excavations by Dr Sigrid Kaland at Westness have revealed a large pagan Norse cemetery on Moaness, and a pair of rectangular stone buildings representing a Late Norse farmstead, with a boat-house (*noust*) nearby (Kaland 1993). Described in the *Orkneyinga Saga* as the home of Sigurd of Westness in the early 12th century, this was indeed a favoured location. The farm buildings, which are located almost on the present-day beach, were linked by a paved area. One of the structures was 35 m long and 6.5–7 m wide and had been a dwelling, with the interior subdivided into two large rooms separated by a third small room; it had been rebuilt during its lifetime. Side-benches beside the large central hearth were found in the north room which had an eastern entrance, whilst the southern room, some 10 m long, had a protected western entrance leading into a paved interior. The adjacent structure comprised two conjoined elements: one 15 m long and 5–5.5 m wide, with curving outer walls, its sunken paved access suggesting a byre with room for 18 cows; the other element was a possible sheep byre, being much smaller in area, only 5 m × 5 m, with a paved floor enabling good run-off for the waste products.

The boat house, or *noust*, had been built at the best location, the most sheltered from the winds and fierce currents of Eynhallow Sound. It has been truncated by the sea, but some 8 m survived of the length and as the width was 4.5 m, it may have housed a single large vessel or two small *faering* (rowing boats).

Tuquoy, Westray

A different type of site has been excavated at the badly eroded cliff edge near Crosskirk Church on Westray. The impressive stone remains, which are falling from the cliff, have been assessed and partially excavated by Olwyn Owen (Owen 1993). Potentially associated with Thorkel Flettir and his heir Haflidi – although not specifically mentioned in the *Orkneyinga Saga* – the well-preserved massive structural fragments, covered with lime plaster, comprise only one edge of a large settlement. The exposed remains cover 150 m at the cliff edge, and have been traced up to 50 m inland. Other isolated buildings and field remains remains cover a larger area.

It is a substantial structure of at least 3.75 m wide and 6.65 m in length, with walls 1 m–1.4 m thick; had a well-paved floor and underwent several phases of modification, suggesting varying functions at different times. The recovery of a runic inscription (translated as 'Thorstein Einarsson carved these runes') and a distinctive kidney-ringed pin indicate a date range of the late 11th to early 12th century. Initially, it was suggested that this structure might have been of a defensive nature, similar to Cubbie Roo's Castle on Wyre, but the preferred current view is that it was a well-built dwelling of some high status, conceivably more similar to the hall-type structure at the Wirk, near Westness, Rousay. The Wirk has a small square tower with an attached hall (26 m long and c. 7 m wide) and the main accommodation was on the first floor. The structure is similar in scale to that surviving from the 12th century Bishop's Palace in Kirkwall.

New Developments

Continuing excavation programmes in the islands yield new information about the Norse earldom, and of particular note in this respect is the work being undertaken by Dr James Barrett at the site of Quoygrew on Westray. Thorough integration of environmental issues with targeted excavation continue to investigate the relationship between a substantial stone structure of Late Norse date, and an extensive midden with a clear infield–outfield system. This work is of crucial significance for increasing understanding of the local topographical impact such settlements can have, as well as providing an insight into the dietary balance of the population. In a related project, he is also examining the wider implications of the expansion of fish consumption in terms of local eating patterns and export activities, perhaps in relation to the demands of the Church (Barrett et al. 2000).

Renewed active interest in the role of the Church and Christianity in Late Norse Orkney can also be seen. Important work undertaken at the Brough of Deerness – arguably one of the most evocative and picturesque of the sites of the period in Orkney – as long ago as 1975–77 by Morris (Morris & Emery 1986) placed the form of chapel construction identified in the Northern Isles within the North Atlantic context. Survey programmes by both Morris and Lowe in the Northern Isles have provided – and continue to provide – an invaluable database for broader study.

Finally, there is an on-going Scotland-wide re-examination of all the pagan burial evidence including all old finds and reinterpretation of the earlier evidence by Professor James Graham-Campbell and Caroline Paterson. This will go a long way towards ordering this complex record, particularly for Orkney, and the results are eagerly awaited. It is clear that although there has been a disproportionate amount of archaeological activity in Orkney over the last centuries, there is more to be discovered, more to be understood and probably more to be explained.

CHAPTER FIVE

Orkney in the Middle Ages

A Unique Norse Earldom Dynasty

The history of Orkney in the Middle Ages is the history of the earldom. The whole archipelago of islands was controlled and ruled by a single dynasty: from Orkney the earls extended their authority over the Shetland islands to the north and southwards over the province of Caithness, which included Sutherland, on the north Scottish mainland. Indeed, as we will see, for a period they also exercised some control over the Hebrides. At the same time the earls themselves had to submit to those kings of Norway who were powerful enough to be able to enforce their superiority in the islands in the west which had been settled by Norse Vikings. This was part of the process by which medieval hierarchies were established, and rulers of large units with the title of king asserted supremacy over chieftains of provinces, or (as in this instance) groups of islands ruled by a family with the title of earl.

The earls of Orkney were also earls of Caithness, which from c. 1100 came under the authority of the Scottish kings, and this made their position historically distinctive and very interesting. Nowhere else in Scotland, or in Norway, do we have a situation where an earldom dynasty owed allegiance to two kings. As earls in the islands they were nominally subject to the authority of the king of Norway, as earls of Caithness they owed homage to the kings of Scotland; and in both roles they had to face the same relentless growth of royal power encroaching on their insular and highland domains. It is a gripping story of challenge and response to change, although inevitably the earls of Orkney failed to maintain their independence in the political climate of developing nation states. It is not always easy to understand the mechanisms of power which led to the demise of the earldom, the weakening of Norway's control and the inexorable growth of the Scottish kingdom. The ultimate success of the kingdom of Scotland in reaching its northern territorial and maritime limits was to be achieved in the 15th century.

All over medieval Europe noble families were often at loggerheads with their kings and there were very few dynasties of earls which retained their power and influence for as long as the earldom of Orkney. From its obscure origins in the late 9th century until the 'excambion' of 1470 there was an earldom of Orkney, with very few breaks indeed, and those only because the kings of Norway held the earldom in abeyance, for a brief period, or granted it out to more reliable royal servants, temporarily, until they had assured themselves of the suitability of the family claimant to the earldom. There were breaks in the direct line, but distant Scottish heirs came forward who were willing and able to move north and adapt to a life in the Northern Isles. This is all the more remarkable because during this period the Norse world of the Northern seas lost its coherence and Norse culture started to weaken. But the vacuum was filled by distant Scottish cousins who brought a new language and different culture into the islands. There may have been a glamour – and there was certainly status – attached to possessing the title of earl of Orkney, as well as the acquisition of a wealthy lordship, which was sufficient inducement to the Angus heirs and the Strathearn cousins and the Sinclair progeny to take on a new role and seek out the Norwegian or Danish king on the other side of the North Sea in order to acquire a formal acknowledgement of their claim. Although we know very little of the process of assimilation there was undeniable continuity of title, and the pride in the dynastic continuity is very evident in a 'Genealogy of the Earls' which was written by cathedral clergy in Orkney in the 15th century at the command of Earl William Sinclair.

Orkneyinga Saga

The 'Genealogy of the earls' went back to the 9th century and the foundation of the earldom, and was based on the remarkable story of the deeds of the earls recounted in the dynastic *Orkneyinga Saga*, the saga of the earls of Orkney. This compilation was written in Iceland c. 1200, based on several different *þattr* or sagas of individual earls, and woven around stanzas of skaldic poetry written in honour of the earls, with added traditional stories. It is one of Scotland's most remarkable surviving pieces of historical and literary evidence, and provides brilliant pictures of a past nordic world when the earls were sea-lords and captains of a fleet of longships with which they dominated the waters around the northern half of Britain. There are also glimpses of life in the islands, of the earls' followings and families who were settled on the good fertile lands of Orkney and Caithness, and who became involved in the rivalries and tensions of their chiefs and overlords. It may not be absolutely reliable as a piece of historical documentation – it would be a lot less entertaining if it were – but it is a valuable source of knowledge about the remote past which is unmatched by any other medieval example of historical evidence from Scotland. It reveals clearly the status which the earls had in the north Atlantic world of the high Middle Ages, and it was still read and known in Orkney in the 15th century.

The 11th Century: Christian Rulers of a Maritime Empire

Although the earls submitted to the growing authority of the kings of Norway in the 11th century, nonetheless this century saw the earldom become an independent established administrative lordship in its own right. The earls were no longer the Viking chieftains who solely based their careers on 'going out and acquiring the wealth of nations' (Adam of Bremen) and attracting and maintaining a warband in permanent readiness for a life of predation, although there was still an element of that. Thorfinn Sigurdsson, who shared the earldom with his half-brothers after the death of their father in 1014, and who then jointly ruled with his nephew Rognvald during the 1030s, was praised for making 'something of a name for himself in Orkney by feasting his men, and others too, people of great reputation, on meat and drink throughout the winter, in the same way that kings and earls in other lands would entertain their followers around Christmas so there was no need for anyone to search for taverns' (*OS* chapter 20).

Important though it still was for a successful earl to attract a loyal following which was militarily well-trained, there were other considerations if he was going to maintain his rule over his conquered dominions. The first of these was to govern and administer his territories, to instal men who could rule them on his behalf and exact regular tribute. The saga of Earl Thorfinn focuses on the battles which he won in northern Scotland and in the Hebrides, and when the saga writer assures the reader that 'it's said on good authority that he was the most powerful of all the earls of Orkney' (*OS* chapter 32), we can have some confidence that this was a well-founded judgement. His skald claims that he ruled a huge maritime zone stretching from Dublin to Shetland, and this is expanded upon in the saga eulogy as including nine Scottish earldoms, the 'whole of the Hebrides' and a 'considerable part of Ireland' (*OS* chapter 32). There is doubtless some exaggeration here, although we do not know exactly what is meant by a 'Scottish earldom'. However, the point is also made that he 'ruled all his lands till he died', and he would only be able to do this with the help of a loyal retinue (*hird*) which was able and willing – and sufficiently organised – to administer the different lands and islands on the earl's behalf.

The Establishment of Church and Bishopric

The change from Viking warlord to ruler of an 'empire' was also helped by the establishment of a Church in Orkney, for the installation of a Christian clergy provided the earl with an educated elite, which could be put to good use in the recording and accounting processes, so important to government. The conversion of the islands is supposed to have taken place after the forced conversion of Thorfinn's father, Sigurd Hlodversson, in 995 by Olaf Triggvason. This event probably initiated the due Christianisation of Orkney and Caithness, for only when the earls had

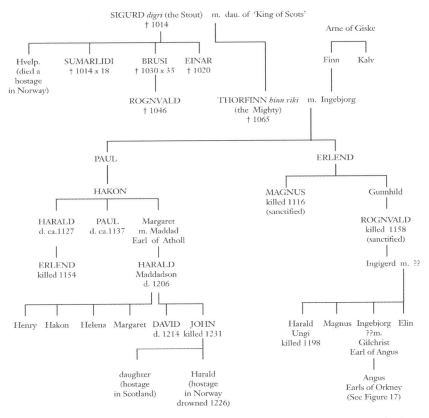

FIGURE 16. The descent of the earldom family (1014–1231)

agreed to allow a priesthood to be established in their earldoms, and
when they had endowed and built churches would the proper process of
teaching and inculcation of Christian morals be applied. Some priests may
have been left behind in Orkney by King Olaf after Sigurd's conversion,
but the saga makes no mention of any permanent Christian establishments
until the sole rule of Thorfinn (1040s), when it is specifically said that he
'built and dedicated to Christ a fine minster, the seat of the first bishop
of Orkney' (*OS*, chapter 31). The absence of any pagan graves from
Orkney datable to the 11th century indicates that pagan burial customs
had ceased during the 10th century. Although this vacuum may have been
filled by an 'underground' spread of belief in Christianity it is unlikely
that any regular Christian worship was established before Sigurd was
prevailed upon to formalise religious conventions in his earldom in 995.

Thorfinn, Sigurd's son by his second marriage to the daughter of the
Scottish King Malcolm II, was brought up at the court of his grandfather
after his father's death. This undoubtedly meant that he would have been

educated in a very Christian environment and influenced in the way in which a ruler should be protecting the Church in his kingdom and fostering the spread of belief. His famous pilgrimage to Rome c. 1050 was an indication of the role Thorfinn wished to be seen to be playing as a model Christian ruler, for many other kings and lords from northern Europe also went to Rome at this same period. There was probably an element of penance involved, as Thorfinn had been responsible for the murder of his co-earl, Rognvald Brusisson, in 1046. It is very likely that the papacy imposed conditions for the remission of his sins, among which would have been the establishment of a bishop with proper endowment of lands and ecclesiastical facilities. The saga writer also says that after his return from Rome Thorfinn gave up piracy and 'devoted all his time to the government of his people and country and to the making of new laws' (OS chapter 31). The church which he built for the first resident bishop, Thorolf, was at the same place as his own permanent residence, Birsay, in the west Mainland of Orkney, a pattern seen in other Viking lordships, such as Dublin, where the Viking ruler Sigtrygg Silkbeard built Christchurch Cathedral in the 1050s. The official establishment of Christianity in the kingdom of Norway took place at much the same time. This process is a very important stage in the assimilation of the Viking world into the wider medieval Christian culture of Europe. It is certain that the earl's lead would have been followed by other landowners and the *bonder* (farmers), so that in the second half of the 11th century small private chapels would have been constructed around the islands and in Caithness. In the next century some of them developed into parish churches.

Earls and Kings

Thorfinn's long reign saw Orkney become the seat of a powerful earldom dynasty and the centre of a maritime network which reached from Norway to Dublin and from Scotland to Iceland. Scandinavian involvement in the internal situation in England, and Scotland, meant that the earls participated in the stirring events which were happening further south, such as the battle of Stamford Bridge in 1066 when the joint earls Paul and Erlend Thorfinsson accompanied their Norwegian king, Harald Hardrada, but survived to return home.[1] At the very end of the century their sons were coerced into joining Magnus Barelegs on his expedition to the Northern Isles, the Hebrides, Ireland and the Isle of Man, when he intended to re-assert Norwegian supremacy over the Western world. In connection with this show of aggrandisement Paul and Erlend were taken back to Norway, under some sort of duress, where they both died. Magnus' attempt to bring the earldom under direct royal control did not long outlast his death in Ireland in 1103.

The 12th Century: Cultural Achievements and the Cult of Saintly Earls

Any permanent encroachment by the kings into the private empire of the earls of Orkney did not happen until the end of the 12th century. For most of this century the earls ruled their island world untroubled by the financial demands of national kings or the control mechanism of an international Church. However, there were plenty of internal disputes over inheritance of the earldom lands and rights, especially because there was no right of primogeniture, as all male heirs had equal claims, even those who inherited that right though the female members of the earldom *aett* (dynasty). In the strife which inevitably accompanied the growth of young heirs to manhood and the pressing of their claims, six earls were killed during this century, two of whom, Magnus Erlendson and Rognvald Kali Kolsson, came to be revered as saints.

The veneration of royal holy men and the growth of national saints' cults was a phenomenon of the recently converted Scandinavian world. It reflects the burgeoning of deeply pious societies, but ones which needed to replace the local gods that had been banished with the coming of the monotheistic Christian religion. There was a clear tendency among the Scandinavian peoples to invest their royal leaders who met violent deaths with the attributes of sainthood, and thus acquire national martyrs who could represent the aspirations of the political units which were developing at this time in Norway, Denmark and Sweden. The earldom of Orkney is an insular example of a patriotic community with a separate and distinct identity and with a strong ruling dynasty. Hence when Magnus Erlendsson was killed in April 1116 on the island of Egilsay by his cousin Hakon Paulsson, who was ruling the islands jointly with him, the family of Erlend very quickly turned the situation to the advantage of their earldom line and represented his violent death as the martyrdom of a peaceful and noble young man sacrificed to the ambitions of his rival. Magnus' relatives and supporters would appear to have been very important in the establishment of the cult, from which they, and particularly Magnus' nephew Rognvald, the only male heir to the Erlend line, directly benefited.

Cathedral Patrons and Builders

There were of course other important factors in the creation of a saint, such as proof of miracles, and the support of the local bishop. The Church to begin with appears to have been unhappy about the growth of fervent local feeling around the memory of the dead Magnus, but of course the bishop was closely connected with the sole rulers, Hakon and his son Paul. Indeed the bishops' first cathedral in Orkney was built for them by the earls, close to their residence at Birsay, and no bishop could afford to alienate his powerful secular patrons and protectors. Bishop William is represented in the saga as being antagonistic to the growing belief in Magnus' sanctity, which he decried by calling the stories 'sheer heresy' (*OS*, chapter 56). His remarkable conversion to belief in the earl's sanctity is described in the Miracle Book as having been caused by miraculous happenings (*OS*, chapter 57). A more rational explanation would see Bishop William's change of heart as being due to a shrewd recognition of a change in the political wind, and the prevailing of Rognvald Kali's claim to possession of his murdered uncle's estates. Promises by Rognvald and his father Kol to build a magnificent cathedral at Kirkwall dedicated to Magnus, and endowed with land and income which would be at the bishop's disposal provide sufficient explanation for Bishop William's decision to initiate the due process required for canonisation. The corporeal relics were disinterred from their resting place in the bishop's church in Birsay, submitted to ritual testing in fire and 'translated' and enshrined, before being transferred to Kirkwall, first to the church of St Olaf and then to the magnificent cathedral which Rognvald started to build in 1137.

Even today St Magnus Cathedral impresses every visitor to the small market town of Kirkwall, where this remarkable example of Romanesque architecture is still the centre of island life and culture. How much more impressive must it have been in the mid 12th century, when the nearest comparable ecclesiastical building was far away in the south of Scotland! It is testimony to the wealth and widespread cultural connections of the earldom dynasty at this time. The effort and resources invested in the building must have paid off in many ways. Apart from the income which came pouring in from pilgrims to the shrine of the murdered earl, there was the intangible prestige which accrued to the saint's descendants, and made the Orkney earldom unique among earldom dynasties; it was in fact on a par with the royal Scottish and Norwegian dynasties, both of which had acquired their own family saint in the previous century. This must have been of inestimable advantage in the game of medieval power politics.

Rognvald Kali Kolsson, pilgrim-poet and earl-saint
The achievement was Rognvald Kali Kolsson's and helps to explain why he himself acquired a martyr's crown. He was a most successful earl, weathering many rival claimants and controlling some notable trouble-makers, whose adventures are recorded in the saga. He was skilled in sporting and artistic achievements, being one of the finest skalds in the Norse world, and, as the saga writer tells us 'he was immensely popular there in the Isles and far and wide elsewhere' (*OS*, chapter 104).[2] He symbolises the northern world's assimilation of the wider medieval Christian culture, although retaining its own distinct qualities. The saga account of his pilgrimage to the Holy Land is a remarkable literary record which is an unusual survival. The poetry which Rognvald composed in honour of the lovely lady Ermingard, while tarrying at the court of Narbonne,

shows strong influence from courtly love poetry, possibly the first such examples in skaldic verse. But this attractive and much-loved earl met his death in a sordid fight-out while pursuing an outlaw in upper Thursodale, Caithness. This was a sufficiently violent end in the pursuance of his duty as a Christian ruler to provide the right credentials for martyrdom. He was buried in St Magnus Cathedral and very soon miracles occurred at his grave, so that the current bishop had his relics translated: this time, it is said, with the permission of the pope (*OS*, chapter 104). Ecclesiastical pressure certainly led the move to canonisation on this occasion and it must have been Rognvald's remarkable achievements in founding and endowing St Magnus Cathedral which earned him saintly status in the eyes of the bishop and chapter, and led to their promotion of his cult. So the cathedral was the resting-place of two earldom saints! An unprecedented situation in the whole of the northern world, marking the peak of the Orkney earldom's status and the islands' unique contribution to medieval life and culture.

The 13th Century: Royal Encroachments and the Earldom reduction in Land and Power

At the very end of the 12th century the northern world was changing, and the Orkney earls were to suffer from increasing royal authority in both Scotland and Norway. As earls of Caithness they were subject to the kings of Scots, and in the late 12th century these kings were intent on expanding their power to the very north of their kingdom. The kings of Norway were also determined to bring the 'skattlands' in the west fully within the administrative network of their kingdom, insofar as they had the ability to do so. For both rulers it was only possible to extend their authority to these remoter outposts when they were free of civil war and feudal uprisings, and there were plenty of these in both kingdoms in the 12th century. But the illegitimate claimant Sverre fought his way to a very powerful position as sole king of Norway by the end of the century, and was intent on imposing royal officials and administrative control throughout his kingdom and 'skattlands'. The earldom of Orkney had been free of such impositions hitherto, only having to render a tax when each new earl was accepted and entered into a relationship with his acknowledged over-lord, the king.

Harald Maddadson's Encounters with Powerful Kings

The earl who happened to be ruling at the time when powerful, ambitious kings were on the thrones of both Scotland and Norway was Harald Maddadson, who shared the government of Orkney and Caithness with Rognvald until the latter's death in 1168, and who then dominated the northern earldoms alone until his own death in 1206. Throughout this

latter period he was challenged by rival claimants to the earldoms, and
was unable to retain his power untouched by royal encroachments. The
story of his involvement in the political situation in north Scotland, and
his attack on the bishop of Caithness in 1201, which led to his humiliating
submission to King William, is a salutary lesson in the mistake of alienating
the Church.[3] As far as his relationship with his Norwegian overlord is
concerned he made another disastrous mistake; this was to become impli-
cated in a rising against King Sverre in 1192–93, which was hatched in
the islands, by the earl's brother-in-law, with the intention of placing the
illegitimate son of Sverre's ousted rival on the throne. Although not
participating in the battle of Floruvåg, fought near Bergen, by the Eyias-
keggjar ('Island-Beardies') with King Sverre, Harald was considered
responsible for the gathering of forces against Sverre and he had to undergo
another humiliating submission in 1195. This meeting is fully described
in *Sverre's Saga* and Harald was accompanied to the king's presence by
Bishop Bjarne of Orkney, who pleaded his case. He was fortunate to retain
his earldom, but he forfeited the Shetland Islands, and lost half the judicial
dues from Orkney, also having to suffer the indignity of having a royal
official appointed to sit beside him in his earldom. The crown acquired
the estates of those members of the island aristocracy who had been
involved in the battle of Floruvåg.

In this way, one of the most powerful earls of Orkney was constrained
and his position severely weakened. But the kings could only maintain their
dominant position if they had sufficient resources themselves to keep officials
in the islands, or in Caithness, and if they had the support of the Church.
This depended on whether they were able to control the appointments to
the bishoprics, as the Scottish kings did, although in Orkney, at this time,
the right of episcopal appointment lay with the earls. So, once the powerful
Sverre had died in 1202 and civil war broke out in Norway again, Harald
had the royal official murdered, and took Shetland back under his authority.
However, the breach in the independent status of the earldom had been
made, and once the kings were again in a strong enough position to do so
they were able to crack down and bring the earls to heel, with the threat
of more sanctions and tighter methods of control.

The End of the Norse Line and Arrival of Scottish Earls

The process of assertion of royal rights in the two earldoms continued
during the rule of Earl John Haraldson, who does not seem to have learned
the lessons of his father's turbulent life. He first made the mistake of
becoming tainted with complicity in the shocking murder of Bishop Adam
of Caithness in 1222, which provided Alexander II with all the excuse he
needed to send expeditionary forces north and impose fines and conditions
on the earl. Earl John then ended up on the wrong side of the powerful
Hakon Hakonsson in Norway and was summoned to Norway in 1224 on
suspicion of conspiracy. Finally he quarrelled with the royal official in

Orkney, which led to a feud in which rival earldom claimants became involved and the earl himself was murdered in the cellar of a house in Thurso in 1231. This event had long-term consequences for the earldom as there was no apparent direct heir, and after all the parties involved had been summoned to Bergen for retribution – and presumably the appointment of a new earl – the ship carrying the earl's kin back home went down with the loss of all on board. With this dramatic event the old Norse earldom line died out, at just the same time as the saga itself also dries up, and the history of Norse Orkney can be regarded as coming to an end.

The history of the earldom did not, however, come to an end. It gradually becomes more of an outpost of Scottish feudal history, and increasingly tied into events in Scotland. The remainder of the 13th century is a very obscure period, for without the narrative of the earls' saga and with the decline of the social, cultural and economic links with the north Atlantic there was a hiatus in the history of the islands which was filled by very few Scottish sources. We know that the earldom passed to members of the Angus family, who certainly moved north, and maybe even adopted the mantle of their Norse predecessors, but there is little evidence of their lives and achievements. Only at the time of the famous expedition of King Hakon Hakonsson to assert Norwegian sovereignty in the Western Isles do we catch a glimpse of one of these earls, but his failure to follow the fleet of his Norwegian lord west, and his absence from Orkney during the months following the battle of Largs, when King Hakon died in Kirkwall, reveals something about his priorities, and his divided loyalties. It was of course exceptionally difficult for an earl with two overlords when they came to blows, and to be in such a position was becoming very anomalous in the northern world of 13th-century kingdoms. Earl Magnus III was compelled to take a position of enforced neutrality, and received a crushing series of fines from his Scottish overlord, while he had fresh conditions eventually imposed on him when he was reconciled with his Norwegian overlord in 1267.

A very important factor affecting the earls' power and position was the occurrence of minorities during this period. Because of the prevailing system of primogeniture and the rejection of any rights of inheritance of illegitimate sons there were several occasions when heirs were under age at their father's death. This provided opportunities for feudal overlords to get involved in the administration of the earldom, the Scottish kings in Caithness and the Norwegian kings in Orkney.

The 14th Century: Plague, Schism and Scots

The 14th century was a difficult era all over northern Europe, and the effects of the Black Death in the middle of the century were disastrous for Scandinavia, particularly Norway, where, it is estimated, nearly half of the population may have died. The only information we have about the incidence of plague in Orkney is an entry in the *Icelandic Annals* (sub anno 1349) that the 'same sickness came to Shetland, Orkney, the Sudreys [Hebrides] and Faeroes'. The abandonment of farms meant that economic values deteriorated making it very difficult for the land-owning classes who lived off the rents and income from their estates. This led to a power struggle between nobles and the monarchy, and there is certainly evidence of some turbulence in the islands with different factions fighting for control. Another hiatus in the male line of heirs meant that inheritance of the earldom had passed to the earl of Strathearn in 1330, and on his death c. 1350, leaving five heiresses, the door was opened to rival claims by his sons-in-law, and eventually grandsons.

A growing body of documentary evidence tells us something about the political situation in the islands, and the later 'Genealogy of the earls' gives some details of the turbulent events. The winner playing for the high stakes was the grandson, Henry Sinclair, a member of a southern Scottish noble family, who succeeded in persuading King Hakon VI Magnusson in 1379 that he was the best claimant to be given the lands of the earldom and the ancient title of earl. This dramatic development in the fortunes of the Sinclair family must have entailed a certain amount of adaptation to the completely different political and cultural circumstances which prevailed in the islands. One can glean that they took on the challenge with energy and determination.

Certainly the period of the three Sinclair earls forms a memorable epilogue to the ancient Norse earldom, but it was of a very different character from the earlier dignity. The North Atlantic links were gone (unless one believes the contentious evidence of the Zeno letters!),[4] and even contacts with Norway must have been much weaker, for the Union of Kalmar (1397) had created a single Scandinavian monarchy with its main base in Denmark. What maritime network existed was mostly between Orkney and the Scottish mainland, and especially southern Scotland, for the joint earldom with Caithness was temporarily in abeyance when the latter earldom was resigned to the Scottish crown in the 1370s. The situation in Shetland was of course very different, and the social and cultural links with Norway, particularly Bergen, remained strong and significant in the life of those islands.

It is difficult to know to what extent the Sinclair earls regarded their Orkney earldom as merely important for the dignity it brought them. They probably ruled their island earldom mostly as absentees; certainly the second Earl Henry was fully occupied in central Scottish affairs, and through his prestigious marriage to Egidia Douglas, granddaughter of King Robert II, very close to the royal court, as can be seen from his witnessing of important royal charters. He probably never even visited his Scandinavian overlord, but was represented in the north by relatives or members of his feudal following. The Church in the north was also being strongly

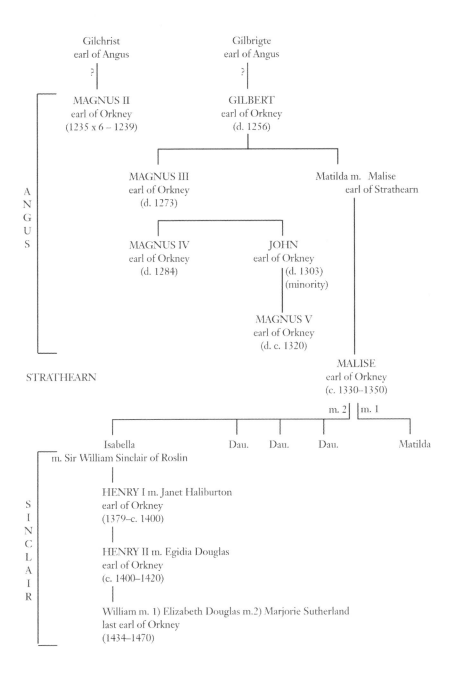

FIGURE 17. The Angus, Strathearn and Sinclair earls (simplified) following the 15th-century 'Genealogy of the Earls'

influenced by Scottish incomers, who appear to be moving north in the later decades of the century to fill the vacuum left after the Black Death by the decimation of Norwegian Church personnel. There is certainly evidence of turmoil in the Church in Orkney in the second half of the 14th century, perhaps due to clashes between those of different nationality, and certainly due to tensions between bishop and earl. From the 1380s the effects of the Schism and the existence of rival popes in Rome and Avignon can be seen in double appointments being made to the bishopric because Norway continued to adhere to Rome, while Scotland accepted the authority of the Avignon popes. Scottish candidates included a Sinclair bishop, so the earl must have been trying to put in his own nominee, but all indications are that the candidates who would have been consecrated by the Trondheim archbishop were more successful in getting possession. This cannot have led to very easy relationships between earl and bishop, and the Icelandic Annals refer to the 'distressing news from Orkney' already in 1382–83 that Bishop William had been killed.

The 15th Century: The End of the Norse Era

This century sees very big changes, and a dramatic reversal of fortunes for the earldom. It demonstrates that the power and unique position of the Sinclair earl rested ultimately on the plans and ambitions of the Scottish king. The anomalous situation in which the Norwegian earldom was held by one of the most powerful nobles in the Scottish kingdom could not last. Although one admires the adroit way in which the last earl attempted to maintain the pretence of a relationship with his Dano–Norwegian overlord[5] in the circumstances, the situation of double allegiance could not last in the era of nation states, when it was a matter of national pride that the kings of Scotland controlled all the islands around their coast. The way they managed to get possession of Orkney and Shetland was extraordinary in terms of diplomatic conventions, and very revealing of the ruthless nature of the Stewart kings' foreign policy.

   The earl who dominates the 15th century and who plays the leading role in the political upheavals was William Sinclair, son and heir of Henry II. He may have been under age at his father's death in 1420, and the king of Denmark–Norway seized the opportunity to put royal officials in control of Orkney – first the bishop, Thomas Tulloch, and then the earl's uncle, David Menzies of Weem. The documents appointing these two provide us with some information as to the political situation in the islands, and the remarkable 'Complaint of the people of Orkney' against David Menzies in 1425 provides a wealth of unprecedented detail about the social and economic situation. There was a determination from the Scandinavian side to govern the islands and to make the appointment of earl dependent on good behaviour. It was regarded not as a hereditary dignity automatically confirmed to the previous earl's son and heir, but as an official appointment which could be granted to the candidate who promised to adminster the islands in accordance with restrictions imposed at the installation. The members of the earldom family only had the right to claim the title, not automatically to inherit it. So thanks to the king's insistence that the young William Sinclair prove his inherited right to the dignity the 'Genealogy of the earls' was drawn up by the bishop and chapter of St Magnus setting out his inheritance, which was sent to the king.[6] It was not until 1434 however that William succeeded in getting a grant of the lands and title of earl – with stringent precautions and attempts to make his continued possession of the honour dependent on his adherence to the promises he had made to be a good and faithful vassal.[7]

However, this new earl of Orkney was deeply involved in the political life of his country, and married to Elizabeth Douglas, of one of the most powerful noble families in Scotland at the time. Although William's career in Scotland is hardly part of the history of Orkney, yet his relationship with James II and III was very relevant to the fate of Orkney, and the royal ambitions towards the islands deeply affected the earl's position. In the 1450s foreign affairs were dominated by the question of the 'annual of Norway', a sum of 100 marks which the Scottish crown was supposed to pay each year to the king of Norway in acknowledgement of the cession of the Hebrides to Scotland in 1266. Resistance to the continuation of this payment in the early 15th century led to strained relations with Denmark–Norway and negotiations took place in the late 1450s when it became clear that James II was determined to try and force the cession of Orkney and Shetland as part of an agreement between the two countries. However, his untimely death in 1460 led to the abandonment of that plan and allowed Earl William a breathing-space to prepare himself better for the time when royal ambition would once again focus on his rich northern possessions.

Events suggest that Earl William tried to implement delaying tactics, and evidence shows that he used these years to purchase land in the Northern Isles in order to build up a private family estate which could not be touched by the Scottish king, forseeing a day when the islands would come into Scottish possession. So when the young James III had grown to manhood and was looking for a wife in the late 1460s and the daughter of Christian III of Denmark–Norway was considered to be a highly suitable match, the Scottish envoys demanded that Orkney and Shetland be handed over as part of Princess Margaret's dowry. Christian, desperately short of cash, only offered to pledge Orkney, in 1468, followed by Shetland, in 1469, as part-payment for the dowry which he was unable to raise. A short-term measure which turned into a long-term situation.

The Marriage Contract does not make it absolutely clear what was actually conveyed to the Scottish crown by the pledging of 'the lands and islands of Orkney', and there have been differing interpretations as to exactly what was included in this phrase.[8] But there was no doubt that the title to the ancient and long-established earldom had to be acquired in addition to immediate rights over lands, if the Scottish kings were going to make permanent gains in the islands in the event of redemption of the pledge by the Dano–Norwegian crown. James became the earl's feudal superior by the pledging to him of royal rights over the islands and he could exercise pressure on the earl to yield to his authority. So, in 1470 the earl was persuaded or compelled to give up all his rights to his Orkney earldom in return for the grant of the royal castle of Ravenscraig in Fife, several remarkable privileges and a handsome annual pension of 400 marks.

Conclusions: Earldom and Community

Thus the ancient Norse earldom of Orkney passed into the hands of the Scottish crown, and a remarkable phenomenon of the early medieval period disappeared. It had of course been much changed over the centuries. The Angus, Strathearn and Sinclair earls had been increasingly Scottish-based and Scottish-orientated. Evidence suggests that they ruled their earldom as an independent lordship, with only sporadic active intervention by the Dano–Norwegian kings. The dominance of the northern seas by Norwegian longships was replaced during the later Middle Ages by the cogs of Scottish merchants (and English fishermen). The Northern Isles became a land of opportunity for Scottish entrepreneurs who moved north in the wake of the earls and the bishops, intermarried with local families and became integrated into the political, ecclesiastical and economic life of the islands, especially in Kirkwall. Their impact on the native language and culture by 1500 was profound, much more so in Orkney than in Shetland. The conversion of the Norse world of the Northern Isles to a Scottish colonial outpost happened much more easily than in the Gaelic west. The Norse and Scottish languages blended in a way which was not possible with the Gaelic language, while the earldom connection with southern Scotland provided an easy access route for the inbringers of Scottish influence.

These factors created a hybrid social community which was a melting pot of North Sea cultures, and a fiercely independent one. Already in the 11th century we have an account of the dramatic occasion when one of the Orkney farmers stands up to Earl Einar, who is imposing 'his usual harsh levy', and pleads for leniency, much to the earl's fury; 'the earl was in such a rage, he swore that only one of them would see the assembly next spring' (*OS* chapter 14). Exactly 400 years later, c. 1424, a letter of the 'whole country' of Orkney to the Danish authorities itemises 37 examples of the mis-rule and abuses of the Orkney governor (David Menzies of Weem): from taking the law-book and seal of the Lawman for his own

FIGURE 18 The seal of the 'Community of Orkney' from letters to the Danish authorities and Queen Philippa in 1424 and 1425

use, to introducing foreigners who 'were a veritable pest to the country', to imprisoning a skipper who 'did not go to him on the instant at the first summons'. Precious surviving records like this reveal the existence of an independent community of farmers and merchants well able to defend their rights and organise their communal resistance to overbearing earls and feudal governors. In the 15th century they called themselves *comunitas Orcadie* ('the community of Orkney') on a common seal which was used (Figure 18). Such medieval provincial seals were a Norwegian phenomenon, whereas in Scotland it was only the urban communities in burghs which used seals. The Orkney seal depicts what appear to be two farmers ('odallers') supporting the royal Norwegian lion. It represents another side of medieval Orkney from the powerful earls (who of course had their own seal). Both community and earl were manifestations of a medieval society which had no equal in Scotland, and which developed its own particular form and nature from Norse roots in a Viking past.

Notes

1 *Anglo-Saxon Chronicle* sub anno 1066, where the earls are said to have been left at Riccall in charge of the ships.

2 It may be, as the present writer has argued (Crawford, 1995) that a statue on the Bishop's Tower in Kirkwall represents Earl Rognvald.

3 The details of this story can be read in Crawford, 1993, 129–147.

4 See W. P. Thomson's comments, 2001, 168.

5 The kingdom of Norway was by this time united with Denmark, and the kings were primarily based in Denmark.

6 The copies of the Genealogy which have survived are in much later manuscripts and there are mistakes in the dating of the Latin and the Scots texts. It has been argued that these are based on an original drawn up in the 1420s (see Crawford, 1976, 166–7).

7 The 1434 installation document is based on the 1379 one agreed with William's grandfather, Henry I, but with some significant changes.

8 See the recent statement on the comprehensive nature of the transaction regarding the pledging of Christian's rights in Orkney by Thomson, 2001, 201–2, building on my early study in 1967–8, and developed at length in my doctoral thesis, *The Earls of Orkney – Caithness and Their Relationship with Norway and Scotland 1158–1470*, St Andrews, 1971, 333–38.

CHAPTER SIX

The Reformation and
the Stewart Earls

B ETWEEN 1468 AND 1615 lies a period of historical twilight for old
Orkney. During it, Norse Law is still in force, there are still periodic
attempts by the Danes to redeem the islands, and the descendants of the
last Sinclair earl are still trying to regain something of what they have
lost. Effectively, all this comes to an end with the fall of Earl Patrick, and
his execution in 1615. Roughly halfway through this period, in 1540, Robert
Reid was appointed bishop of Orkney. A vigorous man, he restructured
the cathedral chapter and added extensively to the Bishop's Palace in
Kirkwall. It has been said that Reid might have spent more time on pastoral
care and less on buildings and dignitaries, but Orkney was suffering from
the effects of feuding among the Sinclairs, and Reid's regime, among other
things, restored order. The governance of Orkney after the death of James
V in 1542 was unusually uneventful under M. Bonot, the representative of
Mary of Guise, the king's widow, who inherited the royal estates as her
portion.

The Sinclair feud began after the death of Lord Henry Sinclair at the
battle of Flodden in 1513, when his branch of the family fell out with that
of his brother, Sir William Sinclair of Warsetter. The chief bone of
contention was the *conquest* lands – acquired (through purchase) by William,
the last Sinclair earl, and remaining his personal property after he lost his
earldom to the king of Scots. The squabble culminated in the battle of
Summerdale of 1529, when the Warsetters, led by James Sinclair of Brecks
and Edward Sinclair of Strom, defeated William, Lord Sinclair, and his
supporter the earl of Caithness, with much bloodshed. This left the
Warsetters in control of the conquest lands, though their opponents
retained a lease of the royal lands, granted to Lord Henry's widow on his
death. Initially condemned, James and Edward Sinclair were rehabilitated
through the influence of another relative, Oliver Sinclair of Pitcairns. Oliver
Sinclair was a favourite of King James V, and had probably induced his
royal master to visit Orkney in 1541, the only Scottish monarch to do so.
Their followers were pardoned, and James Sinclair was knighted and
granted estates in the islands. Oliver Sinclair received a lease of the royal
lands, and the office of sheriff. Unfortunately for the Sinclairs, this was to

be their last good fortune. James Sinclair went mad and killed himself, and Oliver Sinclair fell from grace with the Scottish defeat at Solway Moss in 1542 and the king's death shortly afterwards. The conquest lands were swept up in the portion of the queen dowager, and although the Sinclairs made various attempts to get them back, they were never successful.

In 1558 Robert Reid died. Adam Bothwell, his successor, had Orkney connections. He was a stepson of Sinclair of Pitcairns, and had visited the islands in 1555. During the vacancy, the income from the bishopric estates was granted to Bothwell's cousin, Sir John Bellenden of Auchnoull. These estates were very extensive – more so in fact than either the former royal or earldom land; the greatest concentration was in Birsay, but there was also land in Westray, St Ola, Evie and Stenness. Bothwell arrived in Orkney in the spring of the year of the Reformation, 1560. As momentous events unfolded in the south, he closed his kirk doors and forbade the saying of mass. In parallel, he was forced by his relatives to consent to the dismemberment of the bishopric lands. Westray went to Gilbert Balfour, his brother-in-law, and Birsay to Sir John Bellenden. Oliver Sinclair, in Orkney again and probably still after the conquest lands, received lands in Eday. Sir Patrick Bellenden, Sir John's brother, became the laird of Evie and Stenness.

At this time there were disturbances in Orkney. Ostensibly, they were about religion, but in fact they were inextricably mixed up with the complex problems of the Sinclairs, and Bothwell, with his connection to Oliver Sinclair, could not escape involvement. Sinclair's arrival created consternation in Caithness, and the earl offered protection to the Orcadian Sinclairs in return for supporting an invasion of the islands. This never took place, but contrary forces in Orkney did make life difficult for the new bishop. One faction attacked and occupied Mons Bellus, his palace at Birsay. The Sinclairs were irremediably split amongst themselves. On the one hand James Sinclair of Brecks's son-in-law, Magnus Halcro, pledged himself to Caithness, Brecks's old enemy. On the other, the faction that attacked Mons Bellus was led by Henry Sinclair, son of Edward Sinclair of Strom, the surviving Summerdale victor. Henry Sinclair submitted petitions to the bishop against the 'mutation' of religion. Bothwell showed these to Edward Sinclair, who was a sheriff depute. Sinclair, while deploring his son's action, felt that peace was best served if Bothwell replied to them. Bothwell refused to do so until his palace was returned. Later, as the bishop was lying ill in his chamber, the Sinclairs had mass said within earshot and marriages conducted 'in the auld maner'.

It may be that neither religion nor Sinclair enmity lay behind Bothwell's humiliation. Henry Sinclair's followers no doubt supported the old religion, but he had also told them that they might 'leiff frelie, and ... knaw na superiouris in tymis cumyn'. Exactly what this means is unclear. Older historians might suppose that these were udallers – independent proprietors holding their lands by traditional Norse tenure, without feudal superior –

who were defending their lands against encroachment. Alternatively, Henry could have been suggesting that he and his followers might repossess the (udal) conquest lands and parcel them out among themselves. Whatever the truth, it was clear that religion was but one stick with which Bothwell might be beaten. Bothwell had continuing disputes with Gilbert Balfour, his relative and recent beneficiary, and Thomas Tulloch of Fluris, a former bishopric administrator. Balfour was pressurising him for money, complaining that he was out of pocket from trying to defend Mons Bellus. Tulloch was said to owe money from the bishopric revenues, and to be in league with Henry Sinclair and Sir John Bellenden of Auchnoull. The latter, whom Bothwell felt was behind all his troubles, clearly hoped for further rich pickings from the bishopric, including pensions so large that the bishop could not sustain himself. In the end there was a settlement of sorts between Bothwell, Bellenden, Balfour and Tulloch, but this was completely upset by the appearance on the scene of another, more powerful player.

Sir Robert Stewart of Strathdon, commendator of the abbey of Holyrood, was an illegitimate son of James V. He had dabbled in the politics and wars attending the Reformation, but had changed sides at least once, and was regarded as untrustworthy. He was among the first to greet Queen Mary on her return from France in 1561 and cultivated Lord Darnley as he rose in royal favour. In December 1564 he received a feu of the royal estates in Orkney and Shetland, and had the earldom in his sights, but his plans were thwarted by the queen's estrangement from Darnley. Robert was present when her secretary David Rizzio was murdered, but took little part in events up to her abdication in 1567. His fortunes reached their lowest ebb in February of that year when Darnley was murdered. Four months later, the earl of Bothwell was briefly created duke of Orkney. After his defeat at Carberry, Bothwell escaped to Orkney, pursued by Murray of Tullibardine and Kirkcaldy of Grange, accompanied by Adam Bothwell, on his last visit to his diocese. The fugitive earl sought help from Gilbert Balfour, himself suspected of involvement in the king's murder, but Balfour would not allow him ashore at Kirkwall or at Noltland Castle, the hefty bolt-hole he had erected in Westray. Bothwell was forced to go to Shetland, and thence to exile.

Now was Robert Stewart's opportunity. With public attention still on the deposed queen, he made his way to Orkney. He does not give the impression of being a man of particular intelligence or breadth of mind, but he does seem to have inherited the vision of the Sinclairs. Both the Bellendens and Oliver Sinclair were his vassals as commendator of Holyrood, and it must be this connection that aroused his interest in the Northern Isles. His aim was to obtain a feu of the same lands which Oliver Sinclair had enjoyed briefly in 1541–42, then add to them control of those bishopric lands over which Bellenden, Bothwell and Balfour had been squabbling. As children, he and his fellow bastards had received major ecclesiastical benefices, in his case the rich Holyrood estates, chiefly stretching along the south banks of the Forth. Robert sought to exchange these with Adam Bothwell for the bishopric lands of Orkney – except for those of Birsay, which were the subject of a separate deal with Sir John Bellenden, who was to receive the Holyrood barony lands of the Kerse, centred round modern Grangemouth.

The bishop negotiated hard over the exchange of lands, but when Robert's men seized the cathedral by force, killing two of his followers, he feared for his safety and, facing the power of both Robert and Sir John Bellenden, was forced to capitulate. Bellenden, having supported Robert against the bishop, now found out for himself that the man was not to be trusted. The new feuar obstructed his attempts to uplift arrears from the Birsay lands, tried to wriggle out of undertakings he had given and fell out with Patrick Bellenden over the Stenness and Evie lands. Bothwell and the Bellendens were to be Robert's enemies for years to come, and although Robert was successful in cornering much of what he wanted, it was at a cost which he was never quite able to meet.

For the time being, he was able to consolidate his mastery. He toured Orkney and then Shetland, of which he had appointed his half-brother, Laurence Bruce of Cultmalindie, *foud* and chamberlain. He held courts. He had himself made provost of Kirkwall and, it is said, destroyed the contents of the burgh's charter chest. He conducted campaigns against Gilbert Balfour, now conveniently abroad, and Edward Sinclair of Eday, son of Oliver of Pitcairns, whom he arrested, together with other Sinclairs – Warsetter, Essinquoy and Strom. Among the charges later levelled at Robert were those of banishment, unlawful imprisonment, confiscation of property and controlling the ferries to prevent his victims going south to complain. While seeking to reduce all opposition to his power, he also began to symbolise that power in stone, constructing his palace at Birsay. This was not as impressive architecturally as the magnificent achievements of his son, but it was an advanced and civilised building, perhaps by the same hand as Balfour's Noltland. Using the old Bishop's Palace as a quarry, it was probably built in two phases, the first being three sides of a courtyard erected between about 1569 and 1575, with the north range completing the structure in the 1580s. In between these phases lay a crisis in Robert's life.

When the earl of Morton became regent in 1572, the voices of Robert's enemies began to be heard. In August 1575 he came south to answer them and Morton placed him in open confinement in Edinburgh. A list of complaints was drawn up and commissioners were appointed to investigate the Shetland activities of Bruce of Cultmalindie. Among the complainers were the Sinclairs, as well as other families which had supported Bishop Bothwell and Patrick Bellenden – Halcros, Moodies, Giffords. Besides allegations of oppression, there was the suggestion of graver crimes. He had sought, they said, to usurp the king's authority by declaring quasi-monarchic powers in the islands. He had ruled according to the laws of Norway (though these had been acknowledged by parliament in 1567). Most importantly, he had sent his servants to Denmark to render homage. This charge was obscure and inconclusive, but potentially a very grave one indeed.

Robert was no doubt guilty of oppression, but guilt or innocence was less important than who his accusers were, and how much support they had in high places. During 1577 he was reported to be 'very poor', owing to Morton's demands, including a bond for more than 10,000 merks. The regent, seeking to bring order to the country, was dealing ruthlessly with supporters of the former queen, but in Robert's case he may have been more interested in his wealth than his crimes. As the 1570s drew to a close Robert began to find support. Morton had alienated too many people and had neglected the favour of the young king. Robert made no such mistake, and when James VI emerged as a force in his own right he was moved to more open ward and invited to meetings of the privy council. Patrick Bellenden was compelled reluctantly to conclude a bond of friendship, and Laurence Bruce was appointed admiral depute of Orkney and Shetland. In 1579 Robert returned to Orkney, and the following year had the pleasure of observing Morton's arrest, imprisonment, trial and execution. On 28 August 1581 he finally realised his ambition of becoming earl of Orkney.

He was now at the zenith of his power. He controlled more than twice the territory the Norse or Sinclair earls had enjoyed, and only two areas lay outside his direct control – the udal lands and those feued out by Bishop Bothwell. Despite his reputation as a land-grabbing oppressor, he did not acquire udal land on any very large scale, though it is highly probable that he manipulated his legal powers to enforce forfeiture in some cases. It was rather the bishopric lands that remained a particular problem for Robert. Disputes regarding them meant that he was never able to enjoy what he had achieved and the outcome was a second drastic decline in his fortunes. Robert had still not satisfied the Bellendens over the exchange of Birsay for the Kerse, and in 1588 the family, in the shape of Sir Lewis Bellenden, son of Sir John and like him justice clerk, found the ear of the king, supported by the secretary, Maitland of Thirlestane. There was more talk of oppression, and the reaction of the king, who had revised his favourable opinion of Robert, was much more decisive than the equivocal investigations under Morton. James revoked all grants made during his minority, including that to Robert as earl, and commissioned Bellenden and Maitland to bring Robert to justice. They sent Patrick Bellenden to Orkney to enforce the confiscation of Robert's lands, while setting in hand a detailed survey of their revenues.

Patrick Bellenden's trip was unsuccessful, since Robert was supported by his nephew Francis Stewart, earl of Bothwell, but Robert's position had been fatally weakened. He had to make his way south to answer for his conduct.

The king effectively removed him as earl, replaced him with his son Patrick, and forced him to part with large sums of money, including 8,000 merks to Maitland, and major grants to Patrick Bellenden. To raise cash, he had to regrant land confiscated from various udallers, and feu out large tracts to his own supporters, such as the Scollays of Tofts and Strynie, the Feas of Clestrain, the Gordons of Cairston, the Hendersons of Holland, and the Kincaids of Yinstay. These now joined the Bellendens, Balfours and the rest to swell the ranks of a whole new class of proprietors in Orkney – feudal lairds on the Scottish pattern. These were to continue to flourish after the fall of the Stewarts, in some cases right down to the 20th century.

Robert's family life was not peaceful either. Jean Kennedy, his wife, only visited Orkney twice (once she returned having been 'aucht dayis ... veray seik upone the sey'). She too had been involved in the Kerse/Birsay exchange, since the Kerse had originally been her marriage portion, and the state of things pleased her no more than it did the Bellendens. She was also aware of his mistresses, of which he had at least three, one bearing him no fewer than five children. At his death, she was suing for divorce on the grounds of adultery. Their eldest son Henry, master of Orkney, proved unruly and was said to be plotting against his father with the earl of Caithness. Aiding Henry in this was a servant, Andrew Martin, who, when Henry died unexpectedly, transferred his allegiance to Robert's second son, Patrick, and supported him till the very end, while the earl remained closer to his older illegitimate sons, James Stewart of Graemsay and William Stewart of Lyking.

When Robert Stewart died in 1593 Patrick, his son and heir, enjoyed high royal favour as a gentleman of the bedchamber and a hunting companion. He had been granted the revenues of the priory of Whithorn and now, for his maintenance at court, he received the lordship of Shetland, confiscated from his father. Even before his father's death we find him designated earl of Orkney. But the king's favour had its limits. Patrick's first attempt to find a wife – a daughter of the earl of Morton – was vetoed. More importantly, the king refused to serve him heir to his father. There were problems over Robert's will, and Patrick and his mother were at odds over what she should receive. The king himself wanted bishopric income for his own purposes. It was said that he was going to 'challenge' the earldom of Orkney, and there were hints of an increase in duties. A major survey was made in 1595, producing a new rental.

But it was the lands bequeathed by the old earl to his younger sons that were to be the cause of one of the most turbulent episodes of Patrick's first seven years. In the early 1590s Patrick and his brother John, master of Orkney, concluded an agreement allowing Patrick to redeem land in the South Isles which John had received from their father. Despite this, Patrick imprisoned both John and their illegitimate brother Stewart of Graemsay, pulling down the latter's house. A settlement was reached, but in 1595–96, Henry Colville, parson of Orphir and Patrick's chamberlain, hatched a plot to incriminate John Stewart in plots to kill the earl. In June 1596 John was tried for conspiracy, but acquitted. Less than three weeks later Henry Colville was murdered in Shetland. Colville appears to have been playing an extremely dangerous game, aimed at avoiding the desperate problems that had beset his predecessors as Patrick's chamberlain, Patrick Monteith of the Fair Isle and William Bannatyne of Gairsay. These men had been engaged in turn by Patrick to gather his dues, and were required to raise, very quickly, the enormous sum of £24,000 – about a third more than the total annual income of earldom and bishopric. Bannatyne in particular was afraid of violence from the proprietors, especially John Stewart – so much so that he tried to earn favour by getting involved in Colville's murder. It did him no good. Afraid of John, and pressured by Patrick for money, he was forced to provide the funds himself, before being 'chaissit and ejectit' from Orkney.

Other complainers included Sir Patrick Bellenden, the Hendersons of Holland, and the Sinclairs of Campston and Flotta, all of whom spent time in the cellars of Kirkwall Castle. Michael Balfour had been one of Robert Stewart's agents in the feuings of the late 1580s, and he was pursued for money Patrick felt himself owed as a result. His lands of Noltland were invaded and thoroughly stripped by William Stewart of Lyking. Despite this service to Patrick, Stewart was also jailed, deprived and threatened with starvation and torture. Patrick's clear intention was to ruin these families and appropriate their lands. The relationship of Orkney's udallers with Patrick was also uneasy, though the likes of Malcolm Groat of Tankerness and William Irving of Sebay were minor figures. In Shetland, matters were rather different. The royal and bishopric estates were much smaller, and Patrick's main opponents were udallers – the Shetland Sinclairs and, most active of all, his own uncle, Laurence Bruce of Cultmalindie. Patrick's earliest challenge to the udallers came in 1592, when he sought to impose himself upon them as superior. A representation to parliament against this, led by Bruce, seems to have been successful, but support for Bruce as a focus of dissent soon dropped away, though he remained in the background, building up his estates and constructing his castle of Muness in Unst.

Patrick was showing clear indications of extravagance and conceit, the main motives for his rapacity. In June 1590, sailing south to attend the court, his ship was captured by Captain Gwynn, an English pirate, and he lost valuables to the tune of £36,000 Scots, three times the annual income of the earldom. He made repeated efforts to seek restitution without success, but it is the folly of travelling with a cargo of such value that is the most striking feature of the episode. Two years later he set out on a much grander matrimonial adventure, his target being Princess Emilia, sister of Prince Maurice of Nassau, stadtholder of the Netherlands. He lost further sums to no avail and had to settle a year later for a less pretentious match with Margaret Livingston, widow of his old adversary, Sir Lewis Bellenden. In 1593 he began his building works, modestly by comparison with what was to follow, erecting a gallery for himself in the cathedral; shortly after this he began to build a new house at Sumburgh.

In 1600, he was finally confirmed as earl, apparently for no greater price than putting his affairs in order. It was a signal for the construction of two buildings – the castle of Scalloway, a civilised L-plan tower-house, and the astonishing palace of Kirkwall. This, marrying a stunning new structure with elements of the Bishop's Palace, has been described as the finest piece of renaissance architecture in Scotland; it is said to have been built with stone worth £200,000, hewn without leave or payment from the Sinclair quarries of Eday. Against this backdrop, Patrick's pomp became notorious, with liveried servants, musketeers accompanying him to the kirk, and trumpeters at his table.

The two periods of Patrick's active rule, on either side of the century's turn, are characterised by two quite different approaches by his opponents. In the 1590s both the Crown and the lairds used the device of the 'general band', a mass finding of surety for good behaviour. This was not a popular procedure. The sums demanded were too great, and obliged those charged to make their way to Edinburgh in time of harvest. After 1600, complainers against Patrick followed either of two approaches. Firstly, there was the use of *lawburrows* – compelling Patrick to find surety not to harm the complainer. Balfour found lawburrows against Patrick in the sum of 10,000 merks, Robert Monteith of Egilsay, Stewart of Lyking, and Bruce of Cultmalindie each in the sum of £5,000. Failure to find surety resulted in *horning* – judicial outlawry by spoken denunciation at the mercat cross, followed by three blasts of the trumpet. Failure to purge this led to repeated fines of the sum named. Patrick made execution of the horning as difficult as possible. Executions in Orkney had to be suspended because of threats to the messengers, and in the south they had to be at his dwelling place rather than in his presence, since on at least one occasion he simply refused to answer the door. These antics resulted in the personal intervention of the king's advocate, Thomas Hamilton of Monklands, and finally the king himself.

Secondly, there were attempts to seek exemption from Patrick's juris-diction. Laurence Bruce and Robert Monteith in particular pursued Patrick continually before the session in Edinburgh in the years to 1609. The king's advocate began to attend hearings of these causes, and it was he who enabled Patrick's opponents to obtain a personal commission to pursue him. The king overruled the privy council's objection that Patrick's actions were a civil rather than a criminal matter, saying that Patrick's 'contemptuus rebellion … is become of the natour of a criminall'. Though Monteith and Bruce could not apprehend Patrick personally, their actions forced him to come south in the summer of 1609, and he was never to know complete freedom again.

Besides the accumulation of penalties at the instance of his main opponents, Patrick had amassed a host of other creditors – the merchant William Fairnie, who was owed 7,300 merks; his brother-in-law Patrick, commendator of Lindores, who had lent him 12,000 merks in 1591 and was still chasing it 15 years later; Thomas Craig and Thomas Henryson, advocates, seeking bishopric pensions; the tradesmen and merchants of the capital; and finally his own servants – James Annand and John Livingston of Baldorran, together due well over 20,000 merks. Patrick had to grant repeated bonds to Sir John Arnot, his chief financial adviser. In 1601 his liabilities stood at 80,000 merks. Six years later he owed more than three times as much, and was truly 'drownit in debt'.

The king's impatience had grown over the years. In the 1590s, Patrick had intrigued with the queen in pursuit of her income from the bishopric of Orkney and had taken her part against the king over custody of her son Henry. He had doggedly refused to listen to the various counsellors who were put his way, including Sir John Arnot and his own kinsman, the earl of Cassillis. Arnot warned Patrick about the folly of ignoring the courts, which would move the king to 'extreme anger'. In 1605 James appointed James Law to the bishopric of Orkney, which had been a dead letter since Bothwell left. The king's motives may have been mainly ecclesiastical, but Law too was expected to influence Patrick, though even he found it difficult to enforce a contract with Patrick over the bishopric lands, despite the king's insistence.

Attempts to bring Patrick to heel – a charge of treason before parliament by Hamilton of Monklands in 1606, a trial for oppression in 1610 – came to nothing. Law pressed the case for outright confiscation of the earldom, but the council and officers of state were very reluctant to go to such unprecedented lengths. Patrick was offered the keepership of one of the royal palaces in exchange, but refused. Not until 1611, when he had been in ward for almost two years, was the decision finally made to take the whole matter out of his hands. The Norse laws of Orkney and Shetland were abolished and replaced by those of Scotland. A tacksman was appointed in the person of Sir James Stewart of Killeith, and a thorough reassessment and reorganisation of the royal and bishopric lands was undertaken, with the intention of direct administration under the Crown.

It was this deprivation of his estates that precipitated the first step towards the end, Patrick's incitement of his illegitimate son Robert to rebellion – first, obscurely, in 1612, then more spectacularly in 1614. By the latter date Patrick was in close ward in Dumbarton Castle. Robert visited him there in the spring, then left for Orkney to begin what was soon seen as outright revolt. He was only the nominal head of his forces, the actual commander being the Orcadian Patrick Halcro. Within a very short time they mustered forces and made their way to Birsay, where they seized the palace. Robert had Andrew Martin, his father's aged servant, draw up a 'bond of association', stating the aims of their enterprise. These purported to be the restoration of good government in a country where it was threatened by 'extraniers ... corruptioun of the lawis, partialitie of juges, the greid of officers and oppressioun of magistratis'. The signatories appended earnest subscripts – 'to the dethe', 'with the hart and handis' – a very dangerous thing to do, to be treated as concrete evidence of treason.

Robert's forces moved on Kirkwall, taking control of the three great strategic objectives – the cathedral, the castle, and the Palace of the Yards. The cathedral was a massive stronghold, despite its holy purpose. The castle was a Scottish tower-house, built on the east side of the Peedie Sea and surrounded by curtain walls. The Palace of the Yards was the least defensible of the positions, but Robert billeted himself there, probably in obedience to his father's wish to repossess a building dear to his heart. The erstwhile defenders were allowed to leave Orkney while the new occupants prepared for the response of the government.

On 20 August a punitive expedition set sail under the earl of Caithness and Bishop Law. After an abortive attempt to charge the rebels to surrender, the earl brought his forces and one of his cannons ashore. He was surprised and exasperated by the support for the rebels which he found in the islands. He himself saw the antipathy of the Orkney Sinclairs at work, not without reason, since Orcadians were well aware that he saw his commission as something of a return match for Summerdale. In addition, the new administrative arrangements were no more popular than the old. Sir James Stewart had appointed a sheriff, John Finlayson, who was hated 'to the deith' for his demands. Moreover, the totally unprecedented situation left people without guidance. Patrick had threatened to return, and if he did – where would supporters of Caithness be then? Of the lairds, only Monteith of Egilsay actively supported Caithness, and some actually encouraged the rebels. The men of Birsay and Harray, nearly 100 of the minor landowners, were mustered in support of Robert and his men.

Caithness brought the first of his cannon to Weyland, where it was trained on the castle. An early shot shattered the turnpike head, but others simply broke against the massive stonework of the keep like golfballs. The weapon was then trained on the 'Chapel Tower' of the palace, where Patrick Halcro had positioned musketeers. After some exchange of fire, Caithness brought his second, larger cannon to bear on the great oriel windows of the palace. The threat of this caused Robert to surrender the building and retreat into the castle. Shortly afterwards the cathedral also yielded. Caithness was now able to deploy his forces at will and fire his cannon on the castle ramparts, straight across Broad Street. Initially, he hoped to beat the building down, but still the massive walls held out and and gunpowder and ammunition were running low. He began negotiations. Robert for a time would not compromise, fearing the wrath of Caithness, his father, and the council. It was the impatience of Patrick Halcro, who pursued his own discussions with earl and bishop, that forced Robert Stewart finally to capitulate.

The boy himself and his associates were sent south to Edinburgh, where they were interrogated, tried and hanged. To the end, Robert protected his father from any accusation of complicity, and Patrick denied any knowledge of what his son had been planning. Even at this stage it was difficult to pin any criminal wrongdoing on Patrick, but the death of his son undid him. He broke down, confessed and threw himself upon the unlikely mercy of the king. He was tried before an assize of nobles and councillors and condemned to death, the execution to take place on 3 February 1615. His mental state was such that he required a further three days for the clergy to prepare him to behave appropriately on the scaffold (the story that he was too ignorant to rehearse the Lord's Prayer seems unlikely, to say the least). On Monday, 6 February, the Maiden ended his life.

Patrick Stewart is an extraordinary figure in the history of Scotland. Rarely has anyone so high-born brought himself so low by his own extravagantly unwise efforts. The impossible situation of chaos, debt and disaster in which he found himself was almost entirely of his own creation. It derived from a fundamentally unrealistic view of the world; an overweening conceit regarding his place in that world; an inability to listen to good advice; a continuing belief in his personal influence on the king against all evidence to the contrary; a desire for self-aggrandisement which took no account of his obligations to kin, allies or followers, and which caused him to make enemies where he could reasonably have looked for friends.

His image in the islands too is out of the ordinary. Although his ghost walks more in Shetland than in Orkney, he is the exemplar of the bogey-man, the 'Bad King John' of the Northern Isles, of whom bizarre stories are told. He and his father, more than any other figures in the Scottish history of Orkney and Shetland, lie at the heart of the common belief in the malign nature of Scottish rule. Yet the real story is more complex. Patrick's earldom died with him, despite the efforts of his brother John to revive it. The lairdly dynasties lived on – the Bellendens, the Monteiths, the Bruces. If we compare the tales told by their descendants with the general support given by the ordinary people to the rebellion of Robert Stewart, and if we look at the frantic efforts of Scottish councillors to contain the activities of their wild compatriot, then we realise that the picture of Patrick is one painted by the class which replaced him, and that Scottish government had in fact made strenuous efforts to bring him to heel – which, in the end, they did, permanently.

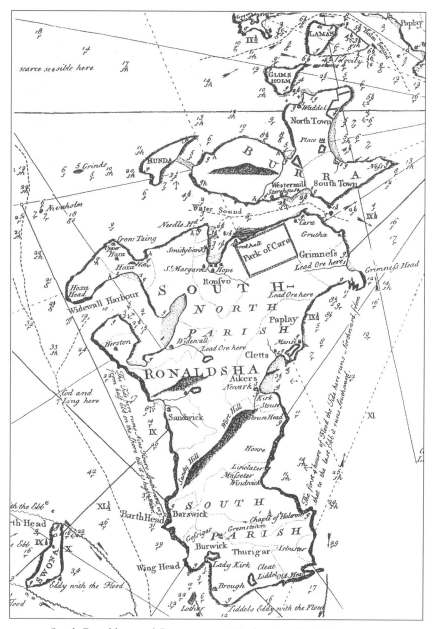

MAP 4 South Ronaldsay and Burray, 1750 (Mackenzie, *Orcades*)

CHAPTER SEVEN

Agricultural Improvement

In 1750 Murdoch Mackenzie (1712–1797) published his *Orcades*, an atlas of sea charts which provided the first reliable guide to the navigation of the difficult waters which surround Orkney. He was interested in the sea rather than the land, but navigation depended on landmarks, so he mapped the prominent turf dykes which surrounded the townships, and he annotated his maps with symbols such as g (= grass) and (h = heather) (Map 4). The result was a remarkably good picture of pre-Improvement Orkney, and one which is particularly valuable as so little of the old landscape remains. The townships, hill-dykes and common grazings which Mackenzie recorded had existed with little modification since the medieval period, or perhaps ever since Viking times, but they were entirely swept away when land was reclaimed and squared in the middle of the 19th century.

Mackenzie's township dykes were the most prominent feature of this old landscape because farmland was otherwise unenclosed. The function of hill dykes was to keep animals away from the corn. In spring the parish bailie court would issue instructions that the dykes, which being built of turf required annual repair, were to be 'put up', and it would set dates by which cattle, horse, sheep and pigs were to be banished to the common grazings, after which any animals still inside the dyke had to be tethered. Farmers were obliged to keep their neighbours 'skaithless' (free from harm), and they were liable to fines if they allowed their animals to damage their neighbours' corn. There was no very effective way of managing common land, so the more accessible parts were invariably over-grazed, and were often cut down to the subsoil by the haphazard extraction of shallow 'yarpha' peats. The pasture was further damaged by the removal of divots for building material and the stripping of turf to add to middens in order to replenish the fertility of the arable land and keep it in continuous infield cultivation. Then in autumn, when the harvest had been secured, the 'slaps' and 'grinds' in the hill-dyke (gaps and gates) were opened and the hungry horde of animals returned to range over the entire arable land of the township. In winter this stubble grazing was sometimes open from one end of a parish to the other.

Inside the hill-dyke the land was a mixture of arable rigs, plots of grassland and meadow sections forming a maze-like landscape which was entirely incomprehensible to an outsider. Around the house sites there was land permanently attached to each house, the 'toft' and 'tunmal', but the main part of the arable land, the 'townsland', lay in blocks of rigs known as 'sheads', and was worked in run-rig. A whole range of terms such as 'flaa', 'tie', 'geyro', 'skutto', 'spieldo', 'reeb', 'dello', 'outbreak' and 'out-tilling' were used to describe plots of land of different size, shape and location. Run-rig in Orkney did not involve annually changing plots of land – rigs might sometimes be in the possession of the same family for several generations – but ultimately the run-rig holding was defined as a share, rather than by fixed boundaries. A farmer who, for example, was entitled to one pennyland in a three-pennyland township would insist on receiving one-third of the good land, but he knew that he also had to take his proportion of land that was ill-drained, which had shallow soil or suffered from sea-gust or other disadvantages. The greater the number of farmers the more inevitable it was that the demand for fairness could only be satisfied by dispersal, with the result that, particularly at times of population increase, the run-rig landscape could become bewilderingly fragmented. If there were complaints that the shares had for some reason become unfair, a 'perambulation' was required. The 'honest men' would descend on the township and, under the supervision of the parish bailie, set to work with measuring rod and line to redistribute the run-rig lands. Agricultural improvers had nothing good to say about run-rig: it was thoroughly inconvenient, and the practice of stubble grazing prevented the introduction of new crops such as sown grass and turnips – run-rig was 'clean daft'. Yet it had worked well enough as long as everyone farmed by the same methods and grew little else except oats and bere (barley) – it was only when run-rig clashed with improvement that its drawbacks became apparent.

Robert Scarth of Binscarth (c. 1795–1879), who managed several Orkney estates as well as his own, was more than any other single person the architect of improvement. When he looked back on the pre-improvement period, he remarked that small farmers who had accumulated modest savings 'would as soon have thought of throwing it in the sea as of laying it out in drainage or lime or any attempt to improve the waste lands'. Farmers had probably been right to be wary of investments as long as their return on capital was uncertain. Improvement was a hobby for the better-off until steamships opened mainland markets and brought higher prices for Orkney cattle. Progressive lairds and agriculturally-minded ministers were often impressed by the prosperous farms of the Lothians and tried to introduce some of the features they admired, but their experiments, although receiving a good deal of favourable publicity, were often a doubtful success in financial terms.

Remarkable evidence of early interest in 'Improvement' comes from the Bu of Burray (the 'Place' on Map 4). When Sir James Stewart died in a Hanoverian prison after the 1745 rebellion, an inventory of his property revealed an astonishing collection of bits and pieces of carts, wagons and improved ploughs, much of it described as 'old' or 'broken'. At that time most Orkney parishes were entirely devoid of wheeled transport, and not many improved ploughs could be found even in more advanced farming districts in Scotland. Even more surprising, a hundred years before turnips were commonly grown as a field crop, Sir James had owned a turnip-drill plough. The neatly enclosed fields, and the 'Dunrobin cattle' which were introduced at the Bu, contrasted with the squalid conditions in the rest of the island. Sir James also owned the 420-acre grazing enclosure, the Park of Cara, in the neighbouring island of South Ronaldsay (Map 4).

Later, Thomas Balfour was the tenant of the Bu and was influenced by the Burray improvements and so, when he bought Sound in Shapinsay, he embarked on a similar programme. He cleared the crofters from the south-west part of the island, and relocated many of them in the new village of Shoreside (now Balfour Village) which is Orkney's earliest example of a planned village. Balfour laid out large, irregular fields surrounded by turf and stone dykes. However, the previous distribution of arable land was little altered and most of his fields contained a mixture of arable land and grass. The Shapinsay fields were typical of those criticised by the agriculturalist, Alexander Wight, when he travelled through Scotland in 1778. He commented on the many large enclosures made by 'followers of fashion' in which there was both corn and grass; this kind of enclosing was 'a snare and delusion', since it did not partition off the pasture from the crops, and consequently herding was just as much needed as if no enclosures existed.

Thomas Balfour was a political ally of Sir John Sinclair, the driving force behind the *Statistical Account* which was published between 1791 and 1799. Orkney is fortunate to have an unusually good series of parish accounts written by ministers who often had a good deal to say about 'Improvement'. They were full of enthusiasm for abolishing run-rig, dividing commons, introducing rotations, growing turnips and sown grass, draining, squaring, enclosing, and introducing better breeds of animals. Sometimes their knowledge was practical since ministers often cultivated their glebes, but more frequently they had only a theoretical knowledge and under-estimated the difficulties of introducing the type of farming they advocated. These same new ideas were enthusiastically propounded by Sir John Sinclair's Board of Agriculture, which was established following the publication of the *Statistical Account*. The board commissioned a series of county studies which included John Shirreff's book, *On the Agriculture of the Orkney Islands*.

The schemes of 'Agricultural Sir John' were derided by his political enemies, as were the improvements made by his friend, Thomas Balfour. Opponents dismissed the Shapinsay improvements as 'chimerical and visionary, as are many other of the childish Don Quixote schemes for which both these gentlemen are so particularly eminent'. The idea of growing grass rather than corn was 'an almost absurd one, made at random without knowledge or experience of the subject', and Balfour's turnip crop was described as 'pitiful'. Although Sir John Sinclair and Thomas Balfour were right to see that the future of Orkney farming lay in sown grass and turnips, there was nevertheless a certain amount of truth in these barbed comments. The success of Thomas Balfour's improvements was limited, although perhaps he did not actually lose money on these schemes. Seventy years later his enclosures were swept away by the more thorough-going improvements of his grandson.

Other important changes were made by the brothers, Malcolm and Samuel Laing, on the farm of Stove in Sanday. Malcolm introduced a large flock of Merino sheep which turned out to be ill-suited to the Orkney climate, but his younger brother's reorganisation of the cottar population had more far-reaching consequences. A farm such as Stove contained a large population of cottars who were 'on ca" (on call) and were obliged to turn out to work on the big farm whenever their services were required, in return for which they were paid in land which was intermingled with the rigs of the main farm. For a farm to be in 'a state of cottarage' was no great disadvantage as long as farmers and cottars farmed by the same methods, but the introduction of new breeds such as the Merino sheep and experiments with new crops made it desirable that the ill-cultivated rigs and half-starved beasts of the cottars should be kept well away from the farmer's neat fields and prize animals. Laing's solution was to relocate the cottars on little self-contained holdings on the margins of the farm. The small size of the holdings and the high money rent made it necessary for these tenants to seek outside employment, and so the old ill-defined customary services were replaced by a new form of economic compulsion. Crofters were obliged to seek casual agricultural employment and, as a result, Laing never lacked 'good and efficient workmen'. Crofting was not so much an age-old way of life – it was to a large extent a 19th-century creation. Laing's scheme was widely copied, notably in the squaring of the Graemeshall estate in Holm, and in the process cottar sub-tenants were usually converted into direct tenants of the laird.

The new laird of Graemeshall, Alexander Sutherland Graeme (1806–94), had little knowledge of Orkney, and indeed made only three visits to his estate over a 50-year period. Initially, he tried to take an enlightened interest in matters he barely understood but, as he was progressively overwhelmed by his debts, his benevolence gave way to oft-repeated complaints that his extensive estate yielded him a very small income. To protect him from his creditors, the estate was eventually administered by a trust from which he was paid an annual allowance, so the effective management of the property was in the hands of an Edinburgh lawyer, John Irving. Irving knew as little about Orkney as the laird, but had boundless confidence both in himself and in the theoretical concept of 'Improvement'. In 1828 he was the driving force behind ambitious plans to re-organise the entire estate, and to bring farming into the modern age.

The third protagonist was the local estate manager, David Petrie, a much-respected old-fashioned farmer and a doggedly faithful servant of the estate. Petrie's dilatory and muddled accounts, often prepared years after they were due, prevented any proper analysis of profitability. The improvement of Graemeshall was a leap of faith, rather than a business venture based on firm financial predictions.

If more grandiose schemes were seldom entirely successful, much was achieved at a more modest level. Eighteenth-century planking brought about the partial consolidation of run-rig by allocating land in larger blocks, often acre-sized squares rather than individual rigs. The introduction of potatoes was also important. They were first grown as a field crop about 1750, and became commoner after 1756, when the grain crop was blasted by an August storm. However, as late as 1780 potato cultivation had still not reached some districts, including Eday and Stronsay. The introduction of the potato provided protection from the terrible famines which had previously struck with such devastating effect on average twice in a century. There had been heavy mortality in 'King William's Ill Years' at the close of the 17th century, and again in the 'Years of the Short Corn' (1739–42). In contrast, there was much less distress in the wet and stormy seasons 1782–85. It was not only the potato which prevented starvation; many people were protected from the worst effects of harvest failure by the money they now earned from linen, kelp-making, fishing and service with the Hudson's Bay Company.

The abolition of common land was a necessary preliminary to large-scale improvement. The commons were not just common grazings, but were 'commonty' – land deemed to be owned in common by the proprietors of the adjacent arable land. Until individual ownership had been established, investment was not possible. An Act for the Division of Commonties had existed since 1695, and common land had already been abolished in most of Scotland, but at the beginning of the 19th century no Orkney common had yet been divided. Proceedings in the Court of Session were lengthy and expensive, and there was the danger that the cost of division might ultimately exceed the value of the land. The first parish whose common was divided was Stenness, where Sir William Honyman, the judge Lord Armadale, instituted proceedings in 1802. Despite his legal expertise it was 1815 before the division was finalised, and other divisions proceeded at the same leisurely pace, yet over the next 50 years every major common in Orkney was divided. The establishment of ownership did not always alter the use of the commons, many of which continued to be used by small tenants as common grazings until wire fences made it possible to attach portions of the former commons to big farms as sheep runs.

The part which kelp played in the Orkney economy was one reason why agricultural progress was slow, and many farms remained in a 'state of cottarage' long after labour services had been abolished in the north-east of Scotland. Kelp-making grew to huge proportions during the Napoleonic

Wars, when alternative sources of alkali needed for glass-making and bleaching were unavailable. At its height some 3,000 people were employed in collecting seaweed and burning kelp, and the profits which could be made by employing a cottar labour force far exceeded what might be made from farming. Kelp survived the end of the war, but the removal of tariffs on imported alkali brought sudden collapse in 1830. The end of the kelp boom left estates impoverished. Thomas Traill of Westove, whose Sanday kelp-making estate was one of the richest, went bankrupt and sought a new life in Canada, and Samuel Laing retired from Orkney to live in reduced circumstances in Norway and Edinburgh, where he made a new career as a writer and as the translator of *Heimskringla*.

The years 1830–40 were a difficult decade, but in 1833 the little paddle-steamer, the *Velocity*, which ran from Aberdeen to Inverness and Wick, extended its August runs to Kirkwall, and a regular summer service to the islands operated from 1836 onwards. In the 1840s steamships were making it much easier to export live cattle to Aberdeen, and railways were opening markets even farther south. Dealers regularly visited Orkney, and the greatly improved price for cattle initiated a period of sustained growth (c. 1846–c. 1875). Not only did the Orkney economy expand at about 10% per annum, but it became more agriculturally based.

The other stimulus to growth was the Public Money Drainage Act of 1846, which made money available for agricultural improvement at low rates of interest. Since these loans became available just as cattle sales were beginning to take off, Orkney was one of the areas to take most advantage of the scheme. The best example of what might be achieved was David Balfour's improvement of Shapinsay. A grid of 10–acre squares was imposed on the island with straight-line boundaries which ran for miles and made hardly any concessions to the existing landscape. These squares were used as a basis for letting, and it was a requirement of the lease that tenants enclosed and drained the fields; if they were unable or unwilling to do so, the work was undertaken by the estate with borrowed money and the cost of the loan was passed to the tenants as an addition to the rent. Previously there had been only 748 acres of arable land on the island, but within the next dozen years or so a further 1,500 acres were added. The irregular rigs of crofting tenants and most of the common hill grazing disappeared under the plough, and Thomas Balfour's once-prestigious 18th-century improvements at Sound were treated no differently, being swept away in their entirety.

The term 'Agricultural Revolution' is one which generally needs to be used with caution, since changes in most parts of Britain were complex and took place over a relatively long period. 'Revolution' is an apt term in Orkney, however, because the changes occurred so quickly. Within the span of a farmer's working life Orkney farming emerged from the Middle Ages, the old landscape was obliterated, the traditional grain-growing economy was replaced, and many of the farmer's expectations, beliefs and values were over-turned. The agricultural expert, R. O. Pringle, visited Orkney at the end of this period of growth, and his paper 'On the Agriculture of the Orkney Islands' (1874) put on record what had been achieved. Pringle's round-up of Orkney's main farms describes Victorian high farming at its most advanced. Large, well-managed and labour-intensive farms were carefully cultivated according to the five-shift rotation, the quality of their beef cattle was universally recognised, and their impressive farm steadings proclaimed a confidence in future prosperity.

Confidence in the future was, however, misplaced. When Pringle described the situation, Victorian high farming was about to disappear, never to return. Orkney's prosperity had been initiated by communications which opened southern markets to Orkney's cattle. Further improvements in the form of transatlantic steamships, American railroads and the ability to transport refrigerated goods meant that Britain was flooded with the produce of the Americas, Australia and New Zealand. By 1880 the period of growth was over, and farming entered a long period of depression.

This crisis was most visible in the crofting community. New crofts had been created throughout the 19th century in response to an ever-increasing population and reached a maximum in 1883, when there 3,373 agricultural holdings. Often crofts had been reclaimed by their occupants, who sought permission to build a house on the edge of the common and set about trenching the heather hillside with the spade. Crofters put in drains and built stone dykes. After a lifetime of effort, the more successful of these places were transformed into little farms. Crofts shared in mid-century prosperity, and their increased profitability resulted in recurring rent increases. The problem in the 1880s was that rents of crofts continued to rise, but the income of crofters declined when prices fell. In 1883 a royal commission, the Napier Commission, was established by Gladstone's Liberal government to investigate the condition of crofters throughout the Highlands and Islands. The commission was established in response to unrest among crofters in Skye, and initially it aroused little interest in Orkney, except in Rousay, where recollections of the Quandale clearance (1845) created the same bitter memories of eviction as in the Highlands. The highly-charged evidence of the Rousay crofters reached a moment of high drama when their landlord, General Burroughs, refused to give an undertaking that he would not victimise crofter-delegates who gave hostile evidence. The hearing was followed by the eviction of the delegates, threats to shoot the general, the sending of a gunboat to Rousay and the beginning of a very public war of attrition between Burroughs and his crofting tenants. The Napier Commission led to the Crofters' Act of 1886 which gave crofters security from eviction and established a land court, the Crofters' Commission, which had powers to set judicial rents and to cancel arrears. During the commission's first visit in 1888 it heard 443 cases, reducing rents by an average of 30% and cancelling 44% of the arrears.

It was not only crofters who experienced economic difficulties. Between 1880 and 1900 the rent of big farms declined by a similar amount without the need for government intervention, and many farmers were also behind with their rent. By the early 20th century agricultural depression had produced a change in the nature of landownership. Many estates had been offered for sale but failed to find buyers, with the result that they were administered by trusts which continued to manage the property, in some cases for as long as 50 years. Other estates had been rescued from bankruptcy, or were owned by absentees. In the mid-19th century David Balfour had been only one of many lairds who invested their own money and had been in the forefront of improvement. In contrast, landowners in the early 20th century had mostly withdrawn from active management and were content to collect the rent without any further investment on their part.

This tight-fisted, unenterprising style of management was compounded by the way compensation for improvements was handled. Previously tenants had seldom been compensated for the work they did during their tenancy, but the Agricultural Holdings (Scotland) Act of 1883 and the Small Landholders' Act of 1911 strengthened the position of tenant farmers. Since compensation was based on the value of the improvements to the incoming tenant, estates, although ultimately responsible, expected the payment to be made by the new tenant, who in effect 'bought' the improvements and therefore expected to occupy the farm at its unimproved rent. Since the farmer might have built the farmhouse and farm buildings, reclaimed and drained land, put up fences and made roads, compensation could in some cases amount to the greater part of the value of the farm. The way these payments were handled was one of the main reasons why rents did not rise in response to the better economic conditions before, during and immediately after the First World War.

These moribund estates, therefore, had to meet the greatly increased cost of national taxation and local rates from an income which was static. Although landowning was not actually unprofitable, the universal conclusion was that the days of the landed estate were over and that a better income might be obtained from other forms of investment. In 1919 the Burness estate in Sanday, which had belonged to the late Captain Horwood, was divided into lots and offered for sale, and other estates, including the two largest, the earldom estate and the property of the Balfours, were similarly offered to sitting tenants. Farmers were not entirely convinced of the advantages of ownership; it was the common wisdom of the time that money was better spent on stock and equipment rather than in buying land. But when the moment of decision came, virtually all farmers decided to buy. The price represented a good bargain and was generally within their reach, since many farmers had accumulated savings during the First World War, when the navy in Scapa Flow had provided a ready market. Farmers were also motivated by the negative consideration that if they failed to buy, they might lose both their homes and their livelihood. As owners they were entering a hard world: the year 1923, when sales peaked, was the worst in living memory, with the kind of harvest failure which had caused destitution in previous centuries. Even more worrying was the economic climate: the support farmers had enjoyed during the war years was dismantled, and by 1923 the index of agricultural prices had fallen by 46% from its 1920 level, although beef prices held up better than grain, at least until the 1930s.

In the long run the owner-occupier revolution was a success story. In the same way that the security provided by the 1886 Crofters' Act had released a burst of energy on small crofts, the new owner-occupiers in the 1920s set about making the most of their farms. This was the period when a good deal of shallow 'breck' land was reclaimed, and the use of wild white clover greatly increased the quality of grassland. Wild white clover was first sown in 1906 but it was only in the post-war period that its use became universal, its nitrogen-fixing nodules enabling grass to be laid down for longer periods, and setting in train the 'greening' of the Orkney landscape which was such a feature of the 20th century. Cattle numbers increased by about 10% during the period of the sales, and all this at a time when farming was in decline in many other parts of Britain. There was also a big increase in egg production. Ever since the price of grain fell in the 1880s there had been a tendency to feed grain to poultry rather than sell it off the farm, but egg production now ceased to be a sideline, and on many small farms egg money rivalled the income from cattle sales.

Improvement in Orkney had made a slow and uncertain start in the 18th century, and progress in the early 19th century was inhibited by an over-reliance on kelp-making. The opening of markets for beef cattle and the investment of capital had transformed Orkney farming in the period c. 1846–c. 1875. Thereafter, depression had resulted in rather static conditions until the early years of the 20th century and then, after the First World War, a second farming revolution transformed tenants into owner-occupiers. By this time farmers were again experiencing difficult economic conditions, but Orkney farming had been modernised. Farmers had a new sense of independence, and they had a confidence in the long-term future of farming despite all the immediate problems.

CHAPTER EIGHT

Modern Times

Agricultural improvement brought profound changes to Orkney, transforming the economy in the mid-1850s from a subsistence farming based on the growing of grain to a commercial agriculture based on the export of beef cattle. With agricultural improvement came a new prosperity and by the 1880s there was said to be £1 million deposited in Orkney banks. Kirkwall had become a thriving commercial centre with banks, businesses and hotels being constructed. Local newspapers like *The Orkney Herald* and *The Orcadian* had a large circulation, providing local, national and international news that was read avidly by a large proportion of the community. Newspaper advertisements opened people's eyes to the range of consumer goods available. The Letters page provided a forum for controversial and sometimes libellous debate, which was followed eagerly, and this of course did no harm to the papers' circulation.

Leisure time became available to many for the first time and societies sprang up catering for a wide variety of interests – antiquarian, scientific, literary, agricultural and musical. In rural areas social activity still tended to centre round the church and school, while local agricultural societies organised ploughing and hoeing competitions, agricultural shows and harvest homes. In addition, both the Temperance Movement and the Volunteers corps were at the forefront of social life, providing outings, concerts and picnics for members and their families. Branches of the Young Men's Mutual Improvement Society sprang up in many parishes and islands, providing a forum for debate and discussion.

Communications with the outside world were facilitated with a year-round steamship service, a rail service as far as Thurso, a regular postal service and telegraph system. Orcadians showed a general enthusiasm to embrace the new opportunities now available in the Victorian world of the British Empire, and to possess the very latest innovations from the south.

This avid interest in innovation, together with the prevailing taste for the Victorian values of the outside world, could not help but be at the expense of local indigenous culture, and inevitably traditional beliefs and customs were thought to be synonymous with everything that was backward and undesirable. The Orkney dialect was denigrated and positively discouraged, especially in schools, where children were reprimanded for using the local idiom. However, local folklore beliefs lingered on in country districts, despite disapproval from the Church for anything that smacked of superstition.

Social comment on contemporary society in Orkney was not just confined to the columns of the local newspapers. Home-made entertainments could also be a vehicle for witty comment on current issues. A local pantomime, *The Deerness Mermaid*, written and performed in Kirkwall in 1894, was based on the factual story of an eccentric character, William Delday, who had the gift of blurring the distinctions between the ordinary and the fabulous. He first saw the so-called Deerness Mermaid in the late 1880s in Newark Bay, and instantly fell in love and announced his intention of marrying her. Many of the populace also saw the creature, probably a mutant seal, and the story hit the national newspapers. The pantomime script was the vehicle for pithy social comment. Although there was a recognition of the undesirability of denigrating local traditions and Orkney dialect as 'uncultured lingo', the pantomime songs were mostly set to the music of the Victorian music hall or Gilbert and Sullivan, rather than to traditional Orkney melodies. The lampooning of politician A. J. Balfour through the comic pantomime character of A. J. Golfer was no doubt acceptable in the town of Kirkwall, but tenants on the island of Shapinsay might have found there were still undesirable consequences, had they dared to ridicule this kinsman of Colonel Balfour, their local laird in Balfour Castle. Town attitudes to the Crofters' Commission are more unexpected, for the script features an excessively greedy crofter, not satisfied with his lot despite being given forty years to pay off his arrears. The general impression, however, is of a self-confident society, liberal in outlook and happy to poke fun at itself.

During the last years of the 19th century cheap imports of beef and grain from abroad meant that Orkney's agricultural economy entered a period of decline which was to last until the outbreak of the First World War. A proportion of the grain that had previously been exported was now diverted to feed poultry, thereby creating a flourishing egg export trade, the proceeds of which were regarded as pin money for the farmers' wives. This was a period when the herring fishing industry was at its height, benefiting especially the islands of South Ronaldsay, Burray and Stronsay, the village of St Mary's in Holm and the town of Stromness.

By the end of the 19th century a small fleet of floating shops serviced the islands and north coast of Scotland. In addition, travelling shops pulled by horses served the Orkney Mainland parishes selling groceries, foodstuffs and draperies. These shops returned to Kirkwall often loaded with eggs and lobsters as payment in kind. Such travelling shops were largely the inspiration of Robert Garden, who treated his employees well, accommodating them in the sturdily-built houses that still stand in Garden Street, Kirkwall. When he died he bequeathed money for the Garden Memorial Building when the Balfour hospital was opened in 1927.

Education at this time was highly prized as a route out of the poverty trap. The Education Act of 1872 meant that universal education in Orkney facilitated the progress of a remarkable number of gifted scholars. Of the Orkney students who passed through Edinburgh University alone during the first quarter of the 20th century, at least nine attained professorial chairs, while four became the principals of colleges and universities. This flowering of Orkney achievement led to the saying that Orkney's chief exports were fat cattle and professors. Andrew Carnegie, a wealthy industrialist who had emigrated to America from Scotland, gave money to build a new library in Kirkwall, and attended the opening ceremony there in 1909. This building has been replaced by a new library with a room for the Family History Society and more space for the County Archives.

Surprisingly, emigration had continued unabated throughout the period of 19th-century agricultural improvement, and newspaper advertisements for new agricultural goods lay side by side with those offering passages and job opportunities overseas. More than 4,000 Orcadians emigrated during the last decade of the 19th century, although the population fell by only 2,471 during this period. Emigration slackened between 1901 and 1910 to 2,870, while the population dropped by nearly 2,000 to 25,791, marking a pattern of decline that was to continue until 1971.

Before the First World War Orkney was a county of landed estates with farms that were cultivated by crofters and tenant farmers. The islands had strayed far from the Old Norse udal system whereby farmers owned their properties outright, and by the end of the 19th century only a few farms were privately owned. The Crofters' Act of 1886 had for the first time established the legal rights of crofters. However, Orkney landowners continued to exercise a paternalistic control over their tenants. These Orkney lairds considered themselves to be in the aristocratic mould, entertaining their guests with such conventional pastimes as shooting parties and trout fishing. Although agriculture was well established on a commercial footing by the start of the 20th century, the older generation of tenants could still recall the harsh days before agricultural improvement. Now, with improved stock and crops, individual farms still supported three generations of the same family. Herring fishing also provided some seasonal work for Orcadians, but the economy was also diversifying in other directions.

From the second half of the 19th century the great natural harbour of Scapa Flow had been used increasingly by the Royal Navy; indeed in 1863 the Home Fleet visited the Flow on exercises. It was to be conflict abroad, however, that was soon to set Orkney firmly on the international stage. The strategic necessity for a northerly base for the Home Fleet in the face of a perceived threat from the German navy soon became apparent. In 1914 Admiral Jellico became Commander in Chief of the navy and, with the likelihood of 100 ships in the Flow, he was appalled at the lack of defences there. Soon a build-up of land-based defences was begun with blockships, nets, booms, artillery, minefields, loops and steel barriers put in place. With the completion of these precautions the Home Fleet returned to Scapa Flow, where they were to remain at anchor for much of the war, occasionally leaving in an attempt to tempt the German fleet out to sea.

It was from Scapa Flow in 1916 that 72 ships sailed to join with 52 other British vessels in the Battle of Jutland. The result was indecisive, but after this battle the Germans never again ventured out of port for the remainder of the conflict. That same year Lord Kitchener, Minister of War, left Scapa Flow aboard HMS *Hampshire* en route for Russia. Just off the coast of Birsay, the ship hit a German mine and sank with the loss of all but 12 survivors.

In 1917 up to 123 ships were using the Flow when further tragedy struck. An internal explosion blew up the battleship *Vanguard* with the loss of more than 1,000 lives. Only two of the total crew survived and the many anonymous headstones in the Lyness naval cemetery demonstrate the impossibility of identifying many of the corpses and bear witness to the ferocity of the explosion. Only two months later two British destroyers, the *Opal* and *Narborough*, became disorientated in blizzard conditions. Both ships struck the rocks at Hesta Head on the island of South Ronaldsay and although many initial survivors clung to the rocks there, only one crew member survived until rescue came. This he did by wrapping the cloth from an inflatable dinghy around him.

The Northern Patrol of 10 cruisers, usually armed merchant cruisers, operated from its headquarters in Kirkwall and made 15,000 interceptions during the First World War. In October 1918 a German U-boat was detected by indicator loops in Hoxa Sound and was destroyed, the first and only First World War U-boat to be blown up in a controlled minefield. Activity was not only confined to the surface of the waters of Scapa Flow. The first planes had been brought to the Flow in 1913 and air stations were built at Houton and Swanbister in Orphir, and also at Stenness loch. The first successful landing of a plane on the deck of an aircraft carrier under way was made by Commander Dunning in a Sopwith Pup, which alighted on the deck of HMS *Furious* off the coast of Orphir. Tragically, however, Dunning died on the unsuccessful second attempt.

It was at the end of the First World War that Orkney waters provided a scenario for a unique drama to unfold. At the Armistice in November 1918 the German High Seas Fleet was interned in Scapa Flow, 74 ships in all – heavy and light cruisers, battleships and destroyers. These vessels were disarmed but manned by over 4,000 German crew. The British did not go on board, though their patrol boats regularly took round messages to the German ships, who were supplied with food brought direct from Germany. In command of the German fleet was Admiral Von Reuter, who had been warned not to let his ships fall into enemy hands. Von Reuter was afraid that if talks broke down and the deadline for signing the Treaty of Versailles were not met hostilities would break out afresh and the British would seize the entire complement of German ships in Scapa Flow. As the deadline of 21 June approached there was no sign of a breakthrough, and Von Reuter now set in hand elaborate plans to sink his whole fleet. On 17 June he sent round a coded message giving each ship explicit instructions to be ready to scuttle. Ironically it was the regular British patrol boat on delivery duties that, unawares, took this message round. At the same time German supply ships returned to Germany carrying 2,700 returning German sailors on board, leaving a skeleton crew of only 1,700 to man all 74 ships. Four days later, on 21 June, Von Reuter, unaware that the deadline for the signing of the treaty had been extended by two days, sent round a further coded directive by semaphore and signal lamp 'Paragraph 11 confirmed'. Two hours later, when all the ships had received this message, the bell aboard the German flagship tolled and the scuttling began. Five hours later it was all over. Fifty-two German ships lay at the bottom of the Flow, while another 22 lay beached or saved by the British. In the course of scuttling, nine German crew lost their lives while the rest escaped mostly by life raft, some clinging to a small skerry off Orphir known as the *Barrel of Butter*. The following morning British ships delivered the redundant German crews to prison camp on the Scottish mainland at Invergordon. In the Flow there remained an eerie silence. Around the great expanse of empty water the beaches lay littered with detritus of the scuttling – life rafts, tin cases containing bottles of beer, pistols for firing rockets, sailors' caps, lifebelts, pages of books, onions and packing cases.

The local population had watched these events unfold with amazement. A Sunday school outing of children aboard *The Kestrel* had been sailing around the fleet. As the German ships began to list and settle in the water, some of the children believed this was a show specially put on to entertain them. Their parents in Stromness, frantic with worry for the safety of their offspring, watched helpless from the shore. In Orphir a funeral was interrupted as a shout went up to the mourners, 'Boys, the fleet's sinking', and the entire party deserted the minister at the graveside for the dyke to watch the spectacle!

The scuttling of the German fleet may have been a blessing in disguise. Its future had been one of the unresolved sticking points in the Versailles peace talks, and the scuttling certainly solved a difficult political problem. Between the wars the firm of Cox and Danks salvaged much of the fleet, raising the great ships by two methods. The first was to pass hawsers beneath the hull and attach them to cranes on a floating dock. The second method was used to raise the larger ships like *The Hindenberg* when stopcocks were closed and airlocks attached to the hull. Air was then pumped into the hull until buoyancy was achieved. Today what was once seen as a disaster now proves to be an asset to the Orkney economy. The seven great ships of the German fleet that still remain on the bed of Scapa Flow provide an attraction to divers who come to Orkney from all over the world to explore the wrecks, thus boosting the tourist industry of the islands.

By the end of the First World War there was thought to be little money in agricultural land and landowners found it more profitable to invest their money elsewhere. Legislation now meant that farmers could purchase their properties as sitting tenants, and so the process began which transformed Orkney from a population of farm tenants to a county where the majority were owner-occupiers. Men now had an incentive to invest in further improving their own land and farm buildings. However, the prevailing attitude of 'it's the outside that keeps the inside going' often meant modernisation of the domestic quarters in the farmhouse buildings came low on the list of priorities.

Other modernisation was slow to arrive. By 1922 Orkney was the only county in Scotland without a telephone service, though this was installed the following year. In 1924 a generating station was built in Kirkwall to supply electricity to the town. The gas plant, originally installed soon after 1838 solely for street lighting purposes, was updated and mass wireless receivers were installed enabling Orcadians to hear radio broadcasts from around the world for the first time. However, other areas of Orkney had to wait for mains electricity until considerably after the Second World War.

Lyness on the island of Hoy, a naval fuel pumping station for the Grand Fleet during the First World War, acted between the wars as headquarters for salvage operations for the sunken German fleet. As the threat of new conflict increased, a massive operation to create tunnels and great fuel tanks at Lyness was effected by a largely immigrant labour force of some 1,000 men, some of them former miners, who excavated deep within the hillside of Wee Fea. This work, begun in 1938, was finally completed in 1942, the spoil from the tunnels being used to build a new deep water quay at Lyness.

At the outbreak of the Second World War Scapa Flow again became well established on the world map, and once more the conflict impinged considerably on the Orkney way of life, though in some ways it caught the islands unawares. Just three months before war was declared, the crew of a German fishery protection vessel visited Kirkwall and played in a football match arranged at Bignold Park. When they left, a choir from Kirkwall Grammar School sang the German national anthem at the quayside in their honour. At the start of the war the islands were declared a closed area, and access to and from them could only be achieved by obtaining a special permit. All photography of the area was forbidden and the use of cameras prohibited. All correspondence to and from the islands was scrutinised at the government censor's office in Inverness and anything that was thought might compromise national security was swiftly cut out. During the first days of war an 11 o'clock curfew was declared, but this was soon abandoned when it was found that few Orcadians took any notice of such restrictions.

More ships were deliberately and hastily sunk adding to those that already lay blocking the four easterly entrances into Scapa Flow. However, complacency regarding the effectiveness of these defences resulted in a fresh disaster. German reconnaissance had not been idle and a weakness was detected in the effectiveness of blockships in the channel between the Orkney Mainland and the island of Lambholm. Late on the night of 13 October 1939 Commander Prien navigated his U-boat 47 on the surface through a gap between two of these blockships in Kirk Sound and thereupon entered the waters of Scapa Flow. Prien had three factors in his favour; the lighthouse lights were switched on to help guide the British Fleet, which was mostly out on exercise; the Northern Lights were said to be bright that night, and there was an exceptionally high tide. On entering the Flow Prien was disappointed to find a lack of British ships. However, eventually he spotted battleship *Royal Oak* at anchor, left supposedly to guard the radar station at Netherbutton.

It was now early on the morning of 14 October and Prien knew he had to act quickly before the outgoing tide made escape impossible. One of his first torpedoes fired from the bow tubes probably struck the anchor chain. A slight explosion was felt aboard the *Royal Oak* but no cause could be found, and those on duty thought it must be due to some small internal explosion. Torpedoes fired from the stern of the U-boat missed their target completely, but torpedoes from the re-loaded bow tubes struck with deadly effect and the battleship sank in just 13 minutes.

Asleep below, most of the crew simply had no time to get up on deck. Others choked on the heavy fuel oil that leaked from the vessel. Despite the best attempts of the cutter *Daisy*, which rescued many, 833 out of a crew of 1,400 perished. Prien and his crew, meanwhile, escaped undetected through the same channel they had penetrated just a few hours previously. This was a spectacular achievement and the German nation greeted Prien home as a hero, and saw him personally decorated by the Führer.

Winston Churchill immediately travelled to Orkney to inspect the scene at first hand and it was he who ordered the immediate construction of the concrete barriers that eventually bore his name. These would permanently seal the four inadequately blocked channels, leaving the other five entry/exit points to the Flow to be guarded by indicator loops and boom defences. More coastal batteries were now built and searchlights were installed with heavy and light anti-aircraft guns. Barrage balloons were deployed to discourage any close approach from bombers. Four airfields were constructed, at Hatston, Skea Brae, Twatt and Grimsetter, plus two dummy airfields. Orkney could claim a series of firsts at this time. An airfield, HMS *Sparrowhawk*, was built at Hatston and boasted the first tarmac runway in Britain. It was from this airfield that planes took off to sink the German cruiser *Konigsberg* off Bergen, the first ship to be sunk by air power alone. On 17 October 1939 the first German aircraft to be shot down on British soil crashed near the Pegal burn on Hoy, but not before the first bomb to explode on British soil in the Second World War fell on Ore Farm at

Lyness. A month later an aircraft claimed the first British civilian to be killed in the war when a stray bomb fell at the Brig of Waithe in Stenness.

During the war Orkney played host to many ENSA entertainers who visited the islands to entertain the troops. These included Yehudi Menuhin, Flanagan and Allen, George Formby, Evelyn Laye, Will Fyffe, Tommy Trinder and Gracie Fields, who performed in the huge garrison theatre in Kirkwall, and at other garrison theatres in Stromness, Lyness and Flotta. The Second World War also saw the inception of the *Orkney Blast*, a local forces' newspaper, inspired by author Eric Linklater, which kept the garrison in touch and entertained for some four years. Despite dances, concerts, dramatic and arts' societies, time hung heavily for many servicemen. One of them wrote the definitive verse, *Orkney, Bloody Orkney*, which was published in *The Orkney Blast* and sums up the boredom and loneliness experience by many stationed in Orkney during the war years. Two of its many verses run:

> This bloody town's a bloody cuss,
> No bloody trains, no bloody bus,
> And no one cares for bloody us
> In bloody Orkney.

> Best bloody place is bloody bed,
> With bloody ice on bloody head,
> You might as well be bloody dead,
> In bloody Orkney!

The Second World War left an indelible mark on the Orkney people and the Orkney landscape, leaving behind an outstanding system of coastal defences, of interest to present and future generations. There were other assets that remained in the islands as a consequence of war. Roads had been built and improved. The Churchill Barriers, constructed from rubble and concrete blocks and built with the help of Italian prisoners of war, now acted as causeways enabling the population of Burray and South Ronaldsay to travel overland to the Orkney Mainland for the first time. As a result many of them now work and shop in Kirkwall. Tourists come from all over the world to visit the beautiful Italian chapel created by the prisoners of war on the island of Lambholm under the leadership and inspiration of Domenico Chiochetti.

During the years 1939 to 1945 the population of Orkney nearly trebled to some 60,000 with the addition of both military and civilian personnel, while there were often up to 100,000 others on board ship in Orkney waters. These personnel had to be fed, and Orkney's farmers were encouraged to break in and cultivate new land.

When war ended and the armed forces left the islands, a new market had to be found for the surplus produced by the dairy industry, which had supplied vast quantities of milk to the servicemen garrisoned in the islands. In 1945 the North of Scotland Milk Marketing Board was set up and milk supplies were diverted to the production of Orkney cheese.

The egg industry prospered after the war and Orkney became the greatest egg-producing area in Britain. There were 3,200 agricultural holdings at this time, but the average size of each was only 34 acres. In 1950, 50 million eggs were being exported, and by 1957, 78 million eggs were being produced. That year half of Orkney's agricultural earnings came from eggs, but the following year the British Egg Marketing Board warned of the danger of overproduction, and over the next 12 years the industry declined. By 1969 production and transport costs, together with a lowering in the price of eggs, had caused a deficit in the industry costs.

The introduction of modern amenities was gradual. In 1947 the houses and streets of Stromness were lit by electric light for the first time, and four years after that the North of Scotland Hydro Board built a new power station in Kirkwall and soon 3,300 householders were supplied with electric power. The village of St Margaret's Hope on South Ronaldsay became the first island village to have a publicly funded electric supply. The supply of electricity to outlying country areas was slower to be established, the island of Egilsay having to wait until 1981 to be connected to the electricity mains. In 1958 a television transmitter was erected at the former radar station of Netherbutton in Holm, although there were still country areas with no electricity to power a television set. Housing conditions were still quite primitive in country areas at this time, with 55 per cent of the rural population without piped water, 77 per cent with no flush toilet and 82 per cent with no bath.

The pace of change in rural areas was slower than in the towns of Stromness and Kirkwall. Although a bus service and increasing car owner-ship created a more mobile community, leisure time was still parish centred with strong attendance at the local groups such as the SWRI and guild meetings. One commentator declared that the main recreation in his parish was a call on a neighbour, fishing on sea or loch, listening to the wireless or an evening at a parish concert or whist drive, often followed by a dance. However, it was remarked that more people were beginning to travel out of Orkney to take a holiday for the first time.

Over the next years the population of the islands continued to decline. During the war emigration had slackened but between 1951 and 1961 it was estimated that 2,700 left the islands and the population fell by 11.8 per cent during this decade. Even the population of Kirkwall remained static at 5,672. This trend continued over the next ten years when the population figures hit an all time low at just 17,077, nearly half the number who had lived in Orkney at the peak of population in 1861. The outlying islands were particularly hard hit and the population of these isles declined by two thirds during the century following 1861 as a result of what was known as 'the drift from the isles'.

It was not until the building of an oil terminal on the island of Flotta by Occidental in the early 1970s that this trend of depopulation began to be reversed. This was a tremendous undertaking and one that gave wide-spread employment in the short term. Once established, the oil terminal provided regular work, either directly or indirectly, for some 450 people. The building of an oil terminal generated a new air of optimism in Orkney. Prices of property rose and the establishment of this brand-new industry provided a catalyst that kick-started the general economy of the islands and reversed the trend of depopulation. There were soon moves to exploit other sources of energy. In 1977 the South of Scotland Electricity Board asked permission to make exploratory bore holes in a uranium corridor which had been discovered running from Yesnaby to Stromness. Strong local resistance and opposition were successfully voiced in Orkney, the campaign slogan proclaiming 'Uranium never Orkney Forever', and the Electricity Board retired defeated. Three years later three windmills were erected at Burgar Hill to generate power for the national grid. In 2000 these were superseded by three new windmills, built in Denmark and capable of supplying some 20 per cent of Orkney's electric power require-ments. One of them, a two-megawatt machine with a 64-m tower and 72-m blade diameter, is currently the largest windmill in the UK. Other com-mercial wind projects are scattered through the islands.

Over the centuries Orkney had successfully assimilated Picts, Vikings and Scots. Now it was the turn of the English. Back in 1931 more than 90 per cent of the islands' population had been born in Orkney and in the 1950s the Orcadian reaction to incomers who arrived on their shores was reported to be 'rather conservative'. However, the numbers of those arriving from the south to make Orkney their home was increasing, and by 1991 some 14 per cent of those living in Orkney gave their birthplace as England. Many brought professional skills and technological expertise essential to new industries and services. As a result the population of the Mainland rose, but some of the outer isles became increasingly depleted of native-born Orcadians. However, some small communities only remain viable because incoming families from the south have settled on islands like Egilsay, appreciating the quality of life available there.

Some of these new Orcadians have contributed their considerable creative gifts to the arts in Orkney. The composer Sir Peter Maxwell Davies, now living on Sanday, has spent much of his working life composing at his home on the island of Hoy, and it was he, together with author George Mackay Brown, who was instrumental in founding the St Magnus Music Festival. This annual midsummer event draws many visitors to Orkney, who have come to hear such international artists as Vladimir Ashkenazy, John Williams, Evelyn Glennie, the BBC Philharmonic Orchestra and poet Seamus Heaney. This festival also combines professional and amateur performers and regularly involves Orkney schoolchildren. In addition there is a well-supported annual Folk Festival in May and a highly successful

Science Festival in early September. Speakers have included men of international calibre including former astronaut Commander John Young and the eminent geneticist Sir Walter Bodmer. All these festivals have an enthusiastic local following as well as attracting visitors to the islands.

Orkney has its own list of distinguished and well-known writers and poets in Edwin Muir, Eric Linklater and George Mackay Brown, while the genius of artist Stanley Cursiter saw him appointed the Queen's Limner. The Flotta Oil Terminal has been generous to the arts in Orkney. Occidental helped gift a Steinway concert piano to the Orkney Arts Society, and together with the Armand Hammer Foundation donated £50,000 towards the establishment of the Pier Arts Centre in Stromness. This building houses an art collection that includes works gifted to Orkney by Margaret Gardiner, a frequent visitor to the islands. Amongst its outstanding collection are works by Barbara Hepworth and Ben Nicholson.

Orkney is also home to many resident artists and craftsmen and women. Ola Gorie originally introduced silver jewellery-making to the islands in 1959, using her her own distinctive designs, and the firm now employs some 55 people. Since that time others, such as Ortak and Sheila Fleet, have set up their own successful businesses. Orkney silver jewellery is now exported worldwide, and helps promote an increasingly important and successful craft industry. Other crafts include the making of the distinctive straw-backed Orkney chairs, woodcarving, pottery, knitwear, tapestry, felted goods and clothing.

The high quality of Orkney's produce has been emphasised in recent years, and Orkney brands are actively promoted. Local quality beef is marketed as 'Orkney Gold', while Orkney seafood is sold world-wide. Thus you may find Orkney's Grimbister cheese in Harrods, Orkney Herring at the Hilton in Kuala Lumpur and Orkney beef in many of London's top restaurants.

The whisky industry is somewhat older. Once there were three distilleries on the Orkney mainland, including the makers of 'Old Orkney' in Stromness, but that distillery closed down some years ago. Two outstanding single malt whiskies are produced in Kirkwall; 'Scapa', at the distillery of that name, and 'Highland Park', surely among the country's top brands. Now more than 200 years old, Highland Park Distillery attracts many visitors, and is one of only a few distilleries remaining in Scotland to use its own malting floors.

As Orkney's standard of living increases, and as technology makes links with the outside world more immediately available, the elements that make Orkney culture unique have become increasingly important to residents and visitors alike. In 1977 the Orkney Heritage Society was formed, and since then specific parishes and islands have set up their own heritage trusts. There are flourishing traditional dance and music associations. An Orkney Yole Society was recently formed to preserve interest in this traditional craft, which once featured in the maritime economy of the islands. The Orkney Family History Society provides information on genealogy worldwide, especially to those whose forebears left these shores. BBC Radio Orkney has served the islands since 1976, helping maintain a sense of local community. The Orkney dialect, condemned as late as 1952 by the then Director of Education, is now actively encouraged.

The Orkney Archaeological Trust, set up in 1996 by the Orkney Heritage Society, does much to encourage the appreciation and conservation of the outstanding archaeological sites in Orkney. The trust forms the catalyst for archaeological excavation and research. In 1999 UNESCO recognised the outstanding Neolithic archaeological sites at Brodgar, Maeshowe and Skara Brae by giving them World Heritage status, declaring them to be deserving of protection for the benefit of humanity. The Trust has raised the profile of Orkney's archaeology, which is now the main attraction that brings visitors to the islands each year. In recent years the Heritage Society has organised successful international Neolithic and Iron Age conferences. National bodies such as Historic Scotland, Scottish Natural Heritage and the RSPB are also influential and involved in conservation and preservation issues in Orkney.

Orkney continues to place a high value on quality education. Children can be educated mostly on their home island at primary level, and there is also provision for children to stay on at school until the age of 16 on the larger islands of Westray, Sanday, Stronsay and Hoy, should they feel unready to attend the two secondary schools on the Orkney Mainland. The Orkney College once only offered certificate and diploma courses, which meant that it was necessary for young people to leave the islands to follow degree courses. Now, new educational opportunities have become available. Following an extensive building programme, Orkney College is taking its place as part of the new University of the Highlands and Islands, and is offering a variety of degree courses, including an MA course in archaeology.

Since 1971 the population of the islands has risen by 3,000 to around the 20,000 mark. The population participates in a wide range of sports and hobbies and all the usual youth groups are represented; in fact there are few interests that cannot be pursued in Orkney and a local directory lists more than 100 local, national and international voluntary groups active in the islands. There has, however, been a continuing contraction in the numbers of those living in the more remote islands and parishes, as the population becomes increasingly concentrated in the vicinity of Kirkwall.

The main millennium project in Orkney was centred on an £8¾ million leisure centre in Kirkwall, funded mostly from lottery money. While providing excellent sporting and leisure facilities, inevitably it runs at a loss, and some feel the money would more usefully have been spent in spreading recreational facilities more widely among parishes and island communities. Likewise, while there are thriving supermarkets in Kirkwall and Stromness, competition means that the number of small shops is shrinking, and some parishes have lost their small local shops altogether. For those who have to travel long distances to shop or work in Stromness or Kirkwall, the high price of fuel makes for a higher cost of living.

In 1974 Orkney successfully escaped being submerged in the Highland Region local authority, when the Orkney Islands Council became the smallest regional authority in Scotland, nearly all members being elected independent of political party affiliation. In national politics, the islands have maintained an unbroken liberal tradition since 1950 when Jo Grimond, later Lord Grimond of Firth, became Member of Parliament for Orkney and Shetland, followed 33 years later by Jim Wallace, now deputy leader of the new Scottish Parliament. Orkney demonstrated little enthusiasm for devolution, only narrowly voting in favour of a Scottish parliament, and voting against giving it any tax-raising powers.

At the start of the 21st century the people of Orkney continue to value their unique cultural heritage, and have capitalised on some of their past connections to forge fresh links abroad. Twinned with Hordaland in Norway, the islands maintain their past links with Scandinavia. A friendship treaty with Manitoba maintains Orkney's strong past connection with the Hudson's Bay Company in Canada. Cultural links have also been established with the town of Moena in the Dolomites, the hometown of Domenico Chiochetti, creator of the Italian chapel at Lamb Holm.

The oil industry on the island of Flotta is still extremely important to the economy of the islands, but its term as an important industry remains finite. It is essential therefore that new industries be established, but with a delicate hand to ensure that economic development is sympathetic to the local environment. It is fortunate that Orkney's Oil Reserve Fund does enable forward-looking investment.

There are plans for an economic future that will further harness the sustainable energy resources of wind and wave and enable the export of that power south to other parts of the UK. As long ago as 1943 George Bernard Shaw wrote a letter to *The Times* urging that a massive hydroelectric scheme be established in the fearsome waters of the Pentland Firth which he reckoned would provide enough power for the whole nation. Now, nearly sixty years later, the European Marine Energy Centre has established wave test facilities to the west of Stromness, and tide research facilities are expected to follow, adding to the already impressive story of renewable energy developments in Orkney, including the wind research centre at Burgar Hill. Meanwhile, agriculture remains Orkney's foremost industry, though tourism takes a close second place. The population demonstrates distinct and vigorous entrepreneurial skills; in fact the rate of establishment of new small businesses is the highest in the Highlands and Islands. In the 21st century Orkney remains a cohesive, resilient community, forward-looking and appreciative of the natural environment and distinct quality of life available to those who make these islands their home.

CHAPTER NINE

Orkney Place-names

ORKNEY HAS BEEN VERY WELL SERVED by place-name scholars in the past two centuries. The name of the Orkney scholar Hugh Marwick and, in particular, his study of Orkney farm-names,[1] must be known to all who have an interest in the place-names of Orkney and in what they can tell us about the history and language of the islands from the period of Norse settlement (c. AD 800) onwards. Place-name researchers from Scandinavia have also taken a keen interest in Orkney's place-names because they can be used as sources of information by scholars attempting to fill in the gaps in the saga record, as a recent Orkney historian, William P. L. Thomson, has said in his useful discussion of the place-name evidence in his book *History of Orkney*.[2] There is, however, still much that remains uncertain about the past because place-names can only relate part, albeit an important part, of the whole story.

The language (or languages) in which place-names are coined tells us a great deal about early settlement in a region. Sometimes a language is even more significant by its absence than by its presence and that is certainly true of the language spoken by the pre-Norse inhabitants of Orkney. It is necessary to start any survey of place-names in the Northern Isles of Orkney and Shetland by making some comment on the fact that there is a dense coverage of Norse place-names which obliterates almost all traces of the pre-Norse, Pictish place-names which must have existed previously. Archaeological evidence suggests that there must have been some cultural contact between the Norse and their predecessors, but the extant linguistic evidence gleaned from place-names does not, on the face of it, seem to support this suggestion.

One explanation for the lack of surviving Pictish place-names is that contact between the Norwegian invaders and the local Pictish population was essentially 'nasty, brutish and short'. This point of view has recently been given a vigorous airing by the Shetland archivist, Brian Smith, in an article entitled 'The Picts and the Martyrs, or, Did Vikings Kill the Native Population of Orkney and Shetland?'.[3] Supporters of this view argue that an extended period of intermingling of people and languages should have resulted in some survival of pre-Norse place-name vocabulary and, since this did not happen in the Northern Isles, the only logical conclusion is that there was no such period. Smith, in fact, says:

'I suspect that the Norse invaders of Orkney and Shetland didn't just "overwhelm", or "submerge" the native population: I think they killed them.'[4]

The other possible explanation is that, for some reason or reasons, new place-names were created by the Norse and all previous names were deliberately and systematically replaced. This is a persuasive argument because it best fits the archaeological evidence, which consists of artefacts from both cultures, suggesting a probable intermingling of people as well, although a cautionary note about interpretation of this evidence is included in a recent book, *Vikings in Scotland*.[5]

Perhaps the strongest argument in favour of the likelihood that earlier Pictish place-names were deliberately replaced by Norse place-names is based on analogy with other North Atlantic islands, where Norse place-names were being methodically and intensively introduced by the Viking colonists as a means of land management and establishment of a distinct cultural identity. Faroe and Iceland had no indigenous population and, therefore, blanket Norse naming could easily happen. In Orkney and Shetland, the existence of indigenous peoples would have complicated the process of annexation of land, but the Norse settlers would have been keen to stamp their linguistic authority on the islands in a similar way by simply replacing pre-existing place-names and thus making a clear statement of political and economic mastery. The establishment of ownership of farms and of a fresh cultural identity, marking the North Atlantic colonies as being different from the Norwegian homeland, would have been important to all Norse colonisers. In fact, it would have been even more important to use all available means, including place-name creation, to establish Orkney and Shetland as being just as securely Norse as the virgin territory of Faroe and Iceland. The place-names in all the North Atlantic islands make a vigorous statement of national pride, while at the same time signalling the establishment of a new type of national identity outside the Norwegian homeland.

However firmly one may adhere to this latter point of view, lack of toponymic evidence from the earlier period of Pictish settlement means that the history of Orkney's place-names prior to the arrival of Norwegian colonists in the 9th century remains speculative. The name Orkney itself, which is frequently recorded in the 12th/13th century *Orkneyinga Saga* (The History of the Earls of Orkney) recognises the existence of an indigenous island population because it is derived from the name *Orcades*,[6] first mentioned by a Roman geographer in the 1st century AD, the *orc*-element which is generally interpreted as a Pictish tribal name meaning 'young pig/boar', to which the Old Norse (ON) word for an island (*ey*) is added. The name Pentland Firth (ON *Péttlandsfjörðr*: Pictland Firth), given to the stretch of water which separates Orkney from the mainland to the south, also reflects awareness of a neighbouring tribal people whom the Norse identified as Picts. Similarly, the word Caithness (ON *Katanes*: ness or headland inhabited by the Cat tribe) incorporates a reference to an indigenous Pictish population.

The Norse were therefore willing to recognise Pictish inhabitants in the specific or qualifying part of the name for the whole Orkney archipelago, but there is no toponymic evidence to suggest that they were willing to grant any kind of internal status to the Picts because generics, or the definitive parts of place-names, are overwhelmingly Norse in origin. In other words, the Norse were in a superior position because they were choosing what to name and how to name it. One could also argue that they had freedom of choice because by then there were no Picts remaining in Orkney, although this seems less probable.

The Norse name for the central, main island in Orkney (now referred to as Mainland), if it existed, has not survived to the present day. Other names for the larger peripheral islands in Orkney, however, are Norse in origin and contain ON *ey*, the generic term for an island: North/South Ronaldsay, Sanday, Westray, Papa Westray, Eday, Stronsay, Rousay, Egilsay, Shapinsay, Gairsay, Graemsay, Hoy, Burray and Flotta. In these island names, many of which are also parish names, it is possible to detect some of the different types of name formation which are replicated many times over in habitative and topographical names in all the North Atlantic islands.

There are examples of place-names, such as Egilsay, Gairsay and Graemsay, which incorporate personal names and indicate a close connection between the eponymous person and the island, whether that of ownership or some other type of contact. Other names such as Hoy 'high island' and Flotta 'flat island' are given because of the striking topographical contrast between the neighbouring islands. Reference to sand, as in Sanday, is very frequent in Norse naming in all the North Atlantic islands, as is reference to isthmuses (ON *eið*), as in Eday, both of which features would have been significant because of their association with easy landing-places or passage for boats. Points of the compass, as in Westray, are also common and they often occur singly rather than in linked pairs. There is, for example, no eastern island to match Westray. Lying beside Westray and also beside Stronsay are two smaller islands known as Papa Westray and Papa Stronsay, the names of which refer to Celtic priests (ON *papar*), whose presence around the North Atlantic is recorded in many place-names and has been the subject of much debate. Finally, there is Shapinsay, or Shapansay, for the specific of which derivation from the ON present participle meaning 'helping' has been proposed but it seems rather doubtful as a description of an island.[7] Sometimes the modern form of the name is such that there can be little doubt of its origin, but sometimes that is not the case and discretion is generally the better part of valour when etymology is in question.

The visitor to Orkney cannot fail to be impressed by the main town of Kirkwall and its magnificent cathedral. Kirkwall is an interesting place-name because it encapsulates the mingling of Norse, Scots and Scottish English, which is the essence of present-day Orkney speech and naming practices. The spoken dialect of Orkney is now referred to as Insular Scots because it is essentially a dialect of Scots which incorporates some characteristically Scandinavian grammatical and lexical features. There is no scope in this short piece on place-names to write about the decline of the original Norn language spoken by the Scandinavian settlers in Orkney, but the interested reader can refer to the recent book on the subject by Michael Barnes,[8] who is also the author of the excellent recent study of runic inscriptions in Orkney.[9] To return to the place-name, Kirkwall, it is recorded in *Orkneyinga Saga* in the Old Norse form *Kirkjuvágr*[10] 'church voe' or 'inlet of the sea with a church situated at its inner end'. Influence from English orthography on the later Scots form, Kirkwaa, led to the second element in this place-name being recorded with a final -ll, which gives us the modern form Kirkwall (cf. Scots *haa*/English *hall*; Scots *baa*/English *ball* etc.). That this could have happened to the name Kirkwaa suggests that people, or at least the people who were recording the name in writing, had forgotten what the Norse original meant and had, therefore, proceeded by analogy with Scots *waa*/English *wall*. Continued use of a place-name to identify a location does not depend on understanding of its constituent parts, otherwise we would not be able to use place-names such as Helsinki, Manhattan, Tokyo etc. in the confident knowledge that the people to whom we are talking will understand what we mean by them.

Stromness, Orkney's other main centre of population, has an equally attractive location beside an inlet of the sea and a name which is similarly Norse in origin, deriving from ON *straumr* 'a current or tide' and *nes* 'a headland'. Marwick notes that this name does not appear frequently in early written records and it is not mentioned in *Orkneyinga Saga*.[11] His comments make it clear that the early history of the settlement at Stromness is not easy to decipher, unlike the place-name itself. This is true of many purely topographical names, which could have been created at any point in the history of the settlement of an area but which are likely to have been among the earliest created since the name-giver's (or name-givers') first impressions are generally visual impressions of the appearance of a place.[12] For example, tides and currents frequently gave rise to Norse place-names created by the sea-going Vikings and their descendants. Stroma, in the Pentland Firth to the south of Orkney, for instance, incorporates the same element *straumr* which clearly refers to the navigational dangers of the firth around this island.

Headlands are also important features, both from a landward and seaward perspective, and the element *nes*, anglicised to *ness*, is repeated in many place-names, although it is most frequently used of the area along the whole length of a headland rather than the outermost point of the land. For example, the parish name Deerness, recorded in *Orkneyinga Saga* as *Dýrnes*[13] or 'animal ness', is an example of a place-name including *nes* which was used more than once by the Norse in appropriate locations and which certainly referred to an area of land. As Marwick correctly points out, Diurinish in Skye has the same Norse origin, although subsequent Gaelic influence has affected its present pronunciation.[14] Similarly, Stenness, which is recorded in *Orkneyinga Saga* as *Steinnes* or 'stone (or stony) ness'[15] is likewise a place-name which can be found in several other locations which were colonised by Norse settlers, such as Stennes in the parish of Northmavine, Shetland.

The parish name Deerness also gave rise to the Orkney surname Deerness,[16] as often happens when families are identified by association with the place in which they farmed or lived. As with many things in the field of naming, however, while there is an evident link between place-name and personal name, the process of development from one to the other is, to quite a considerable extent, random. There is no guarantee that a particular type of place-name will give rise to a surname.

Returning to the main topic of place-names and to some further parish names of Norse origin which, like Deerness, do not incorporate ON *ey* 'island', the importance of topography as a significant source of place-names is again reinforced. The parish of Holm is interesting because, although it also fits into the broad pattern of parish and island names often being one and the same, the island term used in this instance is ON *holmr* which, unlike *ey*, is an ON word which has certainly survived in the Shetland dialect but, rather surprisingly, does not appear to be listed by Marwick in his dictionary of Orkney Norn.[17] The word *holmr*, unlike *ey*, which is generic in reference, describes a particular size and shape of island (generally relatively small and rounded). In most instances, in fact, it is very probable that where Orkney parishes have topographical names, these place-names predate the creation of the parish.[18] Firth (ON *fjörðr* 'inlet of the sea, fiord'), and Sandwick (ON *sandvík* 'sandy bay'), for instance, are very common place-names and examples are numerous, particularly in the Northern Isles. If such commonly used place-names chance to appear in early documents such as *Orkneyinga Saga*, as in the case of these two names,[19] the researcher is very fortunate in having a date but, for the most part, they are impossible to pinpoint because the elements from which they are constructed remained active as name-forming elements for several centuries.

The chronology of the elements from which habitative place-names were constructed is a topic which intrigued Marwick and which he examines, in considerable depth, in the latter part of his study of Orkney farm-names.[20] Habitative place-names, in this context, are those which are coined to describe farmsteads. Marwick's theories were highly influential and it is only in recent years that the fairly rigid chronological boundaries which he drew have been questioned, by William Thomson among others.[21] Marwick, himself, was aware that 'the task is beset with extreme difficulty; paths are obscure and signposts hard to recognise. The present attempt must thus be regarded merely as a rough blazing of the trail, and the suggestions made as being provisional in the meantime, and subject to amendment or correction in the light of later research'.[22] As Thomson makes amply clear, the great value of Marwick's work to scholarship remains indisputable because he was responsible for drawing attention to these patterns in the naming of Orkney farms, which are of abiding interest and which have informed all discussions of the topic since he wrote his original text. Thomson makes the very valid point that 'Marwick's scheme, although he described it as a "chronology", is strictly speaking a hierarchy based on size, location, and tax-paying status' and, in that sense, it still stands, although there are continuing arguments about the distribution of names within the structure of this hierarchy.

Which element and which names containing that element, for example, should occupy pride of place at the apex of any hierarchy of significance based on the status of the farm by comparison with other farms bearing different names? Many, including Marwick, would give that honour to the bær-names (to use the West Norwegian form bær, meaning 'farmstead'), which can be found variously in Orkney place-names in forms such as Bea/ -bea, -bay, -by etc. On the chronological front, Marwick certainly suggests that these names are 'from the very earliest phase of settlement'[23] although Wainwright, another eminent scholar, would strike a note of caution regarding one piece of evidence cited by Marwick, while agreeing with him in principle.[24] The place-name, Kirkaby, does not occur in Orkney and Marwick argues that its absence suggests that the -by names were created before 'any Norseman had been long enough in touch with Christianity to adopt the new faith'[25] but, as we have already seen at the start when discussing the absence of Pictish place-names, arguments based on negative evidence are always open to question and it is possible that the place-name Kirkaby simply did not survive in Orkney, as Wainwright points out. The survival of the Shetland example of Kirkaby in a remote location in Unst is highly fortuitous and it is a place-name which might easily have faded from local memory. This point of Wainwright's undermines Marwick's argument but Marwick's reference to Kirkaby only forms a relatively minor part of his wider discussion of the chronology of -bær names and, on its own, Wainwright's point would not demolish the whole argument.

Fellows-Jensen (1984) notes that the chronology of name survival may be complicated by various factors such as transference of names and replacement of one name by another and, in particular, she draws a parallel with developments elsewhere in Scandinavia where she notes that 'It is true that the occurrence of the simplex name Bær/Býr and of some compound names in -bær, -bý points to a situation in which there has been a change of name, but in these cases the bær-name is a secondary name that has replaced an older name for a primary farm, perhaps after the older name had come to denote a parish or some other fairly extensive area.[26] Her final conclusion, after discussion of several names incorporating -bær, is that 'All in all, it seems that the generic *-bær* is unreliable as an indicator of the age of settlements in the Isles.'[27]

It is a valid conclusion because the available evidence does not give clear support to Marwick's chronological theories. On the other hand, few would argue that the *-bær* names are not important in terms of status and that they have not played an important part in Orkney's place-name history since the earliest period in the colonisation of Orkney by the Norse. It remains, however, a niggling irritation that there are no Orkney *-bær* place-names in *Orkneyinga Saga* although the Caithness place-name, Duncansby, makes several appearances in the form *Dungalsbær*. Certainly, *Orkneyinga Saga* does not record all place-names in use in the period which it describes by any means and, as has already been said, negative evidence is worthless, but one can and should ask the question 'Why are the Orkney *-bær* place-names absent?'

In addition to their absence from *Orkneyinga Saga*, many of the Orkney examples do not appear in early rentals and, once again, the same question arises. Marwick suggests that 'The explanation of course is that the original units have been broken up, fresh names have been applied to the component parts, and the original name has survived only by chance, if at all, to denote some feature of the former unity.'[28] On the other hand, if the *-bær* farms were of considerable significance in the Orkney Norse world which is the subject of *Orkneyinga Saga*, it is strange that not even one of the place-names creeps into the saga. In my opinion, the question still remains unanswered.

Marwick distinguishes between ON *bú* and ON *bær* 'farmstead', and it does seem that, in Orkney, a clear distinction was made between the common noun or appellative *bú* and the place-name element *bær*, according to Marwick and his fellow Orkney historian, Storer Clouston.[29] William Thomson further defines the element *bú* as a 'technical term for a big farm worked as a single unit, as opposed to a multiple-occupancy township'.[30] There is a very fine line between the technical term which only functions as an appellative and the term which also functions as a place-name element and it is not a line which can easily be drawn in this instance. Most descriptions of 'The Bu of ——' type are indeed place-names and are functioning as such in the early rentals where they appear. The language of this description is English rather than Norse. The immediate purpose of the description 'The Bu of ——' is always to identify the precise location of the Bu, which, when all is said and done, is the essence of any place-name's purpose. An assumption is made that the reader, as well as the writer, although both speakers of Scottish English, will understand what a 'bu' is, although the occasional name which is recorded as 'Bu', suggests that sometimes an erroneous assumption about derivation from 'bull' is in the mind of the scribe at least (cf. the earlier discussion of the name Kirkwall).

A search through a modern Ordnance Survey map of Orkney (20th-century Pathfinder™ Gazetteer[31]) for place-names which contain Bu,

Bea/-bea, -bay or -by produces a number of examples which the visitor to Orkney can still identify in passing. There is, for example, The Bu of Burray (ND4897), The Bu of Cairston (HY2709), The Bu of Orphir (HY3304), the Bu of Aith (ND2989) and the Earl's Bu (HY3304), as well as some examples of Bu (HY2304; HY5041; HY6940; ND4093) on its own as a farm name. Bea also occurs as a farm name in its own right (HY2828), but the majority of examples appear in compound place-names such as Midbea (HY4444), Bea Loch (HY6540), Bea Ness (HY6538) and Beaquoy Farm (HY3021), which, if Marwick's interpretation of the name is accurate, translates as 'farm farm farm' because ON *kví* (which gives rise to Orkney *quoy*) means a small farming enclosure. In word-final position, the most common spellings are now -by and -bay and there are many examples, such as Chuccaby (ND3190), Dounby (HY2920), Grinaby (HY4843), Netherby (HY5804), Yesnaby (HY2215), Everbay (HY6724) and Housebay (HY6821) or Houseby (HY2922). The importance of these latter *huseby*-names in Orkney is considerable and deserves more focused attention than is possible here. William Thomson recognises the uncertainties associated with the interpretation of the names but pinpoints their territorial importance when he says 'whatever uncertainty there may be about the number of husebys, and whatever doubts about the validity of attempting to define the areas they once controlled, it is nevertheless clear that large blocks of land owned by the earls existed in association with these names'.[32]

Among other typical Norse farm-name elements dealt with in detail by Marwick are *staðir*, *bólstaðr* and *setr*. The typical modern reflex of *staðir* in Orkney is -ston, whereas in Shetland the form is, most frequently, -sta, although the occasional -ston does crop up in Shetland (e.g. Benston in Nesting (HU4653)) and also in Caithness (e.g. Borrowston Mains (ND0169)).[33] What has happened to the *staðir* names in Orkney could be explained by scribal familiarity with and, therefore, confusion with Scots *toun* which has the meaning 'an area of arable land on an estate, occupied by a number of farmers as co-tenants', although it may be that the influence, in this instance, is not from Scots but from ON *tún* 'an enclosure' which is common in the Northern Isles and is very specific in its application. Whatever the reason for the development to -ston, it is the commonest form of the name in Orkney and can be found in place-names such as Benstonhall (HY5536), Berston (ND4792), Cairston (HY 2610), Clouston (HY2911), Corston (HY3119), Germiston (HY3311), Grimeston (HY3114), Hatston (HY4311), Hourston (HY2919), Knarston (HY3020), Tenston (HY2717), Tormiston (HY3212); the list is not exhaustive. Early forms such as *Knarrarstaðir* in *Orkneyinga Saga*[34] help to identify these as *staðir* names and the occurrence of many of them in early rentals also confirms their antiquity. Many of these place-names had Norse personal names as specifics and it is no mere chance that many of them have also survived as modern Orkney surnames. Clearly, naming the owner of a *staðir* farm was important and various suggestions have been made as to why that should be so; Marwick outlines Storer Clouston's theory in his chapter on *staðir* names.[35] It is most appropriate that a man named Clouston should be expounding a theory on *staðir* names and it again emphasises the way in which personal names and place-names are interconnected but, regrettably, his theory is difficult to substantiate.

That is, unfortunately, true of many place-name theories about the Northern Isles and, as has already been said, the best route forward is the comparative route which looks at Orkney in conjunction with its other North Atlantic neighbours such as Iceland, where *staðir* was the most commonly occurring farm-name element at the period of consolidation of settlements. It seems that *staðir* occupies a similar slot in mainland Orkney nomenclature, with the significant difference of its later development towards -ston in the Norse/Scots linguistic environment of Orkney. Underpinning the *staðir* names must be the will to consolidate and to define ownership of farms. It is a corollary of the impulse which was earlier suggested as the motivating factor behind the deliberate replacement of earlier Pictish place-names.

Bólstaðr, likewise, is used to define ownership but normally is much wider in its application in that the specifics tend to define the function of the farmstead or its position in relation to the settlement as a whole, as well as sometimes identifying ownership. An important study of *bólstaðr* names in the North Atlantic area has recently been completed by Peder Gammeltoft, a Danish place-name scholar writing in English, and he incorporates the Orkney material in his list of Scottish *bólstaðr* names.[36] Fortunately, the list is alphabetical and it is very easy to find material from the different parts of Scotland which were settled by the Norse. Gammeltoft's interpretations largely follow those suggested by Marwick, although he sometimes disagrees about the specific or qualifying element in a place-name. There can be no certainty about these specifics in the absence of early written records because the earliest forms available to the researcher are often centuries later than the probable date of creation of the name(s), although some place-name elements remained in active use for a long period of time, causing further confusion for anyone attempting to establish chronology. Most of the Orkney *bólstaðr* names can be easily identified by the visitor with a map of Orkney because the modern reflex is -bister, as in the following selection: Bimbister (HY3216), Coubister (HY3715), Easterbister (HY4701), Westerbister (HY4602), Foubister (HY5103), Grimbister (HY3712), Hobbister (HY3212), Isbister (HY3918), Kirbister (HY2414), Mirbister (HY3019), Rennibister (HY3912), Skelbister (HY3609), Wasbister (HY2814).

The other ON habitative element mentioned above – *setr* – has also been the subject of discussion in the wider North Atlantic context because it is absent from Iceland, and various good reasons have been put forward to explain that absence.[37] In Orkney and Shetland *setr* is generally used of a hill farm or a secondary settlement on marginal land. It is very common indeed in Shetland, where marginal land is the norm, but slightly less so in Orkney. Our present perception is that the land is generally more suitable for agriculture and of better quality in Orkney than in Shetland and that was probably also true at the time of colonisation by the Norse because Orkney is much flatter than Shetland, although some of the present quality of the land can be attributed to land improvement undertaken in recent centuries. *Setr* can still be identified in modern Orkney place-names such as: Grimsetter (HY4808), Melsetter (ND2689), Mossetter (ND4486), Setter (HY3415), Settersquoy (HY3009) (cf. Beaquoy above), Stangasetter (HY6744), Vaasetter (HZ2071) Winksetter (HY3416), Yearnasetter (HY6427).

All of the names discussed in this chapter are examples of Orkney nomenclature, but if asked to identify a place-name element which, above all others, is associated with the Norse colonisation of Orkney in particular, that element, in my opinion, would be *skáli*, which seems to typify many of the subtleties and contradictions of Orkney names. There are some *skáli* names in neighbouring Shetland and in Caithness but it occurs much more frequently in Orkney names, where it evidently applied to quite substantial and important buildings rather than the insignificant buildings to which it refers elsewhere in the North Atlantic area, with the single exception of the Caithness example, spelt Skiall (ND0266), which follows the Orkney pattern of being associated with the idea of good, old, fertile land, emphasising the closeness of the political links between Orkney and Caithness. Examples in Orkney are not difficult to identify because many of them take the simplex form Skaill (HY2318, HY4552, HY5806 etc.) and, although it does occur in compounds, the number of specifics with which it occurs is limited, with Langskaill (e.g. HY2414, HY4343, HY5005) being the most common compound. Marwick states that 'many or perhaps most of the skaills represented the chief farms in their several tunships, and a skaill farm is still today associated with the idea of good, old, fertile land. There is little doubt that most of them indicate some of the earliest lands in Orkney to be cultivated by Norsemen, and the very name itself has still a certain air of dignity about it.'[38]

That sense of dignity, combined with elusiveness of interpretation, seems an appropriate note on which to start drawing this brief overview of some of Orkney's place-nomenclature to a conclusion. The visitor to Orkney will certainly feel that he/she has entered an essentially Scandinavian toponymic world on disembarking from the boat at Stromness or stepping off the plane at Kirkwall airport, and travelling through a land where the place-names on the map have much in common with those of western Norway, but also have a local resonance acquired through centuries of contact with mainland Scotland. The Scandinavian influences are indeed remarkably strong in Orkney, but, after a few days of acclimatisation to the place and its dialect, the visitor will depart with the impression that

Orkney is, in fact, a very distinctive part of Scotland. Even its dialect, which, on first hearing, may seem alien to the ear, is, as has already been said, a dialect of Scots, and while it contains a number of Scandinavian words and grammatical patterns, it is firmly linked to neighbouring mainland speech. Thereby hangs another tale, however, and space does not permit its inclusion here. Orkney is an island with a fascinating linguistic and cultural history and the proliferation of archaeological remains, visible at every corner and in every field, is guaranteed to tempt all visitors to prolong their stay, with the aim of finding out more about the past history of these interesting islands.

Notes

1   Marwick, Hugh 1952. *Orkney Farm-Names*, W. R. McIntosh, Kirkwall.

2   Thomson, William P. L. 1987. *History of Orkney*, The Mercat Press, Edinburgh, 24–33.

3   Smith, Brian 2001. 'The Picts and the Martyrs or Did Vikings Kill the Native Population of Orkney and Shetland?', *Northern Studies*, Vol. 36, Stevenson (Printers) Ltd, Dundee, 7–32.

4   *Ibid.*, 7–8.

5   Graham-Campbell, James and Batey, Colleen E. 1998. *Vikings in Scotland*, 163.

6   Watson, W. J. 1926. *History of the Celtic Place-Names of Scotland*, William Blackwood & Sons Ltd, Edinburgh and London, 6, 28.

7   Marwick 1952, 53.

8   Barnes, Michael P. 1998. *The Norn Language of Orkney and Shetland*, The Shetland Times Ltd, Lerwick.

9   Barnes, Michael P. 1994. *The Runic Inscriptions of Maeshowe, Orkney*, Reklam & Katalogtryck ab, Uppsala.

10 Pálsson, Hermann and Edwards, Paul (eds.) 1978. *Orkneyinga saga. The History of the Earls of Orkney*, The Hogarth Press, London, *passim*.

11 Marwick, Hugh 1952, 160.

12 Fellows-Jensen, Gillian 1984. 'Viking Settlement in the Northern and Western Isles', in *The Northern and Western Isles*, Alexander Fenton and Hermann Pálsson (eds.), Bell & Bain Ltd, Glasgow, 148–168.

13 Pálsson & Edwards 1978, 51.

14 Marwick 1952, 76.

15 Pálsson & Edwards 1978, 36.

16 Black, George F. 1984 reprint. *The Surnames of Scotland: Their Origin, Meaning and History*, The New York Public Library, 204.

17 Marwick, Hugh 1929. *The Orkney Norn*. Oxford University Press.

18 Fellows-Jensen, Gillian 1984, 154.

19 Pálsson & Edwards 1978, 168, 40 etc.

20 Marwick 1952, 225–251.

21 Thomson 1987, 26–27.

22 Marwick 1952, 227.

23 *Ibid.*, 247.

24 Wainwright, F. T. 1962. 'The Scandinavian Settlement', in F. T. Wainwright (ed.), *The Northern Isles*, Nelson, 138–139.

25 Marwick 1952, 247–248.

26 Fellows-Jensen 1984, 155.

27 Fellows-Jensen 1984, 157.

28 Marwick 1952, 244.

29 Clouston, J. Storer 1926/27. *Proceedings of the Orkney Antiquarian Society*, Vol. V, Kirkwall.

30 Thomson 1987, 29.

31 Pathfinder™ Gazetteer – 1. Ov – Scotland. Database compiled by Robin A. Hooker.

32 Thomson 1987, 29.

33 Waugh, Doreen 1987. 'The Scandinavian Element *Staðir* in Caithness, Orkney and Shetland', in *NOMINA*, Volume XI, Northamptonshire, 61–74.

34 Pálsson and Edwards 1978, 94.

35 Marwick 1952, 237.

36 Gammeltoft, Peder 2001. *The place-name element bólstaðr in the North Atlantic area*, C. A. Reitzels Forlag A/S, Copenhagen.

37 e.g. Fellows-Jensen, Gillian 1984, 162.

38 Marwick 1952, 238–239.

CHAPTER TEN

Agriculture in Orkney Today

A TOURIST CYCLING IN ORKNEY spotted a lonely figure in the middle of a field and was puzzled to see him still there on the return journey. His curiosity getting the better of him, the cyclist crossed the field, exchanged pleasantries with the man, whom he established was the owner of the field, and asked what he was doing. 'I'm out to win a Nobel Prize,' the farmer replied. The tourist was even more puzzled and asked for further explanation. 'Well,' said the farmer, 'the prize is awarded to a man outstanding in his field.'

While this story is unlikely to win any prizes, it serves to characterise farming in Orkney. The industry has flourished here because, generally, its practitioners are masters of their craft; the fields are owned almost exclusively by the farmers themselves, and many people are concerned that if the present decline in the industry continues much longer, there will be little left for farmers to do but stand in the middle of their fields.

The Background

Farming has been a dominant feature of these islands throughout their history, as other chapters of this book testify. This remains true today as illustrated (Figure 19) by the contribution made by agriculture to gross domestic product in Orkney when compared to other regions of Scotland.

An indication of the importance of agriculture for local employment can be derived from the Scottish Executive Agricultural Census (Scottish Executive 2001). A total of 2,290 people here depend on farming for some or all of their income (full- or part-time owner-occupiers, spouses and all hired and family labour). This represents 24 per cent of the 9,577 'economically active population' recorded in the (albeit dated) 1991 census (Orkney Islands Council 2001). When all those employed in jobs 'downstream' from farming – the suppliers, hauliers, veterinary workers etc. are considered, to say nothing of all those in the service and public sector administering to the needs of this vibrant rural population, the importance of farming to Orkney becomes alarmingly clear.

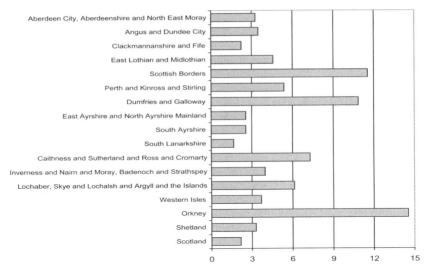

FIGURE 19   Agriculture's share of GDP (%)

It is instructive to consider the reasons for this industry assuming such importance here. Human beings are components of their ecosystems and respond to ecological conditions just as other species do. Agriculture was born when we learned how to manipulate these conditions rather than merely react to them. Our success is influenced by such things as competition, the health of the environment and the resources it provides. We have largely eliminated competitors and the environment in Orkney is not generally considered to pose any major threat to our health. The primary resources in question are the sun and the soil. The former may often seem a stranger, but even at this high latitude (59 °N), it can provide somewhere in the region of 60,000 GJ of energy per hectare at the earth's surface in a year. Considering that a cereal crop in the arable areas in the south will yield about 300 GJ of energy per hectare in a year, light would not appear to be a major limitation. A fortunate combination of geology and climate has left the majority of Orkney with a soil that is potentially suitable for agriculture (Berry 2000) and a topography that presents few barriers.

In other respects, the climate is certainly challenging. An annual rainfall of just over 1,000 mm provides ample water for crop growth but its distribution throughout the year (Figure 20), in combination with the heavy soils prevalent in the county, often make land work difficult and cause stock to spoil their grazing areas (poaching).

There is a perception among farmers in Orkney that their weather, particularly summer and autumn rainfall, is deteriorating. Comparison of the mean annual rainfall for the last 15 years (1,043 mm) with that of the 35-year mean from 1947 to 1982 (982 mm) indicates a 6.3 per cent

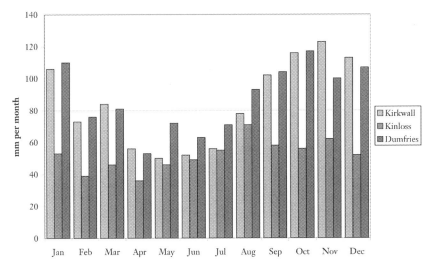

FIGURE 20   Rainfall (1960–90 average)

increase. In 10 of the last 15 years, the total annual rainfall was greater than 982 mm. Considering the combined rainfall for June and July – two months where sustained dry weather is essential for successful hay and silage making – the average figure for the past 15 years (112 mm) is 15 per cent greater than the 35-year mean from 1947 to 1982 and in 5 of these 15 years the total for these two months was over 20 per cent greater than that 35-year mean. Later in the year, when farmers are trying to secure the last of the harvest and prolong the summer grazing period, 9 out of the last 15 Octobers have been wetter than the 35-year mean from 1947 to 1982.

Thanks to the Gulf Stream, the temperature in Orkney is higher than regions at similar latitude (e.g. southern Greenland, the Falkland Islands and Leningrad), but in comparison to other UK regions with similar agricultural systems, the temperature is slower to rise in the spring with consequent effects on early growth (Figure 21). This shortens the growing season and inevitably adds to winter feeding and housing costs.

Wind is possibly Orkney's most notable weather feature (Figure 22) and although its effects are felt not only by farmers, it amplifies the impact of rain and can cause particular problems and losses at harvest time.

Apart from dictating the weather, Orkney's geographical position places other hurdles in the farmer's way. For an industry with a bulky product and requiring equally bulky inputs, the long distances between market and supplier add considerably to costs. Transport can add 10–15 per cent to the cost of fuel, fertiliser and feedstuffs when compared to farms on the mainland. Similarly, remoteness slices about £15 from the value of each beef animal shipped to Aberdeen and £3 from each lamb.

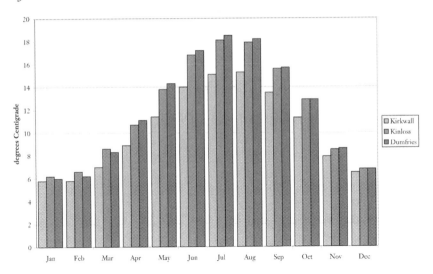

FIGURE 21   Maximum temperature (1960–90 average)

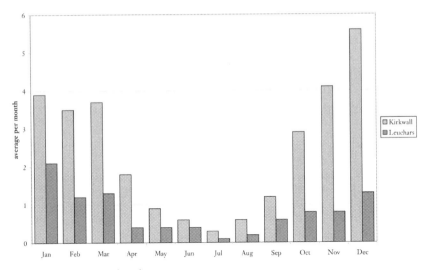

FIGURE 22   Days with gales

Farmers in the outer islands lose almost as much again in getting their stock to Kirkwall for the first leg of the journey to market.

Despite these difficulties imposed by the climate and location, Orkney has been farmed for millennia and today those visitors who understand farming are consistently impressed by the activities they find here. Somehow, the rewards have made the effort worthwhile; many are now asking how much longer that view will prevail.

A Modern Industry

Much that is written about Orkney deals with its rich and fascinating past and the farming depicted can often seem to belong to a bygone era. This would be misleading; farming in Orkney is very much of the 21st century. The reader is commended to study *The New History of Orkney* (Thomson 2001) for an excellent account tracing the development of the industry here and providing an insight into the current situation. This chapter attempts to continue that theme, providing further description and emphasising the vital place of the land in Orkney life and the eagerness of Orkney farmers to examine, employ and adapt new technologies and techniques to help overcome both natural and artificial impediments to their craft. The activities of the Orkney Agricultural Discussion Society over much the past century provide just some of the examples (some published in the society's journals) of the industry's thirst for progress.

Just as elsewhere in the country, the industry has had to strive for efficiency to remain viable. As soon as they offered improvements in output, new terminal sire breeds of cattle and sheep were introduced. Orcadian buyers have for long had a strong presence at breeders' sales in the south and Charolais, Simmental, Limousin and Texel bulls and tups regularly find themselves sailing north on the ferry.

With only a small proportion of dairy blood in the Orkney herd, the adverse effect this can have on beef quality has been largely avoided but producers, ever mindful of the importance of this feature, have tended to retain an element of 'traditional' breeding in the female herd. Many have taken a step further by re-introducing Aberdeen Angus sires and are enjoying the premium price their progeny now attracts. Mr Jim Ironside, managing director of Aberdeen-Angus Producers Ltd, commented recently about the enduring quality of the cow stock and the level to which Orkney farmers are prepared to invest in high quality bulls.

As dedicated stock farmers keeping tight control over their herds and flocks, Orkney farmers are keenly aware that animal health is a priority. On the basis that prevention is better than cure, a number of animal health initiatives have found ready acceptance in the county. Among these is a scheme to eradicate Enzootic Abortion, a highly contagious disease in sheep (HISHA 2000). By becoming accredited as free of this disease, breeders are well placed to expect higher prices for their stock. A similar approach has been taken by the newly established Orkney Livestock Association (OLA), which aims, with the involvement of the veterinary profession and financial assistance from the Orkney Islands Council, to eliminate a number of economically important cattle diseases such as BVD and Leptospirosis from the islands (*The Orcadian* 2001). Once again, freedom from these conditions would enable producers to win premium prices in the marketplace. The high density of livestock keeps the vets busy and Northvet, one of the local practices, is among the biggest in Scotland.

With an increasingly discerning public, several farm assurance schemes have been introduced to define production standards and inform the consumer. Among the first of these was Farm Assured Scottish Livestock (FASL), which appeared in the early 1990s and immediately received a high proportion of its subscribers from Orkney. This has now developed into a broader scheme coming under the banner of Quality Meat Scotland (QMS 2001), whereby qualifying farmers comply with standards which include feeding, health, welfare and traceability of stock. Virtually all of Orkney's livestock farmers have successfully met these standards.

The emphasis on quality will be vital in helping farmers win back markets after the recent BSE and foot-and-mouth disasters. Orkney is well placed to lead this, according to a senior Scottish Executive official who recently referred to the preponderance of high quality beef and lamb produced in the county and to the remarkable initiatives which have been taken here to market beef, lamb and dairy products.

The dairy industry blossomed in Orkney during the Second World War in response to demand from service personnel stationed here (Thomson 2001). This slimmed down significantly when they left but by turning production to cheese manufacture this sector has remained sustainable, with 26 dairy holdings still producing 15 to 16 million litres of milk annually. Once local liquid demand has been met, this produces about 1,000 tonnes of Orkney cheddar, a specialist product with a high reputation and a long tradition of success at agricultural shows and food exhibitions. Recent corporate acquisition activity in the dairy industry raised doubts over the future of the local 'creamery' and so local producers stepped in to take control. A new producers' co-operative, Orkney Milk, was established and now owns 70 per cent of the cheese business; 20 per cent is owned by the firm which previously marketed Orkney Cheese and the remaining 10 per cent is owned by the Orkney Islands Council. Together they form the Orkney Cheese Company which moved production late in 2001 to new premises outside Kirkwall with a state-of-the-art production line and enhanced storage facilities.

Another unfortunate element in the struggle to improve efficiency has been a reduction in the farm labour force. This trend has seen a halving in the number of both full-time owner-occupiers and full-time workers in the last 30 years to about 500 and 330 respectively (Orkney Islands Council 2001). To enable this leaner workforce to manage a bigger herd (through the long Orkney winter), modern farm steadings are commonplace with mechanised handling of feed and waste. Cattle sheds with slatted floors are popular since straw is too precious as a feed to allow its use for bedding. The 'minimal bedding court' with its sloping floor was an Orcadian invention; the 1:16 slope encouraging quick drainage and the location of the feed trough at the top of the slope ensuring that cattle scrape the solid waste and frugal sprinkling of straw to one side with their feet as they 'retire' after a meal.

Erection of these modern steadings has been assisted by a series of grant schemes, the terms of which have ensured that adequate provision is made for waste storage. This has the double benefit of allowing farmers to apply slurry to the land at times when it has most benefit to the crop and does least harm to the environment.

Hay has largely been supplanted by grass silage as the preferred winter forage – there are virtually no opportunities for outwintering cattle. The silage is made in pits or, becoming more common, baled and wrapped in polyethylene. Just as feeding of this material is highly mechanised, so is its production in summer and the use of modern, high-capacity equipment is widespread, often using the services of contractors or other farmers who share their equipment (and labour) through the 'machinery ring'.

The latest high-capacity machinery is also in evidence during land preparation and sowing of arable crops and although the cereal area does not justify enormous combine harvesters, their smaller cousins annually cross swords with the unpredictable autumn weather to secure Orkney's small but valuable harvest. When Orkney farmers eventually bade farewell to the binder and stook and the natural 'sook' of sun and wind, it became clear that, except in a very few situations, the moisture content of the combine-harvested grain rendered artificial drying uneconomic. An essential parallel technology has been the use of propionic acid treatment to prevent microbial degradation of the grain. Critics of 'chemical' farming need fear nothing – this is a natural product of ruminant digestion. A more recent innovation is to harvest the crop at an earlier and moister stage and ensile it after 'crimping' with a specialised machine. Not only does this produce a material ready to feed without further processing, but the option to harvest earlier reduces the risk of harvest losses and spreads the working season for the hard-pressed contractors.

The Scope of Agriculture Today

Out of a total land area in Orkney of just over 111,000 hectares (Mackey, Shewry and Tudor 1998), the area farmed today is approximately 54,000 hectares (Scottish Executive 2001), an increase of 25 per cent over the last 100 years. When over 36,000 hectares of 'sole right rough grazing' is added to this it represents over 80 per cent of the land surface coming under agricultural influence. Table 1 shows a small selection from the vast array of statistics available on the Scottish Executive website – fruit of the meticulous annual data submission exercise carried out by every farmer in the land.

Although pigs and poultry do feature in the data, their numbers are of little significance. Brief consideration of these statistics begins to convey an impression of the significance of livestock farming here with about 12 ruminant animals to every man, woman and child in the county. It is

Land	hectares
Grass for mowing	16,677
Grass for grazing	32,238
Tillage:	5,154
including: barley	4,004
oats	113
fodder crops	542

Stock	number (head)
Dairy cows	3,563
Beef cows and heifers for breeding	31,351
Male cattle over 1 year old	13,905
Non-breeding female cattle over 1 year old	14,591
Breeding ewes	59,557
Lambs and other sheep	90,200

Source: Adapted from Scottish Executive (2001)

TABLE 1   Agricultural Statistics 2000 (*Orkney*)

interesting to make comparison with the overall Scottish picture. Taking the area of 'total crops and grass' plus 'sole right rough grazing', Orkney represents about 1.7 per cent of the national total. This is very similar to the ratio found for breeding ewes and lambs, where Orkney has 1.6 per cent and 1.7 per cent respectively of the national figure. Moving to the data for 'total crops and grass' (an indication of more actively managed farming), Orkney has 2.9% of the national total but the focus of Orkney farming is revealed by studying the ratio for the beef breeding herd and 1–2 year-old male cattle where, in each case, 5.6 per cent of the national herd is found in this small county. Come to 'big cattle country'!

The emphasis on cattle, sheep and grass has not always been so strong. The past century saw a reduction in the area devoted to growing cereals and rootcrops (Figures 23 and 24) and a corresponding emphasis towards grass (Figure 25) and the animals that graze upon it (Figure 26). Today's cereal and root crops produce respectable yields (typically 2.5, 35–40 and 10–12 tonnes per hectare for cereal grain, swedes and potatoes respectively), but the produce is used entirely for stock feed. The local distilleries and brewery have to go south to source raw material with appropriate composition for their needs. Until the 1960s, pig and poultry production systems were profitable and widespread throughout Orkney (Thomson 2001), but rising feed costs and crippling competition from big, highly intensive farms in the south led to these dying out in the islands.

These changes have inevitably meant a move away from rotational cropping, where traditionally a field would have been in grass for three years, then cereals for a year, roots for a year and finally another year of cereals,

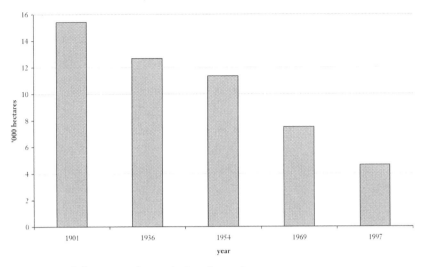

FIGURE 23   Orkney cereal area during the 20th century

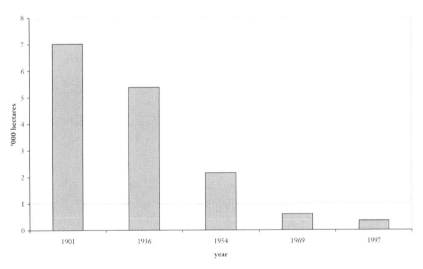

FIGURE 24   Orkney rootcrop area during the 20th century

this time undersown with the grass that would start the next cycle. Reasons for the move to grass monoculture are complex but a key feature is the opportunity that silage-making offers, to produce a high-quality winter feed and thus reduce the need for high-energy cereals and roots. Couple this with the high-capacity mechanisation employed in silage making and it is clear why the diminishing workforce has opted for this system. Farms which at one time would have spent most of the summer and autumn trying to conserve hay and straw crops of questionable feeding value can have the

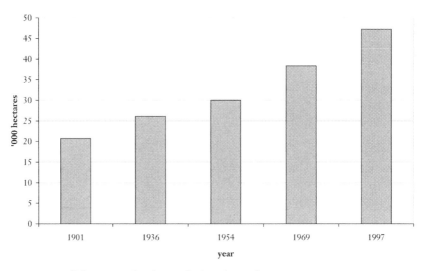

FIGURE 25 Orkney grassland area during the 20th century

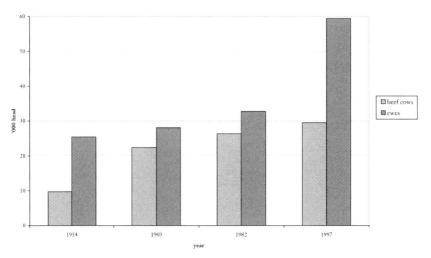

FIGURE 26 Numbers of breeding animals in the second half of the 20th century

entire winter supply of high-quality forage ensiled and under polyethylene in less than a week.

Although this grass monoculture approach reduces the amount of work (and energy cost) needed in spring cultivation and sowing, there are disadvantages in dispensing with rotational farming. Cultivation provides an opportunity to incorporate farmyard manure into the ground and thereby improve soil structure and fertility. Furthermore, pests and diseases and, particularly, weeds thrive when presented with the same crop year after year. This has meant increased reliance on imported fertilisers and chemicals, although not to the extent seen on intensive farms in the south. A significant factor has been the widespread use of white clover in grassland since the Second World War (Thomson 2001). Without the nitrogen-fixing attributes of this little plant, grass swards would, as they did before its introduction, struggle to produce worthwhile crops beyond two or three seasons. Holmes (1989) refers to a survey in England and Wales, where 55 per cent of the grassland was over 20 years old and well-managed swards today can go on yielding profitably almost indefinitely, hence the term 'permanent pasture'.

Leaving aside the agronomic and technical aspects of the trend towards reliance on a limited number of enterprises (grass and ruminants), and accepting that there were viable economic reasons for having done so, there is a real danger of Orkney farmers being found with all their eggs in one basket. This was brought out recently by the successive crises arising from BSE and foot-and-mouth disease. Ironically, Orkney was fortunately untouched by the latter and showed little evidence of the former but suffered considerably because of the overall consequences on the national market.

Financial Support For Agriculture

Since the Second World War successive UK governments have employed a range of agricultural support measures to encourage farmers to provide the nation with secure and affordable food supplies. When the UK joined the then European Economic Community in 1973, the Common Agricultural Policy (CAP) offered our farmers access to additional European funds, although many have argued that our leaders failed to take full advantage of this by often refusing to put up matching UK support. Reports of fraud and featherbedded farmers are legend, but these are largely restricted to the arable sector and of little consequence in Orkney.

Examples of early livestock schemes were based on 'deficiency payments', whereby animals failing to reach a price based on the national average for that week were eligible for 'up-maak' to make up the difference. At the same time, 'Hill Livestock Compensatory Allowances' (HLCAs) were introduced as a headage payment on breeding cattle and sheep to help offset the high cost of keeping these animals in 'less favoured areas' (land with low potential and remote from markets and suppliers). Generous improvement grants were also available to meet the costs of reseeding pasture with improved species, fencing and draining pastures and erecting buildings.

European assistance became available in 1993 in the form of 'premia' for suckler cows, ewes and male beef cattle. The latter can be claimed twice during the lifetime of an animal and is monitored through use of 'cattle control documents' (CCDs), which change colour (by re-issue) when each payment is made. Lay observers may be puzzled by references to white and blue CCDs when cattle prices at the mart are quoted.

The European schemes are still essentially similar but are now monitored under the umbrella of the Integrated Administration and Control System (IACS) (Scottish Executive 2001), which entails the measurement and recording of just about everything that moves and grows on a farm. Cattle have to wear two special ear tags and have to be accompanied by passports wherever they go. Farmers have been turned into unwilling bureaucrats by the sheer financial necessity of applying for these subsidies. There is a system of penalties for late and inaccurate applications, although it has to be said that any discrepancies are handled very fairly by local Scottish Executive Environment and Rural Affairs Department (SEERAD) offices.

This year sees significant changes to the HLCA system. It has been replaced by the 'Less Favoured Areas Support Scheme, 2002', where aid is paid on the basis of area farmed rather than numbers of breeding livestock. By this means, the scheme ought to encourage more extensive stocking rates of livestock. The initial rates of payment have been designed to achieve equity with the previous scheme on a national basis, but areas which have been carrying higher stock numbers than the national average will see the gross subsidy reduce. As discussed under Table 1, Orkney farmers have deployed their stock-rearing and grassland management skills to maximise their access to headage-based support. The change in system will 'move the goalposts onto another field' and is estimated to cost Orkney about £1 million per year.

There are examples of local financial support schemes such as 'interest relief grants' for capital projects from the Local Enterprise Company and Local Authority assistance for purchasing fodder in years when the weather has made harvests difficult. Although many see these as an acknowledgement of the importance of farming in the community, there are those who speak of unfair advantage and the 'preponderance of farmers on the Council'.

The overall cost of agricultural support is widely condemned and there is continual clamour for reform or abolition of the CAP. The extent to which Orkney farmers depend on subsidy was revealed by a study (Table 2) carried out by the Scottish Agricultural College (SAC) in 1998 (Orkney Islands Council 1998).

Source of Income	beef herd only	beef herd and ewes
Cattle	50.9	43.8
Sheep	0.0	13.5
Crops	2.5	1.6
Subsidy	37.0	33.6
Contracting	4.3	2.5
Other	4.8	5.4
Totals	100.0	100.0

TABLE 2 Estimated breakdown (percentage) of income by farm type

Farmers themselves are acutely concerned by the reliance they have on this level of subsidy, a source of income so vulnerable to political whim, and would feel more confident and empowered if a living could be made from what they produce on their land. Unfortunately, recent statistics are far from encouraging, showing that even with current subsidy levels, net farm incomes for 'less favoured area' specialist beef farms and mixed beef and sheep farms (typical of Orkney) were predicted to remain at £4,000 and £3,000 per farm for the year 2000 (Scottish Executive 2000c). Another perspective came from a farmer who recently commented on how the link between income and costs has changed over the years. Taking the cost of a typical stock tractor, he estimated that it took the sale of just over eight cattle to pay for it in the 1970s; now it will take 24 similar animals. Farmers are responding by maximising their access to subsidies by intensifying production of their land. Thirty years ago, a farmer and spouse could live reasonably off the proceeds of a 60-cow herd; today, it would take at least double that number of cows and one of the partners working off the farm for them to make ends meet. Although this has been eased by the erection of modern buildings, it raises questions about how many animals an individual can reasonably care for during pressure points in the season. Another concern is the effect that intensification of farming has on the wider countryside.

Farming and Wildlife

Agriculture, by definition, modifies the natural world. If the process were 100 per cent efficient, the land would yield only the product the farmer (and by implication, society) is seeking. The process has never been 100 per cent efficient despite sterling efforts by improvers and scientists to eliminate competition for resources on the land they influence.

Meanwhile, there has been growing public concern that loss of diversity in the countryside is too high a price to pay for cheap and abundant food. Events such as the publication of *Silent Spring* (Carson 1962) crystallised opinion and led to widespread public support for farming systems that recognise, as farmers had done all along, the value of biodiversity in the countryside.

What of farming in Orkney? The move away from mixed farming with abundant areas of cereals and roots inevitably reduces the variety of habitats available with consequent pressures on wildlife, but the landscape that we see here today has evolved its own characteristic flora and fauna. Berry (2000) describes a predominant farming landscape harbouring many wildlife refuges such as wet grassland, undrained meadow and disused tracks within proximity of moorland edge and coastal fringe. These are all 'oases' for birds feeding off the productive farmland. Curlew and oystercatcher are found in greater abundance here than in many other parts of Scotland

(Charter 1995), responding to the wealth of insect larvae present in the grassland: indeed, their nests are often found in the grassland itself. However, the loss of moorland and its fringes are likely causes of the decline in lapwing and redshank numbers and may be contributing to an apparent disappearance of meadow pipit and skylark. The area of wetland – also important for so many species – has been substantially reduced by widespread drainage. There is strong evidence that the current predicament of the hen harrier, a raptor for which Orkney is well known, is a consequence of the dwindling area of rough grazing land separating moorland and grassland together with the voles which favour this unglamorous habitat. The past 40 years have seen the loss of 2,200 hectares of rough grassland in the West Mainland alone (Uttley 2002). This has led Scottish Natural Heritage (SNH) to initiate and fund a scheme to encourage farmers to adopt management practices designed to restore the mix of rough grassland adjacent to a varied heather habitat, the combination harriers favour for nesting, feeding and rearing their young.

The corncrake is a bird that once epitomised the long, lovely summer evenings in Orkney and to those farmers who remember its distinctive call, it is conspicuous by its absence. When the corncrakes return to Orkney in early May from South-East Africa, they home in on early cover vegetation that is more than 25 cm high (iris, nettles, reeds or early-growing grasses); insect food is abundant and, for this shy bird, the cover is ideal for nesting and rearing their young. Where formerly farmers once had lightly fertilised fields of open swards cut late in the season for hay, there are now dense, highly productive crops of grass cut much earlier for silage. As the old hay reaper came rattling slowly along, it was relatively easy for the hen and her chicks to weave their way through the open hay stalks, keeping out of sight and out of the way. Then, as the farmer wound his way around and around the field, the corncrake population would all end up in the last strip and finally make an unwilling run across open ground when they heard him approaching for the last time. Today's silage mowers are over twice as wide and travel three times as fast as the old reaper. To the corncrake, the silage crop is an impenetrable jungle and the feathered family will do well to travel 200 m in one day. The farmer never even sees them, hidden by the tall grass. A scheme funded by the RSPB, SNH and the Scottish Crofters' Union offers financial incentives to any farmers who find a calling bird in fields destined for hay or silage (Scottish Executive 2000d). The cash helps to offset the costs to the farmer of delaying grass cutting and conserving a poorer quality fodder. A further element of this scheme is to require the farmer to start cutting in the middle of the field and leave the outside strips until last. This saves the birds from having to break cover to make good their escape into the adjacent field. This approach is working well in most parts of the corncrakes' breeding range on the west and north fringes of Scotland. Unfortunately, the results in Orkney to date are disappointing, due to a combination of the greater proportion of relatively intensive grassland management, a small scattered population and insufficient areas being entered into the scheme.

Support measures for agriculture have played an important part in the interaction between farming and wildlife. For a large part of the post-war period, financial incentives derived from the nation's wish to be self-sufficient in food hastened the disappearance of moorland and wetland in Orkney. Once the desire for more environmentally sympathetic farming gained political momentum, one of the first attempts to redress this balance appeared in the Agricultural Development Programme (ADP) of the 1980s. This made provision for management payments to encourage the retention and restoration of moorland and the establishment of shelter belts and other arboreal features which, in turn, fuelled the latent desire of many farmers to foster a diverse and bountiful countryside, full of life. They, together with the RSPB, SNH and others, campaigned for Orkney's inclusion in the Environmentally Sensitive Areas Scheme, introduced in selected areas of Scotland in 1987. This was ultimately unsuccessful but the success of the ADP has led to a series of 'agri-environment' schemes based on the same principle of financially recognising agricultural practices that favour biodiversity. The most recently completed of these, the Countryside Premium Scheme, stimulated a large amount of applications but had only limited success, primarily due to inadequate funding. This has now been replaced by the Rural Stewardship Scheme (Scottish Executive 2000d) and indications to date are that this again has elicited much interest from Orkney farmers. Following the MacSharry reforms of the European CAP (Scottish Executive 1998), payments made in respect of Suckler Cow Premium, Beef Special Premium and Sheep Annual Premium have been graded according to stocking rates, with an 'extensification premium' paid to farmers who maintain these below a specified level. This principle has now been extended to the Less Favoured Area Support Scheme referred to earlier and these measures again serve to help farmers offset the costs of scaling down the intensity of their operations. Conservation groups argue that support measures should reflect the particular benefit of having cattle on the land as well as sheep, as the differing grazing habits of the two species promote greater variety in the pasture, the fodder crops and the wildlife they support.

Much of the effort spent in providing guidance to farmers on environmentally sensitive production methods and helping them apply for and meet the requirements of the succession of incentive schemes has come from the Orkney branch of the Farming and Wildlife Advisory Group (FWAG). Established in 1985 with a committee representing the full range of countryside interests, this group is widely supported by the farming community and has enjoyed consistent support from the local authority. This group is symbolic of the co-operative spirit that will be essential to maintain a healthy balance between farming and wildlife and ensure that the Orkney countryside is enjoyed by farmers and all others who venture into it.

Conclusion

The livelihood of Orkney's farmers has been under sustained pressure for the last six years. The industry has a proud record of innovation, adaptation to change and responding to market demands but recent years have seen unprecedented volatility in the physical and financial environments. Few can remember confidence in the industry being lower. A community that was once eager to hand its capital on to the next generation is now encouraging its children to seek careers elsewhere. Evidence for this is seen in the rising average age of farmers (estimated by the local branch of the Scottish National Farmers' Union to be 60) and falling numbers of students training at agricultural college. It is estimated that 45 per cent of farms have no clear successor to the present owner (SAC, personal communication). Farms are bigger, fewer and cannot afford to employ staff. It has become a lonely business. Loneliness imposes psychological pressures and carries other dangers, particularly when working alone with machinery or unpredictable livestock. There is a growing catalogue of tragic accidents that could have been avoided or mitigated had a companion been around.

There are whispers of hope. Despite widespread calls for subsidy cuts, there seem to be enough strong voices who recognise the strategic value of support for agriculture in socially fragile and environmentally rich areas. There is a steadily growing demand for high quality, sensitively produced foodstuffs, a standard which farmers here consistently meet. Mr Ironside of Aberdeen-Angus Producers echoes the thoughts of many when he suggested that more of Orkney's livestock should be leaving the islands 'in boxes', although he acknowledged this would require a major rearrangement of breeding policies to ensure continuity of supply. There are others who doubt the capacity of the climate and the vast majority of the land to put that last bit of finish on the animals. There are other opportunities for farmers to use their resources in profitable ways, such as meeting the requirements of Orkney's vital tourist industry, providing facilities for equestrian enterprises and in horticulture but realistically, the scope of such activity soon reaches a ceiling imposed by a small population. There is, however, growing excitement about the capacity of the land and its managers to rally to the call for supplies of 'renewable' energy, particularly that harnessed from the wind. Initially by leasing land to developers for the erection of wind turbines, but ultimately by investing in the equipment outright, the farming community would seem to have an opportunity to generate meaningful income directly from resources and, for once, turn the wind to their advantage. Others are interested in growing crops which can be used to reduce our reliance on fossil fuels, either for burning directly, as in the case of short-rotation willow coppicing, or as the basis for fuels that can be used in vehicles. Oilseed rape is the crop most likely to fit the latter category; it has been grown successfully in Orkney and can be processed to produce a 'biodiesel' fuel. A key feature of these ideas is that they follow the same principle adopted by Orkney's farmers for centuries – using their own skills and resources to produce something for which there is a real and sustainable demand. As long as there is a living to be made from this, there will be farmers in Orkney and they are the people who ultimately make these islands worth living in.

CHAPTER ELEVEN

Fishing

Introduction

As is general in island communities, fishing has always been important in Orkney. It has, however, been of less significance than in most of the islands of Scotland, mainly because Orkney has always had a better farming base; as the Orkney fishery officer remarked in 1868, 'In Orkney, farming operates greatly against fishing' (S.H.A. AF29/38:98). At the subsistence level, fish has always been an available and convenient item in the food supply; and in recent centuries it has also had a measure of commercial importance. In the modern period the most consistent element in the Orkney fisheries has been the lobster fishery, mainly operated by crofter-fishermen. Orkney, in common with almost all the coastal communities in Scotland, has also had an interest in the herring fisheries, although its main function has been to be as a base for visiting boats. For a time in the 19th century the cod fishery was also important. In the most recent phases the islands have also developed a small but efficient fleet of modern boats which have contributed an important element of diversity to the economy.

Early Fishing

Archaeological evidence shows that fish has been a component in Orkney's food supply from the time of the earliest human settlement. While thus far it has not proved possible to find unambiguous evidence of people in Orkney prior to the advent of farming, it is intrinsically probable that Mesolithic groups, which are well attested on the Scottish mainland, crossed the Pentland Firth to Orkney as early as the fifth millennium BC or before (Ritchie 1995, 20–21). The first farmers have been recognised at Knap of Howar (on Papa Westray), Skara Brae and elsewhere from 3600 BC on-wards; and in their settlements a variety of bones and shells, especially in middens, is testimony to the importance of fish. As well as species which could be caught from the shore like small saithe and ballan wrasse, the bones from species like cod, ling, halibut and turbot suggest off-shore fishing from boats; and a range of shellfish were collected along the tidal shores. The many thousands of limpet shells that have been found have been interpreted as being more likely to have served as line bait rather than as human food (Clarke and Sharples 1985, 77).

Fish were a prominent diet item throughout the prehistoric period, and this was to continue throughout later history. They also featured in the Pictish and Norse dwelling sites that have been excavated (Ritchie 1985, 199, 228). In better known later times, every man in summer had his 'seat' or share in a boat and saithe and dogfish were both important diet items and sources of oil for lamps and other purposes. They were caught in inshore waters, and the various tide races among the islands were favourite catching places. Many were dried or smoked for preservation (Thomson 1987, 216; Fenton 1978, 527–540).

Boats from the Scottish mainland were active in fishing at Orkney from at least the 16th century; and while there were landlords and merchants in Orkney alive to the potential for commercial fishing, it had a slow beginning, and it is little in evidence before the late 18th century. However, Orkney men were also involved in ventures mounted elsewhere. They were recruited in number from the 1740s for English cod smacks fishing at Iceland (Fenton 1978, 596). Also, when there was encouragement of the Scottish herring buss fishery from government tonnage bounties in the second half of the 18th century there were in the 1750s 300 Orkney crew men, although no busses were owned in the islands (Dunlop 1978, 10).

Fishing and farming were both overshadowed by kelp in the life and economy of Orkney in the late 18th and early 19th centuries; and the first notable commercial fishery in Orkney was actually that for lobsters, which began in the late 18th century. However, after the collapse of kelp in the 1820s fishing for one or two decades had pride of place. In the 1840s it was estimated that the value of fish landed and cured was upwards of £25,000, and this was fairly evenly divided between herring and cod (N.S.A. XV, 214). Although for most of the 19th century a substantial part of the able-bodied manpower had some involvement in fishing, the development of farming from the 1840s put it more and more into a back seat.

The Herring Fishery

Although various outsiders, especially the Dutch, had long fished herring around Orkney, there is little record of serious attempts at commercial herring fishing by Orcadians until the early 19th century, when there was a response to the initiatives provided by the Fishery Board in the shape of bounties on barrels cured to approved standard (Coull 1998, 46–49).

The island of South Ronaldsay, closest to the main Scottish seat of the fishery in Caithness, was prominently involved, and it had been anticipated from 1814 in the private initiative on Stronsay backed by the laird, Samuel Laing (Thomson 1987, 218). In the early stages the fishery developed

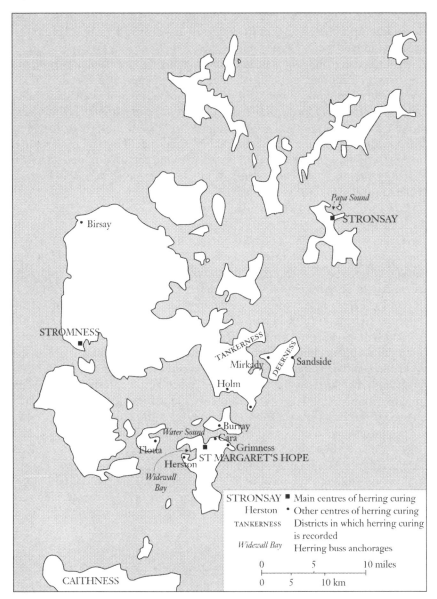

MAP 5 Centres and districts of herring cure in Orkney

relatively rapidly, and in a few years there was a fleet of several hundred open boats operating. By the 1840s it was estimated that the in the season there were over 700 boats fishing for herring, and till late in the century the herring fleet regularly ran into hundreds. The concentration of big numbers of open boats at relatively few centres for the season must have created a big problem of accommodation when crews of the open boats

Top. Knap of Howar, Papa Westray (copyright © Historic Scotland)
Middle. Skara Brae, Sandwick (copyright © William Murray)
Bottom. The Stones of Stenness (copyright © William Murray)

Top. The Ring of Brodgar, Stenness (copyright © RCAHMS)

Bottom left. One of the standing stones at the Ring of Brodgar (copyright © William Murray)

Middle right. The Broch of Gurness, Evie (copyright © William Murray)

Bottom right. The Broch of Gurness, aerial view. The buiding to the right of the broch is a later Pictish structure that was removed from the top of the broch site during excavation (copyright © RCAHMS)

Top. Midhowe Broch, Rousay (copyright © William Murray)

Bottom. Maes Howe runes

Top left. Knowe of Burrian, Pictish symbol stone (Orkney Museums)

Top right. Beachview, Birsay (copyright © Christopher Morris)

Middle left. Pictish symbol stone, St Peter's Church, South Ronaldsay (Orkney Museums)

Middle right. Marwick Head with Kitchener's memorial and the Brough of Birsay
(copyright © William Murray)

Bottom left. Cubbie Roo's Castle, Wyre (Christopher Morris)

Bottom right. Norse Mill, The Bu, Orphir (copyright © Paul Johnson)

Top. St Boniface Church, Papa Westray (copyright © Graham Ritchie)
Bottom. St Magnus Cathedral, Kirkwall, from the air (Orkney Photographic Archives)

Top left. St Magnus Cathedral, Kirkwall, side door (copyright © Graham Ritchie)
Top right. St Magnus Cathedral, Kirkwall, east end (copyright © Graham Ritchie)
Bottom left. St Magnus Cathedral, Kirkwall, tower and transept (copyright © Graham Ritchie)
Bottom right. St Magnus Cathedral, Kirkwall, nave aisle (Orkney Photographic Archives)

Top left. The Earl's Palace, Kirkwall (copyright © Graham Ritchie)
Top right. Tankerness House, Kirkwall (Orkney Photographic Archives)
Bottom. The Earl's Palace, Birsay (Orkney Photographic Archives)

Top. Noltland Castle, Westray (Orkney Photographic Archives)
Bottom left. Balfour Castle, Shapinsay (copyright © Graham Ritchie)
Middle right. Melsetter House, Hoy (copyright © Graham Ritchie)
Bottom right. Covenanters' Monument, Deerness, by Tom Kent (Orkney Photographic Archives)

Top. Martello Tower, Hackness, Hoy (copyright © Graham Ritchie)

Bottom. Crofters' houses in Rackwick, Hoy, in the early twentieth century (Orkney Photographic Archives)

Top. Transporting a cow to *South Isles* steamer, Hoy Head (Orkney Photographic Archives)
Bottom. Fishing boats at Stronsay pier in the early twentieth century

Top. Jack Folster on his way to lay creels, Stromness
Middle. The modern style of Orkney lobster boat, with forward wheelhouse and well deck aft
Bottom. St Margaret's Hope, South Ronaldsay (Orkney Photographic Archives)

1ST BATTLE SQUADRON, 1ST CRUISER SQUADRON AND 4TH DESTROYER FLOTILLA AT SCAPA FLOW. TK.

Top. 1st Battle Squadron, 1st Cruiser Squadron and 4th destroyer Flotilla at Scapa Flow, by Tom Kent
Bottom. Exterior of the Italian Chapel, Lamb Holm (copyright © William Murray)

Top left. Altar of the Italian Chapel, Lamb Holm (Orkney Photographic Archives)
Top right. Windmill at Burgar Hill, Evie
Bottom. St Magnus and *St Nicolas*, by William Leask (1899) (Orkney Museum)

Top. Orkney express sterling bus, 1905 (Orkney Photographic Archives)
Bottom. The *St Ola* and *Hebridean Princess* in Stromness Harbour (James Troup)

Top. St Mary's Village, Holm, by Tom Kent. Far right is the storehouse, built in 1649
(Orkney Photographic Archives)
Bottom. Finstown and the Bay of Firth (Orkney Photographic Archives)

The Black Craig, Stromness
The Old Man of Hoy (Orkney Photographic Archives)
Rough sea near Why Geo, Rousay (copyright © William Murray)

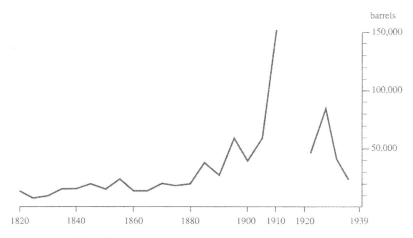

FIGURE 27   Orkney herring cure 1817–1939 (by 5-year means)

were ashore. The herring fishery in fact led to the development of several villages in the south-east part of the archipelago: St Margaret's Hope and Herston in South Ronaldsay, Burray village, St Marys (Holm) and White-hall on Stronsay (W. Thomson, pers. comm.). Various improvements were made in boats, fishing gear and curing practice; and curers from established places in mainland Scotland joined local curers during the two-month season from early July to early September.

An enduring feature of the Orkney fishery until the middle of the century was that busses from the Clyde came and bought herring from the local fishermen to cure on board. While this could mean higher prices to the fishermen, in the long run it inhibited the development of on-shore curing, which was one of the main strengths of the Scottish industry. The engagement system, by which curers guaranteed prices to fishermen before the season began, was late to develop in Orkney, and was never as effective as on mainland Scotland, even if from mid-century enough big mainland curers came for the season to deter the busses, which then faded from the picture. Although by the 1850s an engagement system was regularly in operation, and agents of James Methuen of Leith (the foremost of the Scottish curers) had made an appearance, terms to fishermen were distinctly inferior to those obtained at main centres like Wick, Fraserburgh and Peterhead. The result was that the annual production in Orkney seldom got much in excess of a modest 20,000 barrels. It was also the case that most of the Orkney herring went to Ireland, which constituted the lower end of the market, whereas from mainland Scotland an increasing proportion went to the more profitable market on the continent.

From mid-century Stronsay came to the fore as the leading base for the developing herring fishery, and it had the competitive advantage of being further from Caithness than South Ronaldsay. While the leading Orkney men did improve their boats and gear, from the 1880s the fishery came to be more and more dominated by stronger-going visiting Scottish boats; and some friction resulted from the visitors being given better engagement terms by the curers than the local boats. However, from this time the bulk of the cure went to the continental market.

Stromness had a brief period of prominence in the 1890s when it became the base for the early summer fishing in May and June for a fleet of hundreds of visiting boats, and the total number of fishermen in the peak years exceeded 4000. However, this phase ended when they left for more dependable early season grounds at Shetland and the Hebrides.

It was the early 20th century that was to bring Orkney's peak in the herring fishery; but it was to be the phase most dominated by outside interests. It was at this phase that the steam drifter rapidly came to dominate the Scottish fishery, although sail-boats continued in dwindling numbers until the inter-war years. Steam drifters operated in strength all along the Scottish east coast from Shetland to the Borders during the main summer season but Orkney men never had the resources to take the big step to the steam drifter. In Orkney the fishery concentrated very largely at the village of Whitehall on Stronsay, where the annual cure rose to over 150,000 barrels. In the peak year of 1912 about 300 drifters made landings at Stronsay, where there were 33 curing stations (Coull 1998, 53, 54); but among these was only one Orkney curer, and congestion at Whitehall was such that there was an overspill of five curing stations on the island of Papa Stronsay (Gibson 1984, 27). At this phase the best Orkney boats might make £400 or £500 in a season, although this was well behind that of the leading visitors. The curing staff of coopers and gutting girls were nearly all incomers, but there was considerable work for the local crofters and farmers in providing cartage between the piers and the curing yards (Gibson 1984, 30).

The inter-war period was a very difficult one for the herring fishery in the whole of Scotland, with the serious dislocation of the main continental markets and increasing international competition. Although steam drifters continued to land at Stronsay, the home fleet quickly withered away: the fishery was in decline and Stronsay ceased to be a base for the fishery at the end of the inter-war period.

The White Fishery

Although interest and activity in the commercial white fishery were never so great in Orkney as in the neighbouring archipelago of Shetland, the islands have had an involvement in it in the modern period. It was started by local curers and fishermen at the end of the 18th century, but in the manner so common on the periphery it was stimulated in the early 19th century by merchants and boats from outside – from England (Fenton

1978, 597). By landing to Orkney curers they could get a quicker turn-round to go back to fishing grounds, or could unload part of their catch on the way back to their home bases.

There was further stimulus from 1820 when the Fishery Board gave bounties of 4s per cwt. on cod and ling cured to approved standard. Orkney merchants, especially in the North Isles, engaged men for the open boat fishery; here the men cured the fish themselves before delivering them to the merchant. Merchants also made use of the bounty of £3 per ton to fit out cod smacks, which employed wet salting aboard, and the merchants completed the curing on shore. By the 1830s there were between 30 and 40 smacks owned in Orkney. The smacks might fish at Faroe, Iceland or even north Norway as well as on local banks; and as well as fishing themselves they might buy fish from fishermen at various places. In addition, English as well as Orkney smacks might land in the isles.

Although bounty incentives were withdrawn after 1830, the expanding market continued to prompt production. Orkney was a modest producer on the Scottish scale, but by the later 1830s production was running around 200 to 300 tons annually, and it showed a fluctuating rise until in the 1870s it could reach 1,000 tons or more. There is no precise record of the number of boats engaging in the fishery, but at the maximum it must have run into hundreds; and in 1877 their production was added to by a total of 38 smacks, then at their peak in number.

The main fishing season in Orkney was in the spring and early summer, and at the peak the open boat fishery could itself yield upwards of 500 tons. In the early stages there is mention of three- and four-man crews in local boats employing hand lines, but in the 1860s six-man crews in Stronsay and Shapinsay pioneered improvements with long lines, and there is record of them making the relatively high net earnings of £100 per crew for a three-month season (S.H.A. AF29/83, 65). Such boats sold their fish to merchants by the hundredweight, and they were split, salted and spread on beaches or trestles to cure. The fish which merchants got from smacks, most of which were English, were wet salted aboard; they were bought by the ton, and the merchants completed the curing. Marketing of the cured fish was partly on the mainland of Britain, but Orkney curers might also send their products to Shetland for forwarding with Shetland fish to the Spanish market, for centuries a main destination for cured cod from around the North Atlantic.

However, the part-time character of white fishing by Orkney men was highlighted in the 1870s. At this juncture boats from the south shore of the Moray Firth, which were owned by full-time professional fishermen, began to come north in the spring, and engaged to fish for merchants in the parish of Holm. These men spent most of the year fishing for herring, but as spring was a slack time in the herring trade, they used the time to go lining; and in Orkney they might precede this with several weeks fishing lobsters. They were better equipped than local crews; they were able to get superior engagement terms from merchants, and their level of production was on a bigger scale. Already in 1870 they were capable of making £10 per man monthly at the spring cod, and in 1873 the nine boats which came contributed 1,840 cwt. to the total Orkney production of 21,072 cwt. from boats and smacks (S.H.A. AF29/83, 269). While this pattern of lining in spring by visiting mainland crews continued well into the 20th century, they increasingly fished for the fresh market, by-passed Orkney curers, and landed at mainland ports like Aberdeen.

English smacks continued to land for Orkney curers into the 20th century, but from the end of the 19th century the development of steam trawling was to produce great changes in marketing, which had complicated effects on Orcadian fishing. The exploitation of local grounds by trawlers gave less opportunity for Orkney fishermen; but landings in the islands were supplemented from the 1890s by those of English steam trawlers working at Faroe and Iceland. Such vessels might go on trips of three weeks or more, and their practice was to salt part of their catch in the first stages of a trip, before filling up with fish which would be delivered fresh at their home port after unloading the salted portion in Orkney. However, as time passed the trawlers became more efficient and also carried more ice to preserve their catches, and after the first decade of the 20th century their landings at Orkney dwindled into insignificance.

There were some other sectors of the white fishery. Catching of white fish for domestic consumption has always been practised, and in the modern period in winter there was also catching of 'sillocks' (young saithe) by sweep nets along the shore for selling in bulk to farmers for manure. A fishery in which Orkney became involved in a minor degree from the 1890s was that for haddocks, mainly for the fresh market or for smoking. This was and is a major fishery in Scotland, and by the end of the 20th century the remoteness which had effectively excluded the islands from participation in an expanding market had been alleviated by improved contacts through steamer services. Much of this fishing was in winter, and the sheltered waters of Scapa Flow were the main location of the fishery in Orkney.

The revival of fishing in Orkney from the 1960s has entailed exploiting an expanded range of species, but for a time white fish were the most important (see below).

Shell Fisheries

Shellfish over the modern period have gained increasing importance as a luxury item: as well as being associated with increasing purchasing power, improving transport has allowed the reliable marketing of fresh and frozen species. Orkney has had an involvement in these fisheries from the late 18th century. The first notable development of a commercial shell fishery in Orkney was that for lobsters (Fenton 1978, 531–544): from the late 18th century English companies began collecting them for the London market, and transported them live in well smacks. There has been a directed

fishery for lobsters ever since, and by 1834 about 100,000 were being
exported annually (Fenton 1978, 544). Lobsters gained enhanced importance in the second half of the century with improvement in catching
methods from about 1850 when the lobster creel replaced the pouch net.
The lobster fishery, which was always operated close inshore, was one of
the best suited to men of small capital; and Orkney has some of the best
lobster grounds in Britain.

By the 1860s lobster fishing had enhanced prominence, and for three
months in spring about half of the fishermen were engaging in it, drawing
effort away from the cod fishery. It was stated in 1865 that total lobster
sales from Orkney for the previous year were fully £3,000 and that a man
might make the high total of 18/- in a week (AF29/83, 10). From the later
19th century it was possible to convey the lobsters more rapidly to the
London market by rail from Wick or Aberdeen.

Interest in lobster fishing was maintained as participation in herring and
cod fishing declined from the late 19th century. When values of shellfish
landings began to be recorded at the end of the 19th century, Orkney was
the leading Scottish district, apart from the Ballantrae district of the
south-west, where landings were enhanced by the shrimps and prawns of
the Solway. In the inter-war period the lobster fishery became the main
one for Orkney men despite the continued herring landings of visiting
boats at Stronsay; and after the eclipse of Stronsay herring curing after
the Second World War, lobsters dominated fish landings in Orkney, being
well over 90 per cent by value. The main landings have consistently been
in the bigger and more peripherally located islands of Sanday, Westray,
Stronsay and Hoy. In more recent times the intensively fished lobsters
have become scarcer, but there has been an increase in the catch of a
range of other shellfish species.

Although brown crabs are of lower value, the establishment of processing
plants in Orkney in the 1960s has allowed them to come into the effective
resource base, and the pattern of concentrating on crabs in the earlier part
of the year and on lobsters in the autumn developed, with a low period
for both in mid-summer while moulting was proceeding (Coull and Sheves,
26–27). Shell fishing has continued to expand and diversify, with fishing
for scallops, velvet crabs and cockles (see below). The total landings of
shellfish are now over 3,000 tonnes a year and the value over £4 million.

Numbers of Fishermen

The traditional and age-old pattern of numerous men mainly employed
in farming who spend part of their time in fishing is recorded with a
measure of accuracy from the 1820s when the Fishery Board began esti-
mating each year the numbers of men and boats in the Orkney district;
and the part-time nature of the men's involvement becomes clearer when,
in the inter-war period, it began recording separately the numbers of
crofter-fishermen. These records effectively substantiate the traditional

FIGURE 28   Number of fishermen employed

picture of the Orcadian being a farmer with a boat, contrasting with the Shetlander as a fisherman with a croft.

The broad 19th-century trend appears as an irregular rise in numbers of fishermen till around the peak population levels of the archipelago in the second half of the century, followed by a relatively rapid decline. Almost continuously from the 1830s till the 1890s there were over 2,000 fishermen, although by the First World War there were under 1,000, and there has been a general slower decline since (Figure 28). The rise at the start of the graph is linked to the collapse of the kelp which was Orkney's main resource during the Napoleonic Wars; but it is also related to an expanded effort in the herring fishery (see above), which was then in a growth phase along the east coast of Scotland (Coull 1998, 47–51). The first dip in the rising part of the graph is largely due to circumstances in the main (Scottish) herring fishery: in the 1840s the Irish Potato Famine caused a serious recession in the main market. From the late 19th century a series of factors combined to cause contraction in the effort in Orkney. On top of the general fall in the Orkney population and rising emigration, there was an accelerated move in the herring fishery to bigger and more expensive boats which it was difficult for the part-time fishermen to follow, and in Orkney there was a concomitant increase in the lobster fishery for which crofter-fishermen could more easily equip themselves. There was in Orkney, too, more alternative employment in farming, which, as well as giving a more secure return than fishing, involved less hardship.

FIGURE 29   Number of fishing boats in service

Despite the pressures towards more specialisation in occupation in the
20th century, in 1921 of 862 fishermen recorded, 725 (84 per cent) were
still crofter-fishermen. Decline in numbers continued until in the 1980s
the total of fishermen was under 300. Since then there have been important
changes: there has been some recovery in numbers and a trend towards
full-time commitment in fishing. There has also been the disappearance
of the crofter-fisherman, but there were still 22 per cent part-time in 2001
of the total of 345 fishermen; with shorter working hours in the modern
labour force, men in other occupations can now find time for involvement
in commercial fishing.

Boats

The traditional double-ended type of open boats of Orkney date from
Viking times and were mainly below 20 ft and used by crews of three or
four men. The rise of the herring fishery led to the acquisition of a large
number of bigger boats, some bought from outside, but others built in
Orkney; and numbers of recorded boats peaked at over 700 in the 1860s
(Figure 29). Though numbers then declined, by the end of the century
some boats were decked and over 40 ft.

Although Orcadians subsequently moved out of direct involvement in
the herring fishery, there was from the inter-war period the progressive
motorisation of the fleet. From the 1960s there was new investment in
bigger boats and by 1998 there were 12 modern steel-hulled boats of over
20 m. While most of these were white fish trawlers there was one highly
successful pelagic freezer-trawler, and the catching power had reached its
greatest ever. This was a welcome trend, but the readjustments that have
ensued from recent cut-backs in the Scottish fleet for conservation reasons
have meant that by 2003 the number of boats over 24 m had been reduced

to five. In the same year there were 35 other boats of over 10 m that were engaged mainly in shell fishing, and which were crewed mostly by full-time fishermen, in addition to about 130 boats of under 10 m, most of the crews were part-time.

Modern Developments

There have been important new developments from the 1960s, which have seen a resurgence of the fishing industry. National concern for stimulating activity in the periphery has been linked to local initiatives for innovation and diversification of the Orkney economy, which had become very much farming-dependent. The granting of development status to Orkney was followed by financial help from the Highland Board from the 1960s; and this, along with the Grant and Loan scheme of the White Fish Authority, helped to initiate the acquisition of modern diesel boats. This was to be followed from the 1970s by regional aid from the European Community, and the Orkney Council has also given help from its oil revenues in the acquiring of boats and the improvement of processing and other facilities on shore. The outcome has been the development of a fleet of a range of sizes which includes some of the best-performing boats in the Scottish fleet. There has also been a prominent expansion of the shellfish sector, which now includes brown and velvet crabs, scallops and whelks as well as lobsters. There are processing plants for shellfish at Stromness and on Westray, and there are ponds on several of the islands, where lobsters can be held and marketed to best advantage. The great part of the shellfish caught are landed in Orkney, and give rise to a supplementary employment total between 50 and 100 people. Much of the shellfish is packed and sent to mainland and continental markets by refrigerated and 'vivier' (i.e. in a live state) truck. Orkney fishermen, following the Shetland example, have now applied for a regulating order, which would allow them to manage all shell fishing out to six miles from the shore. With the modern import-ance of shell fishing and the pressure there is on shellfish stocks, this is a prudent positive move. Among shellfish lobsters have long been the most valuable and recent attempts to rebuild lobster stocks from juvenile hat-cheries have produced encouraging results. Orkney fishermen have also, from the beginning of 2000, constituted themselves into a Producers' Organisation (PO), which is another appropriate measure to administer fish quotas and to have a say in national fisheries policy.

Despite the progressive developments in Orkney, the major part of the Orkney catch (in both volume and value) is now landed outwith the islands, and such is the character of modern markets that there is little scope for changing this. For white fish better prices are obtained at auction markets on the Scottish mainland – mainly at Scrabster and Aberdeen; the total catch of white fish up to 2000 had risen to over 8,000 tonnes and the value to over £7 million; but there is now inevitable reduction. Pelagic catches have been landed at a range of ports in Scotland and abroad: as well as Ullapool and Lerwick, there have been landings in Denmark, Norway, Faroe and Holland. While the value of landings made in Orkney in 1998 approached £5 million, the total value of fish caught by Orkney boats was over £13 million.

Orkney also has a share in the modern industry of fish farming, and now produces over 3,000 tonnes of salmon annually.

Conclusion

Fishing has always been part of life in Orkney, and in the modern period commercial fishing has played a varying but significant part in the economy of the archipelago. This has included herring, white- and shellfish. From the end of the 19th century fishing became largely confined to lobsters, but this was followed by new growth and diversification from the 1960s. Throughout the early modern period fishing for Orkney men had been only one of several employments; time had also to be found for kelping, crofting, farm labour, and for the cutting and boating of peat fuel. The Orkney pattern had for Scotland a rare degree of flexibility, which allowed a degree of switching in accordance with changing opportunity; but it was tied to labour-intensive operation, which was ultimately bound to decline. The period since the 1960s has seen more commitment to full-time fishing, and with it an expansion and diversification which has been a welcome element in the economy and employment in Orkney. While modern conservation regulations are part of the environment in which fishing must now function, the fact that shellfish are the main basis for Orkney fishermen has meant that the islands are relatively little affected by modern conservation problems.

CHAPTER TWELVE

Tourism

Introduction

Tourism is the largest industry in the world. By 1993 it employed more than 100 million people, and in 2000 the World Tourism Organization (WTO) reported international tourism receipts had reached US$476 billion. It is significant in Orkney, too, but on a different scale.

Until the 1960s, there was a very *ad hoc* arrangement. Potential visitors would write to the town councils in Kirkwall and Stromness or to Orkney County Council. Sometimes, local legal firms answered individual requests, particularly in the earlier half of the 20th century.

All this was very reactive; there was little or no marketing. Hotels and shipping companies usually undertook the few advertisements that did appear and these were orientated towards their product. Around the turn of the 20th century annual publications such as *Peace's Orkney & Shetland Almanac* were the most informative sources other than hardback books. Guide books evolved about 20 years later. They were commercially produced, mostly Orkney-wide, but sometimes covering smaller geographic areas, invariably supported by advertising, and usually printed on the whim of the business concerned. Market research, product planning, competitive analysis and development strategies were not yet on the agenda.

Management

The business community started professional tourism in Orkney. During the mid-1960s, realising the latent economic benefits of the industry and seeking some cohesiveness to exploit it, the two Chambers of Commerce, one for Stromness & The West Mainland and one embracing Kirkwall, initiated discussion regarding the formation of a tourism body. An approach to Orkney County Council resulted in the societies being requested to form an organisation of their own.

Orkney Tourist Association subsequently appeared with representations from the public and private sectors on its executive committee, an early day public-private-partnership of the voluntary kind. The three local authorities provided some funding and paid membership was sought from tourism interests throughout the islands.

In 1965, the Highlands & Islands Development Board (HIDB) was established by act of parliament. As a new regional development agency, HIDB was given the task of regenerating a large geographic area extending from Shetland to the Mull of Kintyre. The remit included social, economic and demographic rejuvenation. Tourism was quickly recognised as one activity that could broaden the economic base and increase the gross regional product in tandem with the revitalisation of traditional and the attraction of new industries. Consultations were held in pre-defined areas with a view to creating a network of local bodies. At the time the bureaucrats proposed Orkney and Caithness be combined, but this suggestion was firmly rejected on both sides of the Pentland Firth.

Orkney Tourist Association became Orkney Tourist Organisation in 1969, one of 15 local boards. Members continued to pay annual subscriptions but funding was largely from central government through the HIDB budget. That same year, The Development of Tourism Act established national boards for England, Scotland and Wales together with a British Tourist Authority (BTA), the latter being solely responsible for overseas marketing.

The three management tiers worked with relative success throughout the 1970s and early 1980s. Being part of the HIDB network gave Orkney some competitive advantage; marketing, networking and visitor services were generally stronger within the region. This was partly due to funding. Treasury cheifly funded the HIDB network; in the rest of Scotland most finance, with varying levels of suport, came from local authorities.

Two important pieces of legislation now entered the arena. The Orkney County Council Act, 1974, enabled the islands to establish various funds related to oil developments. The Local Government (Scotland) Act, 1973, consolidated the three councils into one island authority, Orkney Islands Council. Gradually, partly due to the oil revenue reserves, the local authorities in both Orkney and Shetland became the major tourism funding sources; in the rest of the HIDB region, the status quo remained.

Simultaneously, membership fees were increased and their structure altered. Accommodation members began paying on a per room basis, business members by size, reflecting their revenue potential. Discounts for those in the rural areas and smaller islands were introduced, taking cognisance of visitor distribution.

Larger budgets enabled more vigorous and flexible marketing. Tourism began to increase, sometimes against national trends, making a significant contribution to the Orkney economy and, behind the scenes, its growth would be used to secure Euro-funding for a variety of projects from island piers to sewerage systems.

Conflicts appeared during the mid-1980s, particularly in interagency relationships, e.g. between HIDB and the Scottish Tourist Board (STB). South of the border, BTA and the English Tourist Board were effectively amalgamated and Scotland began lobbying for separate overseas marketing. In 1985, the Scottish Affairs Committee called for a realignment of responsibilities allowing STB to take over HIDB tourism marketing. The idea was rejected at the time but the transfer did eventually take place.

The desire for the reorganisation was never far away from government eyes and civil servants wanted local boards to generate more non-government revenue. Many tourist offices became retail outlets, rather than visitor servicing points, in all but name. Sometimes the reasons for revision were valid but power plays, even dogma, were at work. Duplication of efforts and the elimination of waste were the favourite arguments. In marketing terms, this made sense, political boundaries are seldom recognised by the consumer, but tourism management involves more than marketing.

By 1992, Orkney Tourist Organisation was re-named Orkney Tourist Board (OTB), becoming a company limited by guarantee with no share capital. Scottish tourism was co-ordinated by STB, many responsibilities were transferred from Inverness to Edinburgh and the number of area boards was again under consideration. In the meantime, Scotland's largest market, i.e. Britain, was showing dangerous signs of slowing down.

The Local Government Scotland Act, 1994, replaced regions and districts with single-tier authorities and tourist boards were more or less halved. Orkney, Shetland and The Western Isles, supported by their local authorities, enterprise boards and chambers of commerce, successfully mounted a campaign to retain their local bodies. Even editorials in the Scottish broadsheets favoured their retention. The legal status of OTB changed once more in 1996 when it became one of 14 'operational statutory tourist boards'.

With the establishment of the Scottish Parliament, tourism responsibilities were given to one of the executive ministers as part of a mixed portfolio. By late 2001, tourism was considered worthy of an individual brief – something the industry had sought for decades. The turn of the millennium also saw another government review. STB became 'VisitScotland' and senior management were culled. More consultations to reduce the number of local boards are taking place; the outcome is unknown at the time of writing.

It would be disadvantageous if Orkney lost its independent tourism body. Historic growth was essentially due to Orkney's ability to simultaneously market individually and dovetail into national promotions. Regardless of reassuring platitudes, to rely upon national/regional efforts, in which Orkney is a small player, seems a recipe for disaster.

Economics

The purpose of tourism is simply economic. There are associated social dynamics, such as the reciprocation of facilities, but in reality it is solely a means to generate revenue.

It is impossible to identify Orkney's first visitor, or the transport operator concerned! But what is a 'visitor' in any case? Various definitions were in operation until the United Nations Statistical Commission adopted WTO proposals in 1993.

Prior to this, most definitions were accommodation-orientated, which caused problems. Neither the spending of day-trippers from Caithness nor the revenue from cruise liner passengers could be credited, yet both make an obvious contribution to Orkney's economy. In addition, attractions world-wide rely heavily on catchments within a one to two-hour drive. There is an obvious sharing of resources between visitors and residents, a local dimension to tourism. So, the lady from Stromness buys a coffee in Rousay and the economy benefits; a family purchasing four helps that little bit more.

WTO defines a visitor as 'any person travelling to a place other than that of his/her usual environment for less than 12 months and whose main purpose of visit is other than the exercise of an activity remunerated from within the place visited'. Visitors are classified into international and domestic and a further distinction is made within these between tourists (overnight visitors) and same-day visitors. There are more detailed explanations but it is sufficient to note denominators are now common.

As a commercial activity, tourism is subject to the laws of supply and demand with some ancillary complications. Using data normally supplied from transport carriers and others, visitor consumption is used to illustrate demand. Other components exist but consumption is the basic constituent.

Volume is the key demand performance indicator, but even when it decreases, provided visitor-spend grows in sufficient proportion, the subsequent increase in consumption could well be measured a success. It depends on perspective and objective.

Numbers to visitor attractions such as Skara Brae normally shadow demand patterns, although figures can include a local element. A reduction recorded against a general increase usually points to inadequate management, ineffective marketing, or sometimes the product itself.

The easiest demand statistic to calculate is occupancy, although it is limited to transport and accommodation. Seat occupancy or bed (against room) occupancy is the important figure; it reflects revenue, yield and other financial issues. Empty beds or unoccupied seats mean the investment return is lost forever, hence the proliferation of multi-priced tariffs.

Orkney can absorb more visitors. There are in excess of 650,000 bed-spaces available per year, roughly broken down into the following sectors: 40 per cent hotels, 40 per cent self-catering, 10 per cent bed & breakfast and 10 per cent others. Give or take 10–20,000, volume floats around 100,000 visitors per season. For the year 2000, OTB estimated 92,000 visitors were hosted between May and October – about 14 per cent of total capacity.

Since 1970, the pattern is mainly of growth although a few dips and plateaus have been seen. Statistics can be found in the yearly economic review published by Orkney Islands Council and the OTB Annual Reports.

Tourism is demand-led, but there is also a supply side. The International

Standard Industrial Classification (ISIC) categorised tourism in seven bands, but as soon as you combine an activity with transport it nearly always qualifies as tourism. Local dimensions cause further difficulties, e.g. Orkney buses carry visitors but their primary purpose is to convey residents. Another dilemma is private car journeys. How do you acquire reliable data as to their purpose, be it tourism, work or other use?

From the ISIC grouping, WTO evolved and established the Standard International Classification of Tourism Activities. This lists over 200 categories, designating them as dedicated wholly, partly involved or totally irrelevant to tourism. An extensive list of Tourism Specific Products has also been officially agreed.

Transport is the fundamental component, the pre-requisite, of Orkney tourism. These lifeline links have seen periods of expansion, containment and contraction. Some developments have been welcomed; others vehemently opposed. Air services from the Faroes and Bergen have come and gone. British Airways flies to Orkney in name only, sub-contracting to Loganair. A car ferry now operates between South Ronaldsay and Caithness whilst the John O' Groats passenger ferry stills ploughs its variation of the 'short sea crossing'. The historic P&O connection was severed in late 2002 when NorthLink took over the principal tourism arteries. Regardless of these changes, one element has remained constant – the cost of getting to Orkney. It is not, and never has been, a cheap destination.

Some tourism revenue leaks out of the economy on imports or savings. The remainder is re-spent to the benefit of the local system. Further re-cycling and re-leaking takes place until the amount becomes minimal. This multiplier concept impacts on income, employment and other areas. It has three main effects: [a] Direct – created in the tourist sectors, e.g. wages to hotel employees; [b] Indirect – created by [a] on purchases from local suppliers, e.g. a restaurant buying local farm produce; and [c] Induced – created by the additional income from [a] and [b] increasing their expenditure locally e.g. a shop owner retaining staff for 12 months rather than making the position seasonal.

Multiplier models have problems; information may be unreliable or inadequate; analyses may be incorrectly applied; and the time-lapse for the indirect and induced effects to influence the economy complicated to establish. Although quantitative data is difficult to collate, the trends are important to strategic planning. That said, for a full 12 months, tourism probably contributes £20–30 million annually to the economy. It is a broad band but it does emphasise tourism's importance to Orkney life.

Product and Development

The total tourism product is – Orkney. More precise products, tangible and intangible, are found within it including a mixture of specialised market segments. With the appeal of the island environment, sometimes its re-moteness, they are fundamental enticements. Several studies also show Orcadian sociability to be a positive factor.

The product has five main elements: attractions, facilities, accessibility, price and image.

Destination attractions include natural attractions – land/seascapes, cli-mate; built attractions – historic towns, sites of interest; cultural attractions – museums, theatres, events; and social attractions – where visitors mix and meet residents, e.g. visits to friends and relatives. The latter plays a significant role in Orkney.

Facilities comprise the spectrum of services: accommodation, restaurants, car rental and retail outlets. Facilities, amenities and attractions can overlap. Sometimes a facility becomes an attraction in its own right, e.g. Disneyland-Europe, Gleneagles Hotel. Orkney lacks a facility at this level. In the right hands, perhaps tourist submarines in Scapa Flow could attain that distinction!

Accessibility is of great significance in Orkney. It is more than a product component and more than service provision. Although dependent upon the foibles of operators, the council and others are vital to infrastructure provision. The new terminal built at Kirkwall by Highlands & Islands Airports is a good example. It could be argued a proper Instrument Landing System should have been a greater priority.

Price includes the cost of travel, accommodation and everything else in the holiday spend. Price varies according to services used but it is a major determinant, usually the most important one, in holiday planning. For an island destination, price and accessibility go hand in hand; they are also related to quality and value for money.

Image is the most influential motivator of all product parts. Customer perceptions are all-powerful. Consumers' ideas of image are not always based on fact or experience, hence the need for qualitative research. Image development is created slowly over time but it is very fickle and can be lost overnight.

Assessing these components, the Orkney product is, on balance, an attractive one. So why aren't the islands inundated with millions of visitors each year? Frankly, there is too much competition. Attractive landscapes are found all over the world, some close to home too: such as Shetland, Caithness and Ireland. The same can be said for all the other product parts.

On the positive side, Orkney contains unique elements. Where else can you dive the German High Seas Fleet? The environs of Brodgar have World Heritage status, although that list, well over 700, is quite extensive and growing. However, there are those who are just not interested in the product and plenty not charmed by the perceived climate either.

Many attractions accounting for mass tourist flows are free; visitors seldom have to pay for the experience. This gratis element means it is often difficult to control visitor entry, but Orkney is fortunate or unfortunate, depending on your viewpoint, in having its own control mechanism – the Pentland Firth!

Tourism can be self-destructive and environmental damage can result from visitor pressure. Historic Scotland's concerns about the erosion of Maeshowe's carvings are well recorded. The Royal Society for the Protection of Birds positively promotes certain locations to protect sensitive sites or species. Responsible tourism management takes cognisance of these anxieties and acts accordingly. The long-term consequence of ignoring expert advice harms the very product the industry sells.

The rise of ecotourism was a feature of the 1990s, where economics were not the only principles applied in tourism development. Although acquisition of money remains the underlying purpose, impacts on both natural and social environments required a more balanced approach. Sustainability, or sustainable development, became very important and 2002 was designated as the International Year of Ecotourism. It is a growing sector and one in which the Orkney product has great opportunities.

In developing tourism, there are a few hurdles besides competition. Some are external factors. Unfavourable currency exchange rates clearly affect overseas visitors, but domestic recession also has a negative affect. The most recent external causes occurred in 2001; the events of September 11th in America influenced international markets and foot-and-mouth created an adverse reaction at home.

At present, visitor numbers peak markedly in the summer months. Nearly half of all visitors arrive during July and August. Bed-space capacity could be doubled, but it is uneconomic in investment terms.

One method of overcoming the seasonality problem is staging special events and festivals, a tactic successfully employed by The Isle of Man for many years. There are success stories in Orkney too. The Folk Festival in May, the St Magnus Festival in mid-June and the Science Festival in September have all helped increase occupancy levels. Prior to the inception of the St Magnus Festival, Kirkwall hotels experienced average bed occupancies of around 40 per cent. The festival increased this percentage to the high 90s. The problem was more acute in Stromness but the Folk Festival pushed up occupancy to a similar ratio.

Recent years have seen the expansion of festivals – writing, story-telling, football, blues, jazz, beer – and more could be created. Combine these with the layer of traditional events, Stromness Shopping Week, the Ba', agricultural shows, regattas, angling competitions and the product acquires a very active and extensive calendar.

In event attractions, timing and service provision are both critical. Timing is crucial to avoid duplication: there is no point staging the Folk Festival during Shopping Week. Services are essential to enhance, sometimes ensure, the visitor experience: a winter break focusing on the Ba' is meaningless if facilities are closed.

Conferences have increased in number and business tourism is a huge industry world-wide. Length of stay is shorter than holiday tourism but spend is significantly higher. It is a specialised market, extremely competitive and difficult to penetrate. Orkney's role is rather subdued due to location, the lack of committed facilities and the quality of existing ones. The islands are restricted to hotel function rooms, some halls and the Pickaquoy Centre. The latter serves too many purposes, mixing too many markets, to be defined as a dedicated facility for this sector.

The cruise market plays a significant role, with Orkney one of the Britain's top destinations. It is a long way behind Bergen, but infrastructure development has been significant and marketing increased. This market is important because passengers get a bite of the Orkney cherry; Orkney gets a chance to convert them into holiday visitors. A similar argument can be applied to same-day visitors.

Orkney's most difficult development obstacle is probably visitor distribution. Town hotels can be full but accommodation in outlying areas can remain empty. Inter-island accessibility is probably the best ever, although improvements to sea transport have resulted in an inevitable downgrading of air services. Bus timetabling necessitates visitors staying in rural areas having their own vehicles and integration of all transport services could be improved.

The council now produce a full colour brochure devoted to the smaller islands and most areas have their own leaflets. Two centre holidays, i.e. a mix of town/mainland and island destinations, provide limited opportunities but the main problem is on the supply side. Rural areas are more attuned to self-catering and in smaller islands bed-spaces are restricted. Other facilities can also be inadequate or operate limited opening hours. Consumers may view these areas as too remote – sometimes a perception of Orkney itself – and the market for solitude/seclusion is narrow. Growth may evolve as the cherry-eater or same-day visitor returns or as new infrastructure such as tunnels or causeways are developed.

There is a development requirement for quality, not just in bricks and mortar but also in service. Higher quality accommodation is still needed in all sectors and some training courses need to be more demanding. The 'Welcome Host' initiative is a fine introduction, but a one-day course does not make a consumer orientated summer.

Being some distance from the marketplace, Orkney has to ensure the quality of its facilities and services match the quality of its attractions – and give value for money. The tourism product and its development is an ongoing mission. It should be a process of setting the goal posts and then changing them. To do otherwise is simply to stagnate.

Marketing

Tourism is so competitive that no related business can ignore marketing. Marketing is a management tool used to increase profit, but it can be costly, so it needs to be structured and planned. In Orkney, where marketing budgets are extremely low, co-operation is also essential.

Successful marketing follows a logical process of market research, product planning and development, advertising and promotion, distribution, and finally a selling price offering perceived value for money.

Quantitative research provides a customer profile, divided into various socio-economic bands relating to affluence, employment, and so on. Research also informs of consumer interests and holiday behaviour e.g. bird-watchers, allowing market segments or niches to be identified. However, findings do need careful interpretation and weighting, e.g. history will always score high in Orkney because it is inherent in the product.

From mid-1972, OTB started an ongoing research programme. Field surveys took place in 1973, the first on board MV *St Ola*. Data is updated through new visitor surveys. Qualitative research was employed by HIDB during the 1980s to ascertain perceived images and develop regional marketing strategies.

Research is integrated into the marketing audit to determine strengths and weaknesses. Once completed, the audit helps build a marketing plan. Key issues highlighted by the plan allow a strategy to be determined. For example, during the 1980s it was clear Orkney could not compete in advertising expenditure and a strategic decision was taken to host press visits to ensure much greater media exposure.

In deploying the strategy, a programme of action is established using a range of techniques. This blend is referred to as the promotion mix, frequently confused with the marketing mix, as it is in the Orkney Tourism Strategy 2001–2005.

Advertising is used in a variety of media – cinema, outdoor, press, radio, television and the internet. Orkney concentrated on press advertising, the main objective being to elicit response. To increase general image awareness, boards combined under a Highlands and Islands banner which has now evolved into a Scottish umbrella campaign. This piggy-back marketing was sensible due to financial constraints and ensured more effective exposure. Independent advertising was generally placed in specialist channels such as angling or bird-watching magazines to penetrate precise segments. There was one independent foray into television. The cost was relatively high but the real expense came in servicing the campaign, response almost leaving a brochure shortage. Some radio advertising took place. It was associated with shopping centre promotions during the late 1970s and early 1980s. Although the cost wasn't excessive, its effectiveness was too difficult to measure.

The main promotional thrust before the 1990s was through public exhibitions. The list of major national and international exhibitions is too long to detail, but again the HIDB network undertook its own programme and pooled resources. Independent promotions included readers' competitions and sponsorship of special Orkney supplements. The council funded

Orkney films timed to fit television slots. For a short time, Caithness and Orkney also had an advanced tourist office situated at the Caithness Glass Factory in Perth.

During the mid to late 1980s, exhibitions were overtaken by the improving quality of the database. Direct mail became the new technique and Orkney spent a considerable proportion on targeted mailings. Despite its critics, direct mail is a very effective tool, the conversion of an existing client being much cheaper than a new capture.

Expenditure on press or media relations, hosting visits by travel writers and media crews, also increased significantly during the 1980s. With editorial coverage being valued at five times the equivalent advertising space cost, annual exposure was well into six figures. For example, the short segment on ITV's peak-time *Wish You Were Here* – promoting bird-watching holidays in the West Mainland – would have exploded the annual budget had it been purchased.

Distribution is mainly achieved through the travel trade and print. The vast majority of island visitors are independent travellers but trade involvement should be encouraged because it represents Orkney's sales force in the marketplace. OTB has a long history of attending specific trade exhibitions, usually with a few commercial partners, and hosting familiarisation visits.

Orkney was actually the first area in the UK to promote inclusive air holidays. Working in conjunction with British Airways, selected travel agents and local suppliers, a range of self-drive, fishing and bird-watching holidays were promoted. P&O Scottish Ferries also marketed a number of inclusive deals, generally car-based. They also sold the first two-centre holidays, combining Orkney & Shetland in one package for the first time.

The annual Orkney brochure is the most important promotional item produced by OTB. It is a far cry from earlier productions, which were little more than folded lists. The first full colour leaflet was produced in 1976, comprising six pages, A5 in size. Eight four-page leaflets covering the niche markets and an accommodation booklet were also printed. With increased funding the first A4 brochures, the present size, appeared in the early 1980s. Content evolved until a separate promotional brochure became superfluous. The latter was produced for a short time as a series of six foreign language editions. The brochure of today is a showcase of the product and its production is of a high quality. Handbooks are also produced, some inserted into the main brochure, promoting events, the food sector, attractions and other services, a gazetteer listing, street maps and transport contacts. Leaflets by the private sector follow a similar pattern of evolution with a gradual introduction of full colour. There is, however, considerable variation in the quality of design and production.

All these items entice prospective visitors to Orkney, but there is a further requirement for written material once they arrive. Enter the guide book – either for Orkney the brand or for specific attractions. The drive for quality is also apparent in their development. The excellent Charles Tait edition, printed from 1991 onwards, is probably the most comprehensive Orkney guide ever produced.

Guide books are retailed, but the free newspaper also entered the Orkney tourism scene in 1988. Produced annually by *The Orcadian*, the *Islander* updates the visitor on new attractions, helps promote smaller islands and presents some of the quirkier aspects of local life. It effectively completes the wide range of distribution items required.

The newest influence in today's market is the internet. Technology has always played a major role in tourism. Aeronautical design and engineering made bigger and faster aircraft, shrinking the planet; computerised systems allowed global distribution and instant purchase. Technology directly affects price because it reduces costs and enables an increased volume of traffic to be handled. The World Wide Web also provides a further marketing opportunity.

There are analogies with printed material; websites are still evolving in design, content and services. The Orkney website at *www.visitorkney.com* is comprehensive in information provision and now provides a booking service. Despite all the 'cyberbole', for the first time ever, one month in 2001 recorded a decrease in the number of people using the internet. Its use and associated enthusiasm must be measured and balanced.

Technological pace is ever-accelerating. Interactive television, broadband, SMS and viral marketing have not yet been tried by Orkney. In Australia, v-mail, or video-mail is already widely used. V-commerce, i.e. voice-enabled, will soon begin to feature on websites. M-commerce, business by mobile devices, is on its way; by 2005 speeds will be 200 times faster and analysts predict that very soon it will be worth billions.

Whatever the future holds, there will be no room for complacency. There are too many competitors out there, both in cyberspace and in the real world. Tourism in Orkney will need to meet these new challenges and, paradoxically, the only way to guarantee success is a very old one – ensure visitors leave totally fulfilled.

Bibliographic Sources

Prof. Alastair M. Morrison, Purdue University and Dr Dimitrios Buhalis, Sussex University, provide comprehensive tourism bibliographies at the following:

http://cc.purdue.edu/-alltson/books.htm and
http:cc.purdue.edu/-alltson/books.htm

CHAPTER THIRTEEN

St Magnus Cathedral, Kirkwall

ANYONE APPROACHING KIRKWALL BY BOAT or by road cannot fail to be impressed by the way St Magnus Cathedral dominates the skyline; a massive monument in red sandstone which gives the impression of permanence and solidity. Enter the building, and this feeling increases, due to the oversized grandeur of the pillars that hold up the triforia, or first floor galleries. Yet why is such a large and impressive building here, so far north, in a town of some 7,500 inhabitants? How did Kirkwall end up with a cathedral? And how has it survived in such remarkable condition?

St Magnus Cathedral owes its origins to the stories and legends that grew up around the apparent sanctity of Earl Magnus, martyred in 1116 for the sake of peace in Orkney, after betrayal by his cousin Earl Haakon Paulson. Various miracles were attributed to Magnus after his death, and when his nephew Rognvald-Kali won the earldom of Orkney from Haakon's son in the 1120s, he did so with the supposed divine help of his uncle, having promised to build a great church of stone in Magnus' memory should he succeed. In due course, both Magnus and Rognvald were sanctified, and the remains of both lie within the stonework of the cathedral, in the choir. The cathedral was founded in the year 1137, and dedicated to Magnus. Master stonemasons were commissioned, probably trained at Durham. The *Orkneyinga Saga* tells us that the work was supervised by Kol, a Norwegian chieftain, who was also Earl Rognvald's father.

The cathedral is laid out in the classic cross formation, with the main door at the west end. It is a blend of the north-west European Romanesque or Norman and early Gothic styles. The first part to be completed was the central area (choir), which was in use for services within 17 years of the foundation. The layout we see today took a further 300 years to complete, an undertaking that seems incomprehensible to us today. Yet some things never change – the project very quickly ran out of money! Earl Rognvald came up with a radical solution, suggesting to his tenant farmers in Orkney that they should pay him a sum of money, based on the size of their farms, in exchange for the freehold on their properties. The tenant farmers were delighted to pay what was perceived as a fair price in exchange for owning their land into the future, and duly complied. The project was now back on stream, with healthy finances. There was more than a hint of Durham Cathedral in the developing building, with plastered internal pillars, ceilings and walls, covered in floral patterns. Only small fragments of this plasterwork now survive in the upper galleries.

Various extensions and changes were instigated over the years, including the building of foundations for twin towers at the west end, which were never built. The original aim of the building work – to create a suitable shrine within which to house the relics of St Magnus – became less important as time went on, until at the Reformation of the Church in Scotland in 1560 the relics were placed in a plain wooden box, installed within a pillar and subsequently forgotten about until they were rediscovered during major restoration work at the beginning of the 20th century. From being an important shrine to St Magnus, visited by wealthy pilgrims from afar, St Magnus Cathedral now became the parish church of Kirkwall. It only survived the Reformation because in 1478, by a decree of King James III, it had been uniquely bestowed upon the people of Kirkwall. However, the organ and much finery were removed, and whitewash covered all of the rich wall decorations.

The local ownership of the building continues to this day, with the current management and care being in the hands of Orkney Islands Council. The author is the day-to-day manager of the building, ably assisted by the custodian and his team. The Church of Scotland is the tenant, in the fortunate position of not having to worry about the cost of running and maintaining such a vast and venerable building, whose upkeep is very much the responsibility of the council.

One minor glitch along the way was the government's decision in 1845 to assume ownership, declaring the cathedral an historic monument and expelling the congregation. They removed the bishop's and earl's seats (the remains of the earl's seat can still be seen in the south triforium at first floor level) and also discovered the bones of Bishop William the Old and Bishop Thomas Tulloch. In 1851 the royal burgh of Kirkwall reclaimed the building, however, reinstated the congregation and fitted new pews and galleries.

By the early 20th century the building had deteriorated to the extent that a full restoration was required, which was made possible by the Thoms Bequest. Architects were invited to submit proposals, and three plans were considered. Happily one rather grandiose scheme, involving bronze doors, pulpit soaring to the roof and paintings in the pre-Raphaelite style across blocked-in archways at first floor level, was rejected. Instead, George Mackie Watson's simpler and more appropriate scheme was accepted. This included replacing the low bell tower roof with a taller steeple, removing galleries and internal dividing screens, tiling much of the floor and fitting stained glass in the windows. It is perhaps unfortunate that his scheme also included the removal of the potential long vista from one end to the other by the insertion of the organ next to the choir.

St Rognvald's Chapel was created at the east end of the building in the 1960s, complete with impressive wood carvings of Rognvald, Magnus and

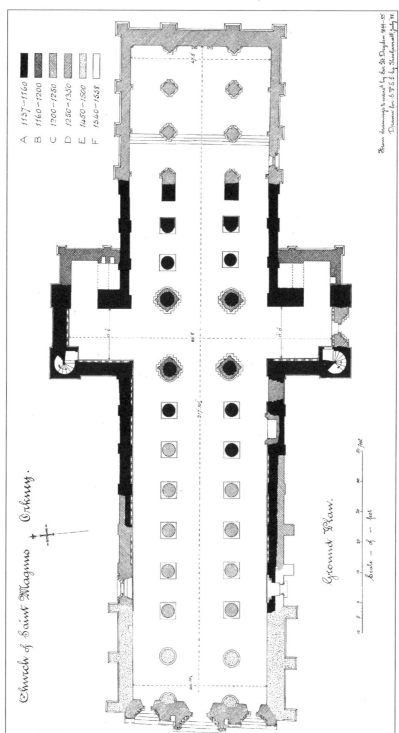

FIGURE 30 Church of St Magnus, Orkney (after Billings)

FIGURE 31   West end of Kirkwall Cathedral and Bishop's Palace (after Billings)

Kol, and some fine 17th-century carved wooden panels were tastefully incorporated. The furniture was designed by Dr Stanley Cursiter, the Queen's Limner and Portrait Painter in Scotland, who has also painted some fine pictures of the cathedral during this period of restoration, some of which can be seen in the Supper Room of the Town Hall opposite the cathedral (now called the Kirkwall and St Ola Community Centre).

A major crisis was thankfully averted in the early 1970s when it was discovered that the foundations were on the move at the west end, with the whole of that end of the building slowly edging towards the sea. £300,000 was quickly raised through a public appeal, and the building is now supported by substantial steel girders. The council's capital repair programme of works on the building, assisted by grant aid from Historic Scotland and funds raised by the Society of the Friends of St Magnus Cathedral, has placed the future of the cathedral in no doubt, with substantial repairs now coming to an end. A stonemason is employed full time at the site, and movement sensors are located on key stonework. Smoke detecting light beams and regular monitoring by the consultant architect allow us all to sleep a little easier! A permanent reminder of what might have been, however, is the rather eccentric slight lean to the west displayed by some of the main pillars.

On entering the cathedral, one is immediately struck by the warmth of the stonework, with its attractive banding of red and yellow. The red sandstone is from the Head of Holland, north of Kirkwall, where a dip in the landscape reveals the location of the original quarry. A small quarry there still provides stone for modern repairs. Much of the yellow sandstone is believed to have come from the north isle of Eday. Some of the stone inside the building is very worn by comparison with other areas, giving clues as to phases in the construction, as some of the pillars were outside for a long period.

The stained glass was mainly fitted in the early 20th century. The windows themselves are far earlier, including the fabulous 13th-century east window and the late 14th- early 15th-century west window, which now contains glass by Crear McCartney, and which was installed in 1987 to mark the cathedral's 850th anniversary. The south transept contains a fine 19th-century rose window, and the north transept has a window depicting St Magnus. Glass depicting various Norse earls and saints can be seen throughout the building, with much only visible from upper galleries and walkways.

The cathedral is noted for its fine stone memorials, which include an extremely worn 13th-century stone in memory of a Knight Templar. Excellent examples of well-preserved 17th-century work can be seen lining the walls down both sides of the building, notably the deep relief carving of the gravestone made for Elizabeth Cuthbert, minister's wife, who died in 1685. As one explores the grave markers, one finds all the classic symbols of mortality and immortality – winged heads, skulls, hourglasses, coffins, bells, spades – among the finest in Britain. There is also a curious wooden artefact which hangs in the north aisle, a large 17th-century *mort brod*, which was hung outside a house to indicate a death in the family – in this case the dead man was Robert Nicolson, glazier. The most impressive monument, however, is undoubtedly the large recumbent statue of Dr John Rae, the Arctic explorer, complete with gun, which dominates the south side of the St Rognvald's Chapel. The missionary William Balfour Baikie is also remembered here with a large memorial on the north side. ('Baikie' is still an affectionate term for 'white man' in some African dialects.) The national saint of Norway, St Olaf, is also depicted in the north aisle by a large wooden statue, which is a copy of the stone original in the cathedral of Nidaros, Trondheim. Interestingly, the original has since been destroyed, leading to a request for permission to copy the copy!

A memorial which lies in its glass case beneath the Royal Oak's bell and an ensign created in more modern times is the book of remembrance for the 833 men who lost their lives when the HMS *Royal Oak* was torpedoed in Scapa Flow during the Second World War.

The cathedral amply repays the observant visitor who elevates their gaze and homes in on the detailed stone-carving around the tops of the pillars. Here can be found much of the symbolism beloved of medieval stone-carvers. The symbolism is now believed to be associated with fertility and with displaying the sins of the flesh, together with other, less obvious, motifs. It is possible to spot four different 'green men', some human-like

but grotesque figures with lizard-like bodies, and even a Sheela-na-Gig –
a squatting female figure with open legs displaying oversized genitals.
Sheela-na-Gig is Irish, meaning 'woman of ill repute'. These carvings date
back to the 11th century in churches in France, but are rare in Scotland.
The cathedral also contains many carved heads, some with hands over
their mouths, one figure wearing a hood, and several dragons.

In the centre of the building, at the back of the choir, can be found the
attractive carved wooden case which contains the bellows and pipes of the
Willis III organ, fitted in the 1913–30 restoration. This triple console
organ is highly thought of, and attracts many students and accomplished
organists.

No visit to the cathedral is complete, however, without a tour of the
upper floors and to the top of the tower. Entry is tightly controlled now,
with strict rules and regulations, unlike in 1934, when the Reverend
William Barclay wrote a famous letter to W. J. Heddle, the town clerk,
venting his spleen about various outrages, including the fact that he 'also
found that the belfry had been used as a urinal' ... These parts of the
building were out of bounds to all but a select few from the mid-1970s
until 2002, when small works such as an extra handrail within the tightest
of the stone spiral staircases and safety rope barriers across the ringing
chamber allowed entry to restart. A small charge allows those sound of
wind and limb to join the guided tours, which are run with a ratio of five
members of the public to one guide, and last about 45 minutes.

The first stop is the south triforium, where an assemblage of carved
stones, stained glass panels, the remnants of the earl's seat and two
ex-pulpits are on show, in what is now a museum for the building. Here,
too, is the famous double hangman's ladder, some 9 m (30 ft) long, which
gruesomely recalls the days when the hangman went up one side, dragging
the unfortunate condemned man up the other. It is said that one side is
more worn, through twice as much use, as only the hangman took that
route back down ...

Next one stops at the crossing, a vertiginous high stone bridge right in
the middle of the building, which commands a stunning view of the whole
interior, and brings home just how massive the cathedral really is. Then
on up to the pendulum chamber and the clock chamber. The current clock
dates from the 1950s, with its predecessor on show in the nearby Orkney
Museum from June 2003. It is wound three times a week, using a tool
very much like a car's starting handle.

The next stop, via some extremely steep stairs within a very tight spiral,
is the ringing chamber. This is unusual, as unlike most British churches,
with their rows of bell ropes, the three bells in the cathedral are rung by
one person, seated in a veritable throne, with a pedal for the foot and two
handles. This system of ringing, known as 'clocking', is Norse in origin.

A wooden staircase then takes one past the bells. These ancient messengers were last worked on in 1987, when the cast iron crown staples,

from which the clappers hang, were changed. They were not tuned on that occasion, however, so they still sound as they must have done for more than 450 years.

The tour takes the visitors out onto the parapet at the base of the spire. There is a breathtaking view from all four sides, out to the north isles, to Inganess Bay, overland to Wideford Hill and up to the Highland Park Distillery. Tankerness House, which now houses The Orkney Museum, can be seen to great effect, as can the ruins of the Earl's and Bishop's Palaces. One can also see close at hand the large metal water spouts in the shape of animals' heads. It is interesting to see, by looking down onto the town, just how many large trees actually grow in Kirkwall, compared with the practically treeless landscape elsewhere in Orkney.

St Magnus Cathedral is very much the centre of the Kirkwall community, with regular services every week and about 60 secular events every year, such as concerts and recitals. It is perhaps best known internationally for the St Magnus Festival, started in 1977 and today going from strength to strength. Now, every June, top orchestras, soloists and choirs transform Orkney into the platform for this prestigious, week-long classical music festival. The cathedral used to be the main venue, and is still used for many of the events, although its 800-seat capacity is insufficient for some of the larger events, which now take place in the nearby Pickaquoy Centre.

Other key events of the year, filling the cathedral until it is standing room only, include the Christmas tree lighting ceremony, performed by a dignitary from the county of Hordaland, Norway, which is twinned with Orkney and donates the Christmas tree every year, and the school carol concerts. The cathedral also blazes with colour during the annual flower festival, when local flower arrangers create ever bigger and more imaginative displays to fit the theme they have been given.

Orkney's links with Norway are nowhere more evident than in the cathedral, with its Norwegian bible on display, the statue of St Olaf, the Norwegian flag hanging in the north transept and a large tapestry hanging in the south aisle, which was presented by the King of Norway to Her Majesty Queen Elizabeth the Queen Mother in 1987 to mark the 850th anniversary of the founding of the building. St Magnus Cathedral was part of the Norwegian archdiocese of Trondheim for its first 331 years, until Orkney became part of the Kingdom of Scotland in 1468, and many modern-day events pay tribute to the building's Norse origins. Every year, whether at Christmas, on St Magnus Day (16 April), on Norwegian Constitution Day (17 May) or during the St Magnus Festival, one can expect at some point to hear the evocative music of the Hardanger fiddle, the blare of a birchbark lur, or the sweet notes of a solo soprano singing Norwegian folk songs. The St Magnus Centre was opened in 2001 by Crown Prince Haakon Magnus of Norway, further cementing the ties which date back more than 1,000 years.

The kirkyard is well worth a visit, and contains some splendid grave markers of all the types represented across Scotland, plus a few curiosities. There is a memorial to a master stonemason, with the masons' marks, or signatures in stone, of all his team.

As one leaves the kirkyard, and turns back for a final look at this grand old building, one of the finest in the north, one again gets an incredible feeling of age and permanence, of a beloved friend growing old gracefully. The bells strike the hour as they have done for hundreds of years and one instinctively knows that this building, this church, will be the centre of the Kirkwall community for a long, long time to come.

CHAPTER FOURTEEN

Kirkwall

D URING THE MIDDLE AGES towns were of major political significance, especially in areas where the king's power was still in process of consolidation. Such a region was Moray (which in medieval terms extended on both sides of the Moray Firth, bounded by the Dornoch Firth, where it met Sutherland, the 'south land' of the mainland Scotland holdings of the earls of Orkney). Moray was prosperous and yielded high revenues, and for that reason its regional rulers were apt to behave with more independence than the Scottish kings liked. But by the second half of the 12th century, David I and his successors had at last got on top of the troublesome *mormaers*. The recipe for successful, central royal control was something we may call 'Normanisation'. Normans were professionals: professional at ruling, and at the military imposition of rule. They had perfected the ultimate armament of the age – the mailed warrior on a big horse. With the knights went castles, and with castles went clearly perceived ideas about feudal lordship. David's successors entrusted the building and manning of the castles to Norman adventurers. Once the castles were in, the towns – the early royal burghs – followed. Elgin and Forres are classic instances. The burghs owed their privileges to the king, and gave him some assurance of support should the new security ever break down.

The oldest towns in the Highlands, then, are these burghs of royal foundation. Moving from the Scottish to the Scandinavian sphere, how does Kirkwall fit in? First, we must face the fact that, in Orkney, the 'Normanisation' is here in a really big way. St Magnus Cathedral may have been paid for with the wealth of the north (although it came near to bankrupting the earldom) but as a tour de force of Romanesque architecture, it is a product of the dominant metropolitan Norman-French culture of the age, and the man who commissioned it, Rognvald Kali Kolsson, although he spoke Norse and had a Norse name, was very much the urban sophisticate – the spontaneous versifier, the elegant flatterer of women, the patron of poets and musicians.

So, was 'Scandinavian' Orkney supposedly just as much connected to the Norman-French culture as were the archetypically Francophile kings of Scotland? There is a significant point in the comparison – St Magnus Cathedral was begun in 1137, fully a generation before Elgin or Forres were laid out. Kirkwall undoubtedly *is* older than any town in the Highlands;

the question is, just how early are its origins, and in what period of history does it start to show the essential characteristics of urban life – of a mercantile town? The first we hear of the place is in the *Orkneyinga Saga*, during a troubled period in the reign of the great 11th-century *jarl*, Thorfinn Sigurdarson, 'the Mighty'.

Thorfinn had been ousted from his earldom by a dynastic rival, his cousin Rognvald Brusason. Rognvald, we are told, established himself and a large household in Kirkwall for the winter of 1046. It is particulary mentioned that he laid in a specially good stock of provisions, but for his Yuletide ale he was not content with the ordinary product. The place at that time for barley malt was the outstandingly fertile island of Papa Stronsay. There went Rognvald with an entourage, and stayed overnight; and in the night came Thorfinn's men and they surrounded the hall and burned it, and although Rognvald managed to escape from the fire, he was quickly hunted down and killed.

We may wonder whether perhaps Rognvald's favouring of Kirkwall might not have been his response to Thorfinn's favouring of Birsay. It was still the norm for a ruler to move around with his household and his personal warband, going from place to place, being entertained, consuming his taxes. With taxes being paid in kind, essentially in foodstuffs, it was easier to move the royal household to the food than the food to the royal household. But the saga writer was aware that Thorfinn was starting to alter this pattern – he established himself at Birsay, built a grand church there, and lived there for the greater part of his life. This echoed the actions of his contemporary, Edward the Confessor, founder of Westminster Abbey (and an early admirer and emulator of the Normans).

Although the saga picks up this special circumstance relating to Birsay, it unfortunately informs us no further at this point on Kirkwall. The establishment here must have included a grand feasting-hall, with all that would have gone with it – kitchens, storehouses, stables, smithies and places where the many people who did all the work of servicing such an establishment would have lived. We do not know whether it existed before Rognvald's time, as one of Thorfinn's (or his predecessors') 'other' places; or was the creation of a deliberate promotion by Rognvald Brusason. We must bear in mind, too, that this was a Christian age; there certainly would have been a church (perhaps the original one which generated the name *Kirkjuvagr*, 'church bay'). But the saga picks up Kirkwall again, nearly a century later, in a way which suggests that the place probably had continued in some form during the intervening period, and by the time of Rognvald Kali Kolsson, it evidently had become a centre of some importance.

The household of a magnate such as a *jarl* of Orkney was a magnet for traders. The cargoes carried by merchant ships of this time were valuable (mostly luxury items like silks and fine clothes and wine), and the customers were the powerful and rich. Where a *jarl* maintained his household, there was the prospect of trade. In fact, trade could not take place other than under the protection of the local ruler. It was even more convenient if the *jarl* had chosen a location where it was easy and safe to unload merchandise. Kirkwall was particularly good in that respect.

The sagas do imply that Kirkwall already existed as a market-centre by the time Rognvald Kali Kolsson seized power in 1136, when Rognvald immediately made it his policy to develop the place as an urban centre. One should be cautious about taking the *Orkneyinga Saga* as straight history, but when it is describing the actions of Rognvald, the incidental details (which its author would have had no reason to falsify) ring true within the wider historical context of the period. Behind it we can see a wise perception that political power (supported by the ecclesiastical power which was its essential concomitant) in future was going to be exercised from towns. In the long run, towns were where the wealth would be concentrated. In the 12th century, power still rested on the control of agricultural production – the ability to levy taxes on the rural population that produced the food – but the wealth that the taxation produced was already being spent in the new towns and cities. For a long time to come, kings and magnates and the high dignitaries of the Church would retain their rural palaces (the Stewart earls were still at Birsay at the beginning of the 17th century, and the bishops kept their own palace there well into the 16th), but the town was becoming the obvious place to be.

Rognvald's relationship with the Church was a special one. His uncle, Magnus, had been murdered on Egilsay in 1116 or 1117; and the saga-writer would have us believe that he quickly became venerated as a saint – a development that his killer, Earl Hakon, is hardly likely to have welcomed, and which it behoved Bishop William therefore to discourage. The miraculous manifestations that persuaded William are told in chapter 57 of the *Orkneyinga Saga*, along with a lengthy catalogue of miracles which demonstrated Magnus' sanctity. Anyone who reads the saga will notice that this long chapter is written in a florid, effusive style which is alien to the terse understated prose which we associate with the Icelandic sagas. It is, of course, a 'miracle-book' – hagiography, an example of the most voluminous class of literature to have been produced in the Middle Ages. This one was probably originally written in Latin and rendered into Norse for insertion into the saga narrative. It is the work of churchmen who were motivated to justify their own faith in a particular figure as a saint, and to emphasize the intercessory power of that saint. This of course would encourage people to make pilgrimages in order to pray before the saint's relics, enhancing the prestige and revenues of the church in which those relics were housed. That church, in the case of St Magnus, was the Christchurch in Birsay, which had been built by Thorfinn the Mighty, probably with the immediate intention of making it a prime seat of an Orkney bishop, at the location where Thorfinn had his own favourite palace.

Hakon was succeeded by his son Paul, and it was with this Paul that Rognvald struggled for the earldom. The struggle came to a head in 1136, which appears to be when the highly significant step was taken of moving – 'translating' – the relics of St Magnus from Birsay to Kirkwall. If this really happened under Paul, what was his motive in either instigating or allowing it? Most likely he was powerless in the matter – intense politicking was going on, to which no doubt Bishop William was party, and the bishop had decided that this was the way the wind was blowing. Certainly when, in the following year, Paul was removed and Rognvald got the earldom, the identification of Rognvald with the *cultus* of his uncle Magnus becomes a very strong motif.

Whether or not the saga narrates the story accurately, the incidental detail is revealing. The 'Short Magnus Saga' tells of Bishop William setting off eastwards to Kirkwall with the sacred relics of Magnus (the saint's bones, which would have been disinterred and reverently washed) which were then enshrined over the altar of 'the church which was there'. This implies that an elaborate shrine was constructed over the altar of a church, either the same one which must have existed to serve Rognvald Brusason's establishment back in 1046, or a successor to it. It was, however, only a temporary measure to house the relics, and foster the cult, until the new cathedral – begun in 1137 – was ready to house them.

In both the *Shorter Magnus Saga* and *Orkneyinga Saga* texts, the account of the translation of the relics from Birsay is supported by a background statement about the appearance of Kirkwall (the wording is closely similar in both versions): 'at that time the market centre at Kirkwall had few buildings'. That it *was* a market-centre – *kaupstaðr* – is taken as known. *Kaup* is related to English 'cheap', the original meaning of which is 'bargain, trade' – so in London we have Cheapside, and there are several English market-towns with the name element 'Chipping'. The Norse form is seen in 'Copenhagen', more obviously in its Danish form, København, 'market-harbour'. The early trading-centre on Oslo-fjord which in due course was supplanted by Oslo itself, was known simply as Kaupang.

So, a decision was taken to move the now officially promoted *cultus* of St Magnus from its old rural location into a mercantile centre; still a modest one in the number of its buildings, but clearly with the implication that it should be encouraged to grow under the earl's patronage. And with the relics of the saint came the bishop himself; he did not give up his rural palace at Birsay, but – as seems likely if Douglas Simpson's identification of the lowest parts of the walls as 12th-century work is correct – he set about building for himself a new palace that from then on would be his main seat. The new Bishop's Palace is a 'first-floor hall' – a building in the Norman-French fashion, the architectural expression of new social mores. We have moved decisively away from the Scandinavian timber-built ground-floor feasting-hall with its central hearth and smoke-hole in the roof, and the heavy ale-drinking which it accommodated. The first-floor hall with fireplaces, its walls hung with tapestries, was a stage-set for the display of the French courtly manners that ushered in the new Age of

Chivalry. Here in Kirkwall, Orkney's ruling class displayed its cosmopolitan sophistication.*

We can identify with reasonable confidence the area where the original *kaupstaðr* of Kirkwall developed, and the site of the feasting-hall where unlucky Rognvald Brusason planned to entertain his household and drink away the winter of 1046. It is important first of all to appreciate that at that time the Peerie Sea was much larger than it is today; by stages, but mostly since the mid-19th century, it has been filled in and land reclaimed. In its natural form it extended southwards nearly a kilometre from the present-day harbour, to where the Catholic church now stands. The main street, as the town developed, followed the shoreline – Bridge Street, Albert Street, Broad Street, Victoria Street, Main Street. The original location of mercantile activity was Bridge Street (facing the Peerie Sea) along with Shore Street, facing north directly into Kirkwall Bay. Both these streets began as waterfronts; Shore Street remained one until the 1990s. In a trading-seaport, the waterfront was where the important business was done; where the life of the town happened. The shores themselves were beaches, which in the 11th century was a convenience. The shallow-draught Viking-Age merchant ships were designed to be beached for unloading; near to high tide ships were allowed to settle on the beach, unloaded at low tide (perhaps into ox-carts driven alongside), and then sailed away when the next tide came along. At the top of the beach, the traders did business with anyone who showed interest in what they had brought. The dealers and merchants wanted to have booths – their modest houses and ware-houses – set just back from the shoreline on the inland side of the street which naturally developed, following the line of the shore, and from which they could look out on the life going on in the street and in the harbour.

Shore Street and Bridge Street, then, almost certainly represent the original area of mercantile activity. The earl, under whose patronage and protection the town grew, had his feasting-hall probably in the same general area. A further clue is the location of St Olaf's Church. This is assumed to be the already-existing church to which in 1136 the relics of St Magnus were first brought; that particular building may have been quite new at the time, but its siting is likely to have been governed by the existence of an earlier church. Its location was beside the Papdale Burn which ran into the Peerie Sea. The Papdale Burn remained open until the 19th century when it was put into a culvert. It interrupted the shoreline at the point where

---

* A similar thing happened to Bergen, which too was a trading-centre that had grown up on a waterfront. The bishop for the area had his seat on the west-coast island of Selje, which was associated with the martyrdom of St Sunniva and her companions (Sunniva admittedly being a somewhat less tangible figure than St Magnus), and there her relics were housed. The move into the town in this case came in 1170, a generation after it had happened in Orkney, and Sunniva was adopted as Bergen's patron saint.

the street now bends sharply southwards to become Albert Street – the place nowadays referred to as Leonard's the Newsagents' Corner. The burn was bridged at this corner, giving the name of the street. The area defined by Bridge Street, Shore Street, St Catherine's Place and the culverted Papdale Burn, is the ancient core of 'the Burgh' and is likely to have included the earl's hall. Any buried remains of an 11th-century trading-centre and earl's hall would be of the highest archaeological importance, and should this area ever undergo redevelopment, investigative excavations would need to be of the most thorough.

I like to think that Pierowall, in Westray, today is something like what Kirkwall would have been in this early phase. There is a big, very sheltered bay – one of the safest places of shelter in Orkney – and today, the main street of the village runs along the shoreline. Most of the houses – and they, or groups of them, are spaced quite widely apart – are on the inland side of the street. At about the midway point along the street is the old parish church. Somewhere at the back of the village, in the 19th century, graves constituting the largest Viking-Age cemetery in Britain were turned up (although none of the surviving grave-goods decisively indicates the presence of merchants). However, Pierowall – in the saga named simply *Höfn* – is also the only location referred to as a 'thorp', which implies something like a village. It is not much to go on, but could Pierowall have been a trading-centre that, unlike Kirkwall, failed to take off? Its location would have been strategic in an earlier period when Dublin was an important trading centre and ships set out from there around to the north of Orkney, into the North Sea. But by the 12th century it was mainly the North Sea that mattered and Kirkwall was better placed to take advantage of that.

The site chosen for the new cathedral was separated by quite a distance from the old nucleus, but it too was built above the shoreline, looking out across the Peerie Sea. As we have noted, an accompanying Bishop's Palace was a feature of the original plan. The west front of the cathedral, with its great ceremonial door, was designed to be approached, probably up a flight of steps, from the harbour. The cathedral was designed to have a cloisters on the south side; the cloisters would have presented a blank wall to the harbour, going south from the cathedral. That wall continued across the line of present-day Palace Road (which was created about 1800; until then there was no road in this position) and was pierced by an entrance, the Watergate, giving access to the close around the Bishop's Palace. (The Watergate arch survives, removed and reset into the Palace wall.) This was, therefore, a cathedral close, an enclosed and protected area around the cathedral and the palace and also the lodgings of the various cathedral dignitaries, which originally occupied the site of the Long Tenement – the range of building which runs downhill and westward from the round tower which Bishop Reid added to the palace in the 16th century. All this was walled-in, and it would have been, in fact, very much like the closes which are a surviving feature of many English cathedrals, and which provide a haven of quiet calm behind the noise and bustle of the commercial street. We should not be surprised at the Englishness of it: the Church in Norway to a large extent was a daughter of the English Church.

Around the corner from the cathedral close, continuing south along the waterfront, was the Laverock (its name now changed to Victoria Street). The part nearest the cathedral is the oldest. In it lived some overflow of officials from the cathedral, but also an increasing number of merchants, for the bishop entered the same mercantile game as the earl by setting up an alternative 'trading zone', in the hope of attracting merchants to do business there and getting a share of the revenues. One may imagine, for instance, that those who brought wine would feel obligated to use the bishop's market, seeing as the Church (which needed wine for the Eucharist) was such an important customer. In the long term it fuelled the rivalry between the bishops and earls, there being in effect two towns – the Burgh and the Laverock – for long separated by the open ground that lay between the cathedral and the Papdale Burn. The rivalry continues to be played out every Christmas Day and New Year's Day along the medieval lines of demarcation (and to the uninformed observer, apparently to a medieval rule-book).

In the 13th century the nature of trade began to change significantly, with the adoption of a new kind of ship, the cog. This was larger and heavier and had a deeper draught than the cargo-ships of the Viking Age; it was less beautiful, but could carry more cargo. It also needed a lower level of craftsmanship to build it, so cogs could be produced in greater numbers. It became economic to carry cargoes of greater weight and bulk in proportion to their value, such as grain or dried fish (it was the exchange of those two commodities between southern-central and northern Europe that founded the wealth of the Hanse merchants). Like a modern cargo-ship, the cog did not take kindly to being run aground; she had to stay afloat during loading and so needed a wharf. The construction of wharfage to replace the original beaches was a new phase in the development of the town. This was probably done (as in other medieval waterfronts) using timber piles, although in front of the cathedral the bedrock was cut back to create a vertical face. The wharves would be extended as ships got bigger or as the harbour, its tidal scouring reduced by these obstructions, silted up. Medieval waterfronts are of great interest to archaeologists because the timberwork usually remains waterlogged, and survives, along with all manner of organic rubbish which accumulated. There has been no recent redevelopment in Kirkwall within this waterfront zone, but if ever it happens, the archaeological investigation deserves to be as rigorous as it has been in places such as London and York.

In Shore Street, the waterfront road remained open and unbuilt-upon on its sea side. The oil storage tanks erected in the 1950s unfortunately replaced what was probably one of the oldest groups of houses in the town (another small group still survives in Main Street, at the opposite extremity of the town). These had their gable-ends to the street, a pattern familiar to anyone who knows any Hanseatic town, such as Bergen, with its Bryggen merchants' area, or indeed Lübeck. The waterfronts that faced the Peerie Sea however were mostly built-up on the sea side as well as the land side of the shoreline street. As ships got bigger, and the Peerie Sea more full of rubbish, it became less practicable for seagoing ships to serve premises there. The seaward side of the street became built-up, and the merchants in those positions therefore had a waterfront, in effect, as their back gardens (perhaps somewhat as still can be seen in Stromness). Barges could be used to transfer goods from ships anchored in Kirkwall Bay into the Peerie Sea for unloading at merchants' premises.

Whether the street was built-up on both sides or just on one, everyone wanted a share of the action. Frontage was valuable – it was where you did your trade – and in accordance with medieval notions about fair play, everyone should have an equal yardage. The inevitable result is the long narrow standard building-plot running backwards from the street. Main houses and commercial premises were built on the street frontage, and if expansion was needed – the addition of a warehouse or a workshop, or on-premises living accommodation for apprentices or employees, for example – buildings had to be constructed at right angles away from the street, creating a long narrow yard. Kirkwall had a good deal of this medieval pattern, much of which in the area behind Bridge Street and Albert Street was lost when the big car-park was created. More of it survives off Victoria Street. These closes often take their names from the prominent merchants who traded from the original premises on the street frontage.

In this respect of layout, Scandinavian trading-towns like Kirkwall follow much the same pattern as English boroughs and Scottish royal burghs of the period. The pattern of the long narrow plots (now built-up as closes running back from the High Street), today is also still seen today in Forres, and to some extent in Elgin. The Scottish word for these plots was 'tenement'. The trading activity itself was in the hands of private enterprise, but private enterprise was not free to do as it liked. The standard narrow building-plot with its strictly rationed share of the street-frontage was planned and imposed by an overarching authority.

The original 'Burgh' at first was bounded by the Papdale Burn, but development soon spilled along the waterfront road towards the cathedral. Before the end of the Middle Ages this had created the 'Midtown' – the original designation of what, in the 19th century, was renamed Albert Street. Where Albert Street became Broad Street, this development ab-ruptly stopped. This was the site of Kirkwall Castle, built by the St Clair earls c. 1380 on the edge of the Peerie Sea. Relationships between earls and bishops at times were acrimonious and this siting of the new castle would have been seen as a confrontational move on the part of the St Clairs. South of the castle there were no further buildings on Broad

Street (the cathedral looking straight across the Peerie Sea) until the Laverock (Victoria Street) began. (The building-up of the west side of Broad Street began early in the 16th century with Tankerness House and adjacent properties, which were built to replace some of the old cathedral dignitaries' residences in the Long Tenement and the Laverock; the rest of Broad Street was built upon only in the late 17th century after the St Clair castle had been abandoned).

In the 16th century the earls got the better of the bishops; in 1568 the notorious Robert Stewart won control of the Bishop's Palace. His son Patrick succeeded him in 1593 and both embellished the Bishop's Palace and built to the east of it a costly new residence in a fashionable Renaissance style. But he did not enjoy it for long; it was briefly repossessed by Bishop Law, got caught up in the rebellion of Patrick's bastard son Robert, and suffered a siege. The suppression of the rebellion ended the line of the ruling earls and by the 1660s the splendid Earl's Palace had become decrepit. After the last (Episcopalian) bishop died there in 1688, it was allowed to fall into ruin.

By the 17th century the town was no longer growing vigorously. In the later Middle Ages, Kirkwall's trading position had weakened. To an extent this may have been due to the growing, and ruthless, domination of Norwegian trade by the merchants of the Hanseatic League. The Hanse were interested in taking stockfish (dried fish), mainly from northern Norway, and, from their base in Bergen, trading it into central Europe (where Catholic observance of Lent and other fast days meant a strong and sustained demand) in exchange for grain, in which Norway was not self-sufficient. Excluding English or other grain from this market was a mainstay of Hanseatic policy. Shetland, a producer of stockfish, slotted into the Hanseatic pattern, but Orkney was a grain-producer, and her trade would have had to turn elsewhere.

Kirkwall did not grow significantly from the end of the Middle Ages until the early 19th century. During the 1840s, the age of agricultural improvement somewhat belatedly overtook Orkney, and there were significant changes in the agricultural life of the county, which continued to produce grain, but increasingly moved into store cattle production. This new trade in live cattle was entirely made possible by steamship services. Kirkwall became a farmers' market-town, and quickly began to experience traffic congestion.

The problem was that the town had developed along a waterfront and so had just one main street. The Oyce (the channel connecting Kirkwall Bay into the Peerie Sea) had never been bridged, and the way in from Stromness and the West Mainland was by the Old Finstown Road across the shoulder of Wideford Hill. Anything coming from Scapa joined the Old Finstown Road shortly before it entered the town, becoming Main Street. At Clay Loan, the traffic already in the street (here nowadays called Victoria Street) was joined by that from Holm and the East Mainland. It all went down Albert Street and Bridge Street, meeting everything that was trying to come the other way. Not infrequently at the Papdale Burn crossing (Leonard's Corner) it all got stuck. Meanwhile, the harbour itself was hopelessly inadequate. Something had to be done.

When we contemplate the scheme which was put into effect in 1865, we have to marvel at the breathtaking decisiveness and scale of the thing as a demonstration – if we need it – of the difference between the mid 19th century and the early 21st. It was an engineering scheme on what, in proportion to the size of the town, was a staggering scale. Firstly, a new harbour was created, with piers at which steamers could come alongside, removing the need for unloading into flitboats. The Papdale Burn was culverted. Then, a strip of land was reclaimed from the Peerie Sea and protected by a retaining wall, to create Junction Road, effectively a bypass. Junction Road was so called because it connects Kirkwall and Scapa harbours. It went from the harbour, where the bridging of the Oyce provided a new route to the west, then ran southwards, parallel to the narrow medieval street and providing a wider alternative to it. To link it to Broad Street, and thus to Palace Road, created at the beginning of the century and providing a new route to the east, the last remnant of the St Clair castle was knocked down, and Castle Street punched through. Further south, Junction Road then connected to Clay Loan before meeting the Old Finstown Road. Here, some buildings on the south side of the medieval street (where Main Street becomes Wellington Street) were knocked down to enable a straight, more or less sea-level, route to run direct to Scapa – the New Scapa Road. In the 20th century, the infilling of the Peerie Sea continued; by the 1930s Great Western Road was in place and Junction Road in its turn had ceased to be a waterfront.

Following the pattern everywhere, 20th-century Kirkwall has become overwhelmingly the economic centre of Orkney, sucking in people from outlying areas. It now contains an increasingly disproportunate share of Orkney's population. Expansion in housing mostly has gone up the hillside to the east of the town, while an industrial estate has been developed at Hatston, on the west side of Kirkwall Bay.

CHAPTER FIFTEEN

The North Isles

THE FACT THAT the seemingly impossible green and russet jigsaw of Orkney's North Isles can be surveyed, explored as a region in its own right, is intriguing. Surely this is just a scatter of far-flung, unusually-shaped, unconnected islands?

Children can spend hours puzzling over the 'pieces' on the map, seeing a Wellington boot or a dragon there, a teardrop or a stooping old lady here. There is no pattern, no symmetry in this strange island collage ... and yet there does seem endless, tantalising possibility for linkage. To the organised traveller on the other hand, the cluster of 18 principal islands and the necklace of attendant reefs and skerries, fanning out for 30 miles north of Orkney's capital, Kirkwall, can often seem a confusing geographical inconvenience. What a miscalculation. A closer inspection will reveal that the children have, instinctively, the rights of it.

The puzzle does resolve itself. The North Isles of Orkney, with a population of some 2,000 souls, is indeed a place apart, where a shared inheritance, a rich and ancient natural and man-made heritage, can be traced. The pieces magically slot together.

Although each of these islands has a unique personality, they form together a distinct sub-archipelago within the Orkney group where social and historical development has often progressed at a different pace from Mainland Orkney and the South Isles.

The sea tracks, romantically styled 'the Swan's Path' or 'the Whale Road' by the Norse settlers, linking the isles with each other and with the Mainland, have been fixed over the centuries, carefully skirting tidal races and treacherous half-submerged saw-edged rocks; sea and stone and salt-splashed timbers – the fabric of this wonderful island puzzle. The ro-ro ferries of the 21st century, with romantic names such as *Sigurd* and *Eynhallow, Thorfinn* and *Varagen*, follow these selfsame tracks in the wake of the longships and the trading schooners.

Above the restless, iron-grey sea in the clear, sharp air swans' wings still beat a pulsing rhythm, but they have been joined for the past four decades by the eight-seater aircraft which provide a lifeline service to the most remote isles such as North Ronaldsay and Papa Westray.

These North Isles of Orkney are also overlaid by a complex web of internal and inter-island boundaries, some solid features of the landscape and others just arbitrary lines scrawled on a civil servant's notepad. In prehistoric times islanders threw up earth ridges, or gairsties, to delineate ownership, while more recently bureaucrats, more interested in balancing numbers rather than recognising established communities, have been at work. Kings, bishops and counsellors have all drawn their lines, trying to divide, partition the North Isles for administrative or political convenience. It has always been a flawed effort.

The simple truth is that much, much more unites these little islands than separates them. What they have in common will always transcend petty human ambition and attempts at pigeon-holing. Whether it's getting behind the last surviving North Isles football team in the Parish Cup, or purring with satisfaction at the Kirkwall mart when a North Isles beast fetches top price of the day, the folk of the green isles know where their allegiances lie.

The islands which we will examine in this chapter, moving out from Kirkwall roughly in a clockwise direction are Shapinsay (with Gairsay); Rousay (with Egilsay, Wyre and Eynhallow); Westray; Papa Westray (with the Holm of Papay); North Ronaldsay, Sanday, Stronsay (with Linga Holm, Papa Stronsay and Auskerry) and Eday (with Faray and the Calf of Eday).

Their most obvious unifying factor is the sea, the constant companion, the backdrop to life in these islands, some of which are so compact and sea-girt that on a stormy day – of which there are many – the salt spray can carry the length and breadth of the isle, coating the windows with a saline crust. It takes a powerful leap of the imagination for a visitor from the Scottish mainland watching a procession of Atlantic breakers smashing into the sandstone ramparts which form the western fringe of these islands to accept the view expressed hereabouts that the sea, though a tough master, rather than dividing communities can form a bridge between them.

Only people with sea salt in their blood, the wind in their hair and the cry of the tern in their ear can make that leap of understanding.

However, it's time to examine the pieces in our jigsaw. Just a 25-minute ferry hop across The String, Kirkwall's gateway to the ocean, lies Shapinsay. The regular boat service allows Shapinsay folk to work in Kirkwall, making it, along with Flotta with its oil terminal in Scapa Flow, an Orcadian commuter isle. Balfour village with its so un-Orcadian castle as a backdrop, is a tidy, welcoming place. It stretches from the Shapinsay pierhead fringing the west side of Elwick Bay, where in 1263 King Haakon of Norway's fleet of 100 longships anchored, prior to their voyage south and defeat at the hands of the Scots at the Battle of Largs. The family of Washington Irving, one of the United States first literary figures, hailed from the north of Shapinsay.

Off to the north-west is Gairsay, a dumpling of an island, which was home for perhaps the most feared of Orkney's Norse sea raiders and pirates, Sweyn Asleifson, who every year after the corn was sown and again when the harvest was over would set off on raiding expeditions to Ireland and the Hebrides.

Rousay lies to the north-west again, a conspicuously massive island with spectacular sea cliffs to the north and high, barren moorland in the heart of the island. With its attendant isles Rousay can boast 166 sites of archaeological interest, an expanse of visible heritage which is surely unmatched in Europe. Most impressive is probably Midhowe Broch on the mile-long Westness Walk, a memorable string of cairns and brochs, where you are literally tripping over history.

Saga stories – murder, kidnap and mayhem – abound on this island, and in more modern times Rousay was one of the few Orcadian communities to experience a major Clearance of people from the land. Ironically, Quandale, one of these deserted communities, now offers sanctuary to some of the most rare and beautiful flowers in Orkney. A rich variety of habitat means that Rousay is a delight for devotees of the natural world.

On Rousay's eastern flank Egilsay claims its place in Orkney's story as the site of the slaying of Earl, later Saint, Magnus, the man to whom the great, red sandstone cathedral of Kirkwall is dedicated. The island has also been a home to the increasingly rare corncrake and renowned for its breeding ducks and waders. The RSPBs own large reserves represent more than one third of Egilsay's acreage.

Eynhallow, perhaps the most mystical of the Orkney isles, is only a kilometre wide. Fringed by dangerous tidal races the island with its 12th-century monastery seems determined to deter visitors but has a magnetism which while difficult to explain is universally felt.

If the settings on Wyre seem familiar it's probably because the spirit of 20th-century writer Edwin Muir, who was brought up here, lives on. Surely as a child he played beside the quaintly styled Cubbie Roo's Castle, a sandstone mini-fortress built by a Viking chieftain in the 1150s. Let's not forget the seals; like so many of Orkney's North Isles Wyre has a viewing perch close to grey and common seal haul-outs. Whichever island you visit seal-watching is compulsive and compulsory. Wherever you go on the isles seek out local information about the best places to spy on the seals, beachcomb, birdwatch or simply soak up the ozone and the atmosphere. Be prepared to spend an extra minute in conversation. That too is obligatory.

To the north is the self-styled Queen of the Isles, Westray. This island, with a record of habitation stretching back to the dawn of history, has remained, more than most, rich in Orkney culture and tradition. Distance from Kirkwall has lent it a dour independence of spirit which persists to this day. With fierce pride the local folk will tell you that they are Westray born and bred.

For many people Westray is the island of the puffin experience. A rock stack called the Castle o' Burrian with a Dark Ages hermitage on its windblown crest is the mecca for puffin enthusiasts where the comics of the updraughts gather in their hundreds, popping in and out of their burrows and squabbling above the swell.

Westray, with its smaller neighbour Papa Westray, is currently striving to regenerate its embattled mini-economy and the islands scored a major success in the late 1990s by being included in the government's Initiative at the Edge programme to promote development. Fishing, farming, tourism and crafts still provide the principal means of livelihood for islanders, but this new connection with the wider world has set imaginations free and unusual new harvests are anticipated.

Priority stopovers on Westray include the heritage centre in Pierowall village, stark and sturdy Noltland Castle, the Noup Head cliffs and light-house and the many archaeological sites which ornament the island.

The shortest scheduled air flight in the world, under a wave-skimming minute from Westray to Papa Westray (Papay to the locals and visitors in the know) is by far the most sensational way to reach the isle of the priests, travel writer Bill Bryson's favourite spot in Britain. If you want a more sedate journey and aerobatics is not your preference, Tommy Rendall will take you across the Papay Sound in his motor vessel.

For an island no more than four miles long by a mile wide Papa Westray, with its fresh water loch and myriad ancient sites, is a world apart in every sense; for many islomaniacs it is the most beautiful piece in our North Isles puzzle. The spectacular cliff, heath and loch settings favoured by birdlife, particularly the Arctic Terns, bring 'twitchers' and confirmed amateur birdwatchers from the world over.

A wall, a windswept community and a way of life which so many envy in the hurly-burly of the 'sooth' – that's North Ronaldsay. This is an island whose conspicuous remoteness finds favour with many visitors, not least Prince Charles, whose trust volunteers have helped repair the famous stone sheep wall which circles North Ronaldsay and keeps the woollies off the cultivated land. The flesh of these seaweed-eating sheep has become popular in some of the top eateries in the land.

Strains and stresses are inevitable in small communities like North Ronaldsay and Papa Westray, where the populations are numbered in tens rather than hundreds, but when necessary people can pull together and pool resources in a way which would astonish more self-seeking societies in the south. Little wonder these little communities hold a fascination for stressed 'soothmoothers', as folk from beyond the Pentland Firth are sometimes known.

South across the cream-topped waves is Tofts Ness, the nearest landfall from North Ronaldsay on the neighbouring island of Sanday. No island in Britain is more appropriately named. Its beaches are second to none – smooth silver sand which in a Mediterranean setting would be crammed with toasting trendies. So, let's thank God that Sanday remains 'cool' only in the literal, old-fashioned sense. The island sustains one of the larger North Isles populations, around the 500 mark, but has welcomed many scores of incomers over the past decades. Some have left again but many have remained, committing their lives to a new Sanday which is slowly emerging.

Spectacular archaeological discoveries including a boat burial indicate Sanday's long history as a settled farming/fishing community. With its light, sandy soils, even the very first farmers must have found Sanday a welcoming place. Being one of the larger of the North Isles Sanday today offers a hotel, cosy bars, trout fishing, acres to explore and a noisy, natural tranquillity of splashing surf and soughing breezes which is the abiding memory for so many visitors.

Stronsay – The Island of the Three Bays – was once a much busier place than it is today. When herring was king the community played host to thousands of seasonal herring workers and it's said that it was possible on a Sunday to walk from Whitehall village to the calf island of Papa Stronsay across the decks of the anchored fleet. The island wears a more tranquil face these days. About one third of the population is non-Orcadian and although detailed statistics are unavailable for the small isles, the perception is that a similar percentage may be found across the sweep of the North Isles.

Stronsay's attendant isles all have special appeal. Papa Stronsay, one of Orkney's holy isles, has recently regained a community of monks maintaining a tradition stretching back to the Dark Ages; Linga Holm and the Holm of Huip are important seal breeding grounds and Auskerry is a lonely outpost to the south, the smallest permanently occupied island in Orkney.

Nipped at the waist is the most graphic description of the long island of Eday. Here you find legends of Orkney's very own Bluebeard, Pirate Gow; strange names like the Bay of Doomy; gloomy, atmospheric chambered tombs; birdlife in abundance, and incongruously, at a grass airstrip in the centre of the isle, London Airport. Natural treasures abound hereabouts and the richness of the botanical environment is illustrated by the fact that the island is recorded as having 120 species of wild plants.

And so the great wheel of islands spins us back to our starting point in Kirkwall Bay.

What are the ties which bind these magical places together? Official information sources which supplement the remarkable island grapevine are among the most significant. *The Orcadian*, the weekly newspaper, has long since achieved saturation cover out in the isles. It is awaited each week with eagerness at the airstrip and pierhead and is devoured before the sun sinks into the Atlantic.

Most mornings the wireless in byre and school bus, bed and breakfast and busy farm kitchen will be tuned to Kirkwall-based BBC Radio Orkney for the news and the all-important weather forecast. And on dark winter evenings the station provides a delightful panoply of Orcadian social life, history and folklore.

But really, the folk of the North Isles need no reminding of their common heritage and achievements. These are not inward-looking, self-centred communities. Over the centuries people, as well as moving within the isles, have voyaged to Kirkwall, and on to the likes of the Hudson Bay or the hills of Otago. A wee lass may point out across the surf to a neighbouring isle and tell you that's where Auntie Robina or Uncle Magnus live. Just as likely she'll then turn to the curve of the western horizon adding: 'And Uncle Willie bides in Canada.'

Nowadays the telephone, and increasingly the internet, provide an electronic bridge across the vast oceans. On Papa Westray, I remember the day when I realised that the new technology was here to stay. We stood in the gloomy wee post office at Backaskaill and watched the then postie Jim Rendall download photographs of a family wedding that happened that same day – in New Zealand.

As well as the encircling sea, these generally low-lying islands also share a big sky, so tall and open that people more accustomed to comfortable Highland glens can feel crushed by the immensity of it. This sky carries great battlements of clouds. It's said with some degree of accuracy that you can often tell what the weather holds hence by watching the activity on the western skyline dozens of miles away. I once saw a group of tourists awaiting a boat trip left speechless and stunned by a prediction from my creeling colleague, Jim, that the rain would stop at precisely 8.13 p.m. – which it duly did. A good guess or centuries of accumulated weather wisdom. Who knows?

Nowadays most of the small isles have tele-centres and distance learning stations where islanders who have not already plugged in to the new technology can make use of the web, fax and e-mail facilities to contact friends and family overseas or even to continue their education. This is a place with its feet securely anchored in a marvellous, colourful past but with an eye very much on the future.

In Orkney's North Isles the people, through their community councils, meeting in the local hall, school or community room, exert far more influence on their destiny than folk elsewhere, due in no small measure to the willingness of Orkney Islands Council to devolve powers wherever possible.

Most of all, any exploration of this scatter of islands must inevitably be a personal journey. Everyone has a favourite island, a favourite view, a favourite anecdote of the couthy Orcadians. Perhaps more than anything, however, you will be struck, as adventurers, landscape painters and photographers have been in the past, by the cascading luminosity of this place where light lays siege to the senses. It spills out of the great vault of the sky, mica-dancing across the surf, out over the loch and field, cliff and croft, a spring tide of sunlight. As George Mackay Brown, the bard of these islands, said: 'At such times the world is drenched in light.'

And so back, finally, to our jigsaw. Just one more piece to place and it will be complete. This depicts a wave, cream-capped, tumbling to the shore, a child of the great encircling ocean which continues to shape and give meaning to the North Isles of Orkney.

CHAPTER SIXTEEN

The West Mainland

THE LANDSCAPE OF THE MAINLAND rises from the low-lying farmlands of the east to the hills and cliffs of the west. Here we find no less than seven RSPB reserves and habitats that support a variety of wildlife. There are three roads that lead west from Kirkwall. The main Kirkwall to Stromness road runs along the coast of the Bay of Firth to Finstown. To the south is the road to Orphir which joins the main road near the Brig o' Waithe, and the old road to Stromness, known as the Old Finstown Road, which runs to the south of Wideford Hill.

If we take the latter road we climb the lower slopes of the 225 m high Wideford Hill before descending towards the parish of Firth. The view from the top of this hill gives excellent panoramic vistas over much of Orkney. Continuing west we travel downwards before the ground rises once more to give a commanding view over the Bay of Firth. On this rising ground is the Old Manse of Firth, home of the late Jo Grimond, one-time leader of the Liberal Party and MP for Orkney and Shetland from 1950 to 1983. In the bay lie two small green islands. The nearest is the Holm of Grimbister, joined to the Mainland by a causeway accessible at low tide. The outer island is Damsay, once the site of a Norse hall and the scene of the slaying of Earl Erlend in 1154. Damsay was later the site of a nunnery, which led to legends that no frogs, toads or any noxious animals could live there. Unmarried women who became pregnant were said to go to Damsay to pray at the abandoned shrine of St Mary in the belief that the nuns would abort the unwanted child.

The road joins the main Kirkwall to Stromness road at the village of Finstown. This village grew up around the meeting place of the roads from Kirkwall to Stromness, Evie and Rendall and the Redland road around Firth. The village, originally called the Toon o' Firt (Town of Firth) was renamed Finstown in honour of David Phin, an Irish soldier and veteran of the Napoleonic Wars who ran an inn called the Toddy Hole. To the west is a deep valley that shelters the Binscarth Woods, while above it sits Binscarth House, the one-time seat of the Scarth family. There is a footpath from the road that leads through woods which have been planted around the burn that runs through the valley, once powering the old watermill before running into the bay. The road north from Finstown leads towards Rendall. By the side of this road we find a large mound, probably containing the ruins of a fortified Iron Age broch, on top of which has been built a concrete pillbox dating from the Second World War. Orkney is filled with this continuity of use from the earliest times to the present day.

The road passes through low flat moorland, while the land to the west rises to a ridge of hills. There is a large and unique 16th-century doocot at the Hall of Rendall, beehive in shape with projecting stone courses to supposedly prevent rats from entering the building. The side roads that lead towards the sea provide splendid views of Gairsay and the Inner Isles. The Lyde road takes you over the hill to Harray, the only parish in Orkney that does not border the sea. This lack of shoreline led to real hardship during times of famine due to crop failure. While other parishes relied on 'ebb meat' to supplement their diet, Harray people were forced to travel long distances to reach neighbouring shores. Certain parts of the coast in Rendall, Birsay and Sandwick were set aside as the 'Harrayman's ebb'. A row of small upright stones among the heather of Milldoe Hill on the border between Harray and Rendall called the 'Harraymen's graves' are said to mark the graves of a group of Harray men who were travelling to the Rendall shore to gather shellfish during a time of famine. They were caught in a blizzard and, in their weakened state, died of exposure. When their bodies were discovered they were buried where they lay. These heather covered hills and moors are an important breeding ground for hen harriers, although their numbers are sadly in decline.

Although Harray has no sea coast it is the home of the largest loch in Orkney. The relatively shallow Harray Loch covers an area of 989 ha, and is home to a population of wild brown trout. Like its neighbour, the brackish watered Stenness Loch (into which Harray Loch flows) the angler will find plenty of sport using either boat or waders. The one thing that surprises many visitors to Orkney is that these wonderful lochs full of brown trout are absolutely free to fishermen. The only thing that is asked of them is that they close gates behind them and respect the countryside. Not too high a price to pay!

On the northern banks of the Harray Loch is the Merkister Hotel, one-time home of the Orkney writer Eric Linklater, who enlarged the original house, built by his father. It is gratifying to know that one of his daughters has recently bought a home in the West Mainland, maintaining the family connection with the isles. Another link with the past is the award-winning Corrigall Farm Museum, a traditional Orkney farmhouse that gives the modern visitor a taste of life in the 19th century. On Harray's western border lies the village of Dounby. This is a relatively recent development that has grown up around the crossroads that leads from Harray to Sandwick, Birsay and Evie.

North of the crossroads, over the moors and peat hills, is Evie village. On the shore below the village lies the Iron Age Broch of Gurness, discovered by local poet and painter Robert Rendall when he was setting up his easel on top of the mound. The leg of the easel opened up a hole which Rendall enlarged, finding the staircase inside the thickness of the broch walls. The Sands of Evie, next to the broch, is a good place to see waders, and to look for 'grottie buckies' (European cowrie shells), once thought of as a good luck charm. Burgar Hill has been home to experimental wind generators since 1980. Three huge windmills feed electricity into the national grid, replacing previous smaller ones. From Burgar Hill there are magnificent views over the Inner and North Isles, as well as a hide where birdwatchers can see a variety of waterfowl, including red-throated divers that nest here. In the sound between Rousay and the Mainland lies the small island of Eynhallow, where the ruins of a 12th-century monastery can be seen. The land rises to the north-west, where Costa Hill gives a commanding view over the Atlantic Ocean. This site was chosen in 1949 to be the home of an earlier experimental wind generator, as it was claimed that it was the most consistently windy place in Britain.

Crossing over the border into Birsay we pass the Loch of Swannay, a place where the trout have the reputation of being fighters. Birsay can boast two other large lochs that are famous for their fishing, the Loch of Hundland and the Loch of Boardhouse. Carrying on past farmland that rises and falls we arrive at Birsay Village, dominated by the ruins of the Earl's Palace. This old seat of power was once the home of Robert Stewart, illegitimate son of King James V and half brother of Mary, Queen of Scots, who bestowed the title of Earl of Orkney and Lord of Shetland on him. Work on the palace was begun in 1569 and finished before Robert's death in 1593. It later fell into ruin and was used as a source of building stone. Robert Stewart was not the first to use Birsay as the seat of power in Orkney, for it was also the site of Earl Thorfinn the Mighty's palace in the 11th century. Here he built Orkney's first cathedral, Christ Kirk, a fine stone cruciform building that was the seat of the early bishops of Orkney. It was to this church that the body of St Magnus was taken for burial after his murder in c. 1117. His relics were later taken to Kirkwall where the cathedral dedicated to him was built to house his remains. The site of this early cathedral has for many years been disputed; some believe it lay in the village while others think it was situated on the small tidal island of the Brough of Birsay. The ruins of the church and graveyard on the Brough of Birsay, with its attendant settlement, are thought to date from the 12th century. Local tradition had it that the ruins of Christ Kirk lay in the village. Under the present day 18th-century parish church, which is dedicated to St Magnus, archaeologists have found the remains of a substantial building with decorative red sandstone corners. Could this be the missing cathedral?

The Brough of Birsay was a Pictish settlement before the Vikings arrived in their longships. This small island is only accessible at low tide but has much to offer the visitor. Its western cliffs, topped by a small lighthouse, are home to colonies of nesting seabirds. A short walk northwards along the coast leads to Skippigeo (ON – 'ship inlet'), where many boat nousts can be seen, along with the restored sailhouse that was used by local fishermen. Heading south the road takes you past the Boardhouse Mill, restored and open to the public as a working watermill. The road leading east opposite the mill takes you to the Kirbister Museum, where the last house in Orkney to still use the traditional central hearth gives the visitor the feeling of what life was like two centuries ago.

Following the main road past Boardhouse Mill takes you back to Dounby, but if you take one of the side roads leading west you will find yourself heading south along the coast. Here Marwick Head looms over the Atlantic, crowned with a square tower built in memory of a war hero from a by-gone age. Kitchener's Memorial was built by public subscription to commemorate the death of Field Marshal Earl Kitchener of Khartoum, supreme commander of British forces in the First World War. He was lost along with most of the crew of the cruiser HMS *Hampshire* when she struck a mine and sank during a storm on 5 June 1916. A small deck gun that was illegally salvaged from the wreck now stands in the car park on the lower slopes of Marwick Head. The towering cliffs of Marwick Head are a veritable seabird city during the nesting season, home to guillemots, auks, razorbills, kittiwakes, fulmars and puffins. There are also important wetlands nearby where waterfowl breed among the reed beds. If you are lucky you may see the rare pintail duck, as half of Britain's breeding population are to be found in this area.

Continuing south the road leads to Sandwick, passing Vestra Fiold ('west hill'). Here on the hillside there is a quarry where very large slabs of stone have been prized off the outcropping rock face. It is thought that this was the site where the stone for the Neolithic monuments of the Stones of Stenness and Ring of Brodgar were quarried some 5,000 years ago. Two stones of the same shape and size as those at Brodgar can still be seen propped up on stone supports, as if they were ready to be transported. An archaeological examination in the summer of 2002 supported this theory.

To the south of Vestra Fiold lies the sandy Bay of Skaill. The sand dunes that stretch inland from the bay have preserved the Neolithic village of Skara Brae. Here archaeologists have found not only the stone tools used by the inhabitants, but also bone artefacts, such as beads and pins, which normally rot away in Orkney's acidic soil. This is one of the most famous sites in Europe, and was granted World Heritage status in 1999. Next to it is the historic Skaill House and Skaill Loch.

The cliffs of the west coast are spectacular, and make an interesting walk. There is no better example than the cliffs at Yesnaby. Here we find a landscape blighted by wind and salt spray, resulting in a maritime heath where plants grow close to the ground. The famous Primula Scotica (Scottish primrose) grows in great abundance during late May and early June and again in August. This tiny purple flower with a yellow centre is a survivor from the Ice Age and only grows in the far north of Scotland and Orkney. It is very rare, and is protected by law, so never pick one, or worse still, dig one up. It will not grow in gardens, as it is too highly specialized to live anywhere but the wind blasted cliff tops. There is also an interesting quarry at Yesnaby, where millstones were made from the harder than usual stone. The remains of the quarry can still be seen as holes drilled into the rock to make the first rough shape of the millstone. Local legend has it that an earthquake at sea in the year 1755 caused a tidal wave, which struck the west coast of Orkney with great force. A local lad was herding cattle at Yesnaby when he saw the wave heading towards the cliffs. He ran down to the millstone quarry and shouted and waved at the men who were working there. They ran for safety, knowing that there must be some danger, and just escaped as the wave hit the quarry, sweeping away both the millstone they had been working on and their tools.

The walk south from Yesnaby is magnificent, with high cliffs, caves and rock stacks rising from the sea. While the Castle of Yesnaby is the best-known stack, the more southerly North Gaulton Castle can rival the Old Man of Hoy for sheer beauty and elegance. There are also numerous caves where the boom of the waves can be heard beneath you far inland. Beware of 'bonxies' (great skuas), who will dive-bomb any unwary person who ventures into their territory. This walk will take you to the Black Craig in Stromness, where a breathtaking view of the hills and cliffs of Hoy makes sore feet worthwhile. There was once a slate quarry on the lower slopes of the Black Craig, next to which is a cleft in the rocks called the 'Naming Stone'. Here the quarry workers carved their names into the rock, a tradition that continued until the rock face is now covered with names and initials. Continuing down the slopes to the Outertown district of Stromness takes you past Breckness, where the ruins of the old bishop's mansion-house can be seen. It is built on top of an Iron Age broch, the remains of which project from the earth banks. A walk northwards along the beach leads to a wonderful view of the Black Craig and the cave in its base called 'Charlie's Hole', named after a sailor who was marooned in it for several days in 1836 after his sailing ship the *Star of Dundee* was wrecked there. He waited until the gale abated then climbed the cliffs to safety.

Taking the road south from Yesnaby you pass hills to the west, with good views over the Stenness Loch to the east. The town of Stromness is the main ferry port into Orkney, and has its roots fixed firmly in Orkney's maritime heritage of fishing, whaling and the Canadian fur trade. The story is told in the wonderful Stromness Museum. The streets are winding and narrow with buildings made from the warm brown local stone. It has a great character all of its own. Stromness was the home of one of Orkney's most famous sons, the poet and writer George Mackay Brown, whose final resting place is at Warebeth kirkyard, which lies by the side of the Atlantic Ocean.

Taking the main road east from Stromness you come to the Brig o' Waithe, the small bridge that spans the inlet from the Stenness Loch to the sea. Here a long low building by the side of the road was the scene of a wartime tragedy. These houses formed part of a group of buildings that were bombed during a German air raid on Scapa Flow on the evening of 16 March 1940. One of the occupants, James Isbister, was fatally wounded, becoming the first British civilian to be killed in the Second World War. Stenness is famous for its Neolithic monuments. The tomb of Maeshowe and the stone circles of Stones of Stenness and Ring of Brodgar (not Brogar as the signs wrongly call it) were granted World Heritage status, along with Skara Brae, in 1999. Between the hills lies 'Happy Valley,' a wooded garden that is the creation of one man, Edwin Harold, who planted trees along the burn that runs past his house.

Further east through Stenness the Germiston road runs through a valley towards Orphir. To the south of this road is the 268 m high Ward Hill, the highest point on the Mainland. Summerdale lies on the borders between Stenness and Orphir, and was the site of the last pitched battle in Orkney. In 1529 a force led by the earl of Caithness landed in Orphir, probably at the long sandy beach of Waulkmill Bay. (They had intended to land at Scapa Bay and march north to Kirkwall to capture the castle that had fallen into rebel hands.) As they marched through the valley they were attacked by the Orkney men who, legend has it, killed the earl and all his men. Legend also has it that only one Orcadian was killed. A man had stripped the bodies on the battlefield and dressed himself with their fine clothes. On returning home he was struck on the head with a stocking filled with stones by his own mother, who did not recognize him. The nearby Loch of Kirbister is a good fishing ground for the less experienced angler.

Taking the main road west brings you to Houton Bay, from where the ferry to Hoy and Flotta sails. The high ground above the bay gives a wonderful view of the South Isles. To the east of Houton is the Bu, where some of the remains of the earl's hall and farm can be seen. Here too is the local kirkyard, which covers some of the buildings. In the cemetery are the remains of an early 12th-century round church, built by Earl Hakon in atonement for his murder of his cousin St Magnus. Continuing east towards Kirkwall the high land to the north slopes steeply to the sea, and is a patchwork of brown moorland and green farmland. Peats cut here are used in the malting process for making the smoky flavoured Highland Park malt whisky. As you reach the borders with St Ola you can look over Scapa Bay and see the buoy that marks the final resting place of HMS *Royal Oak*.

CHAPTER SEVENTEEN

The East Mainland

THE THREE PARISHES of St Andrews, Deerness and Holm make up the East Mainland of Orkney. The landscape here is gentler than the more rugged scenery of the western part of the Mainland. It is an area known for its fertile farmland, where sleek beef cattle and sheep graze the lush green fields. The airport road from Kirkwall first passes through the district of Tankerness in the parish of St Andrews. Over to the left and down by the coast stands the Hall of Tankerness, the former mansion-house and estate of the Baikie family, who owned the property for 300 years. Earlier, in medieval times, a nearby chapel was dedicated to St Andrew, and this gave the parish its name. In 1135 Earl Paul of Orkney engaged in a sea battle off this coast against Oliver the Unruly, an ally of Rognvald (soon to be Earl of Orkney and the builder of St Magnus Cathedral). On this occasion Earl Paul was victor, capturing five enemy ships.

Modern day Tankerness is home to silversmith Sheila Fleet, and a visit to see the beautiful and distinctive jewellery made in her workshop is well worthwhile. Nearby is Kirkwall's airport. Grimsetter was originally one of four operational aerodromes during the Second World War. Now it is Orkney's main airport, and essential to the islands' social and economic life, linking them to Shetland, Wick, Inverness, Edinburgh, Glasgow and Aberdeen. In addition it is possible to take one of the small Islander planes that fly from Kirkwall airport to Orkney's North Isles of Stronsay, Sanday, Eday, Papay, Westray and North Ronaldsay. There is also an ambulance plane that covers the islands and conveys emergency patients to hospital in Kirkwall or Aberdeen.

One of Orkney's eminent sons was born on a croft that stood where now the main airport runway ends. This man was James Petrie Chalmers, who emigrated to America and became fascinated by the motion picture industry. He founded the *Moving Picture World*, a magazine which is now the major source of information for anyone researching early filmmaking. Chalmers was a well-known figure in the United States and when he died tragically in a lift shaft accident, his obituary appeared on the front page of the *New York Times*.

A left turn takes us past the Tankerness Community Centre, close to the outstanding Iron Age site of Minehowe. The main great mound of this exciting site was opened for the first time in 1946, then excavated professionally in 2000. The literature describes it well:

> Over 50 years after last seeing the light of day the mystery of the 29 steps was reborn. Within the mound is a three-chambered structure reminiscent of a tower sunk into the ground. Access to this sunken chamber is by a steep, ladder-like staircase made up of 12 stone steps that takes the visitor down to a narrow landing from which two long, low chambers branch out at almost right angles. From here, there is a second steep flight of steps, leading down into the darkness and a drop of about five feet into the lower chamber, which is around 20 feet below the entrance.

The function of this structure is uncertain, but it almost certainly was of ritual and ceremonial significance. The mound is surrounded by a huge earthen ditch, but the site extends well beyond this and excavation undertaken by Channel 4's 'Time Team' in 2000 is prompting further archaeological investigation.

It is not only the artefacts from Minehowe that remind us of the Iron Age in this area. In 1867 a woollen hood with a deep fringe of two-ply cord was discovered in the peat moss of nearby Groatsetter. It was in a remarkable state of preservation, and is thought to date from the late Iron Age, making it probably the oldest, best preserved textile in Britain.

The main road continues on across a narrow neck of land, which is all that tethers the parish of Deerness to the Mainland of Orkney. To the left is the shallow bay of St Peter's Pool, a good place to watch the waders that feed there at low tide, while on the opposite side of the road, and backed by sand dunes, lies the sandy bay of Dingieshowe. This name derives from the Old Norse 'Things-howe', which infers that it functioned as a local parliamentary meeting place in Norse times. The mound of the howe, an old broch site, can still be seen. Other evidence of Norse occupation in Deerness includes a Christian cemetery in the attractive sandy Bay of Newark. Excavation here revealed some 200 Norse skeletons, one of which was found to be the remains of a 13th century leper.

Poet Edwin Muir was born in this area in 1888, though shortly afterwards he and his family moved to the island of Wyre. The Muirs' close neighbour in Deerness was an eccentric named William Delday who first spied and declared his love for a creature known as 'the Deerness Mermaid' on the rocks of Newark bay. It was Delday who inspired Muir to write in his autobiography, 'A man I knew once sailed out in a boat to look for a mermaid, and claimed afterwards he had talked to her.' The mermaid, probably a mutant seal, spurned Delday's advances, but Edwin Muir used this tale to make the point that in his day there was little distinction between the ordinary and the fabulous in Orkney.

The island of Copinsay with its satellites of Cornholm, Kirkholm, Blackholm and Wardholm, is clearly visible off the south coast of Deerness.

The Copinsay lighthouse is now unmanned and the farmhouse lies empty, but the whole island is managed by the RSPB as a memorial to the ornithologist James Fisher. This is an attractive island with a variety of flora, and spectacular cliffs on the far side that provide nesting sites for myriad sea birds. Nearby, the squat rocky islet with precipitous sides is known as The Horse of Copinsay and has a large colony of great black-backed gulls.

The parish kirk at Skaill lies further on along the Deerness road. Here in the session house an early 12th-century hogback stone from the Norse period may be seen, which was originally found in the north-east corner of the kirkyard. Thorkel Fosterer, a Norse chieftain, lived here during the 12th century; he was foster father to Earl Thorfinn, Thorkel lived at Skaill at a time when three brothers, Paul, Einar and Thorfinn were jostling for power as co-earls of Orkney. Excavations here have confirmed the presence of a high status Norse site close to earlier Pictish remains. It was in Thorkel's drinking hall at Skaill that a grisly murder took place. As champion of Thorfinn, Thorkel had been in dispute with Earl Einar for some time. Eventually it was decided that each man should entertain the other in turn as an attempt to settle their differences. Things, however, did not go to plan. The feast at Skaill ended, and the party was about to move on to Einar's place, when Thorkel out of the blue struck his guest a tremendous blow with his sword. Earl Einar staggered forwards and fell into the fire, where Hallvard, an Icelander, casually finished him off with a poleaxe.

The road continues on to a large car park area, close to a chasm or 'gloup'. This onomatopoeic word describes a cave with the roof fallen in, that opens out landward as a large chimney. The 70 × 40 m Deerness Gloup is a spectacular sight, and it is also possible to access it by boat from the sea in calm weather. Past the gloup, the track leads on to the Mull Head of Deerness, a nature reserve, now owned by the Orkney Islands Council. The cliffs here house a multitude of nesting seabirds – razorbills, guillemots, puffins and kittiwakes. Cormorants, shags and eider duck also frequent the area. This is an excellent place to walk, especially in late spring when the cliffs are a mass of sea pinks and other cliff-top flora, such as the distinctive blue squill. Later in the summer the delicate white flowers of grass of Parnassus are in bloom, and both common and grey seals inhabit the waters and often haul out on the rocks at low tide.

A narrow and precipitous path leads up on to the Brough of Deerness. Here are the grass-covered foundations of a Norse settlement. Excavation of a rectangular chapel shows that it was built on older foundations, and a very worn 10th-century Anglo-Saxon coin was found between the two layers. This promontory, once linked to the Mainland, was almost certainly an ecclesiastical site. Jo Ben, writing in 1529, tells how people came barefoot to the brough and proceeded on bent knees and with hands clasped to circle the chapel three times, every now and again throwing stones and water behind them. This kind of superstitious practice continued well after the Reformation and similar pilgrimages were still being reported in Orkney into the 18th century.

On the opposite side of the Mull Head stands the Covenanters' Memorial, raised to mark the spot where a ship called the *Crown* was wrecked in 1679. This vessel was bound for the English plantations of the West Indies. Aboard and chained below were some 300 Covenanters, captured in Scotland following the battle of Bothwell Bridge. Storm bound, the ship was wrecked off the Mull Head, but when her mast broke it fell shorewards forming a bridge to the land and this enabled her crew to escape.

Chained below, under battened down hatches, the unfortunate prisoners had no chance. Unable to escape, most of them perished, though, when eventually the ship broke up, about 50 managed to save themselves under cover of darkness despite attempts by the crew to hurl back into the sea any poor wretch who made it to the rocks. Those who could find a ship to carry them fled abroad. In the year 2000 a small party from the USA, descended from one of the survivors, visited the site of the tragedy. The stone tower memorial was not erected from money raised locally from public subscription, but through funds gifted by a South American visiting Orkney in 1888.

Off the north coast of the parish is the excellent natural harbour of Deersound, where 18th-century sailing vessels used to gather each year before heading off to the whaling and fishing grounds of the Davis Straits and Iceland. Many Orcadians eagerly signed on as crew here, for a season's work could earn a man as much as £12 and was therefore an important source of income. At that time many Deerness men found employment on the high seas. A native of the parish, James Tait, was a member of the crew on board the ship that took Napoleon to exile on the island of Elba, during which time he had several conversations with the great man. However, James Tait returned home with something more tangible than remembered conversation, for the former emperor, now in sunnier climes, presented the Orcadian with the gift of his now redundant greatcoat. You might have expected to find this souvenir on display in a place of honour at the Orkney Museum, but not so. Tait was a pragmatic fellow, and for many years he was thankful for the warmth the greatcoat gave him as he worked away through many cold winters on his farm in Deerness, until at length the garment was discarded having become quite threadbare and worn out!

Before the advent of agricultural improvement in the 19th century, the land was farmed in runrig. Agriculture was then based on the growing of grain and farmers lived in small interdependent communities called townships, cultivating strips of intermingled land in a pattern of farming that had developed back in Norse times. In such close-knit communities it was essential to have rules and regulations governing farming practice, and a procedure whereby disputes could be resolved and those who flouted these

'Country Acts' could be disciplined. This was done at local level in bailie courts when the whole parish met together, and the bailie dispensed justice, misdemeanours usually not attracting more than a small fine.

Helping the bailie police the parish and resolve disputes were the lawrightmen, local men of good character and standing in the community. Only one Orkney bailie court book has survived, and this is the one for the parishes of St Andrews and Deerness. This record gives an invaluable picture of the methods used to maintain traditional farming practice. While the crops grew, any livestock were banished to the rough hill ground outside the high turf dyke that encircled and protected the townships' arable land. However, disputes when they arose could be fierce, and if one man encroached on another man's land, or his livestock got into another man's corn, the bailie and his lawrightmen acted as arbiters through the local bailie court.

Eagles, common in Orkney at this time, were dangerous predators of the small native sheep that roamed the hill and Orkney bailies were obliged to offer a reward to anyone who managed to destroy one. The son of the miller in Deerness must have been delighted when he managed to kill an eagle in 1657, for which he was rewarded by the Bailie, who decreed that every household in the parish should pay the lad the sum of two shillings Scots, or a hen! Many of the farm and place-names survive from those days, but there have been profound changes in farming practice which is now based on the raising and export of beef cattle. When the land was first improved in the 19th century, most farms effectively supported three generations of one family, but though now agricultural units are much larger, it is often a struggle to make enough profit to support just one generation.

Returning along the road from Deerness to St Andrews, a turn left past the primary school that serves the whole East Mainland, leads over the hill to the farm of Hurtiso in the parish of Holm. This is a good place to pause for it provides a superb view over the South Isles with Scapa Flow in the distance. To the left, on the headland of Roseness, stands a stone Victorian navigational tower known as the 'daymark' together with, nearer the point, a modern lighthouse. Roseness was once a centre for the smuggling trade, providing hidden landing places and easy access direct from the North Sea for ships laden with contraband from the Low Countries. This was the route taken from the North Sea by Commander Prien in U-boat 47, past the headland of Roseness and between the block ships that lay in the channel of water between the Mainland and the island of Lambholm, now connected by the first Churchill barrier.

The district to the left of Hurtiso is known as Paplay, and Castle Howe, probably a Norse castle site built on more ancient foundations, lies close to the shore opposite the ancient church site of St Nicholas. The beach below the church is a good place to watch grey and common seals when they haul out onto the rocks at low tide. Paplay was an important earldom estate in Norse times, and formed a wedding dowry for the sister of St Magnus. It was here that Earl Hakon confessed to Thora, the mother of Earl Magnus, that he had murdered her son. In 1656 Patrick Graham, second son of Bishop George Graham, re-built the substantial old house of Greenwall in Paplay which eventually became the dower house of Graemeshall.

Turning to the right, the road continues past the Holm Battery with its lookout tower and old gun emplacements that lie close to the cliff edge. Past the Holm war memorial and down the hill the road passes between Graemeshall loch and the once sandy but now badly eroded Graemeshall Bay. Until the beginning of the 20th century most of the parish of Holm was part of the Graemeshall estate. The mansion-house of Graemeshall, formerly the House of Meall, was acquired by Bishop Graham in 1626, and his descendants lived there until the late 1950s. The present house was extensively renovated in 1874, and later a chapel was added. Graemeshall is now home to the Norwood antiques: a collection lovingly built up by one man over many years.

The turning to the first barrier across to the island of Lambholm lies a short way past Graemeshall, and opposite is the Commodore Motel, built on the former site of Rockworks, the headquarters of Balfour Beatty, contractors for the Churchill barriers building works. Lambholm was part of the Graemeshall estate, and during the Second World War the Italian prisoners there often visited the mansion-house, and Domenico Chiocchetti, creator of the Italian chapel, formed a lasting friendship with the Graeme family.

The road leads on to St Mary's, a planned village built to promote the fishing industry. The first buildings were erected in the 1830s, but before that only two buildings stood in the bay. The first was the old Storehouse, on the seaward side, built in 1649 to store estate rents, which were paid then mostly in grain and butter. In 1694 French privateers raided the building, clearing it of its contents, and over the years this old structure has functioned, not only for the accumulation of estate rents, but also as a store for kelp and to stow the freight from wrecked sailing vessels. During the days when the herring industry prospered, the building provided a workshop for coopers, who made barrels for the salted herring before they were exported from Orkney to the Baltic ports of Europe.

The house of Westshore, or Whitehouse, also stood in the bay, a substantial building that was converted into The Ferry Inn during the 18th century. The Holm ferry was important to the islands. In the 17th century the ferryman was bound to be ready at a moment's notice to carry the bishop or his followers on the first leg of their journey south. It was from this bay that the Marquis of Montrose embarked in 1650, his army swelled by a body of inexperienced Orcadians, unused to war. They were bound for Carbisdale and bitter defeat, from which few Orkney men ever returned.

During the latter part of the 19th century the herring fishing industry thrived here and the village of St Mary's was a hive of activity, especially after the pier was completed in 1877. This was an occasion marked with due ceremony. There was a parade and speeches were made. All the herring boats were dressed overall, and when the bunting ran out, the decorations were enhanced by the addition of brightly coloured ladies' petticoats that fluttered gaily in the breeze from the masts of the herring boats.

When the brown-sailed boats, laden with herring, were sighted returning to Holm Sound, the village was said to resemble an ant heap when prodded with a stick, as workers hurried down to the pier from every direction. First the herring were unloaded at the end of the pier into carts that trundled down with the catch to the herring gutters. Once cleaned and gutted, the fish were salted and packed into barrels. The village grew and prospered through the herring trade, and at one time there were four shops that sold supplies to the crews of herring vessels. Alas, at the outbreak of the First World War ships were deliberately sunk to block the four channels on the eastern side of Scapa Flow, and this effectively blocked the route the herring boats took out into the North Sea, and the industry here never recovered from this blow.

During the Second World War barrage balloons were manufactured in the building now occupied by Alfie Flett's building firm and, round the corner opposite the Loch of Ayre, a large nissen hut housed a cinema to entertain members of the troops from local batteries. Later in the war, even the Italian prisoners of war were brought here from Lambholm on one occasion to see a show. Now a quieter place, the village is an attractive spot. The local community centre has been transformed with the aid of lottery grants and there is an active and lively community spirit. An Iron Age broch, close to the loch shores, reminds us of earlier human occupation, and evidence of cist burials and implements such as hammer stones have been recovered from local farmland in Holm.

The road that leads back into Kirkwall continues through agricultural countryside past green fields of beef cattle and sheep. As in other districts of Orkney, farm names on the route overwhelmingly echo their Norse origin – Backakelday (ON Bakkar-kelda = slope, spring-well), Blomuir (ON Blo-mor = blue moor or heath), Hestwall (ON hest(a)-vollr = horse moor or heath), Westerbister (ON vestr-bolstadr = west farm settlement) and Easterbister (ON austr-bolstadr = east farm settlement). In some cases there has been remarkably long continuity of occupation. Laughtons were living in the farm of Easterbister back in 1492, and the Laughtons continued to be named as tenants in the rentals until that family bought the property which they still farm today.

We follow a route parallel to the eastern shores of Scapa Flow, and passing the old radar station of Netherbutton. On the night of 13/14 September 1939 the battleship HMS *Royal Oak* was guarding this facility when she was torpedoed and sunk with the tragic loss of 833 lives. Here and there along the route the remains of other buildings dating from the

Second World War can be seen. This was Orkney's first formed road connecting Kirkwall to the Holm ferry on the first leg of the journey south to the Scottish mainland. Now it passes through pleasant undulating agricultural land, descending past the Highland Park distillery back into Kirkwall and completing the circuit of the East Mainland of Orkney.

CHAPTER EIGHTEEN

The South Isles

T HE SOUTH ISLES FORM A CHAIN OF ISLANDS that encircle the great natural harbour of Scapa Flow. Opposite the town of Stromness, the green island of Graemsay supports a small community and the island's children travel by boat each day to school in the town. The two lighthouses on Graemsay are automatic now, and are called, somewhat confusingly, after the neighbouring island, Hoy High and Hoy Low.

The landscape of the island of Hoy was created by its own system of glaciers that carved out corries and created glaciated valleys, making the scenery more reminiscent of the Highlands of Scotland rather than the low and fertile green of other parts of Orkney. Hoy is Orkney's second largest island and its ward hill, the highest in Orkney, rises 434 m from sea level. As a result, the Norse named the island Hoy (Ha'ey meaning 'high island'). While there is good farmland near sea level, much of Hoy remains covered by rough moorland. This is a paradise for walkers and it is possible to climb the heather-clad ward hill from Sandy loch and to continue along the ridge of hills that eventually descend into the Bay of Rackwick. There is also the opportunity to take a walk through deep heather to the Kame of Hoy and up to the spectacular perpendicular cliffs of St John's Head (335 m). The nearby valley of Berriedale boasts the remains of the most northerly natural woodland in the UK including aspen, rowan, willow, hazel and birch, which may well reflect the typical ground cover in Orkney during the Neolithic period before the climate deteriorated. Sub-arctic and alpine plants grow here and may also be found at lower levels. Great skuas can be a hazard in this area as they tend to divebomb visitors who invade their moorland habitat during the breeding season. Mountain hare, with their distinctive white winter coats, also live in the hills of North Hoy, though not elsewhere in Orkney. The Old Man of Hoy (137 m) is the tallest rock stack in Britain and, when viewed from the cliff top looks even more spectacular than when glimpsed from the Orkney ferry as it plies its way between Scrabster and Stromness.

Past the Old Man of Hoy, the cliff path eventually descends into the hauntingly beautiful valley and Bay of Rackwick, once a community of crofter fishermen. Most of the fishermen eventually abandoned their harsh life and by the 1950s the settlement had become virtually deserted. Now many of the small crofts have been renovated and are used by their new owners for weekends and holidays. One of them, the 'Crow's Nest', has been expertly restored to function as a small crofting museum. It was in a croft in this valley of Rackwick that composer Sir Peter Maxwell Davies wrote many of his most celebrated works, and this remote valley has also provided an inspiration for the poetry and prose of Orkney poet and author, George Mackay Brown.

The visitor has the choice of returning to the pier by a track that runs between the hills, or by road from which a short track leads up to the 'Dwarfie stane', Britain's only Neolithic rock-cut tomb with two chambers on either side of the entrance, and a blocking stone close by. The eccentric Major William Mouncey, a Victorian spy in Persia and Afghanistan, spent several nights here in 1850. Dressed in Persian costume, he carved his own version of Persian graffiti that may still be seen on the outside stonework. Much of the rough moorland of North Hoy is managed by the RSPB as a bird reserve. Here and there are small plantations of trees that have met with mixed success.

A turning to the left returns to Moaness pier, while to the right the road continues on towards the southern part of the island, called Walls. On the border between the two parishes of North Hoy and Walls and close by the road, lies the lonely grave of Betty Corrigall, a young pregnant woman who was deserted by her sweetheart, and in despair threw herself into the sea. Suicide was a grievous sin then and instead of burial in consecrated ground, she was interred in a no man's land between the two parishes.

The ro-ro ferry crosses from Houton on the Orkney Mainland to Lyness in the parish of Walls. This was formerly the headquarters of the Royal Navy as base and communications centre during the Second World War. Among the remains of wartime buildings that litter the landscape there is an excellent museum and interpretation centre. Housed in the former oil pumping station, it lies within walking distance of the pier and is well worth a visit, and gives a good idea of Orkney's strategic importance during two world wars. Behind the pump house, one of the great oil fuel tanks has been preserved as an impressive display area with the opportunity to see a short film. Nearby the well-kept naval cemetery is a stark reminder of the cost of war, with burials of crew from the *Royal Oak*, the *Vanguard*, the *Hampshire* and some of the victims of the battle of Jutland. In addition a small section on its own is given over to the graves of German aircrew. Many well-known stars visited Hoy to entertain the troops during the Second World War, including Evelyn Laye, Tommy Handley, Vera Lynn, George Formby and Gracie Fields.

The potential of Scapa Flow as a safe haven was recognised well before the major conflicts of the 20th century. During the Napoleonic wars the English Channel was a hazardous place for merchant ships and many chose to sail north-about Britain to reach the Baltic ports of Europe. It was off Walls in the Bay of Longhope that these vessels would gather, awaiting escort in convoy by armed naval ships. Two Martello towers, built in 1813, stand sentinel on either side of the bay, and the one at Hackness has been restored and is open to visitors.

Situated in the parish of Walls, Melsetter is an exceptionally fine mansion-house of the Arts and Crafts period. The architect was William Lethaby, who also designed nearby Rysa Lodge. At Melsetter he incorporated and extended the existing buildings for the Middlemore family in 1898, keeping the traditional crow-step gables and creating a fine and elegant home. Some of the original furniture and furnishings remain in the house, designed by such as Morris & Co., Ford Maddox Brown and Philip Webb. After staying at Melsetter, the daughter of William Morris wrote, 'For all its fineness and dignity it was a place full of homeliness and the spirit of welcome, a very loveable place.'

The small village of Longhope gives its name to a lifeboat station that has seen its fair share of tragedy. On 17 March 1969 the lifeboat *T.G.B.* was called out in storm conditions to rescue a Liberian-registered vessel, the *Irene*. This ship eventually beached on South Ronaldsay and the crew were able to walk off her onto dry land unharmed. The lifeboat men were not so fortunate and when their vessel turned turtle, all the crew were drowned. A moving memorial to the men of Longhope who lost their lives stands in the kirkyard overlooking Kirk Hope Bay, where the bronze figure of a lifeboatman by artist Ian Scott of North Ronaldsay has been erected, and around which the bodies of those lost in the tragedy lie buried. The memorial stands as a fitting tribute to the traditions of the service. The crew came from just a handful of families, and it is impressive that a replacement crew from this small community had volunteered within a week of the tragedy. One thousand years earlier this bay saw Earl Sigurd undergo forcible conversion to Christianity under threat of death by Olaf Trygesson.

Close to Hoy lie the four small uninhabited islands of Rysa Little, South Fara, Switha and Cava, though the last three supported communities into the 20th century. Indeed, in the 18th century the pirate Gow and his followers raided the island of Cava and made off with three young women. Later they unceremoniously deposited the unfortunate females back on their island shore, but they had been used so badly that one of them expired then and there on the beach, before she could reach her home and family.

The Vikings showed a distinct lack of imagination in their selection of Orkney place-names. Near to Hoy (the high island), lies Flotta, 'Flat-ey' which means 'the flat island'. This island came to the fore when a large oil terminal was built there following the discovery of the Piper Claymore oil fields in the North Sea. Developed by Occidental, the first oil flowed into the Flotta terminal in 1976 and in 1997 oil from the new Foinhaven field began to be brought here by tanker. Ownership of the terminal eventually passed to the Elf Consortium, and at present it is owned by

Talisman Energy (UK) Limited, a Canadian company. The Flotta flare can be clearly seen from far and wide in Orkney, a symbol of the renaissance in the economic and commercial development of the islands. Orkney benefits from the oil industry, both as a source of employment and a source of income.

At the outbreak of war in 1939 there were nine channels leading in and out of Scapa Flow, five of which were protected by boom defence and coastal batteries, while the remaining four separating the islands of Lambholm, Glimsholm, Burray and South Ronaldsay were guarded less effectively by batteries and block ships. Following the sinking of the battleship *Royal Oak* in 1939 by a German U-boat, concrete barriers were constructed which now permanently connect these islands to each other and on to the Orkney Mainland in the parish of Holm.

The building of the barriers was an immense task. First of all half a million tons of rubble in steel cages were dropped into the sea via overhead cableways, and this was followed by one third of a million tons of 5- or 10-ton concrete blocks. Small railways on the islands transported stone from local quarries. To counteract the acute shortage of wartime labour, Italian prisoners of war were brought to Orkney in January 1942 to help with the building work. About 300 were imprisoned on the island of Lambholm and a further 300 on Burray. Although the Italians protested that this type of work was against the terms of the Hague Convention, a certain economy with the truth eventually persuaded them that they were not building barriers to keep out the enemy, but were simply constructing causeways to enhance the islanders' quality of life.

The commandant of Camp 60 on the island of Lambholm, Major Buckland, provided the POWs with two nissen huts for recreational purposes and the Italians decided that one should become a chapel and the other used for educational purposes. In the event they were combined, and under the inspired leadership of Domenico Chiocchetti, artists and craftsmen among the Italian prisoners created a chapel that shines like a sparkling jewel in this small green isle.

The men used whatever resources they could find around them. Bully beef tins became lanterns. Stair rods were forged into candlesticks. Materials stripped from the old blockships were put to good use, as tiles were recycled for the floor of the sanctuary, and salvaged wood made into a tabernacle for the altar. Bruttapasta created this altar and also the concrete façade of the building. Above the entrance, the face of Christ has been movingly modelled in red clay by Pennisi. The wrought iron rood screen is a masterpiece and was created by Palumbo using a 40-gallon oil drum as a forge. Under Chiocchetti's supervision the plasterboard interior was transformed. Painted as brickwork above with a dado of stonework below, it presents an extraordinarily convincing solid three-dimensional effect that visitors are tempted to reach out and touch, just to convince themselves that the materials are not genuine.

The symbols of the four gospel writers, and a dove representing the Holy Spirit decorate the ceiling of the sanctuary, and above the altar is Domenico Chiocchetti's painting of 'Regina Pacis', based on a picture of the Virgin Mother and Child by Barabina, that he carried with him throughout the war. On the rear wall on each side of the altar are windows, painted to give a stained glass effect, depicting St Catherine of Sienna and St Francis of Assissi. Outside the chapel in the former camp square, stands Domenico Chiocchetti's first work, a statue of St George slaying the dragon, constructed in cement over a wire frame and symbolising the triumph of the Italians over defeat and loneliness. Concealed in the base of the statue is a list containing the names of all the prisoners of war who lived and worked on the island.

The Italians left Orkney in the spring of 1945, though Chiocchetti stayed on for a few weeks to complete the font. Following the war the camp was demolished, all except the chapel. The then owner of the island, Patrick Sutherland Graeme, had promised the Italians that Orcadians would cherish this building, but over the years it began to deteriorate. However, a preservation committee was eventually formed and in 1960 Chiocchetti returned to restore the chapel; over the years a warm relationship grew up between the people of Orkney and Chiocchetti's hometown of Moena in the Dolomites. The Italian chapel has become one of the most visited sites in Orkney. Italians, once prisoner here, have returned as honoured guests to celebrate the work of art they created. This small masterpiece on the windswept island of Lambholm moves people, perhaps because it is all that remains of a prison camp and it stands there as a symbol that it is not possible to confine the creative spirit of man.

The Italian prisoner of war camp was not Lambholm's first encounter with European visitors. In 1694 French privateers raided the island. They stayed a week, destroying the growing crops, sinking the fishing boats and eventually making off with all they could lay their hands on. Cattle, bulls, sheep and pigs, meal, grain and butter were all plundered, together with household possessions – boiling pots and pans, woollen and linen webs and yarn, and fishing lines. The farm on Lambholm was eventually destroyed by fire in the 19th century and the Laughton family there were re-housed in what is now the Foveran Hotel outside Kirkwall. Lambholm is uninhabited now, but it boasts a private airfield and hangar, and in the old quarry lobster fry are farmed for eventual release into the waters around Orkney.

The second barrier joins the island of Lambholm to the uninhabited island of Glimsholm. This barrier is the most likely to become impassable during winter storms when great waves break across the roadway, often bearing large stones which can easily smash a car windscreen. Under such dangerous conditions, the barriers are closed to vehicles, much to the delight of the secondary schoolchildren of Burray and South Ronaldsay, who are normally bussed into Kirkwall each day. Here and there along the barriers the jagged remains of rusty blockships protrude from the water, lying where they were sunk to protect the channels between the islands before the barriers were built.

Glimsholm is joined to the island of Burray by the third barrier. This is a thriving little island that sports its own café, museum, shop, school, village, church, petrol station, pub and hotel. Burray was once part of the earldom estate, centred on the Bu of Burray. When the irascible Sir James Stewart lived here in the mid 18th century the island was in the forefront of agricultural innovation and an inventory shows Stewart had an astonishing collection of farm implements, rare in Scotland at the time. Sir James Stewart was involved in a celebrated affray in Broad Street in Kirkwall resulting in the murder of his political rival, Captain James Moodie. A supporter of the Jacobite cause, Stewart ended his days in Southwark Jail.

An earlier barrier, completed in 1941, connects the west side of Burray to the uninhabited island of Hunda. The main road, however, continues across a natural barrier of shingle called an 'ayre' that built up across the bay, eventually cutting off a body of water from the top of the bay, thus forming a loch. According to folklore, ayres were created by giants, and the derivation of the name 'Echnaloch' is thought to stem from 'Yetnaloch', the word *yetna* being the Old Norse word for 'giant', giving a neat illustration of the importance of Norse folklore in Orkney's heritage. The village on Burray, like St Mary's in Holm, was once a centre for the herring fishing industry, but after ships were sunk to block the channels between the islands the industry fell into decline.

The construction of the Churchill barriers has affected the coastline in the vicinity. There has been severe erosion of Graemeshall Bay on the Orkney Mainland, which was once a sandy beach, but is now strewn with shingle and stone that is thrown up and across the coastal road in stormy weather. By contrast, an enormous amount of sand has built up to the east of the fourth barrier connecting Burray to the island of South Ronaldsay, creating new land, and virtually combining the two islands into one. The road continues on round the coast towards the attractive village of St Margaret's Hope. Before the barriers were built this was the trading centre of the South Isles and in the 1890s there were 20 different shops and 18 tradesmen doing business in the village and people came by boat from islands such as Burray, Hoy and Flotta to do their shopping.

Some have suggested that the village owes its name to Margaret, Maid of Norway, last heir to the Scottish throne in the Canmore line. As a small child, she was betrothed to the son of Edward I, Hammer of the Scots, and brought from Norway to Orkney at the tender age of seven to be handed over to the English. However, the little girl sickened and died in Orkney so never reached her future kingdom. There is also a medieval chapel in the bay dedicated to St Margaret and the word 'Hope' derives from *Hjop*, an old Norse word meaning 'bay', so, despite the fact that little Margaret was regarded as a saint in Norway, the name of the village may merely stem from the development on this site of a chapel in the bay.

A regular car ferry service transports passengers and vehicles from St Margaret's Hope to Gill's Bay on the Scottish mainland. Many of the stone houses along the shoreline of this picturesque village have been built with their crow-stepped gables end on to the sea, each house originally with its own slipway. Before the construction of roads, the sea was the main highway, and herring fishing was an important industry in South Ronaldsay until the First World War. There are several restaurants in the village, a small blacksmith's museum, a pottery and a good craft shop that sells the work of local artists and craftspeople from all over the island.

Each August a colourful and unique event takes place in 'The Hope' in Cromarty Square. This is the Boys' Ploughing Match, during which everyone gathers in the square to see the parade of the horses and ploughmen. Little girls dressed in dark jackets and shorts, brightly decorated with ribbons and rosettes complete with harness, play the part of the horses, while small boys with miniature ploughs, often handed down from previous generations, are the ploughmen. After the parade and judging of the 'horses' the event continues on the Sands o' Right outside the village on the Hoxa road. There the boys are judged on their expertise in ploughing furrows in the sand.

Opposite the Sands o' Right, the Howe of Hoxa, a broch site, is said to be the burial place of Earl Thorfinn, 'Skull Splitter'. The road continues on to the Hoxa Tapestry Gallery with a wonderful viewpoint over Scapa Flow, and the area acts as an inspiration for much of the work of tapestry artist Leila Thomson. At the end of the Hoxa road there is a pleasant walk round the cliffs of Hoxa Head, the site of First and Second World War batteries.

The main South Ronaldsay road leads south from the junction to St Margaret's Hope. A turning off to the left leads down to St Peter's Kirk, a building that dates from 1642. There are interesting old gravestones here and a narrow communion table that runs the length of the church interior. A little farther along the main road, a detour to the right leads to the attractive little fishing hamlet of Herston, with gardens that border the shore.

Farther southwards, at Olad's Brae, there is a good view of the small low island of Swona. This island supported a community until 1974 and, although the population abandoned the island at that time, they left behind much of their farm equipment and furniture. More importantly they left their cattle, which over the years have evolved into a wild herd, now officially recognised as a unique breed.

The road continues on past Tomison's Academy, a former school founded by William Tomison, a native of South Ronaldsay and once Governor of the Hudson's Bay Company. Having amassed a considerable fortune, he gave £6,000 to found this free school for the local inhabitants.

When it first opened it had 170 pupils, with just one teacher. The school closed in the 1960s, and it is hoped to transform the building into a museum that will provide information regarding the strong links between Orkney and the Hudson's Bay Company in Canada. William Tomison did not wish to risk his remains being disturbed by pigs rooting for food in the kirkyard, so his body lies buried nearby in the garden of Dundas House, his former home.

The Tomb of the Eagles can be reached by a turn to the left before the road terminates at Burwick. Here, a new interpretation centre has been built where the story of the tomb is told and where unprecedented finds are on display. Ronald Simison's conducted tour of an Iron Age house and adjoining burnt mount is not to be missed; neither is the spectacular Neolithic tomb near the cliff edge where bones belonging to more than 300 human skeletons were found, together with talons of numerous white-tailed sea eagles. It is thought that the bodies of the dead were exposed and picked clean before being interred and that the sea eagle was the totem of this particular tribe. A spectacular walk may be taken back along the cliffs, which are smothered in sea pinks in early summer.

Bordering the bay at Burwick, the ancient church of St Mary contains a large beach stone into which two footprints have been carefully sculpted. A variety of folklore surrounds this boulder. One story tells how the original founder of the church was rescued from shipwreck by a sea monster, which turned to stone after depositing the survivor safely ashore. Another version declares that the stone was once the boat that brought Earl Magnus safely across the sea and home to Orkney. This impressive artefact is almost certainly a Pictish ceremonial stone, one of a type found elsewhere in Scotland, that was used in the inauguration of Pictish rulers.

Off the south coast, lie the Pentland Skerries and lighthouse, visited by Sir Walter Scott with the Lighthouse Board in 1814. Scott records that the lighthouse keeper had been a 'great swearer' when he first took up his post, but the solitary life had quite changed him! Scott found about 50 head of cattle on the skerries, and took his gun ashore, hoping to shoot some seals. Uninhabited now, the skerries offer a haven to a huge number of seabirds and colonies of seals. Burwick is not the end of the road for the short sea foot-ferry crosses the Pentland Firth between here and John O'Groats during the summer months. This service gives many visitors the opportunity to visit Orkney for the day and to take a bus tour through South Ronaldsay, Burray and on to the Orkney Mainland.

CHAPTER NINETEEN

Transport and Communications

Sea Transport

For generations of Orcadians the sea was not a barrier but a highway, which provided the fastest means of transport for people, goods and information. The first permanent settlers of Orkney travelled here by boat some 6,000 years ago, bringing the animals and seeds needed to create their farms. Imported goods are found on archaeological sites, showing that Orkney was not isolated but in contact with the outside world. For generations, small boats were not only used for fishing and setting creels but were also used to carry passengers and goods like grain, peats for fuel, even animals. Until roads were made in the 19th and 20th centuries, the fastest form of transport from one part of the Mainland to another was by boat. In the days of sail the trip to Orkney could be a dangerous one, and very uncomfortable in rough weather. The merchant lairds had their own vessels, which traded Orkney produce with British and European ports. The rise of the kelp industry in the 18th century saw regular sailing between Newcastle and Orkney, while other trading vessels sailed regularly to Orkney from Leith.

In the early 19th century Kirkwall was served by a small pier, which stood opposite where the Kirkwall Hotel now stands. Next to this pier was the Corn-slip, where grain paid as tax was landed. Malcolm Laing of Papdale led a campaign to have proper wharfage facilities built to promote local trade, and pledged £100 of his own money towards the project. A public subscription brought in £1,800, enabling the Trustees to lay the foundation stone on 11 April 1809. The pier was finished in 1811, with work on the West Pier beginning in 1813. The East Pier was still found to be too small, and was extended in 1828. In June 1832 the paddle steamer *Velocity* paid her first visit to Kirkwall. She belonged to the Aberdeen, Leith, Clyde and Tay Shipping Company, sailing fortnightly from Leith to Aberdeen and Wick. The following summer she included Kirkwall in her fortnightly sailings during the months of June to September. In 1836 she was replaced by the larger paddle steamer, *Sovereign*, with weekly sailings and a new service to Lerwick. The coming of a regular steamship service opened up new markets for cattle and soon Aberdeenshire cattle dealers were to be found in Orkney. The brown heather covered hillsides and moorlands were brought under cultivation and transformed into green fields as agriculture gained in importance. Winter sailings were introduced in 1850, prompted by the short-lived Kirkwall Steam Navigation Company which had been running the steamer *Northman* during the winter months from 1847 to 1851. In 1875 the Aberdeen, Leith, Clyde and Tay Shipping Company was renamed the North of Scotland, Orkney and Shetland Steam Navigation Company, becoming a limited company in 1919. It was usually referred to as the 'North Company'.

At the beginning of the century the mail to Orkney was still being carried in open boats over the Pentland Firth from Huna in Caithness to Burwick in South Ronaldsay. This was a dangerous journey; the boat was lost with all hands in 1815 and 1817. As a result the Stromness Town Council petitioned the Board of Trade for a steam service to carry the mail to Stromness. A pier was built at Scrabster, and the wooden paddle steamer *Royal Mail*, built at John Stanger's boatyard at Ness, Stromness, went into service on 1 April 1856, receiving a licence to carry passengers on 8 May. She was replaced in 1868 when Captain George Robertson won the tender to carry the mail. Robertson, a native of Stronsay, had started a service to the North Isles in 1865 with the steamship *Orcadia*, serving the islands of Eday, Stronsay, Sanday, Papa Westray, Westray and North Ronaldsay. It proved so popular that the Orkney Steam Navigation Company was formed in 1868 to operate the route with a larger steamer, also called *Orcadia*. Robertson remained as a manager in the new company. By 1884 the *Orcadia* had become too small, and was lengthened by 20 feet (6 m) and had a new engine fitted. Robertson's new venture on the Stromness to Scrabster route needed a ship, first the paddle steamer *Willington*, then the tug *Pera*. A larger ship was required, and the new steamer *Express* took over the route in April 1869.

By 1874 Highland Railways had reached Thurso, making the Scrabster to Stromness connection an even more important route to Orkney. The directors of Highland Railways petitioned the government to grant them the rights to operate sailings to Orkney and the Hebrides in connection with their trains. This was agreed. Robertson lost the mail contract and the Highland Railway Company built a much larger steamer, the *John o' Groats*, at the cost of £12,750. The service started on 27 July 1877, but the ship proved to be too large and expensive to run. A pier at Scapa was opened in 1880 and became for a time the principal port for the mail to Orkney. With losses mounting, Highland Railways withdrew from the mail route in 1882 and the North Company took over the service with the steamer *St Ola*. Their old steamer *Queen* replaced this ship in 1890, before the *St Ola* took over in 1892, providing a regular service until 1951. From 1874 Matthew Langlands and Sons' steamers called at Stromness once a week from Liverpool, via Oban and Stornoway, and onwards to Aberdeen, Dundee and Leith. This proved popular with tourists, who brought a new source of income to the islands. Seeing the potential of tourism, the North

Company started cruises to the Norwegian fjords with the *St Rognvald* in 1886, and had the luxurious steamer *St Sunniva* built especially for this service and operational from 1887.

Kirkwall pier was once more too small, so a new iron pier costing £12,000 was built between 1865 and 1867. It was designed by R. Denison of London and built by R. Laidlaw & Son, Glasgow. By 1874 more room for shipping was required; moreover, the open-framed iron pier was becoming unstable. A major redevelopment of the pier, completed in 1886, was carried out at the cost of £17,500. The south pier at Stromness was also proving to be too small, and an extension was built between 1893 and 1894. This development also saw the original open-framed timber pier clad in stone. In the 1920s the Stromness Harbour Commission built a new pier for Thornley Binders, a company which intended to make smokeless fuel from coal dust and sodium alginate extracted from kelp. The company collapsed, and the pier is now used as the ro-ro terminal. The Inner North Isles had their own services. The little steamer *Lizzie Burroughs*, owned by the Rousay laird General Frederick Traill Burroughs, served the island from 1879 to 1892. Her route connected the districts of Sourin, Trumland and Hullion in Rousay to Egilsay and Wyre, and the Mainland parishes of Evie and Rendall, and the town of Kirkwall. The *Fawn*, belonging to the Orkney Steam Navigation Company, continued the service from 1892 to 1917. The steamer *Iona*, owned by local man John Reid, served Shapinsay from 1893 to 1914. The *Iona* was bought by William Dennison and continued the service from 1914 to 1964, followed by the *Klydon*, then the government-owned *Clytus*.

The small sailing ship *Elizabeth (Lizzie) Buchan*, which carried the mail from Stromness to Longhope, served the South Isles of Hoy, Graemsay, Flotta, Cava and Fara. The South Isles Steam Packet Company was formed to bring a steamer service to these islands, and the new ship *Saga* was built at Copland's boatyard, Stromness. Launched on 28 April 1893, she soon completed her sea trials and went into service. This service proved to be unreliable – more through poor management than anything else – and soon the letters page of *The Orcadian* was full of complaints. The *Saga* only sailed from 1893 to 1895 before she was withdrawn, though she went on to serve in the Dardanelles during the First World War, then sailed the Mediterranean before ending her days working on the Clyde. The *Elizabeth (Lizzie) Buchan* took her place for a time before the *Aberdeen* (which was in fact the old Rousay steamer *Lizzie Burroughs* under a new name) was chartered. She was now the property of Robert Garden, the general merchant who also operated shop boats to the isles. After the South Isles Steam Packet Company went into liquidation in October 1895, Robert Garden won the mail contract to Longhope and decided to have a steamer built for the service. The *Hoy Head* went into service in 1896, and continued to operate on the route, serving six different owners, until 1956. Burray and South Ronaldsay still relied on sail packets right up to the 1920s, when Captain Arcus introduced a steamer service with the *Countess Cadogan* (1921–28), in competition with the *Hoy Head*, which now sailed to St Margaret's Hope. The motorboat *Hoxa Head* also provided a mail service for over 20 years.

By the end of the 19th century the North Company had a fine fleet of ships that served the Northern Isles and a second weekly sailing was added during the summer months from 1866. The *St Magnus* (1867–1904) was the last paddle steamer operated by the company, and the first ship to carry a saint's name. In addition the *St Clair* (1868–1937), *St Nicholas* (1871–1914), *St Rognvald* (1883–1900), *St Sunniva* (1887–1930) and *St Ninian* (1895–1948) all served the islands well over the years. The *St Rognvald* was lost when she ran aground in thick fog on Burgh Head on the east coast of Stronsay on 24 April 1900. She had been sailing from Lerwick to Kirkwall with 68 passengers on board. Fortunately all passengers and crew were rescued, but the cattle, sheep and Shetland ponies she was carrying were lost, with the exception of one pony that escaped from the hold and swam ashore. The ship soon broke up, and became a total loss. Her chief officer was found guilty at a Board of Trade inquiry for allowing her to drift six or seven miles off course, and for failing to reduce speed in poor visibility. His master's certificate was suspended for three months.

The outbreak of the war in 1914 saw hundreds of thousands of servicemen and women travelling to Orkney to join the Grand Fleet in its northern base at Scapa Flow. The North Company steamer *St Ninian* sailed the Pentland Firth carrying the sailors and troops, while the *St Ola* continued to provide a regular civilian service. Orkney was designated a restricted area due to the base, and special travel permits had to be carried by everyone wishing to travel to and from the islands. With Orkney playing such an important part in naval strategy there had to be radical travel arrangements to keep the Grand Fleet supplied with men, stores and mail. A train service that ran straight from London's Euston Station to Thurso in Caithness operated throughout the war. This train was known as the 'Jellicoe Special', named after Admiral Sir John Jellicoe, Commander-in-Chief of the Grand Fleet. It was a full day's journey if the weather was fine, but if there was snow on the line it could take several days. Conditions on the train were poor, with no heating or toilets; voluntary groups handed out the only hot drinks available when the train stopped at a station to change drivers and take on water. Another train ran from King's Cross, joining up with the 'Jellicoe' in Perth. On arrival in Thurso personnel still had to face the crossing of the Pentland Firth, a trip that earned the nickname the 'soldier's misery'.

The end of the war saw sailings return to normal. In 1919 the Orkney Steam Navigation Company acquired the *Countess of Bantry* to join the *Orcadia* on the North Isles route. In 1903 the company had seen off a challenge from the short-lived Edinburgh, Aberdeen and Orkney Shipping

Company, whose steamer the *Hebridean* traded between Orkney and Leith. William Cooper was also running a service carrying cattle from Orkney to Leith. In 1898 he chartered the *Express* from S. Reid & Son, Kirkwall. This was the same ship that had sailed the Stromness to Scrabster route for George Robertson. In 1917 the *Express* was sold to the North Company, but was lost on 4 April that same year after a collision off the coast of France. Cooper bought the *Hebridean*, renaming her *Express*, but she was lost in February 1918 after a collision near the Pentland Skerries. He then bought the *Amelia*, which sailed with passengers and cargo from Kirkwall to Leith from 1920 to 1955. She was taken over by the North Company in 1940, and remained on the route for the next 15 years.

In May 1928 the *Earl Thorfinn* joined the Orkney Steam Navigation Company's elderly steamer *Orcadia* on the North Isles route. The slightly smaller *Earl Sigurd* joined her in 1931, replacing the old *Orcadia*. These two ships would faithfully serve the islands for many years. The *Earl Thorfinn* survived being caught at sea during the hurricane of 31 January 1953, when she was forced to run before the wind. With no radio to inform the authorities of her position people feared the worst, until she arrived battered but in one piece in Aberdeen. With the outbreak of the Second World War there were fears of enemy spies gathering information in Orkney, where the Royal Navy was once more established. As a counter-espionage measure the old 'eek-names' (nicknames) for the different islands were used on sailings lists instead of their proper names. One such sailing reads, 'From Starling at 7.30 a.m. for Limpet, Gruellie, Scarf Pier, Dundies and Auks'. This meant, 'From Kirkwall at 7.30 a.m. for Stronsay, Sanday, Eday Pier, Papa Westray and Westray'.

The 'Jellicoe Special' was once more in action, but with slightly more comfortable carriages and catering by the Salvation Army. The *Earl of Zetland* accompanied the *St Ola* this time, while the old *St Ninian* once more carried sailors from Scrabster to Lyness, Hoy. The journey across the Pentland Firth was no better than in the previous war. One sailor quipped that the *Earl of Zetland* was torpedo-proof, as it wasn't in the water for long enough to be hit. To make matters worse the *St Ola* was once mistaken for an enemy vessel by a British cruiser, and a coastal defence gun at Ness Battery also shelled her on another occasion, but this saved her from hitting a mine. One story that has passed into legend concerns a king's messenger who demanded that he be ferried across the Pentland Firth in very severe weather. Captain Swanson thought he would teach him a lesson, and they set sail. The voyage was truly dreadful, and the king's messenger was confined to his cabin with a bad case of seasickness. They arrived in Stromness, but the messenger did not appear for a very long time. Captain Swanson used to remark: 'It was only the hope o' deein' that kept him alive!' In 1951 a new ship of the same name replaced the old *St Ola*. In 1953 the North of Scotland, Orkney and Shetland Steam Navigation Company Ltd changed its name to the North of Scotland,

Orkney and Shetland Shipping Company Ltd, as steam power gave way to diesel.

The last firm to run the old *Hoy Head* was the Stromness-based Bremner and Company. They bought out the previous owners, Swanson and Towers, in 1938 and ran the South Isles service for many years. During the Second World War they carried passengers and cargo, including stores for the naval base at Lyness. The Admiralty also ran a ferry service from Houton to Lyness until 1959. Bremner and Co. had operated both passenger and cargo services with several vessels, but by the mid 1950s rising costs forced the company to approach the government for assistance. In 1958 they were given a vessel to run on behalf of the Secretary of State, which they named the *Hoy Head* and a second government ship, the *Watchful*, went into service in 1961. Bremner and Company's South Isles service was taken over by the Orkney Islands Shipping Company in 1973; the same fate later befell the other small companies which operated services to the Inner Isles.

The North Company was taken over by the Liverpool-based Coast Lines in 1961, which in turn was taken over by P&O in 1972. P&O built a new *St Ola*, the first roll-on, roll-off car ferry to operate on the Pentland Firth route. It arrived in Stromness in November 1974, and went into service in January 1975. The larger *St Sunniva* carried out the Aberdeen–Stromness–Lerwick route, while the *St Rognvald* carried freight. A larger, but older ro-ro ferry was bought in 1992. At the turn of the new millennium P&O lost their contract to NorthLink Ferries, who run four ferries to the Northern Isles. The *Hamnavoe* is on the Stromness to Scrabster route, while the *Hrossey* and *Hjaltland* run the Aberdeen–Kirkwall–Lerwick route. The fourth ship, the *Hascosay*, carries livestock and freight. A new pier complex has been built at Crowness outside Kirkwall to handle these new ferries, and also the ever-increasing volume of cruise liners that visit the islands.

The Orkney Steam Navigation Company changed its name in 1962 to the Orkney Islands Shipping Company, as it had just acquired a new diesel-powered ship, the *Orcadia*, to replace the *Earl Thorfinn*. The old steamer *Earl Sigurd* continued in service until the cargo and passenger ship *Islander* replaced her in 1969. They in turn were replaced by two roll-on, roll-off ferries that serve the North Isles, the *Earl Thorfinn* and the *Earl Sigurd*. New ro-ro ferry terminals were built in the islands, except for North Ronaldsay and Papa Westray where tidal conditions proved too strong. They received a subsidised air service instead. Kirkwall's east pier was extended, and ro-ro facilities installed as part of a huge refurbishment. Smaller ro-ro vessels also serve the Inner Isles. The *Shapinsay* serves the island of Shapinsay, while the *Eynhallow* serves Rousay, Egilsay and Wyre. The *Hoy Head* and the *Thorsvoe* serves Flotta, Lyness and Longhope, while the passenger ship *Graemsay* serves Graemsay and North Hoy. In 1964 there were trials of a hydrofoil, called *Shadowfax* (named after Gandalf the wizard's horse in J. R. R. Tolkien's *The Lord of the Rings*), which was to provide a fast service to the North Isles. It ended in disaster when the hydrofoil caught fire on leaving Kirkwall, with its ten passengers having to abandon the vessel. In 1993 the company changed its name once more, to Orkney Ferries.

A new livestock service was started in 1992 when the Orcargo ship *Contender* began sailings from Kirkwall to Invergordon. The ship had the capacity to hold 500 sheep, or 130 cattle, and proved popular with farmers. When Orcargo went out of business the Streamline Shipping Group took over the run, but the ban on the movement of livestock due to foot-and-mouth disease forced the closure of the route in April 2001.

The dream of a short sea crossing from John o' Groats to Burwick has rumbled on since Victorian times. By 1973 there were two crossings; Thomas & Bews (now John o' Groats Ferries) ran a passenger-only service with the *Pentland Spray* followed by the *Souter's Lass* and *Pentland Venture*, while Captain Bill Banks ran the *Pentalina* from St Margaret's Hope. In 1989 a company who intended to operate a ro-ro service from Gills Bay to Burwick approached the Orkney Islands Council for finance. The council invested in the company, which eventually went out of business. The council found themselves caught up in spiralling costs and eventually withdrew, having spent millions. The ship that was built to sail the route, the *Varagen*, was transferred to the North Isles service. In May 2001 Andrew Banks restarted the family business by operating a ro-ro service from St Margaret's Hope to Gills Bay in his ship the *Pentalina B*. This has been done without any support from the Orkney Islands Council.

Land Transport

Up until the mid 19th century Orkney's roads were little more than dirt tracks, difficult in summer and virtually impassable in winter. People generally did not move far from their own district, unless to go to a market or some such event. This involved a long journey (on foot or on horseback) which was planned well in advance. When government grants were made available to establish proper hard-surfaced roads, made from crushed stone topped with finely broken stone mixed with sand and clay, Orkney's main road network was established. The new roads met with mixed reaction, as small farmers and crofters were enraged at the prospect of losing land to the development. Local man George Marwick recalled how he had received insults and threats from some of the inhabitants of Birsay and Harray when he was carrying our surveying work for the new road around 1860. A road linking South Walls to the neighbouring land mass of Hoy and North Walls was constructed around the end of the century. Up until then it had only been accessible at low water.

During the 19th century the only vehicles were horse-drawn gigs and carts. A stage coach operating on the Kirkwall to Stromness route took 2¾ hours, including stops to water and rest the horses. The parishes also had horse-drawn coaches providing transport to Kirkwall and Stromness. A plan to build a railway between the two towns was proposed, but failed to materialise. In March 1901 the first motor car arrived in Orkney. The Daimler was brought north by the *St Nicholas*, and caused great excitement. By 1905 a Sterling motorbus was bought by E. J. Robertson Grant, who began a Kirkwall–Stromness service with his company Orkney Express. Travel time was halved to 1½ hours. More buses followed, including a double decker, with the pioneer mechanic W. R. Tullock carrying out maintenance. The Orkney Express went out of business in 1908, with the bus fleet sold off and mostly converted into lorries. Horse-drawn coaches carried on without competition until after the First World War, when returning servicemen started bus services using a Model T Ford chassis with a wooden coach body built over it. The most notable innovators were Robert Nicolson, then John G. Nicolson (1920–63) and D. Wishart & Son (1922–65), both running a service from Kirkwall to Stromness. William Laughton (1920–77) operated from Deerness to Kirkwall, and was the longest running family motor bus operator, as his sons continued the service after 1945. Carrying parcels was a major source of income, and helped subsidise services. Bus tours for cruise liner passengers were established in the 1930s, and are still growing in popularity. The Second World War saw Burray and South Ronaldsay linked to the Mainland's road network by the Churchill Barriers, which were closed from 1947 for a couple of summers, as three of them suffered from subsidence. Local bus operator Mansie Spence solved the problem by using a small boat as a link between two buses.

Mansie Spence sold his bus service to James D. Peace in 1962. Peace's buses came to dominate the services, gaining the lucrative schools runs. Shalder Coaches provided a rival service, as did Alistair Rosie's coaches. All three bus companies have now been sold to Rapson's Coaches, trading under the name Orkney Coaches. The only independent bus service is Alec Rosie's Causeway Coaches, which operates the Kirkwall to South Ronaldsay route. The motor car is now the most common method of transport on the islands.

Air Transport

On 4 December 1910 history was made when the first men to arrive in Orkney by air landed near Berstane Road. They were two German balloonists, Herren Distler and Joerdens, whose balloon had been blown off course from Munich. A third crew member, Herr Metzger, had been lost when the balloon bounced off the North Sea. They had sighted a light, possibly the Auskerry Lighthouse, and descended. After a rough landing at Berstane outside Kirkwall they made for the nearest house, Park Cottage, belonging to the Leonard family.

On 18 April 1931 Captain Ernest Edmund (Ted) Fresson landed a Gipsy Moth aircraft near the Balfour Hospital. Accompanied by his friend Heloise Pauer (who owned the plane), he inspected possible landing sites for an air display. He returned in August, bringing with him two fare-paying passengers from Wick – a first for Orkney. He left that afternoon, taking with him Agnes Shearer, a reporter for *The Orcadian*, who became the first fare-paying passenger from Orkney. His 'barnstorming' air display was held in September at Hatston outside Kirkwall, and Garson near Stromness. While in Orkney he sounded out the prospects for an air service to the islands. He subsequently formed Highland Airways Ltd, with backing from *The Scotsman* newspaper, copies of which he carried to Orkney. The service began on 8 May 1933 with Fresson flying a Monospar aeroplane from Inverness to Wideford, east of Kirkwall. Knowing that the powerful North of Scotland, Orkney and Shetland Steam Navigation Company Ltd could put his firm out of business, Fresson shrewdly offered the North Company a share in Highland Airways. It was the first continuous scheduled air service in Britain. By July 1933 a new eight-seater D.H. Dragon gave him the opportunity to fly chartered flights to the islands and to Shetland. In November 1933 he was contracted by the Balfour Hospital to fly patients south, leading to the founding of the Air Ambulance Service in 1934. On 29 May 1934 Fresson won the mail contract to Orkney, the first internal airmail service in Britain and he expanded the service to Dyce, near Aberdeen. Dyce was taken over by Fresson's rival Eric Gander Dower of Aberdeen Airways Ltd, who flew to Orkney, landing at Howe near Stromness, Berriedale in South Ronaldsay and Quanterness near Kirkwall.

From 1933 onwards Fresson had been providing an inter-island air service. In August 1934 a community meeting in North Ronaldsay had decided to welcome the air service, so the islanders gathered at a field to remove a wall and clear stones to form a runway. People power at its best! In May 1935 Highland Airways Ltd was taken over by United Airways Ltd, who in turn merged with British Airways in October that same year. In 1936 the newer and faster D.H. Dragon Rapide aircrafts were introduced, along with links to Glasgow and London. In 1939 the Civil Aviation Authority consolidated flights to Orkney, giving Gander Dower exclusive rights to Aberdeen while Fresson got Inverness.

With war imminent, the Royal Navy Fleet Air Arm sought Fresson's advice as to where to build an aerodrome. Hatston was recommended, as were hard-surfaced runways that could be used in all weather. Fresson was allowed to continue flights to Orkney during the war, but with the side windows of the plane painted over. He received an OBE in 1943 in recognition of his service to civil aviation. Despite this award, when the war ended and the airlines were nationalised as British European Airways (BEA) Fresson was given the post of area manager for the north of Scotland, a position junior to less experienced men. After his six-month contract expired he was made redundant on 5 March 1948, causing fury in the north and questions to be raised in the House of Commons. Fresson emigrated to Kenya where he continued to fly, but retired to Inverness in 1963 and died later that same year. BEA continued to run the service, first with Dakotas, then Viscounts. The wartime aerodrome at Grimsetter, east of Kirkwall, became Kirkwall Airport and still serves the islands. The Viscounts were replaced by HP748s, then ATPs, and now Saab aircraft. BEA was renamed British Airways, which now sub-contracts the routes to other airlines. The air service to the islands did not resume until 1967 when Loganair started flights with Islander aircraft. A new state-of-the-art airport terminal was opened in 2001, the latest chapter in Orkney's long history of air travel.

CHAPTER TWENTY

The Canadian Connection

W HEN GRINDING POVERTY is the fate of most members of a community, how can an individual escape its toils? How can he improve his prospects and those of his family? The classic problem of the Third World in our age: quite familiar, too, to generations past in Orkney.

Probably one of the earliest indications that a cure might lie across the Atlantic is an authorisation in 1702 to Captain Grimington of the ship *Hudson's Bay* to enlist '10 or 12 stout able young men' to work in Canada. At the time, that great fur-trading enterprise, the Hudson's Bay Company (HBC), was just 32 years old. Strikingly, in an age highly suspicious of foreigners, an English company was offering to employ nationals of Scotland. For a century the two states had shared the same monarch, but it would be a further five years till they became one country with the same parliament and government.

In 1708, the year after the Act of Union, Grimington was asked to use his contacts in Stromness to ensure a supply of suitable young men to work in Canada: a temporary response to labour shortages due to war conditions. Brilliant French tactics in Hudson Bay had left only Fort Albany in British hands. With the coming of peace the forts were restored; but Orkneymen were employed only when it became clear that the wages on offer were too low to entice men of quality from London. Thereafter, HBC ships called in Orkney each spring for new men. Thus began the strong involvement with the 'Nor Wast'. The term is a misnomer: Churchill, the most northerly post on Hudson Bay, lies almost due west of Stromness.

Orcadians have a capacity to endure without open complaint. At Hudson Bay there was much to endure: Joseph Hargrave, for example, wrote of '9 months of winter, varied by 3 of rain and mosquitoes'. Most of the Orcadians joined as labourers and their main employment was cutting and hauling firewood, of which a vast quantity was needed to face the bitter sub-Arctic winter – at York, for example, two huge heaps each 40 m in circumference. When the annual ships arrived great bustle replaced the normal routine. Sloops sailed to and fro to the anchored vessels bringing ashore a year's supplies, official and private mail and trade goods of all kinds – guns, gunpowder and shot, blankets and coloured beads. Back to the ships went carefully sorted and graded furs, compressed into 41-kg

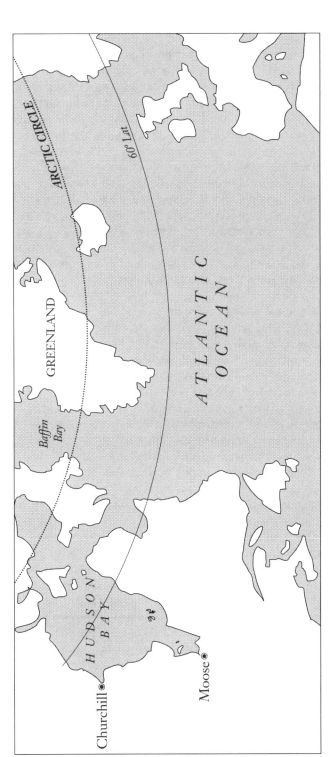

MAP 6 Orkney and Hudson Bay

bundles. Goods sent inland had also to be packed to that size for convenient loading of canoes and carrying at the frequent portages.

Sir John Franklin had high praise for the skills of Orcadian boatmen when the HBC aided the transportation of his expedition to its start point on the Mackenzie River: 'The necessity they are under of frequently jumping into the water, to lift the boats over the rocks compels them to remain the whole day in wet clothes, at a season when the temperature is far below the freezing point. The immense loads too, which they carry over the portage, is not more a matter of surprise than the alacrity with which they perform these laborious duties.' (20 September 1819)

Promotion from labourer was slow and depended as much on luck as talent. Most officers were English, who entered the service as writers (clerks) or were recruited as apprentices from the Greycoat charitable school for orphans in London. Sometimes a clash of cultures led to animosity and to complaints of clannishness, but mostly things worked well and Orkney men were greatly appreciated.

For much of the 18th century trade was conducted at the big forts by the bay when the Indians brought down their annual harvest of furs. However, this casual attitude, described by one former employee as having 'for 80 years slept at the edge of a frozen sea', was challenged by more aggressive traders based in Montreal who carried trade goods deep into the continent and cut off the trade to the bay. HBC had to move into the interior too, instead of relying on the rights granted by royal charter to a monopoly of trade in Rupert's Land, that is the whole area that drained into Hudson Bay and constitutes roughly two-thirds of modern Canada.

More trading posts meant more employees: if the company had to carry pelts to the bay and trade goods to the interior then more men were needed. Often 100 recruits might be required; 70 was normal. Between 1771 and 1799 the HBC labour force increased from 181 to 529. Of these, 80 per cent were from Orkney. Given this increase in labour needs, it was no longer practical to enlist men when the ships arrived in Stromness. Thus, the HBC appointed David Geddes, a leading merchant of the town, as its agent in Stromness. Not only did Geddes enlist labour; he also handled a lot of money, having the responsibilities of a banker for the wages of the Orkney men.

Some Orcadians rose to considerable importance in Rupert's Land. Earliest of these was Joseph Isbister, son of a Stromness merchant with landed property in Harray. He entered the HBC's marine service, making his way slowly to post-master through command of the sloop *Eastmain*. Gritty, determined, autocratic and full of self-confidence, he proved his worth to the company, imposing a man o'war's discipline on Albany and the subsidiary post he established 200 km up-river at Henley House. It was the first inland post. As the River Albany was shallow, barges, not canoes, were used to maintain contact. That the company was pleased with his efforts was indicated by several bonus payments awarded to him, including one he received after he stopped working for the HBC due to the high-handed and ruthless way in which he handled the Henley House Massacre.

Hearing of the murders of his employees, Isbister hastened to the spot. Once the three perpetrators were in custody in separate rooms he fired two pistol shots in the courtyard. Interviewing each Indian thereafter, he assured him that his relatives had admitted their guilt and had been executed. Hangings followed on the basis of confessions obtained in this way.

Justice was done! Or was it? The London committeemen desired their employees to live as a monastic community in the wilderness. That was the theory: the practice was that close temporary liaisons with Indian women became commonplace over the years and helped foster good relations; but the Henley affair was a different kind of sexual politics where the Indians were avenging the forcible abduction and violation of their womenfolk.

Shortly after Isbister's star set a new figure of note emerged from Orkney. In 1760, William Tomison, aged 20, left the island of South Ronaldsay contracted as a labourer. Against all the odds he rose to greater significance in the fur trade than any other native of Orkney, reaching the new rank of Chief Inland, which put most of HBC's activity in Rupert's Land in his hands. An unlikely figure to rise to the highest rank, Tomison was scantily educated and often seems weak in communication skills, save with the Indians, with whom he established a good rapport.

Luck put Tomison in the right place at the right time. He might have spent his career beside Hudson Bay while trade shrank away to nothing and HBC ran into bankruptcy. Instead he had a much more interesting life, but a long hard haul of almost incessant travel.

His first venture inland, living amid friendly Indians and seeking to encourage others to bring their furs down to Severn, proved an almost complete failure. The questing traders from Montreal were cutting off trade far inland. Contention with them as they formed shifting alliances and eventually grouped together in 1779 as the North West Company (NWC) was central to Tomison's life.

At last HBC pushed far inland. In 1774 Cumberland House (near The Pas) was set up, on the Saskatchewan River, 40 paddling days from York, and a year later Tomison was sent there to take charge. The rest of his time would be spent on that river system. When given full authority in 1786, it was on the basis that he continued to live inland.

To a great extent he had to play catch-up against Nor Westers who had captured most of the trade. They were better manned and much better supplied with trade goods. As if that were not enough, there were unreasonable expectations in London, of success on the Saskatchewan, but also in pushing northwards into the Athabasca region, where his rivals were solidly entrenched.

Tomison managed to hold and improve the position in the Saskatchewan valley, establishing trade posts close to those of NWC from Manchester

House to Edmonton and beyond, till within view of the Rockies. Comments by leading Nor Westers suggest not only that they recognised a man of great ability, but felt that without him the HBC would have been forced out of business. Usually he made the annual trip to York with the harvest of furs with a fleet of canoes, or later of big York boats, not behaving as a high official, but steering the lead canoe.

The most serious problems faced by Tomison were not due to trade rivals. In 1782 he reached York fort to find a blackened shell. A French naval expedition, aiding the Americans in their bid for independence, had been intent on commerce destruction. When no ship had arrived by 8 September he built a log tent on a wooden platform and left his furs secure before returning to Cumberland without supplies and trade goods. To survive the winter he needed the aid of bitter rivals.

The timing could hardly have been worse. In the previous year he had been coping with an epidemic of smallpox that swept through the tribes of the great plains. It was the first time they had met this white man's disease and it took a devastating toll. Tomison and his men buried many and nursed survivors, even though the only protection they possessed was fumigation with sulphur. They were fortunate that none of the HBC party contracted the disease. But many of their most loyal Indian trappers were lost and a big effort was needed to rebuild a commercial structure, and to restore confidence.

William Tomison spent more than 50 years in the service of the company. His lack of education had left him with a zeal to provide it for others. When at Edmonton he set up a school for employees' children, and in Orkney he established a school in his native parish in 1793, committing £20 a year from his salary. On his retirement to South Ronaldsay he lived frugally and bequeathed half of his considerable savings to build an academy that was in use till the 1960s, and which is now due to become a research centre for this aspect of Orkney's past.

Some of Tomison's contemporaries, like Mitchell Omand of Stromness, achieved high positions despite being wholly illiterate. That was possible in the 18th century; but not in the nineteenth, which would see officers of good schooling like John Rae from Orphir and the Watt brothers from Stromness.

Rae was a very special case – a man of many talents, a keen observer and a first-class shot. The son of the HBC's agent in Stromness, John Rae was a newly qualified doctor when he agreed to fill a vacancy on a vessel to Hudson Bay and back (1833). Unexpectedly frozen-in for the winter, he fell in love with the wilderness and stayed on as doctor at Moose Factory. The next ten years saw him honing his skills in a forbidding environment. Like any good Bay man he knew that the natives could teach much about survival. Although Rae rose to the rank of Chief Factor his career in Rupert's Land involved more exploration than fur trade administration.

MAP 7 Hudson Bay

John Rae guided four major investigations in the Arctic, the most amazing being in 1851, when what would normally have involved two years was completed in one. That was on the coast of Victoria Island and the Wollaston Peninsula; on foot in spring when the ice still dominated, averaging 27 miles a day in snowshoes; by boat when it became impossible to walk in conditions described by a modern adventurer as 'like porage sown with razor blades'. This achievement earned him the Gold Medal of the Royal Geographical Society.

He might have expected more: many naval officers received knighthoods for less intensive exploration and map-making. Rae's methods were tough and physically demanding. Everyone, the leader above all, had to pull his weight. By choice he led small expeditions so that it was possible to live off the hostile land.

Despite the hazards and wintering in the Arctic in igloos (whose construction Rae studied carefully on his first expedition) there was only one fatality in all of his journeys, when a steersman's error led to the drowning of an Eskimo interpreter.

All this was forgotten when in 1854 he discovered details of the deaths of the members of Sir John Franklin's venture to find the final link in the North-West Passage. Nine years earlier the two ships *Erebus* and *Terror* had sailed with three years' supplies. Then silence. Sea and land searches had found nothing. Rae included evidence from Inuit that in desperation as they struggled south, starving survivors had turned cannibal. Led by the Admiralty, Victorian society was outraged. No British sailor would ever stoop so low! Rae was vilified.

Concentration on these great figures has bypassed important developments. The value of HBC stock fell sharply when for six years after 1809 no dividends were paid. Lord Selkirk took his opportunity to buy a controlling interest in HBC. He purchased from them land in modern Minnesota and Manitoba – roughly four times the size of Scotland. In part his motives were altruistic: to resettle Highlanders evicted in the Sutherland Clearances. His first settlers (who included some Orcadian labourers and craftsmen) were sent to winter at York Factory in 1811. They struggled overland during 1812 to their refuge and farming settlement on Red River.

In fact Selkirk's land lay athwart the Nor Westers' river trade routes. This roused them to fury, leading to a period of violence and murder and subsequent heated legal cases. A private war in a British overseas territory was quite unacceptable. Westminster put pressure on the commercial companies and this led, in 1821, to the merger of HBC and NWC under the name of the former. The HBC regained Selkirk's land and set up an administration for an area they named Assiniboia. The settlement became a retirement home for HBC men who wished to stay with their Indian wives and children.

At the end of the American War of Independence in 1783 thousands of loyalists moved north to Canada. A further war (1812–14) with the infant USA exposed a major danger to those British territories. In an attempt to resolve this and ease social problems at home – post-war depression and high unemployment – emigration was encouraged and also the resettlement in Canada with substantial grants of land to serving soldiers demobilised there. Much of the advertising by land companies was enthusiastically over-optimistic, suggesting a perfection of land and climate.

Emigration soared. Mrs Susanna Moodie depicted Upper Canada (i.e. Ontario) as being 'The great landmark for the rich in hope and poor in purse'. Otherwise, she and her husband, Dunbar, would probably have sailed for South Africa where he had already spent ten years and where his brothers had become prosperously settled. The Moodies were deceived

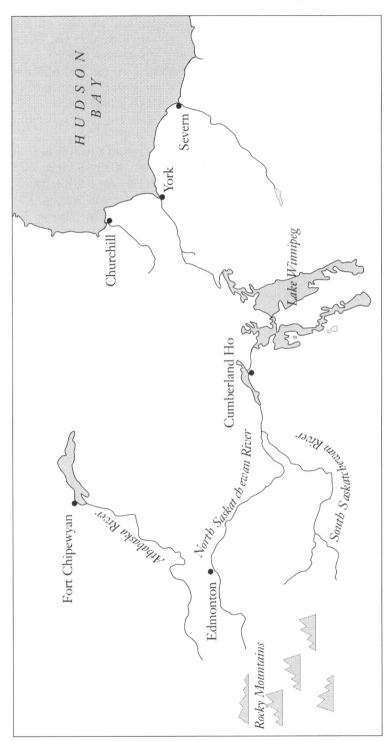

MAP 8 Rupert's Land – river communications

more than once and found themselves farming in an undeveloped and unsuitable area. Hired labour was expensive and very hard to retain. When seeing their first home, Mrs Moodie thought that she was looking at a pig sty rather than a log cabin. In writing *Roughing it in the Bush* she was relating their experiences, partly at least, as a warning for others who might be tempted by opportunities abroad that were best suited to physically strong farmers and labourers who could improve their wealth and status by many years of heavy labour.

In Susanna's case, however, there was the comfort of relatives near at hand. Her sister had married Thomas Traill of Westove in Sanday. Bankruptcy due to the collapse of kelp prices made him and his family emigrate too. Both sisters contributed greatly to Canadian writing. Catherine Parr Traill seems much the happier, possibly because of her absorption in the study of Canadian plants, on which she became expert. Their brother, too, was not far away and made a better success of farming in the new conditions.

Dunbar Moodie had sold his army commission, hoping to invest the capital to realise an income at least equivalent to his peacetime half-pay; but he put it into a canal and steamboat venture that came to nothing. His appointment as sheriff of Hastings County rescued them from penury and allowed them to move to the congenial town of Belleville.

Even in the last quarter of the century discomfort was still the lot of those journeying to their homestead. When William and Jane Aim and their friends emigrated they travelled by train to the terminus with so few seats that some had to sit on up-turned buckets. There followed nearly a day by ox wagon to Saltcoats, NW Territory (now Saskatchewan), where Mrs Aim was treated for sunburn and mosquito bites in the country fashion with an application of buttermilk. Each emigrating male had an allocation of land to break in and also further work for the land company in payment for timber supplied for him to build his new home.

Wiser heads than Moodie's assessed the situation better and took advantage by settling close to already developed transport. For instance, after five years at York, Alexander Aitken returned to Orkney to marry. He then returned to Canada till he could afford to bring out his wife. Frugal to the last he walked from Edmonton to the rail-head at St Paul, Minnesota to meet her. They settled at Portage la Prairie (Manitoba), where he farmed while plying his trade as blacksmith and making his own charcoal from willow. He was very much alive to economic possibilities and during the property boom that followed the arrival of the Canadian Pacific Railway sold up and moved on to Moosomin (Saskatchewan) to set up in business at 'the end of the steel'.

However, not all Orcadians followed this independent route. Possibly their mindset was against direct emigration. Possibly even the subsidised cost was beyond them but they could visualise a bright future if paid off in Canada by HBC.

Certainly there are plenty of examples of men who took this option, sometimes after only one basic five-year contract. At Edmonton, John Walter from Stenness, a qualified carpenter, built York boats for the HBC. Thereafter he was one of the HBC men who took up the first river lots that were made available and he was so successful that his corner became the district of Walterdale. The key to his prosperity lay with the award of a licence to operate a ferry across the North Saskatchewan at Edmonton and using his skills to repair wagons and continuing in boatbuilding. From this it was a natural step to major involvement in the timber industry.

Further west HBC made more positive attempts at colonisation. When the Confederation of Canada came into being the company lost its vast privileges, but was compensated with large chunks of real estate. On Vancouver Island it had the further obligation to develop settlement. Hence the shipping out of a mixed bag of Ayrshire miners and Orcadian labourers. After a false start, mines were successfully developed at Nanaimo.

Orcadians made up a significant element of the Canadian population, particularly in the north and west. Otherwise, one could hardly have found Cree chiefs called Drever or settlements like Orkney, Stromness, Binscarth and Clouston spattered across the continent. They played a role in politics, both local and national, greater than their numerical strength, the highest office held being premier of Manitoba by John Norquay (1878–87), whose family were original Red River settlers.

Many Orkney families have maintained contact with their Canadian relatives through letters and occasional visits. Others have a more remote sentimental recollection. Hence the success of the Orkney Homecoming in 1999, when enthusiastic Canadians came seeking their roots. At the political level a treaty of friendship was signed in St Magnus Cathedral by the Convenor of Orkney Islands Council and the Deputy Minister of Rural Development of Manitoba; equally important was the joy in 'Strings across the Sky' in which Inuit and Dene youngsters celebrated with local young fiddlers a common musical heritage based on a fiddling tradition carried across the Atlantic by Orkneymen in the service of Hudson's Bay Company.

CHAPTER TWENTY-ONE

Stromness

Stromness grew up by the sea and because of the sea. No one who has stood on the deck of the vehicular ferry *St Ola*, or, more recently, the newly built *Hamnavoe*, as she slides majestically into Stromness harbour and who later wanders through the fine conservation area which encompasses the bulk of the street with its lanes and stone piers can have any doubt of that. Despite the quality of the buildings the street has a strangely unplanned air – an uncertainty as to where it is going. Distinguished writer, George Mackay Brown, a native of the place, described its growth in this way:

> Tall houses with gardens and piers,
> Where the stylish merchants lived,
> Small slipways for the fishermen,
> A new kirk, inns and ale-houses,
> The street uncoiled like a sailor's rope from north to south.
>
> And closes swarmed up the side of the hill
> Among gardens and clouds,
> And closes stepped down to the harbour
> And the nets and whitemaas.

> *Per Mare*: *The Stromness Pageant* –
> Performed June 1967

No longer do the fifty or so small stone piers house gutting and curing sheds for the early herring season, as was the case during the quarter-century boom from 1881. The schoolboy morning route in that exciting era from deck to deck of big 'fifies' and 'zulus' to the foot of the Boys' Lane has long passed into folk memory.

Fishing is still important to the local economy, as is the production of quality foodstuffs, but the small distillery and brewery of a century ago have vanished, as has the rope walk. Time was when boats were under construction at several 'nousts' (boat landings on shelving beaches). Today just one boatyard survives and this at a distance from a slipway.

Plainly a much wider area is served by Stromness's numerous facilities than just the town itself; otherwise a community of nearly 2,000 could not be so well stocked with shops. Tourism, too, has an influence in supporting these businesses, as well as hotels and cafes. It has also provided a fresh raison d'etre for some former fishing boats, which now provide specialist services for visitors diving on wrecks in Scapa Flow. When the marina is completed in 2004 the harbour will have an attractive new feature for yachtsmen.

Stromness has the advantage of a fine, sheltered bay, first noted by Jo Ben, probably in the late 16th century: 'This is the best outlet for a fleet. The French and Spanish very often avoid storms here. No winds can harm ships here.'

Stromness was in an ideal situation for vessels awaiting a fair wind to set out on the Great Circle route across the North Atlantic. It was therefore no accident that the first building by the bay was an inn to serve the needs of seamen; nor was it an accident that the growing village had a remarkable number of carpenters, who found plenty of work repairing storm-damaged ships. Traders (often younger sons of lairds) settled here too. Some did well and left their mark in the shape of fine substantial homes along the main street; some even bought their own ships, though most depended on passing vessels to transport their goods.

Outsiders found that food and men could be obtained cheaply in Stromness, as Hudson's Bay Company discovered in the early 18th century (see Chapter 20, *The Canadian Connection*).

The development of Stromness might have been slow had Britain not been at war with France for much of the period between 1689 and 1815. Although The Royal Navy could normally deal with major naval forces, commerce raiders, licensed privateers, were a different matter. In fact, the English Channel became so unsafe that many merchant ships took a route round the north of Britain, finding Stromness a convenient place to shelter while awaiting a Royal Navy frigate on escort duty to Aberdeen or the Firth of Forth.

There was, therefore, no alarm in 1725 when the *George Galley*, a well-armed ship of some 200 tons, anchored outside the Holms (tidal islets on the east side of the bay). Indeed, they were happy to see the good fortune of local boy John Gow that had made him master of so fine a ship while still in his twenties. Gow was a welcome guest of Stromness's merchants and regarded by them as a potential son-in-law. Soon, however, rumour buzzed that he was a notorious pirate who had been causing havoc to shipping on the Spanish coast and the approaches to the Mediterranean. At this point people recalled that he was not in fact a true Stromnessian, having been born in Wick and brought to Stromness a year later.

While careening his vessel Gow dreamt of the opportunity afforded by Orkney: Bailie Robert Graham could be seized in his home in Stromness and ransomed for around £1,000, and the Lord Advocate's house at Hall of Clestrain across the wide Bay of Ireland from Stromness would afford even richer pickings. However, these proved to be just dreams. When suspicion fell on Gow the bailie hastily went to earth. Shortly after an attempted raid on the Hall of Clestrain, Gow ran his ship aground in the North Isles of Orkney and was tricked into captivity with astonishing ease. Trial in London led to his being hanged below the high-water mark.

During his time on Orkney, Gow's wooing had been successful and his engagement to a Miss Gordon (the daughter of a leading merchant) was made binding at the Odin Stone, where the young couple clasped hands through a large hole in the prehistoric standing stone and vowed eternal loyalty. This could be rescinded easily enough, but the involvement of both parties was required and so her family forced the unhappy girl to journey to London and renounce her engagement by touching the dead man's hand where he hung in chains. According to one account the ordeal drove her out of her mind.

More drama came to the anchorage later in the century. During the search for Bonnie Prince Charlie after his failure at Culloden, various warships made use of Hamnavoe, the bay of Stromness. It may have been distant from the search area, but it had the nearest port facilities at a time when there were none at Stornoway and Ullapool.

Throughout this period of war, concerns persisted that the Admiralty neglected the safety of merchant shipping and that Stromness in particular and Orkney in general required fortification. It was, however, not until the two world wars of the 20th century that this happened.

From 1939 to 1945 the Stromness Hotel was the key headquarters for the defences of the north of Scotland and the islands. The town was ringed about with military camps. Some structures survive – gun emplacements by the shore of Hoy Sound and the Ness Battery hutted camp, for example.

Each war brought change; increased numbers of ships and men brought extra trade. Thus by the end of the Napoleonic Wars the traders and property owners campaigned for civic rights for their village which had nearly doubled in size to its peak of 2,236 (1821 census).

The first councillors of the new burgh of barony had high ambitions: they dreamed of their own MP at a time when the neighbouring royal burgh of Kirkwall shared one with four other northern royal burghs, and offered the government their advice, for instance on the handling of the Indian Empire. On an everyday level they grappled – mostly unsuccessfully – with the problems of pigs running free in the town and of people dumping refuse in street and noust.

Law and order was of some concern. Each councillor was given his own district to oversee, but one problem area concerned all. At the first meeting of the burgh council (June 1817) they considered the hazards of the harbour and decided 'against the mischiefs arising from the outrageous and turbu- lent proceedings of seamen and others who frequent the harbour to create a police of the respectable inhabitants of the burgh in the character of constables'.

The greatest concentration of seamen would be when whaling ships from Aberdeen, Hull and Dundee arrived in springtime to recruit extra

FIGURE 32 Stromness – 19th-century lithograph by J. Irvine (by kind permision of the Trustees of Stromness Museum)

men. They arrived well-manned for sailing purposes, but whale catching was conducted from open six-oared whaleboats. It was a labour-intensive occupation, as was stripping and chopping the blubber and scraping the baleen of whales that were killed. Before going to Arctic waters and again on their return the crews were likely to drink heavily in the many inns.

The creation of the burgh coincided with an easing of ice conditions, giving a new lease of life to a dying industry for a further dozen years. Then the ice bit back with a vengeance causing disasters in 1830, 1836 and 1837. In the latter years several ships were trapped by ice in Baffin Bay and the crews were forced to spend a miserable winter short of fuel and fresh foods. Death and disease took a heavy toll as Stromnessians discovered when the first ships finally struggled back and scurvy-ridden seamen were brought ashore to a makeshift hospital set up in the town.

Whale ships continued to come, but in diminishing numbers. Those from Dundee called at Stromness almost till the First World War, but by then they no longer needed to supplement their crews with Orkney recruits.

When the well-to-do petitioned for burghal status the buoyancy of local business may have aided their self-confidence, but they also had the recollection of a successful bid half a century earlier to loosen Kirkwall's control over Stromness trade. Under Scots law the royal burghs had an exclusive right to engage in foreign trade and in return paid one-sixth of the cess (land tax) of Scotland. The Treaty of Union (1707) joined England and Scotland into one country and absorbed the Scots parliament into Westminster. The commercial clauses tried to keep the status quo, but in fact weakened the position of the royal burghs.

The Convention of Royal Burghs allocated the share of tax to each burgh. When one pleaded for a reduction it was often allocated the 'unfree trade' of its area, that is, it could tax the merchants who lived outside the burgh. Thus in 1719 such an arrangement was made with Stromness that lasted for almost a generation.

Then came trouble. Led by Alexander Graham, the Stromnessians refused to make their contribution to Kirkwall. There followed seizure of chocolate and other foreign goods held by Stromness merchants and a prolonged legal tussle (1743–1758). It ended with the decision of the House of Lords that the procedure used against the Stromness traders was illegal. It was clear that there would be no repeat claim. Legal costs had spiralled far beyond the original tax burden. Kirkwall citizens had suffered the billeting of soldiers to recoup the unpaid tax; but their heavy legal bills would be refunded by the Convention. Graham had no such redress: he was bankrupted.

The burgh coat of arms of a stylised viking galley emphasises the importance of the sea in the story of Stromness. Victorian writers made great play with that too. No one today uses their high-flown rhetoric that described Scapa Flow as 'the Orkney Mediterranean' and Stromness as 'the Venice of the North'. Yet, not many years ago, an eminent Scottish academic, only half in fun, described the town as 'the Athens of the North'. The phrase does have a ring of truth about it. Not only is there quality education through the highly-regarded Stromness Primary School and six-year secondary, Stromness Academy, to the International Centre for Island Technology (ICIT) of Heriot-Watt University, but culture and heritage have a high-profile role too. The Pier Arts Centre has an out-standing collection of modern art, and Stromness Museum (created by Orkney Natural History Society in 1837) has fine displays weighted towards wildlife and environment and the maritime side of Orkney's history.

CHAPTER TWENTY-TWO

Tales and Legends

I N THE COLD DARK NIGHTS OF WINTER the Orcadians of centuries long past would gather together around their open fires and tell stories to while away the time. No television sat in the corner of their room, no radio chattered and no newspapers brought the world's events into the homes of our long forgotten ancestors. It was not always an idle time, as work could continue by the light of the fire and the small glow of light that the old cruisie lamp cast across the corner of the room. The spinning wheel whirred and the knitting needles clicked together as new clothes took shape. Creels and nets had to be mended and fishing lines baited to ensure that food could be won from the sea. Visitors came to pass the time with friends, providing an ideal opportunity for storytelling.

The evening might start with stories of people who, although long dead, were remembered for some strange behaviour or great deed of courage. Old women who had sold themselves to the Devil and become witches were a popular subject, though the ending was usually the same. They were led into the great red sandstone cathedral of St Magnus to hear their doom – to be strangled at the stake by the hangman and their body burned to ashes. While these women were alive they had the power to take the profit from a cow's milk so that she produced no cream for butter. They could put a limpet shell into a tub of water and sink it by stirring the water as they chanted their spell, so ensuring that an enemy's boat would be lost at sea. They had the ability to transform themselves into an animal like a cat or a hare. One witch went to the harbour in Kirkwall in the form of a cat to try to steal fish. A keen-eyed fisherman thought that he recognised the cat as the witch and he threw a stone at it, striking the beast on the head. The next day the witch was seen with a cut face and a black eye.

The sea could provide food to keep a family alive, but it could also extinguish life. Shipwrecks were common around the coast of Orkney, and many sad tales were told of fine sailing ships smashed against the rocks and broken as if they were eggshells. One such tale recalls the story of how a ship was wrecked at Aikerness in Westray in the 1730s. The only survivor was a small boy who was found tied to his mother's body. The child was taken in by a local family and cared for. The only clue as to the ship's origin was a piece of wood with its port of registration written on it. The ship came from Archangel in Russia, so they gave the boy the name of Archie Angel. There were Angels in Westray until the late 19th century.

Tales of ghosts and the supernatural usually brought the evening to a close. This would bring on a feeling of dread in the people who had to walk home in the dark by themselves, especially if their journey brought them near a kirkyard or a large mound where the trows were believed to live.

A well-known Orkney ghost story is of the black wife of Scar in Sanday. She was an Indian woman who married John Traill, the son of the laird of Westove, who had business interests in India. When John heard that his father was dead and that he had inherited the estate he planned to return home, but without his wife. She followed him in secret and confronted him on the deck of the ship one night, saying that she would follow him to Sanday alive or dead. Traill saw that there was no one around, so he threw her over the side. He returned home and married a woman whose father also owned land, and they lived in the house of Scar. One night the dairymaid was milking the cow when the light of the cruisie lamp went out. She thought that the cow had flicked it with her tail, but to her surprise the flame came back. She looked and saw a black hand putting the flame back onto the wick, then taking it away again. The black wife had returned as she had said she would.

Another 'black lady' haunted Melsetter House in Hoy. In the 19th century the Moodie Heddle family, who had business interests in Sierra Leone, owned the house. A black woman was seen to arrive at Melsetter, but she never left. Soon rumours started to circulate that the laird had murdered her and that her ghost walked at night. A third story says that a black woman haunts the grounds of Old Nisthouse in Harray, the one-time home of the Clouston family, who had connections with the slave trade.

Many stories were told about the supernatural creatures that were believed to roam the land and seas of Orkney. The creature that gave most trouble to Orcadians was the trow. Trow was the Orkney word for fairy and derived from the Old Norse word *troll*, which could mean an evil spirit as well as a mountain dwelling ogre. Trows were evil, mischievous creatures who would steal newborn babies or even women who had just given birth. A baby was replaced with a changeling, a trow child who would constantly cry and never grow even though it would eat plenty. The trows wanted new mothers to feed their own children whose mothers had died in childbirth. A new mother was replaced in her home with an object such as a log of wood that had been bewitched to look like the corpse of the stolen woman. Sometimes trows would steal people for no good reason. It was recorded by the Kirkwall lawyer and writer Duncan J. Robertson (1860–1941) that old people who were senile were said to be 'in the hill', meaning that their spirit was held captive in a fairy mound.

One old Rousay man was very angry with his son and daughter because they would not bring him 'out of the hill', even though he told them where he could be found. Trows also stole cattle and horses and anything else that took their fancy. As has been mentioned already they made their homes in large mounds, which were usually closed to mortals. At certain times of the year, most commonly midsummer and midwinter, mortals might find a door standing open in the side of a mound. If they entered they might not return for a year or more, although they thought that they had only been away for a few minutes. Fiddlers were always welcome visitors for the trows, as they loved music and dancing. The American writer Washington Irving, the creator of Rip Van Winkle, who fell asleep for twenty years, was the son of William Irving from Quholm in Shapinsay.

A relation of the trows was the hogboon, who would be your friend if you treated him well. The name hogboon (or hog boy) comes from the Old Norse word *haug-bui*, meaning 'mound dweller'. Hogboons differed from trows in that they lived alone in mounds near houses and would bring good luck to the farm if they received a share of the produce. Milk and ale were poured on top of the mound, as was meal and butter. If the hogboon got its share then all went well on the farm, but if you neglected him then you had better beware! An old story from Sanday tells of the hogboon of Hellihowe, who stopped receiving his offerings when the farmer took a wife who did not know about the creature. She even scraped the porridge pot clean before she put it away, so the poor hogboon went hungry. He took his revenge by playing practical jokes on the couple until the man could stand it no longer. He went to the laird and was given a new home far away from his tormentor. He packed everything he owned onto a string of horses and set off. The sun was shining and the birds were singing, and the farmer was as happy as the day is long. Eventually his new home came into view. Suddenly the lid flew off the butter kirn (churn) that was tied to the leading horse and the hogboon stuck out his head and said, 'We're getting a fine day to flit on, Goodman!' The farmer was not aware that hogboons are attached to a family rather than a place.

There was also a race of trows who lived in the sea. These sea trows had been driven there by the more powerful land trows, but they would return to dry land if they had the chance. They were ugly creatures with faces like monkeys and sloping foreheads. They had round flat feet, were covered with scales and had seaweed for hair. They were very lazy and would try to steal fish from fishermen's hooks, but more often than not they would get themselves caught. There is a story of a creature from the sea that went to live on the island of Copinsay. Only one solitary man lived on the island, but he was due to be married in the near future. One night as he lay in bed he saw a sight that made his blood run cold. There in the doorway stood a creature, the like of which he had never seen before. It was small with a flat bald crown, but around its head grew seaweed instead of hair. It was naked, and glowed with a soft phosphores-cent light. The man remembered that cold steel and the word of God were a sure protection against all things evil, so he took his razor and a psalm book and went to do battle with the creature. It stood gibbering at him in a language he did not understand. An attempt to throw the fire irons at the creature failed, as it was too fast, so he set upon it with his fists. The creature fled the house and the man retired to his chair by the fire to recover. Soon the creature returned, smiling and waving its hands in the air in an attempt to make itself understood. The man listened closely and soon began to understand what it was trying to say. The creature told him his name was Hughbo, and his home was the sea, but he was tired of gnawing on dead men's bones and wanted to live on land. If the farmer would let him live on Copinsay he would work for him, grinding enough meal for him with the quern to make his breakfast porridge. The man was happy to have any help, and so it was agreed. This continued for some time, but soon the man's thoughts turned to his sweetheart, who lived on the Mainland. He went to see her and told her about the 'broonie' who lived with him and asked her to come over to the island and meet him. She agreed, and went to Copinsay to meet the broonie for herself. She assured her future husband that she had no problem with the broonie, and the wedding day was set. After she was married she lived on the island quite happily, but eventually the broonie's nakedness started to offend her. She got an old cloak with a hood and left it on the quern one night, a pointed hint to the broonie to cover itself up. The couple went to bed but were wakened by the wails of the broonie who was running around the quern saying, 'Hughbo's gotten a cloak and hood, so Hughbo can do no more good.' The creature ran out into the night and was never seen again.

The most terrible of all the supernatural creatures was the Nucklavee, a monster that lived in the sea but who roamed the shore in search of victims. It was a large human-like creature with a huge head, which rolled from side to side. It had a pig-like snout, a mouth as wide as a whale's, but most terrible of all, its body had no skin and every muscle and vein could be seen. It rode on, or seemed to grow out of, a horse that was every bit as frightening as its rider. The Sanday folklorist Walter Traill Dennison (1825–1894) recorded a story about a man who was chased by the Nucklavee, but escaped by jumping over a freshwater burn. This was the Nucklavee's only weak point; it could not bear the touch of freshwater on its raw flesh.

Freshwater equivalents of the Nucklavee, but more pleasing to the eye, were the water horses. They haunted the fields and roads near a loch or burn in the form of lovely horses. They would allow themselves to be caught, but as soon as people climbed onto their backs they would run into the loch and drown the rider.

The most beautiful of all the supernatural creatures was the mermaid.

As a child Walter Traill Dennison remembered the old folk of Sanday arguing over the mermaid's tail. The old men said it was part of her body, while the old women said the men were 'foolish' and the tail was in fact a beautiful petticoat embroidered with silver and gold. The mermaids' men were known as the Fin folk, and were dark featured and well built. They were powerful sorcerers who could travel over the sea in boats driven by magic. They haunted the shore in search of mortal women to carry away to their homes under the sea. Mermaids too were always on the lookout for a human husband, and with good reason. Should a mermaid marry a Fin man she was doomed to lose her beauty and become a haggard crone, known as a Fin wife. If she married a mortal man, she would stay beautiful forever. The mermaid tried to lure men to her home under the waves with her beautiful singing, which had the magical power to bewitch any man who heard it.

The town of Finfolkaheem ('home of the Fin folk') lay under the sea. Its houses were made of coral and were studded with precious gems, while its great Foy-Hall, where feasting and celebrations took place, was the finest of all buildings. Inside the hall were curtains of light, just like the 'Merry Dancers' (Northern Lights), which flickered and swayed as the dancing grew faster. One Sanday man, Arthur Dearness, was carried away to Finfolkaheem by a beautiful mermaid called Auga, but he escaped thanks to a local witch who broke all the mermaid's spells.

The Fin folk also lived during the summer months on beautiful green islands, which were usually invisible to mortal eyes. Sometimes these islands were seen floating on the sea where no land had been before, and some people were even said to have walked their shores. These islands were called Hilda-Land ('hidden land') or Hether Blether, and it was said that Eynhallow was originally one of these. It was won from the Fin folk by a man called Thorodale, whose new wife had been abducted by a Fin man. He was told by a witch how to acquire the power to see Hilda-Land, and what to do once he had. One morning he woke to see a beautiful small island lying between Evie and Rousay, and he called to his three sons from his first marriage to get things ready. They pushed off their boat, which was filled with salt, and rowed towards the island as fast as they could. Only the father could see the island, but if he took his eyes off it for just one moment he would never be able to see it again. The Fin folk used their magic to try to stop them by conjuring up phantom whales and by the mermaid's beautiful song, but they eventually reached land. Thorodale leapt ashore to be confronted by a monster that spat fire, but a handful of salt was enough to break the spell. The monster turned out to be the Fin man who had stolen Thorodale's wife, but he was no match for Thorodale, who threw a sticky cross that stuck to the Fin man's face and burned him terribly. (Fin folk were believed to be in league with the Devil, so the sign of the cross was a powerful weapon against them.) The three sons walked three times around the island sowing nine rings of salt while

Thorodale cut nine crosses in the turf. This broke the Fin folks' spell and made Eynhallow part of Orkney. The youngest son had large hands and ran out of salt before he could complete his final ring, and that is why it is said that no rats, cats or mice can live on the island.

Other sea creatures that sometimes married mortal men were the selkie folk. For most of the year they swam in the sea as seals, but at certain times of the tide they had the power to discard their seal skin and dance in human form. It was then that a man could steal a selkie maiden's skin, forcing her to live with him for as long as he possessed it. If the selkie woman ever found her skin she would immediately return to the sea and resume her life as a seal.

Orkney's folktales are a mixture of Celtic and Norse traditions, with parallels in Scotland, Ireland and Scandinavia, as the following tale will demonstrate. It is a tale typical in Northern Europe, and features a hero called Assipattle (meaning a person who rakes through the ashes).

Assipattle was considered a waster as he would not work on the farm or do anything useful around the house. One day news was brought to the farm that the Muckle Mester Stoor Worm had arrived at the shores of the land. The Muckle Mester Stoor Worm was the father of all the terrible stoor worms that lived in the sea – huge sea monsters that destroyed ships and breathed poison over the land. The king had sought advice from a wise man who had told him that the Stoor Worm must be fed with seven maidens every Saturday morning or it would destroy the land. This was done, but the cost was too high. The wise man said the only way to be rid of the Stoor Worm was to give it the king's only child, the princess Gem-de-lovely, as an offering. The king said that it would be done, but offered any brave man his kingdom and his daughter's hand in marriage if he would fight and kill the Stoor Worm. Brave knights came, but on seeing the Stoor Worm their courage deserted them. The king decided to fight the monster himself, and a boat was prepared for him to do battle at dawn. Assipattle stole his father's fastest horse and rode to the coast. He went into a small house and took a pot into which he placed a burning peat. He tricked his way onto the boat and sailed out to the Stoor Worm. As it yawned he sailed the boat straight down the Stoor Worm's throat until he was deep inside the monster. He found its liver and set it on fire with the burning peat. The Stoor Worm was filled with pain and spewed out all the water that was inside it, along with Assipattle and the boat. As it died it shot out its tongue, which crashed to the earth with such force that it made a great hole in the land. Water poured into this hole and it became the Baltic Sea. As the Stoor Worm died it lifted its head out of the water, and fell back to earth with such a crash that its teeth fell out. The first group of teeth became Orkney, while a second group of teeth became Shetland and a third group became the Faroe Islands. It coiled its body into a great lump and died, and remains there to this day as Iceland. The fire that flares up from its mountains is from the liver of the Stoor

Worm, which is still burning. Assipattle was given the kingdom and the princess's hand in marriage.

That story explained how Orkney was created, but other stories served the same purpose. Giants were always throwing stones at each other, and these huge missiles were pointed out by local folk. A giant created the lochs of Stenness and Harray by scooping up earth to fill a 'caisie' (straw basket), which he later spilt, forming the island of Graemsay and the Hills of Hoy. A group of giants dancing to a fiddler lost track of time and were turned to stone by the rising sun. They remain there to this day as the Ring of Brodgar; the Comet Stone in the field next to it is the fiddler.

Occasionally the Devil himself appeared in tales, like the story of a man called Vellyan who took him on in a drinking contest. Vellyan was drinking with three of his friends, but they could not keep up with him and had slid under the table drunk. Vellyan carried on himself until he heard a strange noise from under the table. When he looked he saw a black man throttling one of his friends. He demanded to know what he was doing, and hurled insults to the intruder. The stranger rose from the floor and the sight of him made Vellyan's blood run cold, for it was the Devil himself. He was as black as tar and his eyes burned like coals. Vellyan offered him a drink, and passed him a bowl of punch. The Devil drank it down and placed the empty bowl on the table, leaving sooty finger marks on it. Vellyan cursed him for coming to the table without washing his hands. The Devil told him to take off his waistcoat and fight. Vellyan had a few pages of a psalm book sewn into the lining of his waistcoat as a protection from evil, and the Devil knew that he had no power over him while he wore it. Vellyan knew this too, and refused to take it off. The Devil told him to take the waistcoat off or he would kill him like the others. Vellyan said they were not dead, only drunk, but he discovered to his horror that they were indeed dead. To prove it the Devil clapped his hands, sending sparks flying, and the ghosts of his three friends appeared behind him. Vellyan said that any fool could take the ghosts out of drunk men, but it would be a clever man who could put their spirits back in. The Devil grabbed one of the ghosts and thrust it back into the lifeless body. As he tried another Vellyan picked at the lining of his waistcoat and brought out the pages of the psalm book. He would have run out of time if the Devil hadn't tried to put the wrong ghost into the wrong body and found it wouldn't fit. Vellyan put the pages into a keg of gin, and when the Devil was finished he threw the keg at his head, sending him flying up the chimney with a roar that shook the house. His friends were alive again, and stone cold sober. Vellyan told them his story, saying that he had baptised the Devil with gin, seasoned with a psalm book.

A Kirkwall girl appeared before the minister of the cathedral charged with smiling during his sermon. She explained that she had seen the Devil sitting on one of the roof beams, writing down the names of the people who were asleep. When he ran out of paper he tore the tail from his shirt and wrote on that. When this proved too small he tried stretching it, using his hands and teeth, but the cloth tore and he banged his head on the rafters, and that was why she laughed. The minister replied, 'Wonderful vision! Wonderful vision!'

CHAPTER TWENTY-THREE

The Orkney Tongue

THE DIALECT 'Orcadian' has grown out of the original Norn language universally spoken in the islands 500 years ago. Norn was a form of the Norse language introduced into the islands by Norwegian settlers certainly from the 9th century onwards; it was written *Norraen* and was the old word used to describe northerners and their tongue. The word *Norraen* died out in the 14th century in Iceland to be replaced by the word *Norskr*, but in Orkney and Shetland it continued to be used in the spelt form Norn. In Orkney the language of the new settlers replaced what we assume to be an earlier Celtic language. Such slight evidence as we have of the Celtic language comes from place-names and dialect vocabulary. That most enduring Celtic word for stream or river, *esk* or *axe*, is found throughout Britain and several instances occur in Orkney too. A small stream in a valley in the Harray Hills combines both Celtic and Norse in Eskdale, applied to the whole valley. In Evie the related place-name Asiday is recorded. The 'k' is lost in the Burn of Ess which forms part of the boundary between Harray and Sandwick, and in Esgro, a field-name on Clestrain in Stronsay. This latter name Esgro, which is best translated 'water course', is also half Celtic, half Norse; on the island of Graemsay a burn by the name of Ogru shows the complete Norn form.

Celtic elements in the vocabulary are extremely rare. Where they exist, the possibility that they have been introduced through Scots must be considered; however, the word *iper*, from Gaelic *eabar*, mire and commonly used to describe midden slurry seems to have survived Norse occupation and is found in the place-name Aber, applied to a loch, now drained, in Sanday. The word *keero*, describing a small sheep in the North Isles, stems from Gaelic *caora*, sheep, and it could be argued that the word came in through Scots; however the word *kersey*, used for the native sheep, combines both Celtic and Norse and strongly suggests that *keero*, like *iper*, predates the Norse occupation. After a period of 1,200 years it comes as no surprise that these two words, *iper* and *keero*, the former common, the latter rare, represent the final spoken remnants of our Celtic tongue.

Although Orkney became officially part of the kingdom of Scotland in 1468, it was governed by Scottish earls from the first quarter of the 13th century, for whom Gaelic must have been a first language. Despite this, official documents continued to be written in Norn. This state of affairs persisted for almost 50 years after the St Clairs, a Lowland Scots line, took over the earldom in 1369. The last document written in Norn was penned in 1424, which suggests that, among those who wielded power at least, there was a degree of bilingualism for a period of 200 years. But what of the mass of country people? For them it seems that Norn continued to be used as a spoken language well into the 18th century, though by that time they would have been bilingual too. Our sources for the state of the language after Orkney was pledgeed to Scotland are meagre but positive. When at the castle in Kirkwall in 1542 Sheriff Redpath, the first justiciar in Orkney to bear that title, sat in judgment on the grinding of meal at the Mill of Sebay in Tankerness, James Irving of Sebay and the parishioners spoke 'in the common tongue'. The common tongue must have been Norn, but examples of the language in deeds and charters are rare. True, there are many Norn legal terms relating to officials, courts and land divisions, but unfortunately there is no reference to how ordinary folk spoke. Jo Ben, a 16th-century visitor to Orkney, merely said of the language that Orcadians hailed each other with the words 'Goand da boundae'. What a pity he said no more. In the trial for witchcraft of the Sanday witch Marrione Richart in 1633 a witness said that Marrione had herself admitted that, as part of her cure for Elspet Sandison's sickness, she 'aunditt in bitt'. The clerk of the court, as he would be called now, explained in his report of the proceedings that such a phrase was a Norn term meaning that she 'blew into (the) bucket'.

We are allowed a little insight into the state of the Norn language at this period from an unusual source – the study of surnames. In 1625 an Annie Voir lived at Byness (perhaps Lyness?) in Walls on the island of Hoy. Her surname is a complete puzzle until we realise that *voir* represents Old Norse *vágar*, 'bays', the original name of the parish of Walls. In official documents the parish had been called Wawis or Walls since the late 15th century, but here we have local folk still using the pure Norn term more than 100 years later. From a Shetland witch trial of 1645 we get confirmation that our interpretation of *voir* is correct. In the trial of Marion Peebles a place-name Voir is mentioned in the Hillswick district of Northmavine, which clearly relates to the 'voes' there such as Hillswick and Ronas Voe. Another example of an informative Orkney surname comes from the North Isles where, in 1708, a James Kvilo is recorded as living in Stronsay. This most unusual surname is no longer recorded. It is the original form of what today we would write as Quoyloo, which derives from Old Norse *kví-ló*, an enclosure in a marshy area. The written form of the surname Kvilo shows that at the beginning of the 18th century an enclosure was still pronounced 'kvy'.

Birsay man George Moar was interested in antiquities and in 1785 corresponded with George Paton, a well-known Edinburgh antiquarian on the subject of the Norn language in Orkney, giving some examples. A common curse used by local people, he said, was 'swarta suit'. What a fascinating curse this is. It is the exact equivalent of English, 'Plague on you!'. 'Swarta suit', as written by George Moar is Old Norse *svarta sótt*, Black Death, literally 'black sickness'; the obsolete dialect word 'gulso' for jaundice has a similar derivation from *gulusótt*, 'yellow sickness'. *Svarta sótt* is a native Norn form and is not known in Norse speaking countries either as the illness or the curse. It is extraordinary that this curse is still known in Orkney where it is corrupted to 'blacksight', but it has completely lost its venom. In his letter to Paton, George went on to say, 'I am fifty years of age. When I was young, about five or six old men (in the parish) spoke mostly Norse, but they were never taught to read or write any of it for a long time before so that their words and what does remain can be but imperfect.' This echoes the words of Rev. George Low in 1773, when he wrote, 'I believe there is scarce a single man in the country who can express himself on the most ordinary occasion in this language.'

By the 1800s Norn as a spoken language was dead. Why did it die? It died for the same reason that most languages and dialects die: it became unfashionable to speak a language associated with the old and the poor – and indeed the awkward! By an extraordinary piece of fortune two dialect words corroborate this. They are 'norny/nornaway', meaning cantankerous or old fashioned and 'nory', ill-tempered. It goes without saying that both words are derived from the original word *norraen*.

Two principal sources exist for the student of the Norn language. These are firstly, the place-names of the islands, which are discussed elsewhere in the book; secondly, dialect words and phrases which are in current use or which have been recorded. In the late 1980s the writer collected more than 6,000 dialect words and phrases, all of which formed the basis of his *Orkney Wordbook*. If we consider words with correlates in Old Norse only, 60 were commonly used in the writer's home as a child and would have been part of the currency of everyday speech in the 1950s. Of these 60 words, two thirds were nouns and one third verbal forms; adjectives and adverbs are rare. Here are some examples, chosen at random:

An 'aizer' o a fire; he 'brett' ap his sleeves; whit a 'eun' wi that cloot; the bull gid clean 'eum'; the car wis stuck in a big 'fann' in the road; whit are yi 'gaanan' at?'; me eyes are fill o 'gurr' the day; luk at the 'ime' on the buddum o the kettle; pit a runnan 'raes' on that string tae me; luk at the 'rittos' gan efter the ploo; whit a 'skry' o bairns ahint that wife; the bairn's gin an 'spret' his breeks; come an play among the 'skroos'; me finger's fairly 'sweean'; I hid tae 'tepp' the water in the burn; when the 'teebro's' flyan the grund's dryan; thir's a piece o maet stuck in me 'yackles'. If we cast the net wider to include Norwegian and Nynorsk correlates there are very many more.

Orcadian is, however, essentially a Scottish dialect. The 60 words with direct Norse correlates known to the writer as a child are in steep contrast to 500 familiar Scots entries. Here is a small selection of Scots entries used in context: the wind's in a bad 'airt' the day; Ah'm right 'blide' thoor come; the 'bairns' were hintan 'buckies' on the shore; the bike skidded on the 'chingly' stones on the road; yi'll hiv tae 'pit' a 'dwang' in 'atween' that pieces o wid; he covered the paet stack wi 'divots'; granny's wardrobe is aal covered wi 'eerieorms'; wir 'flittan' on Tuesday; for whit a 'gutter's' aboot the door; that 'coo's hostan aafil'; don't touch me feet for Ah'm aafil 'kittly'; this 'neep's' aal 'mozy'; stick a 'preen' in hid; thir's a great 'rive' in yir coat; hid's a peety thir's no a market for 'tattie-shaas'; whit a 'stoor's' coman fae the combine; whit a 'trachle' wir hin wi the crop the 'ear; I deu like the soond o a 'whaup'; Ah'm no seen a 'yellow-yarleen' for 'ears.

The proportion of nouns in the familiar Scots forms, two-thirds, is exactly the same as in the Norn, but verbs are rarer. This is compensated however by a greater number of adjectives and adverbs. One of the most common Scots adjectives, 'wee', is strikingly absent from the dialect of Orkney where 'peedie', formerly 'peerie', is universal. On the other hand Scots 'bonny' and 'bairn' are surely among the most common dialect words in use. A characteristic of the dialect of Orkney, probably due to its insular position, is that special usages have developed, unknown on the Scottish mainland, which these two words 'bonny' and 'bairn' serve to illustrate. 'Bonny' in Orcadian dialect, apart from meaning 'fine' or 'beautiful' can also mean 'dreadful' as in these examples. 'That's a bonny mess yir made!' or 'Yir a bonny like sight wi hair like that!' (the hair had been died green!). 'Bonny fine hid' means 'That's OK by me'. Scots 'bairnly' with the meaning 'childish' takes the form 'bairny' in Orkney dialect and 'bairny bugger', applied to a spoiled adult, is a popular phrase because of its alliteration. Among old folks and indeed among the not so old where a feeling of warmth and familiarity is to be conveyed, 'bairns' is used vocatively in special senses as in these examples. 'Bairns! bairns!' means 'What is the world coming to!' 'Weel bairns, Ah'll hae tae go', carries the meaning 'Well folks, I'll have to go'.

As can be seen, dialect is much more than a collection of words. We have to go beyond the word to the meaning of the word. In the above examples we can see that Scottish dialect words carry different meanings in Orkney settings. Here is an example of an English adjective used entirely differently in Orkney. To say to an English guest 'I wis right *annoyed* when yi didna come last night' might be understood to be tactless and offensive but the real meaning conveyed is 'I was really worried when you didn't come last night', which shows a genuine concern at the non-appearance of the visitor.

What are the principal characteristics of Orkney dialect today? To answer this question we have to make considerable generalisations since the dialect of the 18-year-old is very different from the dialect of the 80-year-old and there are considerable variations within the county. The dialect of Kirkwall, in common with all urban areas throughout Britain, reveals special characteristics.

I was told this story by an Orkney girl, let's call her Sandra, who lived in north east England. She telephoned an English friend with whom she had previously worked and asked for 'Lucy'. 'Oh I doot thir's nobody here caaled Lucy', the reply came. Sandra immediately recognised the voice as Orcadian. By the strangest of coincidences an Orkney girl had moved into the flat previously occupied by her English friend! What were the characteristics of the dialect that helped Sandra to instantly recognise the dialect as Orcadian when others might have assumed the voice to be Welsh or Irish, certainly not Scots!

Firstly, despite the short sentence, the vocabulary contained a pure Orcadian usage. The English verb 'to doubt' has the opposite meaning in Orcadian where 'tae doot' is 'to express a degree of certainty about something negative'. 'I doot hid'll rain', means in the dialect of Orkney, 'I feel fairly certain that it is going to rain', whereas English, 'I doubt it will rain' implies that it will not rain. In the telephone conversation described the expected English reply would have been, 'I'm afraid ...' Another give-away in this brief reply was the use of 'nobody'. Of course 'nobody' is used in English and Scottish dialects, but the use of 'no one' would have been expected in this situation. 'No one' in this sense is unknown in the dialect of Orkney and were it to be pronounced it would be spoken 'no wan' and would sound nonsensical, indeed laughable since it would be immediately apparent that the speaker was 'chantan', i.e. attempting to avoid the use of dialect and ending up with a hybrid language! 'No wan' can be used in Orkney dialect but only in a phrase such as 'Thir's no wan buddy aboot the hoose at aal'.

So far we have drawn attention to two identifiers of the Orkney dialect in this context, but Sandra's ear would have been attuned to other differences. The pronunciation of the vowels for example would also have been striking as the written form partly suggests. When 'there' is used in the sense 'there is' it is pronounced 'thir', but where the sense 'over there' is implied the pronunciation is quite close to the English. As for the pronunciation of 'thir's', it shows an Orcadian peculiarity also characteristic of the Norse languages. 'Thir's', is pronounced 'thirsh', the 'th' being pronounced as in English but the 's' having a marked 'sh' sound. An 'r' followed by an 's' in Orkney dialect is invariably pronounced 'sh', the reason being that the 'r' and the 's' are very close together phonetically. What this means is that since the 'r', unlike the Scots 'r', is not trilled, the tongue is pushed into the 'sh' rather than the 's' sound. This is such a characteristic of Orkney dialect that a request to pronounce 'Birsay' would immediately help to identify one as a native. It is a sobering thought that, in history, such language tests have been used to settle tribal disputes among peoples, often with appalling consequences.

Lastly we look at the pronunciation of two of the remaining words in the reply. The 'o' in dialect 'no' is a very long vowel indeed, pronounced with rounded lips in such a way that it rhymes with English 'dough'. The English 'o' is pronounced with pursed lips. If the speaker had been an elderly Orcadian and had wished to emphasize the fact that Lucy wasn't there, she would have replied 'Na'. A more emphatic 'na' was frequently pronounced with a tremor in the voice reminiscent of the bleat of a sheep! With regard to the pronunciation of 'called' as 'caaled', it is characteristic of the dialect that where an 'a' is followed by a double 'l', then the 'a' is short as in English 'pallet'. Words such as ball, fall, etc., would be pronounced in this way though older people, in common with the Scots, would not sound the final double 'l' as in 'Watch and no faa when yi keek the baa'. What has been said about the pronunciation of the 'a' followed by a double 'l' is an example of the danger of generalising about Orkney dialect since on the island of Rousay and in the parishes of Evie and Rendall 'a' before double 'l' is pronounced in such a way that has no equivalent in English – a short 'a' but pronounced deep down the throat.

Two characteristics of local pronunciation cannot be illustrated from the sentence we chose to show peculiarities of the Orkney dialect. In common with some of our Highland neighbours 'j' and soft 'g' in initial position are pronounced 'ch' throughout the whole of Orkney as in 'Yi wid chenerally need tae wear a warm chumper or chersey in Chanuary'. The conventional English pronunciation of 'j' and soft 'g' comes to the tongue only with great difficulty and where a sentence includes such consonants and 'ch' in initial position, the Orcadian will often get them confused if he/she is trying to speak 'properly'. This often causes much amusement as for example when 'Gerry's a right fine chap' becomes 'Cherry's a right fine Jap'!

The other aspect of pronunciation which we have not been able to illustrate is the Norse vowel ø which still exists in the dialect of older people. The listener will hear 'do' being pronounced *dø*; 'moon', *møn*; 'soot', *søt*, and 'shoes' as *shøn*, the latter showing the Old English plural! From these few examples it can be seen how, in addition to the dialect of Orkney having a vocabulary peculiar to English (though often shared by Shetland), it is characterised by: 1. use of English words with different meaning 2. the absence of words common in English 3. different vowel sounds from standard English 4. unique vowel sounds 5. unique consonant sounds 6. local differences in pronunciation.

Another useful indicator of Orkney dialect is what may be described its intonation or song. Every dialect has a characteristic song but some are more tuneful than others. Orkney dialect is particularly tuneful and it is this which to the uninitiated is perhaps its most striking aspect. If we were to use a simple representation of pitch to represent the song of the telephone reply it might be represented thus:

```
                              caaled      cy
No I doot thir's        here         Lu
              nobody
```

There is a marked tendency to end sentences on a high note in contrast to e.g. Glaswegian where sentences are ended on a low note. The song of the dialect is frequently responsible for Orcadians being identified as Welsh abroad, particularly where there are Welsh immigrants.

From a study of this brief sentence we have not been able to illustrate any of the peculiarities of grammar, some of which are shared with other English dialects. Take for example the verb 'to be':

First person singular	*Ah'm*	First person plural	*wir*
Second person singular	*yir/thoor*	Second person plural	*yir*
Third person singular	*he's/she's/hid's*	Third person plural	*thir*

It is not particularly different from the verb 'to be' in other dialects but it does emphasize the fact that the pronoun and the verb are very compressed – and even more than in English, are sounded as one word. An illustration of this verb also shows that two less familiar pronouns are in evidence here. 'Hid' meaning 'it' is a relic of the original form of 'it', which in Middle English was *hit*, also recorded in Scots but which was readily accepted in Orkney by Norn speakers where the equivalent pronoun was *hitt*. The other pronoun of note is 'thoo' used familiarly by the older generation particularly in the parish of Birsay where the forms 'thee' and 'thine' are also current. It is understandable that such pronouns have been so resilient in Orkney, and indeed in Shetland, where the Old Norse equivalents of 'thoo' and 'thine' were *þú* and *þín*. The familiar form of 'you' died out in Scotland at the beginning of the 19th century.

The main purpose of introducing the verb 'to be' however is to show that it is universally used to represent the perfect tense with all verbs. Let us illustrate this with the present perfect tense of the verb 'to give' which in English begins 'I have given', 'You have given' etc.

First person singular	*Ah'm gin*	First person plural	*Wir gin*
Second person singular	*Yir gin/thoor gin*	Second person plural	*Yir gin*
Third person singular	*He's/she's/hid's gin*	Third person plural	*Thir gin*

Here are examples of usage: 'Wir gin a lot tae charity; Ah'm gin her aal I hiv tae gae'. These examples serve to show also that many Orkney dialect verbs are irregular. The verb 'tae gae', i.e. 'to give' is declined:

Present	*I gae*
Simple Past	*I gid*
Present Perfect	*Ah'm gin*
Past Perfect	*I wir gin*

Some of the more common irregular verbs are:
tae come = to come: *come, cam/kam, come/comed*
tae find (rhymes with 'grinned') = to find; *find, fand, fund*
tae gae = to give; *gae, gid, gin*
tae git = to get: *git, got, gotten*
tae go = to go: *go, gid, gin*

tae hiv = to have: *hiv, hid, hin*
tae ken = to know: *ken, kent, kent*
tae pit = to put: *pit, pat/pot, pitten*
tae strik = to strike: *strik, strak, strukken*
tae tak = 1. to take 2. to bring: *tak, tuk, tin*

It will be noticed that the past tense forms of 'go' and 'give' are identical.

Some common English verbs are unknown in the Orkney dialect, e.g. 'become'. It would always be rendered by the verb 'tae git'. However the sentences 'I wondered what had become of you' would be spoken as, 'I windered whit hid come o yi'. The common English verbs 'talk' and 'bring' are never used. 'We talked about bringing the cattle in' would be expressed as 'We spok aboot takkan in the kye'.

What is true of verbs applies equally to nouns. The noun 'talk' like the verb does not exist. 'We had a talk about bringing the cattle in' becomes 'We hid a spaek aboot takkan in the kye'. The word 'woman' is used only vocatively and then only familiarly and jocularly when a man might persuade his wife to hurry up by saying 'Come on 'umman'. In every other case 'wife' would be substituted. 'Thir's a wife at the door wantan tae spaek tae yi'. Oddly the plural of 'wife' is 'weeman'! As in the case of 'wife' the plural of nouns in Orkney dialect is worthy of attention. Orcadians speak of 'wan teeth' meaning 'one tooth' and 'wan feet' meaning 'one foot'. The plural of English 'foot' where 'foot' is a measure is 'foot' but in the dialect of Orkney it is 'feet'. Ironically 'over six foot' in English translates as 'ower six feet' in Orcadian! 'Trout' which in dialect is 'troot' has the plural 'troots'; the plural of 'horse' on the other hand is 'horse'. 'Year' which is pronounced 'ear' also stays the same in the plural if it is preceded by a numeral as in 'fower 'ear', i. e four years, but the English plural is used in 'hunders o 'ears'.

In common with other dialects of English Orkney dialect has developed characteristic turns of speech. The common greeting 'How are you?' is 'Whit like the day?'; English 'I'm quite happy about that' can be rendered succinctly in dialect by 'Fine hid'. Equally the sentence 'You can go if you wish but it won't be with my approva'l needs no more than 'Had gan'. It might seem quite offensive to say 'had yir tongue', i.e. 'hold your tongue' to someone who is telling you something but this is a mere reaction to an unbelievable piece of news and should not be interpreted literally. The same is true of the phrase 'Nivver spaek!' which when uttered by someone means merely 'I am wholly in agreement with you about that unspeakable thing'. Many common paired phrases in English are reversed in Orkney dialect for some inexplicable reason. Here are some examples: 'sole stockings' = stocking soles; 'knifes and forks' = forks and knives; 'headlight' = light headed; 'needles and preens' = pins and needles. Such a characteristic of our dialect cannot be very old when we realise that 'wire netting', which was invented towards the end of the 19th century, is spoken of as 'netting wire'!

Within the island group there are considerable differences in pronunciation though these are not so marked today as they were formerly. Every Orcadian can immediately recognise an older native of Westray by his pronunciation of the short 'a' as 'ay' in which 'apples' becomes 'ayples' in contrast to the Mainland pronunciation 'ehples'. Unlike all other Orcadians Burray and South Ronaldsay folk made no distinction between the pronunciation of the participle of the verb and the gerund or noun which was made from it. A man from Birsay for example would say 'Ah'm gan tae the fisheen for I like fishan' but a Burray man would utter 'Ah'm gan tae the fishan for I like fishan'. The South Isles of Orkney as well as Deerness and Stromness is characterised by the use of the diminutive 'ack/ick' frequently used are familiar forms of names e.g. 'Billack' whereas on the Mainland and in the North Isles 'Billo' would be the regular form.

Orkney dialect, like all dialect, is changing rapidly. The glottal stop before 't' and 'ck', the use of which has existed in Kirkwall dialect for some time, is spreading rapidly throughout the islands especially among the young. 'Tatties' are no longer 'tatties', they are 'tah-ies' and 'tak hid oot' is likely to be pronounced 'Tah ih ooh'. Smart young Kirkwallians will still address one by saying 'Whit like the day?' – and they will expect the conventional reply, 'No so bad ither' to which they will reply 'Good, good', but this is a rejoinder hitherto unknown in dialect.

Linguists marvel at the fact that the Eskimo, or Inuit, have 35 different words to describe snow. The rich dialect that once was Orcadian cannot compete with the Inuit on that score but we also had a few words for snow, such as – 'ask', 'blindroo', 'erdrift', 'fann', 'figgerin', 'fleuk', 'glush', 'haily buckies', 'lambing sna', 'moor', 'pirlie sna', 'skutch', 'smoor', 'smook', 'stark moor', 'stikkid stoor', 'stirling sna' and 'teeick sna'. Snow being quite rare in the islands our vocabulary developed in other more meaningful ways. It will come as no surprise to Orcadians that there are 74 words in our dialect to describe different ways of walking, all of which can be found in the *Orkney Wordbook*!

Walking is not so important now; we rarely see anyone walk. The only type of locomotion we have to be familiar with today is the speed, colour and model of the vehicle! All language is in a constantly changing state of flux and who can say that changes are for the better or for the worse? As long as we can be mutually understood what difference does it make?

CHAPTER TWENTY-FOUR

Orkney Literature

THE LITERATURE OF ORKNEY has powerful precedents, stretching back to the Icelandic sagas of 700 years ago; it also has its roots in more modern myths, woven by two remarkable writers, Edwin Muir and George Mackay Brown. A third, larger-than-life figure on this literary landscape is the popular novelist, Eric Linklater. While Orkney has long been credited with the production of university scholars and the export of professors it is a signal tribute to the qualities of its imaginative life that it has produced three writers of international stature who have contributed to the current shape of literature in English.

Edwin Muir was born in the parish of Deerness on Orkney Mainland in 1887. His father was a tenant farmer and moved to the Bu, a farm on the island of Wyre, when Edwin was a few years old. His childhood years in this tiny rural community were the wellspring of his poetic impulse, drawn up by powerful memories and set against the later horrors of his adolescence in industrial Glasgow. The family moved first to Kirkwall, then when Edwin was 14, south to Glasgow, where his family life disintegrated with the death of his parents and his brother.

The remembered rural idyll of Wyre provides a very physical base for Muir's Eden, a complex racial memory of innocence and purity that contrasts starkly with the brutal realities of his century: war; political power struggles; poverty and institutionalised violence. At its best, Muir's poetry speaks figuratively of the big human questions – love and hate; hope and despair; guilt and innocence; heaven and hell – in language that is profound yet simple and everyday.

He came to poetry late, at the age of 35, following psychoanalysis and a spiritual reappraisal of himself. By this time he was a cosmopolitan European, writing incisive literary criticism and translating Franz Kafka and contemporary German novelists with his wife, Willa, a Shetlander. He was closely engaged with the intellectual currents that were circulating in post-First World War Europe, yet he grounded his poetic voice in the fabled landscape of his Orkney infancy. This timeless tranquillity is caught in an early poem *Childhood*, that hints at future knowledge, but is bounded by the certainties of his parents:

Long time he lay upon the sunny hill,
  To his father's house below securely bound.
Far off the silent, changing sound was still,
  With the black islands lying thick around.

He saw each separate height, each vaguer hue,
  Where the massed islands rolled in mist away,
And though all ran together in his view
  He knew that unseen straits between them lay.

Often he wondered what new shores were there.
  In thought he saw the still light on the sand,
The shallow water clear in tranquil air,
  And walked through it in joy from strand to strand.

Over the sound a ship so slow would pass
  That in the black hill's gloom it seemed to lie.
The evening sound was smooth like sunken glass,
  And time seemed finished ere the ship passed by.

Grey tiny rocks slept round him where he lay,
  Moveless as they, more still as evening came,
The grasses threw straight shadows far away,
  And from the house his mother called his name.

The landscape is physically very real: it is the Orkney that Muir recalled and wrote about in *The Story and the Fable*, an autobiographical account of his early life that he later expanded into a fuller autobiography. However, it is also a spiritual landscape transmuted by poetic vision and symbolic of a purer world unsullied by the depredations of industrial society and its concomitant evils of materialism and the loss of innocence.

The symbol of Eden constantly recurs in his work. In *Outside Eden* he speaks of a landscape in which the people have spiritually lost their way; retelling poetically the oldest of myths:

Such is the country of this clan,
Haunted by guilt and innocence.
There is a sweetness in the air
That bloomed as soon as time began,
But now is dying everywhere.

One Foot in Eden is the title poem of a collection that deals largely with religious subjects. Muir's concern, however, is typically an observation of the human condition framed in everyday imagery and expressed in conversational tones;

One foot in Eden still, I stand
And look across the other land.

> The world's great day is growing late,
> Yet strange these fields that we have planted
> So long with crops of love and hate.

The informal tone that characterises much of Muir's poetry is a remarkably effective vehicle for carrying some fairly heavyweight ideas. His austere vision of the contemporary world is tempered by the intimate rapport he creates with his reader. Thus his poems have a simple profundity that is not marred by a preaching intellectualism.

Sometimes the puzzling ambiguity of dreams provides the scenario for striking poetry. *The Combat* is a mythological narrative about strange, nameless creatures, unequally matched in a deadly fight. The brutal aggressor is archetypical:

> Body of leopard, eagle's head
> And whetted beak, and lion's mane,
> And frost-grey hedge of feathers spread
> Behind – he seemed of all things bred.
> I shall not see his like again.

The apparent victim is its polar opposite:

> As for his enemy, there came in
> A soft round beast as brown as clay;
> All rent and patched his wretched skin;
> A battered bag he might have been,
> Some old used thing to throw away.

The duel is soon over, yet the forlorn creature would not die:

> For ere the death stroke he was gone,
> Writhed, whirled, huddled into his den,
> Safe somehow there. The fight was done,
> And he had lost who had all but won.
> But oh his deadly fury then.

And the deadly combat is played out again and again, never ending:

> The champions took their posts again.

> And all began. The stealthy paw
> Slashed out and in. Could nothing save
> These rags and tatters from the claw?
> Nothing. And yet I never saw
> A beast so helpless and so brave.

> And now, while the trees stand watching, still
> The unequal battle rages there.

The killing beast that cannot kill
Swells and swells in his fury till
You'd almost think it was despair.

The deliberately wry twist of the final stanza lends a positive slant to the
poignant humanism of the poem; and the use of the present tense in these
lines confirms the poem as Muir's comment on the human condition. It
is an optimistic assertion of the resilience of the human spirit in the face
of overwhelming odds.

A specifically Christian spiritualism that was always distinct in Muir's
poems more explicitly pervades his later work. He was too good a poet to
allow it to topple into piety; rather it informs his verse with an ingenuous
humanism. This is seen in his most widely read poem, *The Horses*, the
account of a group of survivors coping with the aftermath of a nuclear
holocaust. Muir eschews apocalyptic visions, instead sketching the story of
a people's sad bewilderment that is transformed by the dramatic and
symbolic arrival of a herd of wild horses. The narrator's voice is simple
but measured in the enormity of what has happened. The poem opens
with 'The seven days' war that put the world to sleep'. Mankind ironically
destroys in equal time what God created. The trappings of our human evil
are the products of modern technology, now useless:

The radios dumb;
And still they stand in corners of our kitchens,
And stand, perhaps, turned on, in a million rooms
All over the world.

However the survivors, living on a remote seaboard, have acquired a
certainty born from their bitter experience:

But now if they should speak,
If on a sudden they should speak again,
If on the stroke of noon a voice should speak,
We would not listen, we would not let it bring
That bad old world that swallowed its children quick
At one great gulp. We would not have it again.

The ravaged world is conjured with powerful simplicity:

Sometimes we think of the nations lying asleep,
Curled blindly in impenetrable sorrow,
And then the thought confounds us with its strangeness.

Into this twilit sadness come the dramatic semi-wild horses. They are
powerful but frightening, a visitation from before their fathers' time:

We did not dare go near them. Yet they waited,

Stubborn and shy, as if they had been sent
By an old command to find our whereabouts
And that long lost archaic companionship.

The horses provide that broken bridge between the horrors wrought by
20th century technology and the prelapsarian society of older times. They
allow the survivors to re-establish the innocence of the past, leave behind
the evils of the present, and forge a new world:

Among them were some half-a-dozen colts
Dropped in some wilderness of the broken world,
Yet new as if they had come from their own Eden.
Since then they have pulled our ploughs and borne our loads,
But that free servitude still can pierce our hearts.
Our life is changed; their coming our beginning.

Muir's vision is optimistic. All the more remarkable for the painfully honest
way he observes the events of the 20th century. His poetry recognises the
inevitable duality and conflict of good and evil in the world, and seeks to
explore its sources and possible resolutions. His poetic recreation of an
Edenic Orkney, at first accessed through dreams and recovered memories,
is central to the vision of his poetry. Despite the intensely metaphysical
character of many of his poems, they are rooted in the imagery and
metaphor of a rural landscape; they are peopled by characters bound in
close-knit small societies; they are rigorously rhymed but flow with a diction
that is limpid and simple. It is a poetic voice that is grounded in Orkney,
but has spoken to the world.

Eric Linklater (1899–1974) is in many ways a complete contrast to Edwin
Muir. Primarily a novelist, with a range of other writings including essays,
history and autobiography, his prose is breezy and light, his characters
often comic but worldly men of the upper classes. His life also contrasts
curiously to that of Muir. The poet spent his formative, childhood years
in Orkney and left it permanently at the age of 14, returning only on
holiday; Linklater was born in Wales of an Orkney father and spent his
first 14 years in that country. If Muir was proud and particular about his
Orcadian origins, Linklater was fanatic in creating a persona for himself
as an ingrained Orcadian with a bloodline tracing back a thousand years
to the Viking times of Norse sovereignty. It is a streak of romantic
autobiography that finds parallel expression in his variously located novels.

He was a prolific writer, producing more than 70 books, including war
histories, plays, biographies, children's books, three collections of short
stories and 23 novels. His first novel was *White Maa's Saga*, a comic
romance set in Aberdeen and Orkney, published in 1929. It is an assured
piece of autobiographical fiction retailing the adventures of the epony-
mously nicknamed hero as he drinks, fights and romances his way through

university to find fulfilment and love in Orkney. Despite a final slide into melodrama the novel catches faithfully the careless exuberance of university life and gives perceptive pen pictures of Orkney characters and institutions such as the County Show. Although an apprentice work, its motifs and concerns are rehearsed throughout much of Linklater's remarkably varied fiction. The 'saga' of the title, consciously identifying with the classic Icelandic tales of the Viking period, marks the importance of strong narrative and manly challenge in the novels.

These traits are clear in the exotically picaresque novels such as *Private Angelo* and *Juan in America*, in which the heroes episodically face ludicrous predicaments that potently satirise the Italian War campaign of 1943 and Prohibition USA respectively. The intentions in both novels are largely comic, but Linklater was well aware of the power of comedy, as he observed in a letter to a friend: 'I have always thought ... that the comic attitude to life is just as valid as the tragic attitude. In fact it's probably more valid, because tragedy ends in death and with comedy you've got to go on living ... In ancient Greece, which sets the standard for all things, comedy and tragedy were regarded on the same plane, of equal validity as criticism, as comment on life.'

However, there are similar challenges in the more satisfying Orkney novel, *Magnus Merriman*, which is buoyed up by Linklater's characteristically mock satiric tone. The hero of the title stumbles from bayonetting the backside of his commanding officer in the trenches of the First World War, to a parliamentary by-election of the '30s in the heady early days of Scottish Nationalism. Magnus Merriman, one of his creator's most likeable heroes, plunges into the Rabelaisian adventures of the bulk of the novel with a zest born of ingenuousness and irresponsibility. However, a moonlight escapade with an Orkney lass while home on holiday results in impending fatherhood, and he rather manfully accepts his responsibilities and returns to his roots. To his dismay he is tamed finally by a stolidly sensible wife and the realities of farming. In the closing pages, however, he is delighted to discover academic precocity in his infant son who can apparently speak Greek. He invests this prodigy with his final enchanted dream of greatness and rests content.

In many ways *The Men of Ness* is his most enduring novel. It is set in Rousay at the height of Norse power and tells the tale of Ragnar, Thorlief Coalbiter and his sons Kol and Skallagrim, and of Thorlief's wife Signy who drives the sons to avenge the death of their step-father Bui, slain by Ivar the Boneless. It is also the story of Gauk, who is the antithesis of the Saga hero – timid, cunning, henpecked – in his own words, 'a little man', yet a survivor who enlarges the frame of the novel with his human frailties.

Linklater admired greatly the Icelandic saga literature and has interwoven incidents from the great 13th-century saga of Orkney, the *Orkneyinga Saga*, with his own fictional creation. Adopting the spare, laconic style of the sagas, he is at his most effective in deploying his powers of storytelling and description. The account of the voyage of Skallagrim's ship, the *Skua*, and the loss of her sister ship, the *Scarf*, in the Swelkie of Stroma shows Linklater at his best:

> They came by the edge of the whirlpool and a curving wave took the ship and twisted it inwards. Another wave caught the stern and flung it high, and the ship was drawn into the roost. The mast broke. The *Scarf* rose high like a rearing horse, and the sail dragged down one side. It was thrown sideways and fell on its side. The men clung to the thwarts, but some were hurled into the sea. Then a confusion of waves leapt upon it, and broke it and beat it down, and the Swelkie of Stroma sucked the *Scarf* under, and Erling's crew with it, and drowned them.

Linklater was an enormously popular writer in the '30s, '40s and '50s – he has been more widely read than any other Orcadian writer, although his work never achieved critical acclaim. His popularity has waned with later generations who are out of sympathy with the upper class milieu of his characters' lives: his heroes and their friends seem to belong to an unacknowledged but potently exclusive club that refuses entry to the ruck of humankind. There is also a pervasive flippancy of tone that denies human access to the struggles of many of his characters who fail to engage our sympathy.

Yet he is a writer of great power and originality. His range of reference, witnessed by the varied writing disciplines he mastered, is rarely equalled by other Scottish authors of the 20th century. His command of language in both his fiction and non-fiction has a deceptive easy muscularity that has not been bettered by other Scottish writers of his time.

George Mackay Brown (GMB) has established an imaginative identity for Orkney more effectively than any other author, past or present. His *oeuvre*, from *The Storm and other Poems* published in 1954, through to the post-humous *Travellers* of 2001 is a loving exploration of the culture, history and above all, the people of Orkney. He produced poetry, short stories, novels, plays, essays, childrens' tales and collections of journalism. Varied though his work is, it is uniformly crafted and balanced with the poet's eye for the telling symbol and ear for the falling cadence.

GMB lived all his life in Stromness, excepting his years of higher education in Edinburgh, firstly at Newbattle Abbey College under Edwin Muir, then university in the city. He rarely left Orkney, and made a virtue of his reluctance to travel. Instead he turned inwards to fashion a vision of Orkney that was laden with symbol and set in an unspecified earlier time, yet peopled with living men and women. In his novels he is happiest recreating Orkney's past, often drawing on the inspiration of the *Orkneyinga Saga*, both stylistically and materially. The clipped economy of the saga narrative and the historical detail of Orkney's Norse period were employed in *Vinland* (1992), the story of Ranald Sigmundson from his boyhood voyages in fabled Vinland to old age and death as a prosperous but sea-hungry farmer near Hamnavoe. Behind this family saga the larger tale of violent power politics amongst the ruling earls of Orkney is played out. The novel sets the fledgling Christian values of humility, contemplation and reconciliation above the careless bloodletting of the Viking earls.

The victorious earl of *Vinland* was Earl Thorfinn, grandfather to Earl Magnus Erlendson, a central figure in GMB's work. As man, saint and symbol he provided a rich source that GMB worked into poetry, play and prose – most notably in his 1973 novel *Magnus*. The life story of Magnus, from conception through murder on Egilsay at Easter 1117 to sainthood, is presented in an explicitly Catholic religious framework. Even at conception on the wedding night of his parents, Magnus is marked out, chosen: 'a great sacrificial host surged between the loins of bridegroom and bride, and among them a particular chosen seed, a summoned one, the sole ultimate destined survivor of all that joyous holocaust'.

As a young man in the war galleys of the Norwegian king, Magnus eschews the axe, reading aloud from his psalter in the thick of battle. His spiritual detachment from material things is singular and sets the scene for his martyrdom at the hands of his cousin Hakon. GMB makes clear that Magnus went willingly to his death as a sacrifice to ensure the future stability of a divided Orkney. Typically the religious message is leavened with the earthy peasant character Mans, a counterpoint to the saintly Magnus: he is cynical, coarse, resentful of all masters and gloriously human. It is a strength of the novel that it opens with Mans and Hild toiling on the land, watching from afar the aristocratic wedding party; and closes with the accidental pilgrimage of the tinkers Jock and Mary to the Birsay kirk. Albeit the reluctant visit of the faithless, drouthy Mary results in a miracle of restored sight, the prologue and epilogue to the saint's story gives us the best dialogue and most vividly human characters of the novel.

Greenvoe (1972) deploys a delightful range of characters with an economy of observation and a light deftness of touch that has ensured its enduring popularity. GMB portrays a close knit community, largely unchanged for generations, and now under threat by Operation Black Star, a military/ industrial project that requires the island of Hellya for unspecified purposes. The island's destruction follows, resulting in the enrichment of a few and the displacement of a community and its history. Operation Black Star fails abruptly and the novel ends on a note of hope with the silent return of a group of islanders who celebrate the ritual rebirth of Hellya's fertility.

The strength of the novel lies in the close observation and delineation of the island community. It is achieved with ironic detachment tempered by authorial affection. The opening chapter introduces the whole cast of players: The Skarf, failed fisherman and Marxist chronicler of Hellya's history; Ivan Westray, boatman and dallier with the heart of the student

Inga, and the more difficult affections of the schoolteacher, Miss Inverary; the pious creelman Samuel Whaness and the drunken fisherman Bert Kerston; the poison-tongued Olive Evie at the shop and her silent husband Joseph; the unmarried but fertile earth-mother Alice Voar; the paranoiac and guilt-ridden Mrs McKee; Timmy Folster the simple-minded meths drinker.

The Skarf's history of Hellya and his account of the religious rituals of The Master Horsemen give the novel a spiritual dimension that provides the basis for the resurrection of the island despite the destructiveness of Black Star.

Elsewhere GMB has mourned the loss of our creative cultural identity. He speaks of

> Someone like me who sees poetry draining away remorselessly from even the quiet legendary places of the world, as 'the word' loses its power increasingly to 'the number', the richness and strength of a people are not in oil terminals and overfishing (the breaking of the ancient treaty between man and the creatures) and literacy, but in their inheritance from the past, the riches of music and love and imagination.

Certainly his power to deploy 'the word' effectively makes *Greenvoe* a remarkable novel. Johnny Singh's letter to his uncle is hilarious and true to his character: it is also redolent of GMB's poetry. Here is Johnny unable to resist a clandestine visit to the allures of Alice Voar: 'In the window of the much-loved one the half-deflowered rose hangs in a jar. Sweetly it smoulders in the gathering darkness. The village is all asleep. I knock at her door.'

It is no accident that one of the qualities of *Greenvoe* is its episodic form. In the short story GMB achieves his greatest mastery of prose, particularly in the two volumes of short stories *A Calendar of Love* (1967) and *A Time to Keep* (1969). These two collections are central to his artistic achievement, displaying an incisive understanding of human behaviour: the human dramas of love, death, jealousy and passion – both carnal and spiritual – are acted out in the brief compass of small, close-knit communities. The stories are peopled by briefly sketched but solidly real characters who live out their tragedies and comedies through the sharply observed mundanities of peasant life. His storytelling is apparently artless, yet is carefully crafted, setting age-old human conflicts in a symbolic ritual of our dependence on land and sea. GMB's genius was intensely humane. His vivid evocations of the powerful sea, sky and landscapes of Orkney are of relevance to him only in their relationship to human aspirations of love, suffering and redemption. At the end of *A Time to Keep*, the Rackwick fisherman, stricken by unspoken grief for his dead wife, turns to the ever expressive sea:

> Before morning, I knew, the valley would be a white blank. And the sea would be flat with the first frost of winter. And, beyond the Kame,

fathoms down, the shoals of cod would be moving, bronze soundless streaming legions.

    I went out to the shed where I kept my fishing gear.

The vivid understatement of his prose is honed to a bone-clean economy in the poetry that established GMB as a major writer, particularly in the two collections *Loaves and Fishes* (1959) and *Fishermen with Ploughs* (1971). The same storyteller chronicles with ritual and symbol the lives of working people, as in *Crofter's Death*:

> They will leave this keening valley,
> The daylight come.
> They will dig skulls and bones
> From a loaded tomb.
> They will lay the hungerless back
> In the old corn womb.
> They will carve a name, some years
> On withered stone.
> The hill road will drag them back
> To hunger again.
> In the valley are creels for baiting,
> A field to be sown.

Much of his poetry is suffused with the rhythm of the seasons: both of the year and of human life. These subjects also provide potent symbols of religion and ritual: sowing, harvest, bread; and GMB deploys them to give meaning to the mysteries of life. The secular pleasures of life are celebrated equally in *Hamnavoe Market*, a terse, funny and vivid account of the separate adventures of seven men on market day. For some, such as Halcro, the pleasures were deceptive:

> A gypsy saw in the hand of Halcro
> Great strolling herds, harvests, a proud woman.
> He wintered in the poorhouse.

An Orkney Tapestry (1969), a subtle interweaving of essays, poems, stories, drama and folklore, has served as an imaginative introduction for many thousands of readers who have only visited Orkney in their mind's eye. In it GMB celebrates the life of Ikey Faa the tinker, a character gloriously free of man and God's law whose day is filled with a shameless gaiety:

> A ditch awakening,
> A bee in my hair.
>
> Egg and honeycomb,
> Cold fare.
>
> An ox on the hill,
> Gulls, ploughman, ploughshare.

A sharp wet wind
And my bum bare.

A fish-brimming corn-crammed house,
But a hard door.

Chicken, thief, and crab
Round a blink of fire.

A length of bones in the ditch,
A broken prayer.

The character of Ikey runs like a red thread through the centuries of GMB's work. He is loaded with frailties but is an archetypal survivor, taking his pleasures in the immediacy of material life. It is fitting that the last poem of GMB's posthumous final collection *Travellers*, should be *Ikey: His Will in Winter Written*. The tinker, with sardonic humour and the genuine generosity of the dispossessed, leaves the birds, the fish, the flowers and the land to the poor folk of the island who have succoured him. His bequest is touched with an enduring sense of wonder and celebration of Orkney and its people that is the hallmark of the poet. It is equally characteristic of GMB that he gives Ikey, despite the fine words of his will, a last speculative and dourly optimistic hope:

> (Will I manage to struggle to the ale-house
> before closing time? If I do, will the thin-lipped
> prevaricator that keeps the place give me the loan of a
> last whisky?)

This survey has looked at the work of three writers who in different ways have been shaped by Orkney and in turn have given imaginative form to these islands. It is fitting to conclude with Robert Rendall (1899–1967), whose dialect poems give a written expression to the powerfully evocative Orkney voice. Rendall was a draper who combined devotion to the Plymouth Brethren with wide-ranging scientific interests: he published the authoritative account of Orkney's marine shell life. He was also a poet, producing rather stilted and derivative English verses. However, when he turned to his own dialect he found a voice that was unforced and evocative. Reviewing one of his poetry collections, GMB observed that 'Half a dozen lyrics from *Orkney Variants* hold most of the essence of Orkney.'

In *Cragsman's Widow* there is a Greek stoicism and understated observation that lends poignancy to the old woman's monologue:

> He was aye vaigan b' the shore,
> An' climman amang the craigs,
> Swappan the mallimaks,
> Or taakan whitemaa aiggs.

It's six year bye come Lammas,
Sin' he gaed afore the face,
An' nane but an aald dune wife
Was left tae work the place.

Yet the sun shines doun on a'thing,
The links are bonnie and green,
An the sea keeps ebban an' flowan
As though it had never been.

The easy narrative of the cragsman catching the birds and collecting the
eggs gives way to the simple statement of his death and a bitter reflection.
The key opening word of the last verse sets the tone for the unforced but
profound reflections on life and death.

In a similar way, *The Fisherman* concerns itself with the daily business
of living, expressed in language as distinctive as the work it describes. Auld
Jeems' undramatic death is rendered in the alliteration of the cruisie oil
lamp guttering out: an image rendered effective by the powerful negative
sibilance of 'unslockt'. The final tone of 'his yamils' – his contemporaries
– lends the poem a collective dignity that speaks for an era:

Aald Jeems o' Quoys, wha erst wi' leid and line
  Keen as a whitemaa, reaped the Rousay Soond,
And in his weathered yawl a twalmonth syne
  Set lapster-creels the Westness craigs aroond,
Nae stroke o' fortune cloured wi' bluidy claa,
  Nor glow'ring daith wi' sudden tempest mocked,
But in his wee thatched croft he wore awa'
  E'en as a cruisie flickers oot unslockt.
Nae kinsman raised, nor wife, nor weeping w'ain,
  But we, his yamils, this memorial stane.

When Robert Rendall finds his poetic voice in the use of Orcadian
language, he moves from the local to the universal. It is the distinctive
quality of all these writers that their specific Orcadian identity, realised in
language, character and culture has been the key to their universal appeal.

CHAPTER TWENTY-FIVE

Customs and Traditions

I N CENTURIES PAST the lives of ordinary Orcadians were governed by a set of customs that had to be observed if they wished to lead a happy and successful life. These customs differed depending on where they lived, but many were universal. The following are some of the customs and traditions relating to birth, courtship, marriage and death.

Birth

When a woman became pregnant it had to be concealed from the trows in case they stole the baby. A rainbow's end over a house heralded a baby boy; baby girls arrived unannounced. It was bad luck for a pregnant woman to enter the byre when a cow was about to calf, as she risked having a miscarriage. If a married woman helped to deliver a baby, she would fall pregnant immediately afterwards. With no painkillers available home brew was liberally administered to the mother-to-be, while the 'howdy wife' who delivered the child joined in with the drinking.

When the baby was born its first drink had to be off silver if it were to be wealthy in life. If a silver spoon was unobtainable then a silver coin in a horn spoon was acceptable. The drink was usually whisky and sugar in warm water. The baby might have a silver coin placed in one hand while the other was thrust into a container of grain until it grabbed a handful, meaning it would never want for food or money in life. A mother and child should never be left alone until the child was baptised, and a Bible and an object made from steel (usually a knife) were kept in the bed for protection from trows. It was bad luck to let someone borrow fire from the house before the child had cut its first tooth. You should never cut a baby's nails with scissors as it would grow up to be a thief; nails had to be bitten off with the teeth. If a child died unbaptised it could not enter Heaven without a name, but a slip of paper with the name written on it pinned to the shroud would do. If a baby was stillborn the father should not see it or he would become sterile. When more than one child was to be baptised the boys had to be done first or the girls would grow whiskers while the boys would remain beardless. It was bad luck to reveal the child's name before it was baptised, or to praise a child without saying a blessing afterwards as the child could fall prey to evil spirits.

Courtship

When a young girl's thoughts turned to marriage she would often try to discover the identity of her future husband. Several methods could be used to determine this at Hallowe'en. If a girl went to the barn at night and winnowed 'three wechts of nothing' in a sieve containing scissors and a knife she would see the image of her future husband walking past the door. If she threw a ball of wool through the door of the barn kiln and said, 'Who takes hold of my clew's end?', she would hear the voice of her future husband. Another method was to wet the sleeve of her slip and put it in front of the fire to dry; the image of her true love would come into the room at night to turn the sleeve to prevent it burning. Eating a salt fish before going to bed on Hallowe'en would ensure that the image of the girl's future husband would come to her in the night with a drink of water.

If a girl let a pot or kettle boil over this meant that she would lose her sweetheart, but it could be avoided if she immediately dropped a piece of burning peat into the pot. If she wanted to test her relationship she could put two straws on a burning peat in the fire and give one her name and the other the name of her sweetheart. If her love's straw jumped towards her one, all was well, but if it jumped away they would never be married. You could find out the colour of your future husband's hair by taking a glowing peat from the fire and extinguishing it in a tub of water (or urine), then leaving it under a turf overnight. When you broke the peat in two the next day you would see fibres inside that were the colour of his hair. It was once accepted that a young man could spend the night with his sweetheart in her bed, as long as nothing went on. This was done secretly and was known as 'running in the night' or 'bed courting'. During the Lammas Fair in Kirkwall, which lasted 11 days during mid August, young couples could become Lammas brothers and sisters, temporarily giving them the same rights as courting couples. At the end of the fair they were free to go their own way.

A more permanent binding together was a marriage at the Odin Stone in Stenness. The Odin Stone was a Neolithic standing stone with a hole through it that once stood near to the Stones Of Stenness. Here a young couple could take the Odin's oath (now lost) to be true to each other, then hold hands through the stone which made their relationship binding. It was considered so powerful that the only way to break it was to go to the old kirk of Stenness, which had two doors, stand back to back in front of the pulpit and walk out of either door without looking back. If your sweetheart died the oath could only be broken by holding the deceased's hand and renouncing the oath. If your sweetheart was lost at sea, then you were doomed to remain unmarried. Sadly both the Odin Stone and the old kirk have been destroyed.

Marriage

When a young man wanted to marry his sweetheart he first had to ask her father's permission. This was known as 'speiring [asking] night,' and he had to take a loaf of bread and a bottle of whisky with him as an offering. If this went well the next step was 'booking night', when the couple's names were entered in the kirk session clerk's book. While the intended groom did this, his bride-to-be had a party at her house. Money was paid to the minister to ensure the good behaviour of the couple; they would get it back after they married if the bride was not pregnant, but it would go into the poor fund if she were. The marriage was 'cried in the kirk' on three Sundays (or less if paid for).

Before they were married couples had to go through a ceremony of 'feet washing'. The bride's father would take off her shoes and her mother would take off her stockings and give a blessing to her daughter. She would then lift her daughter's feet in the air, then turning her with the sun she would bring her feet down into a tub of water with a splash. It was then the turn of the bride's friends to wash her feet, with much splashing and horseplay. A ring was dropped into the tub and the first girl to find it would be the next to marry. The groom was subjected to feet washing of his own, but his friends were none too gentle with him. Sometimes the couple had their feet washed together in the same tub, which had to be prepared in a certain way. The empty tub had to stand in the sunlight for twelve hours, and it was important not to let a dog look into it, so all the dogs in the neighbourhood were kept locked up. The water was sometimes made up of a bucketful of fresh water from the well and a bucketful of salt water from the sea. When the 'feet washing' was over the water was sometimes kept until the night before the wedding, when it was used to wash the couple's hair. When the water was finished with it could not be poured away in the conventional manner, but was poured into a hole by the oldest woman of the house while she spoke a charm over it. After the 'feet washing' was over the couple had to eat the 'kissing meat', traditionally limpets boiled in milk.

The day of the wedding was traditionally a Thursday, but Tuesdays and Sundays were also lucky. The wedding day had to coincide with a growing moon and a flowing tide if the marriage were to be prosperous. Invitations were issued by the groom and best man, who rode from house to house on ponies whose manes and tails were decorated with ribbons. If the groom came from a different parish to the bride he had to pay local children 'ba' money' which was used to buy a football. If this was neglected then the wedding party could be tormented on the way to the kirk.

On the wedding day the guests gathered at the bride's house. When it was time to leave for the kirk the groom led the wedding walk, accompanied by the best maid, followed by the bride and best man and then the couple's parents. As the young girls left the house they were snatched by the young men who wanted to be their partners, though this sometimes led to scuffles before the girl made her choice. Married couples walked together, while young single people who had no partners brought up the rear. This was not a popular place to be, as the last couple were called the 'tail sweepers' and were given a heather broom to drag behind them. These unfortunate people would try to get in front of someone and hand the broom to them. It was lucky for single people to trip on the walk, as they would soon be wed themselves. A piper or fiddler led the wedding walk and played all the way to the kirk and back, which could be several miles each way. It was considered lucky to cross running water twice on the journey, but it was bad luck to meet a funeral party on the road. Guns were fired as the walk proceeded in order to frighten away the 'peedie folk' (trows). When the wedding ceremony had taken place the bride joined her husband to lead the wedding walk back to the house. However, it was considered an ill omen if the wind was in their faces.

On their return home they were met by an old woman and an old man called the 'hansel wife' and the 'mester hoosal' (master of the household), who made sure everyone was given some food and drink. It was also the hansel wife's task to hand the bride the 'hansel bairn', usually the youngest child in the parish. If the 'hansel bairn' lifted its left leg first the bride would have mostly boys, while the right leg meant girls. All eyes then turned to the doorway of the house to await the arrival of the wedding cake, which was made from oatmeal and butter, sweetened with sugar and caraway seeds. The 'hansel wife' brought out the cake and held it over the bride's head in one hand before bringing her fist down on it. The pieces fell over the bride's head, which had been covered for the occasion, and a scramble ensued to see who could get the biggest piece. If it contained a ring, it meant the finder would soon be married; a button meant he or she would remain single. For a single girl the cake had the power to show her future husband in a dream if she put it under her pillow.

Everyone had provided food for the wedding, which was an opportunity to have meat, usually eaten only on special occasions as it was so expensive. The barn was cleaned so that the dancing could take place, which lasted throughout the night. Ale in 'cogs' (a bucket-like container with handles) circulated all night, until the 'bride's cog' was passed around. This was a heady drink of hot ale and spirits, sweetened and spiced. It was designed to finish off anyone who was still standing! It is still a feature at Orkney weddings and brings the wedding to a close.

It was then time for the bride and groom to be put to bed. The bride, attended by her friends, was undressed and put to bed first. It was then the groom's turn to be put to bed by his friends, who would try to steal some part of the bride's clothing. It was the task of the bride's friends to make sure that they didn't succeed, or to retrieve any garments that were stolen. Towards the end of the evening the bride's mother and some of her oldest friends carried out the 'sweeing of the sneud'. The 'sneud' was the narrow ribbon that tied up the girl's hair and was a symbol of her maidenhood. Her mother removed it on the morning of the wedding and kept it for this ceremony. It was burnt on a flat stone that had been heated on the fire; the shape it took as it shrivelled up and burned gave an indication of her future. This secret ritual was for the women only, and the meanings behind the shapes are unknown.

The evening after the wedding saw the old people who had served the food being entertained as a 'thank you'. The best man organised a 'back-treat' in return for the wedding feast, which involved eating, drinking and dancing. When the bride moved into her new home she gave a party called the 'hame-fare' in celebration. The Sunday after the wedding was known as 'kirking Sunday', when the bride and groom, dressed in their finery, entered the congregation as a couple. A melancholy task that the bride had to perform as soon as she was married was to make shrouds for both her husband and herself. These had to be ready in case of sudden death, which was an all too frequent occurrence. The bride's shroud was some-times made from her own wedding dress.

Death

Certain signs and omens could foretell the coming of death. If you heard the 'death jack' ticking, someone's time was near, although this sound was nothing more than woodworm or deathwatch beetle. Crows flying around a house, or worse still, landing on it, was another sign, while a rainbow with both ends inside the old township dyke meant that someone in that township would soon die. To hear heavenly music, or the howling of the Varden, an animal spirit that follows you during life, was also a deadly sign. To dream of a ship sailing over land, or the loss of teeth, was a warning that someone close to you was about to die. Another omen was to see a 'ganfer', the ghost of a person not yet dead. If you saw it in the morning the person would live a while longer, but the later you saw it the nearer death was.

When someone died the body was 'straiked' (laid out), usually by a 'howdy wife' (who also acted as midwife). A Bible was placed under the chin and a plate of salt placed on the chest to prevent swelling. The feet of the corpse were pointed towards the door, while all mirrors had to be covered. All cats were locked up, and a watch, known as a 'leek-wak', was held over the body for as long as it remained in the house. This could be as long as three weeks, as burying someone too quickly was looked on as a mark of disrespect. A light had to be kept burning in the room at all times, along with a Bible to keep away evil spirits. The dead person was never to be spoken of by name in case he or she returned to haunt the house. One man in Orphir put corn between his late wife's fingers and toes, in her mouth and over her chest. This was to prevent her returning to haunt her stepdaughter. When people left the house they first had to touch the corpse to prevent its ghost from following them.

On the funeral day the lid was screwed down on the coffin for the first time; it was then carried to the kirkyard. This could be a considerable distance, so resting-places were situated along the road and ale or spirits were provided. The resting place took the form of four stones set in a cross, called the 'wheelda-kros' or 'wheeling-stanes', as it was considered bad luck to set the coffin down on the ground outside the kirkyard. The kirk officer who rang a hand bell preceded the coffin, but it was bad luck for anyone to enter the kirkyard before the coffin. It was bad luck, too, if a dog crossed the path of the procession, as the dead person's family would never prosper unless the dog was killed. Should you meet a rival funeral party going to the same kirkyard it was important that you entered the gate first, even if it meant a race! The coffin was carried around the grave, following the course of the sun, and the next of kin were expected to throw in the first shovelful of earth.

Suicides were not allowed a Christian interment but were buried on the boundary between two parishes, or lands belonging to two different lairds. When suicides were eventually allowed burial in the kirkyard their coffins had to be passed over the wall rather than taken through the gate. The bodies of drowned sailors washed ashore were traditionally buried by the side of the shore, as the sea might try to lay claim to its prey and flood the kirkyard. When this custom faded into memory, sailors' bodies were buried in the north end of the kirkyard, as the south end was reserved for the more important members of the community.

Bibliography

CA	*Current Archaeology*
GAJ	*Glasgow Archaeological Journal*
JGSL	*Journal of the Geological Society of London*
NOAJ	*New Orkney Antiquarian Journal*
NSA	*New Statistical Account*
OS	*Orkneyinga Saga*
POAS	*Proceedings of the Orkney Antiquarian Society*
PRPSE	*Proceedings of the Royal Physical Society of Edinburgh*
PSAS	*Proceedings of the Society of Antiquaries of Scotland*
QJGSL	*Quarterly Journal of the Geological Society of London*
RCAHMS	Royal Commission on the Ancient and Historical Monuments of Scotland
ROSC	*Review of Scottish Culture*
SAF	*Scottish Archaeological Forum*
SAR	*Scottish Archaeological Review*
SHA	*Scottish Historical Archive*
SHR	*Scottish Historical Review*
SHS	Scottish History Society
SJG	*Scottish Journal of Geology*
THAS	*Transactions of the Highland and Agricultural Society*
TRSE	*Transactions of the Royal Society of Edinburgh*
MS	Manuscript
p.p.	privately published
rp.	reprinted

Adam of Bremen (2002), *History of the Archbishops of Hamburg–Bremen*, trans. F.J. Tschan with introduction by T. Reuter, New York

Adams, I.H. (1971) *Directory of Former Scottish Commonties*

Anderson, P.D. (1982) *Robert Stewart, Earl of Orkney, Lord of Shetland, 1553–93*, Edinburgh

Anderson, P.D. (1983) 'Birsay in the Sixteenth Century', in *Orkney Heritage* 2, 82–96

Anderson, P.D. (1988) 'The Armada and the Northern Isles', *Northern Studies* xxv, 42–57

Anderson, P.D. (1992) *Black Patie: The Life and Times of Patrick Stewart, Earl of Orkney, Lord of Shetland*, Edinburgh

Anderson, P.D. (1992) 'The Stewart Earls of Orkney and the History of Orkney and Shetland', *Northern Studies* xxix, 43–52

Anderson, P.D. (1996) 'Earl William to Earl Patrick: A Survey of the History of Orkney and Shetland from 1468 to 1615', in *Shetland's Northern Links: Language and History* (ed. D. Waugh), Scottish Society for Northen Studies, Edinburgh, 174–85

Anderson, P.D. (1999) 'Earl Patrick and his Enemies', *NOAJ* 1, 42–52

Anderson, P.D. (2003) 'Cathedral, Palace and Castle: the Strongholds of Kirkwall', in *The Faces of Orkney: Stones, Skalds and Saints* (ed. D. Waugh), Scottish Society for Northern Studies, Edinburgh, 81–92

Armit, I. (ed.) (1990) *Beyond the Brochs: Changing Perspectives on the Atlantic Scottish Iron Age*, Edinburgh

Astin, T. R. (1985) 'The Paleogeography of the Middle Devonian Lower Eday Sandstone', *SJG* 21, 353–375

Astin, T. R. and Rodgers, D. A. (1991) 'Subaqueous shrinkage cracks in the Devonian of Scotland reinterpreted', *J. Sed. Pet.* 61, 850–859

Baikie, S. (2001) *Reminiscences of the Cathedral Church of St Magnus since 1846 by an Eye Witness*, St Magnus Centre Management Committee, Kirkwall

Bailey, P. n.d. *Orkney*, Newton Abbott

Baillie, M. (1999) *Exodus to Arthur*, London

Ballin Smith, B. (1994) 'Reindeer Antler Combs at Howe. Contact Between Late Iron Age Orkney and Norway', *Universitets Oldsakamlings Arbok*, 207–11

Ballin Smith, B. (1994) *Howe: Four Millennia of Orkney Prehistory; Excavations 1978–82*, Society of Antiquaries of Scotland Monographs 9, Edinburgh

Barber, J. 'Scottish Burnt Mounds: Variations on a Theme', in Buckley 1990, 98–101

Barber, J. (1997) *The Excavation of a Stalled Cairn at the Point of Cott, Westray, Orkney*, Scottish Trust for Archaeological Research Monograph I, Edinburgh

Barclay, R. S. (1965) *The Population of Orkney 1755–1961*, W.R. Mackintosh, Kirkwall

Barnes, M. P. (1994) *The Runic Inscriptions of Maeshowe, Orkney*, Reklam and Katalogtryck ab, Uppsala

Barnes, M. P. (1998) *The Norn Language of Orkney and Shetland*, Lerwick

Barrett, J., Beukens, R., Simpson, I., Ashomre, P., Poaps, D. S., and Huntly. J. (2000) 'What Was the Viking Age and When Did it Happen? A View From Orkney' Norwegian Archaeological Review 33, no. 1, 1–39

Barron, W. (1895) *Old Whaling Days*, Hull

Barry, G. (1805) *History of the Orkney Islands*, rp. Edinburgh 1975

Batey, C. E. (1993) 'A Norse Horizontal Mill in Orkney', *ROSC* 8, 20–8

Baxter, A. N. and Mitchell, J. G. (1984) 'Camptonite-monchiquite Dyke Swarms of Northern Scotland; Age Relationships and Their Implications', *SJG* 20, 297–308

Benn, D. I. and Evans, D. J. A. (1998) *Glaciers and Glaciation*, Edward Arnold

Berry, R. J. (1985) *The Natural History of Orkney*, London

Berry, R. J. and Firth, H. (1986) *The People of Orkney*, Kirkwall

Berry, R. J. (2000) *Orkney Nature*, Academic Press

Bennett, M. R. and Glasser, N. F. (1996) *Glacial Geology*, John Wiley & Sons Ltd

Black, G. F. (1903) *County Folklore* 3, Orkney and Shetland Islands

Black, G. F. (1946) *The Surnames of Scotland: Their Origin, Meaning and History*, New York Public Library, New York

Blaeu, W. J. (1663) *Le grand atlas. Theatrum Orbis*, Terrarum Ltd 1996 (vol. 6, facsimile)

Bowman, G. (1964) *The Man Who Bought a Navy*, Harrap and Co., London

Brock, J. M. (1999) *The Mobile Scot*, John Donald, Edinburgh

Brown, J. Flett (1975) 'Potassium–argon Evidence of a Permian Age for the Camptonite Dykes: Orkney', *SJG* 11, 259–262

Brown, J. Flett (1992) 'Flint as a Resource for Stone-Age Orcadians', *Bulletin of Orkney Field Club*

Brown, J. Flett (2000) 'Rocks and Scenery', in Berry, S. (ed.) *Orkney Nature*, Scottish Academic Press, 23–48

Brown, M. and Meehan, P. (1968) *Scapa Flow*, Penguin, London

Buckley, V. (1990) *Burnt Offerings: International Contributions to Burnt Mound Archaeology*, Dublin

Bumsted, J. M. (1982) *The Scots in Canada*, Ottawa

Burgher, L. (1991) *Orkney: An Illustrated Architectural Guide*, Royal Incorporation of Architects of Scotland, Edinburgh

Burl, A. (2000) *The Stone Circles of Britain, Ireland and Brittany*, Yale UP, New Haven and London

Burrows, C. W. (1921) 'Scapa and a Camera', in *Country Life*

Buteux, S., (1997) *Settlements at Skaill, Deerness, Orkney* (British Archaeological Reports, British Series, 260), Oxford

Buteux, S., Dingwall, L., Hunter, J. and Lowe, C. (1999) 'St Nicholas' Chapel, Papa Stronsay, Orkney, Data Structure report, 1999', University of Birmingham/Headland Archaeology Ltd

Callaghan, S. and Wilson, B. (eds) (2001) *The Unknown Cathedral – Lesser Known Aspects of St Magnus Cathedral in Orkney*, Orkney Islands Council, Kirkwall

Cant, H. W. M. and Firth, H. N. (eds) (1989) *Light in the North – St Magnus Cathedral Through the Centuries*, The Orkney Press, Kirkwall

Carson, R. (1962) *Silent Spring*, Penguin, London

Chalmers, W. S. (1951) *The Life and Letters of David, Earl Beatty*, Hodder and Stoughton, London

Charter, E. (1995) *Farming with Wildlife in Mind*, Orkney Farming and Wildlife Advisory Group

Carver, M. (1999) *Surviving in Symbols: A Visit to the Pictish Nation*, Birlinn/Historic Scotland, Edinburgh

Childe, V. G. (1931) *Skara Brae: A Pictish Village in Orkney*, Kegan Paul, Trench, Trubner, London

Childe, V. G. and Grant, W. G. (1939) 'A Stone Age Settlement at the Braes of Rinyo, Rousay', *PSAS* 73, 6–31

Clarke, D. V., Cowie, T. G. and Foxon, A. (1985) *Symbols of Power at the Time of Stonehenge*, National Museum of Antiquities of Scotland/HMSO, Edinburgh

Clarke, D. V. and Maguire, P. (2000) *Skara Brae: Northern Europe's Best Preserved Neolithic Village*, Edinburgh

Clarke, D. V. and Sharples, N. (1985) 'Settlements and Subsistence in the Third Millennium BC, in Renfrew C. (ed.) *The Prehistory of Orkney*, Edinburgh University Press, 54–82

Clarke, D. V. and Maguire, P. (2000) *Skara Brae: Northern Europe's Best Preserved Neolithic Village*, Historic Scotland, Edinburgh

Clegg, P. V. (1986) *A Flying Start to the Day*, p.p.

Clegg, P. V. (1987) *Flying Against the Elements*, p.p.

Clegg, P. V. (1988) *Rivals in the North*, p.p.

Clouston, E. (ed.) Notebooks of J. Storer Clouston (MS)

Clouston, J. Storer (1914) *Records of the Earldom of Orkney 1299–1614*, Scottish History Society, second series, Edinburgh

Clouston, J. Storer (1919) 'The Orkney Townships', *SHR* 16

Clouston, J. Storer (1928) *The Orkney Parishes*, Kirkwall

Clouston, J. Storer (1936/37) 'Orkney and Hudson's Bay Company', *The Beaver*, December 1936 and September 1937

Clouston, J. Storer (1948) *The Family of Clouston*, p.p.

Cormack, A. (1971) *Days of Orkney Steam*, Kirkwall Press

Cormack, A. and A. (1990) *Days of the Steam 'Earls'*, Orkney View

Cormack, A. and A. (1991) *Days of Orkney Buses*, Orkney View

Cormack, A. and A. (1992) 'Bolsters Block Barriers', *The Orcadian*, Kirkwall

Coull, J. R. (1998) and Sheves, G. T. (1979) *The Fisheries of Orkney. A Study in Conservation and Development*, Orkney Fisheries Association, Orkney Islands Council and Highlands and Islands Development Board

Coull, J. R. (1998a) 'Herring Fisheries in Orkney', *Nothern Scotland* 18, 43–55

Coward, M. P., Enfiled, M. A. and Fischer, M. W. (1989) 'Devonian Basins of Northern Scotland', in *Inversion Tectonics*, Cooper M. A. and Williams G. D. (eds), Geological Society Special Publication Classics, 275–307

Crawford, B. E. (1967–8) 'The Earldom of Orkney and Lordship of Shetland: Reinterpretation of their Pledging to Scotland in 1468–70', *Saga-Book of the Viking Society* 17, 156–76

Crawford, B. E. (1969) 'The Pawning of Orkney and Shetland: A Reconsideration of the events of 1460–9', *SHR* 48, 35–53

Crawford, B. E. (1976) 'The Fifteenth-Century Genealogy of the Earls of Orkney and its Reflection of the Contemporary Political and Cultural Situation in the Earldom', *Medieval Scandinavia* 10, 156–78

Crawford, B. E. (1977) 'Scotland and Scandinavia', in *Scottish Society in the Fifteenth Century*, J. M. Brown (ed.), London, 85–101

Crawford, B. E. (1983) 'Birsay and the Early Earls and Bishops of Orkney', *Orkney Heritage* 2, 97–119

Crawford, B.E. (1983a) 'The Pledging of the Islands in 1469: The Historical Background' in *Shetland and the Outside World, 1469–1969*, ed. D.J. Withrington, Oxford, 32–48

Crawford, B. E. (1985) 'The Earldom of Caithness and the Kingdom of Scotland, 1150–1266', in *Essays on the Nobility of Mediaeval Scotland*, K. J. Stringer (ed.) Edinburgh, 232–251

Crawford, B. E. (1985a) 'William Sinclair, Earl of Orkney and His Family: A Study in the Politics of Survival' in *Essays on the Nobility of Mediaeval Scotland*, K. J. Stringer (ed.) Edinburgh, 232–251

Crawford, B. E. (1987) *Scotland in the Middle Ages vol. 2: Scandinavian Scotland*, Leicester University Press, Studies in the Early History of Britain (rp. 1993)

Crawford, B. E. (ed.) (1988) *St Magnus Cathedral and Orkney's Twelfth-Century Renaissance*, Aberdeen University Press

Crawford, B. E. (1990) 'North Sea Kingdoms: North Sea Bureaucrat. A Royal Official Who Transcended National Boundaries', *SHR* 69, 178–90

Crawford, B. E. (1993) 'Norse Earls and Scottish Bishops in Caithness. A Clash of Cultures', in *The Viking Age in Caithness, Orkney and the North Atlantic* (Proceedings of the 11th Viking Congress) Batey, C., Jesch, J., Morris, C. D. (eds), Edinburgh, 129–147

Crawford, B. E. (1994) 'Earl William Sinclair and the Building of Roslin Chapel', in *Medieval Art and Architecture in the Diocese of St Andrews*, J. Higgitt (ed.) (BAA Conference Transactions), 99–46

Crawford, B. E. (ed.) (1995) *Northern Isles Connections – Essays From Orkney and Shetland Presented to Per Sveaas Andersen*, The Orkney Press, Kirkwall

Crawford, B. E. (1996) 'Bishops of Orkney in the Eleventh and Twelfth Centuries: Bibliography and Biographical List', *The Innes Review* 47, 1–12

Crawford, B. E. (1998) 'St Magnus and St Rognvald – the Two Orkney Saints', in *Records of the Scottish Church History Society* 28, 23–38

Crawford, B. E. (2000) 'Medieval Strathnaver', in *The Province of Strathnaver*, Baldwin, J. R. (ed.), Edinburgh, 1–13

Crawford, B. E. (ed.) (2002) *Papa Stour and 1299*, Lerwick

Crawford, B.E. (2003) 'The Bishopic of Orkney 1152/3–1472', in *Ecclesia Nidrosensis. Jubileumsbok i 850 år*, Imsen, S. (ed.), Trondheim, 143–58

Crawford, B.E. (in press) 'Thorfinn (II) Sigurdsson', 'Harald Maddadson', 'Magnus Erlendsson', 'Sigurd II Hlödvisson', 'Sinclair family' in *New Dictionary of National Biography*, Oxford

Crouther Gordon, T. (1985) 'Early Flying in Orkney, Seaplanes in World War I', BBC Radio Orkney, Kirkwall

Curle, A. O. (1941) 'An Account of the Partial Excavation of a "Wag" of Galleried Building at Forse, in the Parish of Latheron, Caithness', *PSAS* 75, 23–39

Curle, C. L. (1982) 'The Pictish North Finds from the Brough of Birsay, 1934–74' Soc Antiq Mon Ser no. 1, Edinburgh

Dalland, M. (1999) 'Sand Fiold: The Excavation of an Exceptional Cis in Orkney', *Proc Prehist Soc* 65, 373–413

Daniell, W. (1821) *A Voyage Round Great Britain*, Longman, Hurst, Rees and Brown, London

Davidson, J. L. and Henshall, A. S. (1989) *The Chambered Cairns of Orkney*, Edinburgh University Press, Edinburgh

Davies, K. G. (1963) *Letters From Hudson's Bay 1703–40*, London

Dawson, A. G. (1992) *Ice Age Earth*, Routledge

Defoe, D. 'An Account of the Conduct and Proceedings of the Pirate Gow' in *A General History of the Pyrates* ed. Manuel Schonhorn (1999) Dover Publications

Dennison, W. Traill (1880) *The Orcadian Sketch Book*

Dennison, W. Traill (1995) *Orkney Folklore and Sea Legends*

Donaldson, G. (1966) *Northwards by Sea*, Beekman Pub

Donaldson, G. (1966) *Scots Overseas*, Greenwood Press, London

Dorman, J. (1996) *Orkney Coast Batteries*, Orkney Island Council, Kirkwall

Downes, J. (1995) 'Linga Fold', *Current Archaeology* 142, 396–9

Downes, J. (1999) 'Orkney's Barrows Project', *Current Archaeology* 165, 324–9

Downes, J. and Richards, C. (2000) 'Excavating the Neolithic and Early Bronze Age of Orkney: Recognition and Interpretation in the Field', in Ritchie, A. (2000), 159–68

Dunlop, J. (1978) *The British Fisheries Society 1786–1893*, John Donald, Edinburgh

Earl, D. W. (1999) *Hell on High Ground vol. 2. World War II Air Crash Sites*, Airlife Publishing Ltd, Shrewsbury

Enfield, M. A. and Coward, M. P. (1987) 'Structure of the West Orkney Basin, Northern Scotland', *JGSL* 144, 871–883

Farrer, J. (1862) *Notice of Runic inscriptions Discovered During Recent Excavations in the Orkneys*, p.p.

Fawcett, H. W., Hooper G. W. W. (ed.) (1921) *The Fighting at Jutland. The Personal Experiences of Sixty Officers and Men of the British Fleet*, MacLure, Macdonald and Co., Glasgow

Fellows-Jensen, G. (1984) 'Viking Settlement in the Northern and Western Isles', in *The Northern and Western Isles*, Fenton, A. and Pálsson, H. (eds) Glasgow, 148–68

Fenton, A. (1978) *The Northern Isles: Orkney and Shetland*, John Donald, Edinburgh

Ferguson, D. M. (1985) *The Wrecks of Scapa Flow*, Orkney Press, Kirkwall

Fereday, R. P. (1971) *The Longhope Batteries and Towers*

Fereday, R. P. (1980) *Orkney Feuds and the '45*, Kirkwall

Firth, J. (1974) *Reminiscences of an Orkney Parish*

Fisheries Inspectorate Annual Fishery Reports

Fitzpatrick, A. P. (1989) 'The Submission of the Orkney Islands to Claudius: New Evidence?', *SAR* 6, 24–33

Flett, J. D. (1900) 'The Trap Dykes of the Orkneys', *TRSE* 39 (4), 865–908

Forsyth, K. (1995) 'The Ogham-Inscribed Spindle Whorl from Buckquoy: Evidence for the Irish Language in pre-Viking Orkney?', *PSAS* 125, 677–96

Foster, S. (1996) *Picts, Gaels and Scots*, London

Forsyth, K. (1997) 'Language in Pictland: The Case Against "non-Indo-European Pictish"', *Studia Hameliana* 2

Franklin, J. (1859) *Thirty Years in the Arctic Regions*, University of Nebraska 1988

Gammeltoft, P. (2001)*The Place-name Element* bólstadr *in the North Atlantic Area*, C. A. Reitzels Forlag A/S, Copenhagen

Geddes, D. 'David Geddes Whom You Pronounced a Dunce', p.p.

Geikie, A. (1878) 'The Old Red Sandstone of Western Europe', *TRSE* 28, 345–452

Gelling, P. S. (1984) 'The Norse Buildings at Skaill, Deerness, Orkney, and their Immediate Predecessor', in Fenton and Paalsson (eds), *The Northern and Western Isles in the Viking World*, 12–39

Geography of the Dominion of Canada (c. 1905) Interior Ministry, Canada

George, S. C. (1981) *Jutland to Junkyard*, Paul Harris Publishing, Edinburgh

Gibbon, J. Murray (1911) *Scots in Canada*, London

Gibson, J. S. (1967) *Ships of the '45*, London

Gibson, W. M. (1984) *The Herring Fishing. Stronsay vol. 1*, BPP, Edinburgh

Goldring, P. (1985) *Governor Simpson's Officers: Elite Recruitment in a British Overseas Enterprise*, Regina, Saskatchewan

Gordon, J. E. (ed.) (1997) *Reflections on the Ice Age in Scotland*, Scottish Association of Geography Teachers and Scottish National Heritage

Goudie, A. (1992) *Environmental Change* (3rd edn), Oxford University Press

Graeme, P. N. S. (1936) 'Pateas Amicis', *Orkney Herald*, Kirkwall

Graham-Campbell, J. (1985) 'A Lost Pictish Treasure (and two Viking-age Gold Arm-rings) from the Broch of Burgar, Orkney', *PSAS* 115, 241–61

Graham-Campbell, J. and Batey, C. E. (1998) *Vikings in Scotland: An Archaeological Survey*, Edinburgh University Press

Graham-Campbell, J. (1993) 'The Northern Hoards of Viking-age Scotland', in Batey *et.al* (eds), 1993, 173–86

Grant, W. G. (1937) 'Excavations of Bronze Age Burial Mounds at Quandale, Rousay, Orkney', *PSAS* 71, 72–84

Hall, A. M. (1996) *The Quaternary of Orkney Field Guide*, Quaternary Research Association, Cambridge

Halliday, A. N., McAlpine, A. and Mitchell, J. G. (1977) The Age of the Hoy Lavas, Orkney, *SJG* 13, 43–52

Hamilton-Baillie, J. R. E. (1979) *Coastal Defences in Orkney in Two World Wars*

Hansom, J. D. and Evans, J. A. (1995) 'The Old Man of Hoy', *Scottish Geographical Magazine* 111(3), 172–174

Hazell, H. (2000) *The Orcadian Book of the Twentieth Century*, Kirkwall Press

Hedges, M. E. (1977) 'The Excavation of the Knowes of Quoyscottie, Orkney: A Cemetery of the First Millennium BC', *PSAS* 108, 130–55

Hedges, J. W. (1975) 'Excavations of Two Orcadian Burnt Mounds at Liddle and Beaquoy', *PSAS* 106, 39–98

Hedges, J. W. (1978) 'A Long Cist at Sandside, Graemsay, Orkney', *PSAS* 109, 374–8

Hedges, J. W. (1983) *Isbister: A Chambered Tomb in Orkney*, British Archaeological Reports, British Series, 115, Oxford

Hedges, J. W. (1983a) 'Trial Excavations on Pictish and Viking Settlements at Saevar Howe, Birsay, Orkney', *GAJ* 10, 73–124

Hedges, J. W. (1984) *The Tomb of the Eagles*, John Murray, London

Hedges, J. W. (1987) *Bu, Gurness and the Brochs of Orkney, Part II, Gurness*, British Archaeological Reports, British Series, 164, Oxford

Hedges. J. W. 'The Broch Period', in *Renfrew*, 1985, 150–75

Henderson, G. (1987) *From Durrow to Kells. The Insular Gospel-books 650–800*, London

Henshall, A. S. (1968) 'Scottish Dagger Graves', in Coles, J. M. and Simpson, D. D. A. (eds) *Studies in Ancient Europe: Essays Presented to Stuart Piggott*, Leicester University Press, Leicester, 173–95

Henshall, A. S. (1985) 'The Chambered Cairns', in Renfrew 1985, 83–117

Hewison, W. S. (1985) *This Great Harbour Scapa Flow*, The Orkney Press

Hewison, H. S. (1995) *Scapa Flow in War and Peace*, Bellavista Publications, Kirkwall

Hewison, W. S. (1998) *Who Was Who In Orkney*, Bellavista Publications

Highton, A. J., Hyslop, E. K., Noble, S. R. (2002) 'U-Pb zircon geochronology of migmatization in the northern Central Highlands: evidence for pre-Caledonian (Neoproterozoic) tectonometamorphism in the Grampian block, Scotland', *Journal of the Geological Society* v 156, 1195–1204

Hillier, S. J. and Marshall, J. E. A. (1992) 'Organic Maturation, Thermal History and Hydrocarbon Generation in the Orcadian Basin, Scotland', *JGSL* 149, 491–502

HISHA (2000), Highlands and Islands Sheep Health Association

Hogarth, K. (1996) *Orkney Tourist Guide Association Notes*

Holmes, W. (1989) *Grass – Its Production and Utilization*, Blackwell Scientific Publications

Hossack, B. H. (1990) *Kirkwall in the Orkneys*, Wm Peace and Son

House, M. R. and Gale, A. S. (1995) *Orbital Forcing Timescales and Cyclostratigraphy*, Geological Society Special Publication no. 85

Huck, B. (2000) *Exploring the Fur Trade Routes of North America*, Winnipeg

Hunter, J. (1997) *A Persona for the Northern Picts*, Groam House Lecture, Rosemarkie

Hunter, J. R. (1986) 'Rescue Excavations on the Brough of Birsay 1974–82' *Soc. Antiq. Mon. Ser. 4*, Edinburgh

Hunter, J. R. (1997) 'The Early Norse Period', in K. J. Edwards and Ralston, I. B. M. (eds) *Scotland, Environment and Archaeology 8000 BC–AD 1000*, Chichester, 241–54

Hunter, J. R. (2000) 'Pool, Sanday and a Sequence for the Orcadian Neolithic', in Ritchie 2000, 117–38

Imsen, S. (1999) 'Public Life in Shetland and Orkney, c. 1300–1550', *NOAJ* I, 53–65

Imsen, S. (2000) 'Earldom and Kingdom. Orkney in the Realm of Norway 1195–1379', *Historisk Tidsskrift* 79, 163–80

Isbister, A. (2000) 'Burnished Haematite and Pigment Production', in Ritchie, A. (ed.) *Neolithic Orkney in its European Context*, 191–5, Cambridge

Journal of the Orkney Agricultural Discussions Society, annual vols 1925–38

Jellicoe, J. (1919) *The Grand Fleet 1914–16. Its Creation, Development and Work*, Cassell, London

Johnson, A. M. (1967) *Saskatchewan Journals and Correspondence 1795–1802*, Hudson's Bay Record Society, London

Judd, C. M. (1980) 'Mixt Bands of Many Nations 1821–70' in Judd, C. M., and Ray, A. J. *Old Trails and New Directions*, Toronto

Kaland, S. H. H. (1993) 'The Settlement of Westness, Rousay', in Batey *et al.* (eds) *The Viking Age in Caithness, Orkney and the North Atlantic* (1993), 308–17

Kellock, E. (1969) 'Alkaline Basic Igneous Rocks in the Orkneys', *SJG* 5(2), 140–153

Kinny, P. D., Friend, C. R. L., Strachan, R. A., Watt, G. R., Burns, I. M. (2002) 'U-Pb geochronology of regional migmatites in East Sutherland, Scotland: evidence for crustal melting during the Caledonian orogeny', *Journal of the Geological Society* v, 156 , 1143–1152

Kirk, S. van (1980) *Many Tender Ties*, University of Oklahoma

Knight, C. and Lomas, R. (1999) *Uriel's Machine*, Century Books Ltd

Lamb, G. (1991) *Sky Over Scapa*, Byrgisey, Orkney

Lamb, G. (1993) *Testimony of the Orkneyingar*, Byrgisey, Orkney

Lamb, G. (1995) *Orkney Wordbook*, Byrgisey, Orkney

Lamb, R. (1995) 'Papil, Picts and Papar', in Crawford, B. E. (ed.) *Northern Isles Connections*, Kirkwall, 9–27

Lamb, G. (1997) *Langskaill*, Byrgisey, Orkney

Lamb, R. (1998) 'Pictland, Northumbria and the Carolingian Empire', in Crawford, B. E. (ed.) *Conversion and Christianity in the North Sea World*, St Andrews, 41–56

Lamb, G. (2003) *Orkney Family Names*, Bellavista Publications, Kirkwall

Linklater, E. (1934) *Magnus Merriman*

Linklater, E. (1946) *Private Angelo*

Linklater, E. (1929) *White Maa's Saga*

Linklater, E. (1931) *Juan in America*

Linklater, E. (1932) *The Two Men of America*

Linklater, E. (1970) *Fanfare for a Tin Hat*

Linklater, E. (1965) *Orkney and Shetland*

Linklater, E. 'The Forgotten Herd of Swona', *The Scotsman* 27 November 1988

Macdonald, I. (ed) (1993) *Saint Magnus*, Floris Books, Edinburgh

MacDonald, J. (1987) 'Churchill's Prisoners. The Italians in Orkney', *The Orcadian*

MacDonald, J. (1987) *Churchill's Prisoners. The Italians in Orkney 1942–1944*, Orkney Wireless Museum, Kirkwall

Macdonald, R. (1990) *Dive Scapa Flow*, Mainstream, Edinburgh

Macdougall, R. (1998) *The Emigrant's Guide to North America*, Toronto

MacGregor, A. (1974) 'The Broch of Burrian, North Ronaldsay, Orkney', *PSAS* 105, 63–118

MacInnes, I. (1981) 'The Alexander Graham Case. The Royal Burgh of Kirkwall and the Unfree Traders of Stromness', in *Orkney Heritage* 1, Kirkwall

Mack, A. (1997) *Field Guide to the Pictish Symbol Stones*, Balgavies, Angus

MacKay Brown, G. (1959) *Loaves and Fishes*

MacKay Brown, G. (1969) *An Orkney Tapestry*

MacKay Brown, G. (1971) *Fishermen With Ploughs*

MacKay Brown, G. (1972) *Greenvoe*, Lempman

MacKay Brown, G. (1995) *Vinland*, John Murray

MacKay Brown, G. (1996) *Collected Poems*

MacKay Brown, G. (1998) *For the Islands I Sing*, John Murray

MacKay Brown, G. (1998) *Magnus*, Canongate

MacKay Brown, G. (2001) *A Calendar of Love*, Hogarth Press

MacKay Brown, G. (2001) *A Time to Keep*, John Murray

MacKay Brown, G. (2001) *Travellers*, John Murray

Mackenzie, M. (1750) *Orcades*

Mackenzie, M. (1750) *Survey of Orkney etc.*

Mackey, E. C., Shewry, M. C. and Tudor, G. J. (1998) *Land Cover Change: Scotland from the 1940s to the 1980s*, The Stationery Office, Norwich

Mackintosh, W. R. (1889) *The Orkney Crofters: Their Evidence and Statements*, Kirkwall

McKinley, J. I. (1997) 'Bronze Age "Barrows" and Funerary Rites and Rituals of Cremation', *PPS* 63, 129–45

Marwick, E. (1975) *The Folklore of Orkney and Shetland*, Batsford, London

Marwick, E. (1991) *An Orkney Anthology*

Marwick, E. (1991a) 'The Story of Stromness Lifeboats 1867–1967', in *An Orkney Anthology*, J. D. M. Robertson (ed.), Edinburgh

Marwick, G. (1903) 'Birsay and Its Old Traditions', *The Orcadian* 1903

Marwick, H. (1929) *The Orkney Norn*, OUP

Marwick, H. (1934) 'Two 18th Century Orkney Inventories', *POAS* 12

Marwick, H. (1951) *Orkney*, Robert Hale

Marwick, H. (1952) *Orkney Farm-names*, W. R Mackintosh, Orkney

Maxwell, G. S. (1975) '*Casus Belli*: Native Pressure and Roman Policy', *SAF* 7, 31–49

Marshall J. E. A., Brown, J. F. and Hindmarsh, S. (1985) 'Hydrocarbon source rock potential of the Devonian rocks of the Orcadian Basin', *SJG* 21, 301–320

Marshall, J. E. A. (1996) 'Rhabdosporites langii, Geminospora lemurata and Contagisporites Optivus: An Origin for Heterospory Within the Progymnosperms', *Rev. Paleobot. Palynol.* 93, 159–189

Marshall, J. E. A., Rodgers, D. A. and Whitely, M. J. (1996) 'Devonian Marine Incursions Into the Orcadian Basin, Scotland', *JGSL* 153, 451–466

Miller, J. (1994) *A Wild and Open Sea*, Kirkwall

Miller, J. (1999) *Salt in the Blood*, Edinburgh

Miller, J. (2000) *Scapa*, Birlinn, Edinburgh

Miller, R. (1976) *Orkney*, London

Molleson, T. (2002) 'The Leper of Newark', in *NOAJ* 2, 45–48

Moodie, J. W. Dunbar (1866) *Scenes and Adventures as a Soldier and Settler*, Montreal

Moodie, Mrs S. (1853) *Life in the Clearings versus the Bush*, London

Moodie, Mrs S. (1852) *Roughing it in the Bush*, London

Mooney, Rev. H. (1995) *St Magnus Cathedral, Orkney*, Jarrold Publishing, Norwich

Morris, C. D. with Emery, N. (1986) 'The Chapel and Enclosure on the Brough of Deerness, Orkney: Survey and Excavations 1975–1977', *PSAS* 116 301–74

Morris, C. (1982) *The Birsay Bay Project Vol. 1: Coastal Sites Beside the Brough Road, Birsay, Orkney 1976–1982*, University of Durham, Department of Archaeology, Monograph Series 1

Morris, C. D. (1989) *The Birsay Project. Volume 1. Brough Road Excavations 1976–1982*, University of Durham Department of Archaeology, Monograph Series 1, Durham

Morris, C. D. (1996) *The Birsay Project. Volume 2. Sites in Birsay Village (Beachview) and on the Brough of Birsay, Orkney*, University of Durham Department of Archaeology, Mon. Ser. 2, Durham

Muir, E. (1940) *The Story and the Fable*, Rowan Tree Press

Muir, E. (1954) *An Autobiography*, Canongate, Edinburgh

Muir, E. (1984) *Collected Poems*, Faber, London

Muir, T. (1998) *The Mermaid Bride and Other Orkney Folktales*, Kirkwall Press

Muir, T. (1999) *The Storm Witch and Other Westray Stories*, Westray Buildings Preservation Trust

Murchison, R. I. (1859) 'On the Succession of the Older Rocks in the Northernmost Counties of Scotland; With Some Obsvervations on the Orkney and Shetland Islands' *QJGSL* 15, 353–417

Myhre, B. (1998) 'The Archaeology of the Early Viking Age in Orkney', in Clarke, H. B., Mhaonaigh, M. Ni. and O'Floinn, R. (eds) *Ireland and Scandinavia in the Early Viking Age*, Dublin, 3–36

Mykura, W. (1976) *Orkney and Shetland* British Regional Geology, Edinburgh

Napier Commission. Evidence Taken by HM Commissioners of Inquiry into the Condition of the Crofters and Cottars in the Highlands and Islands of Scotland (1884)

Newman, P. C. (1985) *Company of Adventurers*, London

Newman, P. C. (1987) *Caesars of the Wilderness*, London

New Statistical Account. The Statistical Account of the Orkney Islands (NSA) (1842)

Nicks, J. (1980) 'Orkneymen in the HBC 1780–1820', in Judd and Ray (1980)

Old Statistical Account (OSA)

The Orcadian

Orkney Archive: D1/110 Misc. Canadian publications; Census returns for Stromness; Minute books of Stromness and Kirkwall burgh councils

The Orkney Herald

Orkney Islands Council (1998 and 2001) *Orkney Economic Review*

Orkney Islands Council (2000) *The Orkney Development Plan 2000* consultative draft 1999

Orkneyinga Saga, Pálsson, H. and Edwards, P. (trs), London 1978

Orkney Heritage (1983) *Birsay: A Centre of Political and Ecclesiastical Power*

Øvrevik, S. (1985) 'The Second Millennium BC and After', in Renfrew 1985, 131–49

Owen, O. A. (1993) 'Tuquoy, Westray, Orkney: A Challenge for the Future', in Batey et al. (eds) *The Viking Age in Caithness, Orkney and the North Atlantic* (1993), 318–39

Owen, O. and Dalland. M. (1999) *Scar: A Viking Boat Burial on Sanday, Orkney*, Tuckwell Press

Pálsson, H. (1996) 'Aspects of Norse Place Names in the Western Isles', *Northern Studies* 31, 7–24

Pathfinder Gazetteer – 1. Ov – Scotland. Database compiled by Robin A. Hooker

Peach, B. N. and Horne, J. (1880) 'The Old Red Sandstone of Orkney', *PRPSE* 5, 329–342

Pethick, J. (1984) *An Introduction to Coastal Geomorphology*, Edward Arnold

Pococke, R. (1887) *Bishop Pococke's Tours*, SHS, Edinburgh

Pottenger, J. (n.d.) *The Salvaging of the German Fleet*, Stromness Museum, Stromness

POW Chapel Preservation Committee (n. d.) *Orkney's Italian Chapel*, Stromness

Pringle, R. O. (1874) 'On the Agriculture of the Islands of Orkney', *THAS* 4th series, 6

Quality Meat Scotland (2001)

RCAHMS (1946) *Inventory of the Ancient Monuments of Orkney and Shetland*, HMSO, Edinburgh

RCAHMS (1999) *Scotland From The Air 1* (catalogue of the Luftwaffe World War 2 photographs in the National Monuments Record of Scotland, Edinburgh), HMSO, Edinburgh

RCAHMS (2000) *Scotland From The Air 2* (catalogue of the RAF World War 2 photographs in the National Monuments Record of Scotland, Edinburgh), HMSO, Edinburgh

Rendall, R. (1946) *Country Sonnets*

Rendall, R. (1951) *Orkney Variants*

Rendall, R. (1957) *Shore Poems*

Renfrew, C. (ed.) (1985) *The Prehistory of Orkney*, Edinburgh University Press, 2nd edn, 1990

Rich, E. E. (1959) *History of Hudson's Bay Company 1670–1870*, Hudson's Bay Record Society, London

Richards, C. (1990) 'Postscript: The Late Neolithic Settlement Complex at Barnhouse Farm, Stenness', in Renfrew 1990, 305–16

Richards, C. (2002) 'Report of the Field Survey at the Quarry Site of Vestra Fiold, Sandwick, Mainland, Orkney'

Richards, Robert L. (1985) *Dr John Rae*, Whitby

Ritchie, A. (1972) 'Painted Pebbles in Early Scotland', *PSAS* 104, 297–301

Ritchie, A. (1977) 'Excavation of Pictish and Viking-age Farmsteads at Buckquoy, Orkney', *PSAS* 108, 174–227

Ritchie, A. (1983) 'Excavation of a Neolithic Farmstead at Knap of Howar, Papa Westray, Orkney', *PSAS* 113, 40–121

Ritchie, A. (1985) 'The First Settlers', in Renfrew 1985, 36–53

Ritchie, A. (1985a) 'Orkney in the Pictish Kingdom', in Renfrew, C. (ed.) *The Prehistory of Orkney*, Edinburgh, 183–209

Ritchie, A. (1989) *Picts*, Edinburgh

Ritchie, A. (1995) *Prehistoric Orkney*, Batsford/Historic Scotland, London

Ritchie, A. (1997) 'The Picts in Shetland', in Henry, D. (ed.) *The Worm, The Germ and the Thorn*, Balgavies, Angus

Ritchie, A. (ed.) (2000) *Neolithic Orkney in the European Context*, McDonald Institute Monograph, Cambridge

Ritchie, J. N. G. (1976) 'The Stones of Stenness, Orkney', *PSAS* 107, 1–60

Ritchie, J. N. G. (1985) 'Ritual Monuments', in Renfrew 1985, 118–30

Ritchie, J. N. G. (1988) 'The Ring of Brodgar', in Ruggles, C. L. N. (ed.) *Records in Stone: Papers in Memory of Alexander Thom*, Cambridge, 337–50

Roberts, N. (1998) *The Holocene*, Blackwell Publishers Ltd

Robertson, D. J. (1923) 'Orkney Folklore', *POAS* 1

Robertson, J. P. 'Account and letter books of Mrs Christian Robertson' (MS)

Rodgers, D. A. and Astin, T. R. (1991) 'Ephemeral Lakes, Mud Pellet Dunes and Wind-blown Sand and Silt: Reinterpretation of Devonian Lacustrine Cycles in North Scotland', *Spec. Publs Int. Ass. Sediment* 13, 199–221

Ross, S. (1957) *Orkney's Wrecked Ships*, Orkney

Rotherham, G. A. (n.d.) *It's Really Quite Safe*, Hanger Books, Canada

Ruggles, C. (1999) *Astronomy in Prehistoric Britain and Ireland*, New Haven and London

Ruggles, C. and Barclay, G. (2000) 'Cosmology, Calendars and Society in Neolithic Orkney: A Rejoinder to Euan MacKie', *Antiquity* 74, 62–74

Saville, A. (1996) 'Lacaille, Microliths and the Mesolithic of Orkney', in Pollard, T. and Morrison, A. *The Early Prehistory of Scotland*, Edinburgh, 213–24

Saville, A. (2000) 'Orkney and Scotland Before the Neolithic Period', in Ritchie 2000, 91–100

Saxon, J. (1991) *The Fossil Fishes of the North of Scotland*, Caithness Books, Thurso

Schei, L. K. and Moberg, G. (2001) *The Islands of Orkney*, Colin Baxter

Schrank, G. (1995) *An Orkney Estate: Improvements at Graemeshill 1827–1888*, East Linton

Scottish Executive (1998) *The Common Agricultural Policy Factsheet*

Scottish Executive (2000a) *A Forward Strategy for Scottish Agriculture: A Discussion Document*

Scottish Executive (2000b) *Scottish Agriculture – A Guide to Grants and Services*

Scottish Executive (2000c) *A Forward Strategy for Scottish Agriculture*

Scottish Executive (2000d) *The Rural Stewardship Scheme*

Scottish Historical Archive (SHA) AF29/79–AF29/84, Letters and Reports from Orkney Fishery Office

Sellevold, B.J. (1999) *Picts and Vikings as Westness: Anthropological Investigations of the Skeletal Material From the Cemetery in Westness, Rousay, Orkney Islands*, NIKU Scientific Report 010, Oslo

Sharpe, R. (1995) *Adomnan of Iona: Life of St Columba*, London

Sharples, N. (1998) *Scalloway; A Broch, Late Iron Age Settlement and Medieval Cemetery in Shetland*, Oxbow Monograph 82, Oxford

Shaw, F.J. (1980) *The Northern and Western Islands of Scotland*, Edinburgh

Shirreff, J. (1812) *General View of the Agriculture of the Orkney Islands*, Edinburgh

Simpson, W.D. *Bishop's Palace and Earls' Palace*, HMSO, Edinburgh

Smith, B. (2001) 'The Picts and the Martyrs or Did Vikings Kill the Native Population of Orkney and Shetland', *Northern Studies 36*, 7–32

Smith, P. L. (1989) *The Naval Wrecks of Scapa Flow*, Orkney Press, Kirkwall

Stromness Museum (1972) *Stromness; Late 19th Century Photographs*

Stromness Museum (1976) *Harvest of Silver*

Tait, C. (1997) *The Orkney Guide Book*, Charles Tait Photographic

Taylor, A. B. (trs) (1938) *The Orkneyinga Saga*, Edinburgh

The Third Statistical Account of Scotland: The County of Orkney, Scottish Academic Press 1985

Thomson, D. 226 *Heavy Anti-aircraft Battery 1939–45*, Orkney Islands Council, Kirkwall

Thomson, W.P.L. and Graham, J. (eds) (1978) *The Statistical Account of Scotland 19*, Wakefield

Thomson, W.P.L. (1981) 'Common Land on Orkney', *Orkney Heritage 1*

Thomson, W.P.L. (1981a) *The Little General and the Rousay Crofters*, Edinburgh (rp. 2000)

Thomson, W.P.L. (1983) *Kelp-making in Orkney*, Kirkwall

Thomson, W.P.L. (1987) *History of Orkney*, Edinburgh

Thomson, W.P.L. (2001) *New History of Orkney*, Edinburgh

Tinch, D.M.N. (1988) *Shoal and Sheaf, Orkney's Pictorial Heritage*

Towrie Cutt, N. and W. (1979) *The Hogboon of Hell and Other Strange Orkney Tales*, André Deutsch

Towrie, S. (n.d.) *Minehowe: The Mystery of the 29 Steps*, Orkney Tourist Board

Troup, J.A. and Eunson, F. (1967) *Stromness: 150 years a Burgh*, Stromness

Troup, J.A. (1987) 'Orkney and Arctic Whaling', in *The Ice-bound Whalers*, Kirkwall

Tudor, J.R. (1883) *The Orkneys and Shetland*, Charles Stanford

Turner, V. (1994) 'The Mail Stone: An Incised Pictish Figure from Mail, Cunningsburgh, Shetland', *PSAS 124*, 315–25

Underhill, R. (1997) 'A Place to Prosper or Just Survive? Motivations for the Emigration of Scottish Labourers to Vancouver Island 1848–1852', unpd Mlitt thesis, St Andrews University

Upton, B. G. J., Mitchell, R. H., Long, A. and Aspen, P. (1992) 'Primative Olivine Melanephelinite Dykes from Orkney Islands, Scotland', *Geol. Mag.* 129 (3), 319–324

Upton, B. G. J., Aspen, P. and Hinton, R. W. (2001) 'Pyroxenite and Granulite Xenoliths from beneath the Scottish Northern Highlands Terrane: Evidence for Lower-crust/Upper-mantle Relationships', *Contrib Mineral Petrol.* 142, 178–197

Uttley, J. (2002) *The Orcadian*, 28 February 2002

Vat, D. van der (1982) *The Grand Scuttle. The Sinking of the German Fleet at Scapa Flow in 1919*, Hodder and Stoughton

Wainwright, F.T. (ed.) *The Northern Isles*, Nelson

Watson, W. J. (1926) *History of the Celtic Place-names of Scotland*, Wm Blackwood and Sons, Edinburgh and London

Waugh, D. (1987) 'The Scandinavian Element *Stadir* in Caithness, Orkney and Shetland', *NOMINA* 11, 61–74

Weaver, H. J. (1980) *Nightmare at Scapa Flow. The Truth about the Sinking of HMS Royal Oak*, Cresselles Publishing, Worcestershire

Weber, B. (1992) 'Norwegian Reindeer Antler Export to Orkney and Shetland: An Analysis of Combs from Pictish/Early Norse sites', *Universitets Oldsakamling Arbok*, 161–74

Wenham, S. B. (2001) *A More Enterprising Spirit*, Bellavista Publications, Orkney

Whyte, D. (1986) *Dictionary of Scottish Emigrants to Canada before Confederation*, Toronto

Wickham Jones, C. (1998) *Orkney: A Historical Guide*, Birlinn, Edinburgh

Wilson, B. and Allerdyce, K. (1991) *Sea Haven*

Wilson, B. (2001) *Arthur Dearness and the Mermaid and Other Orkney Plays*, Kirkwall

Wilson, G., Edwards, W., Knox, J., Jones, R. C. B. and Stephens, J. (1935) *The Geology of the Orkneys*, Mem. Geol. Surv. Scot., HMSO, Edinburgh

Withrington, D. J. and Grant, I. R. (1978) *The Statistical Account of Scotland 19, Orkney and Shetland*, Wakefield

Wonders, W. (1993) 'Orkney and the "Nor-Waast"', in *Alberta History*

Wood, L. (2000) *The Bull and the Barriers. The Wrecks of Scapa Flow*, Tempus

Woodcock, G. (1988) *A Social History of Canada*, London

Wright, G. (ed.) (1989) *A Guide to the Orkney Islands*, G. Wright Publishing

Index

Note:

1. 'St' (in names of places, ships etc) is sorted as spelt. Christian saints are sorted under their name ... eg 'Magnus Erlendson, Earl of Orkney, Saint'.

2. References to figures, tables, maps, if not clear from the entry itself, have been indicated by '*fig*', '*tbl*', or '*map*' immediately following the page number.